THE PSYCHOLOGY OF REASONING

EUGENIO RIGNANO

First published in 1923 by Kegan Paul, Trench, Trubner & Co., Ltd.

This edition first published in 2018 by Routledge
2 Park Square, Milton Park, Abingdon, Oxon, OX14 4RN
and by Routledge
711 Third Avenue, New York, NY 10017

Routledge is an imprint of the Taylor & Francis Group, an informa business

©1923 Eugenio Rignano, Translated by Winifred A Holl

All rights reserved. No part of this book may be reprinted or
reproduced or utilised in any form or by any electronic, mechanical,
or other means, now known or hereafter invented, including photocopying
and recording, or in any information storage or retrieval system, without
permission in writing from the publishers.

Publisher's Note
The publisher has gone to great lengths to ensure the quality of this reprint
but points out that some imperfections in the original copies may be
apparent.

Disclaimer
The publisher has made every effort to trace copyright holders and
welcomes correspondence from those they have been unable to contact.
A Library of Congress record exists under ISBN:23011765

ISBN 13: 978-1-138-55588-4 (hbk)
ISBN 13: 978-1-138-56803-7 (pbk)
ISBN 13: 978-0-203-70532-2 (ebk)

Printed in the United Kingdom
by Henry Ling Limited

Routledge Revivals

THE PSYCHOLOGY OF REASONING

The International Library of Psychology

THE PSYCHOLOGY OF REASONING

Founded by C. K. Ogden

The International Library of Psychology

COGNITIVE PSYCHOLOGY
In 21 Volumes

I	The Psycho-Analysis of Artistic Vision and Hearing	*Ehrenzweig*
II	A Source Book of Gestalt Psychology	*Ellis*
III	Common Sense and its Cultivation	*Hankin*
IV	The Nature of Learning	*Humphrey*
V	Eidetic Imagery and Typological Methods of Investigation	*Jaensch*
VI	The World of Colour	*Katz*
VII	Principles of Gestalt Psychology	*Koffka*
VIII	Colour and Colour Theories	*Ladd-Franklin*
IX	Sense-Perception and Matter	*Lean*
X	Invention and the Unconscious	*Montmasson*
XI	Psychology and Education	*Ogden*
XII	Human Speech	*Paget*
XIII	The Gestalt Theory and the Problem of Configuration	*Petermann*
XIV	Surprise and the Psycho-Analyst	*Reik*
XV	The Psychology of a Musical Prodigy	*Révész*
XVI	Biological Memory	*Rignano*
XVII	The Psychology of Reasoning	*Rignano*
XVIII	The Effects of Music	*Schoen*
XIX	Analysis of Perception	*Smythies*
XX	Speech Disorders	*Stinchfield*
XXI	The Psycho-Biology of Language	*Zipf*

THE PSYCHOLOGY OF REASONING

EUGENIO RIGNANO

First published in 1923 by
Kegan Paul, Trench, Trubner & Co., Ltd.

Reprinted in 1999 by
Routledge
11 New Fetter Lane, London EC4P 4EE

Printed and Bound in Great Britain

© 1923 Eugenio Rignano, Translated by Winifred A Holl

All rights reserved. No part of this book may be reprinted or reproduced
or utilized in any form or by any electronic, mechanical, or other means,
now known or hereafter invented, including photocopying
and recording, or in any information storage or retrieval system, without
permission in writing from the publishers.

The publishers have made every effort to contact authors/copyright holders
of the works reprinted in the *International Library of Psychology*.
This has not been possible in every case, however, and we would
welcome correspondence from those individuals/companies
we have been unable to trace.

These reprints are taken from original copies of each book. In many cases
the condition of these originals is not perfect. The publisher has gone to
great lengths to ensure the quality of these reprints, but wishes to point
out that certain characteristics of the original copies will, of necessity, be
apparent in reprints thereof.

British Library Cataloguing in Publication Data
A CIP catalogue record for this book
is available from the British Library

The Psychology of Reasoning
ISBN 0415-20972-2
Cognitive Psychology: 21 Volumes
ISBN 0415-21126-3
The International Library of Psychology: 204 Volumes
ISBN 0415-19132-7

PREFACE

THIS book owes its origin to the indefinable sense of uneasiness and discontent into which I was thrown by the perusal of some of the best treatises on Logic. These treatises had failed to explain the nature of the logical or reasoning faculty, though purporting to indicate the laws which govern its proper functioning. Even the work of John Stuart Mill, which still remains in my opinion the best, was no more convincing than the rest. And the more I read of such books the less satisfied I became and the stronger became my desire to understand clearly what constituted reasoning.

As for the psychologists I found to my surprise that they either omitted reasoning altogether, or alluded to it in a most superficial manner.

My desire to discover the nature of reasoning was due to an instinctive tendency to resolve complex psychical phenomena into more elementary processes; and until this was accomplished the complex phenomenon remained an enigma. At length one day, just when I least expected it, I saw suddenly and clearly what I had long been seeking. The true mechanism of reasoning was manifest to me, as the resultant of the interplay of a variety of mental activities.

But the psychical phenomena of which reasoning consists, far from being elementary, appeared to me also as complex. Attention and reflection which come into play as soon as reasoning begins; coherence and the critical attitude, the vigilant guardians of the laws of logic; imagination and abstraction which determine respectively the fecundity and the greatest technical output of reasoning; synthetic and analytic thought, to which reasoning owes its evolution to higher forms—all these phenomena or modalities of psychical attitude, the immediate factors of reasoning, are evidently not elementary phenomena, but are themselves complex. So that the solution of the problem led me, by a route opposite to that followed in the present book, from the most complex phenomena of all, to phenomena less and less complex. Finally I found that I had arrived on the one hand at sensorial mnemonic reproductions (evocations of past sensations), and on the other at affective tendencies. Either of these I might have regarded as the most elementary of all psychical phenomena on whose combination and interplay all the others depended, but I succeeded in relating both to a quite general and fundamental property of life, which I had already empha-

v

vi THE PSYCHOLOGY OF REASONING

sized in my biological writings, and which appeared in consequence adequate, by itself, to explain all the highly complicated mechanism of the mind.

The result was that this work which was conceived as devoted entirely to reasoning has ended as a complete treatise on Psychology. For the analysis of reasoning, the most complex of all, led me, *via* phenomena less and less complex, to those that are most elementary, and this obliged me to pass in review all the diverse processes of the psyche.

Apart from the psychologists proper—who will, I think, be interested not only by the results attained, but also by the method of analysis adopted—I hope that this work will appeal to other groups of thinkers. Philosophers, for example, will find here a proof of the empirical nature of reasoning, the instrument of knowledge *par excellence*, and they will also see that the lacuna left by Auguste Comte has been filled in. Comte, in fact, though he demonstrated historically the futility of metaphysical speculation, offered no psychological proof. Logicians and mathematicians will observe that psychology can throw light on certain of the subtlest questions of logic, of logistic, and of mathematics itself. Devotees of rhetoric and dialectic will perhaps object to the depreciation of these occupations, which are still so highly esteemed in forensic and political spheres. And whilst the work provides educationists with the theoretical basis for the most important applications of psychology, the pages devoted to the pathology of reasoning may perhaps explain for alienists more than one point relative to strange mental aberrations. Finally biologists will see the close connexion which unites this particular manifestation of vital teleology, reasoning, with the very essence of all biological finalism in general.

In any case, I trust that the care and attention which for years I have devoted to the subject, as well as the novelty of the research involved and of the results reached, will dispose the reader to view with a certain amount of indulgence the omissions, imperfections and errors which such a work can scarcely fail to contain.

It remains only to add that I have had the opportunity of revising the English translation very carefully both in manuscript and proof, and desire to express my indebtedness both to the translator and to the Editor of the series for the care with which they have endeavoured to render individual nuances of thought to which the genius of another language is seldom fully adapted.

Milan,   E. R.
  April 1923.

CONTENTS

CHAPTER	PAGE
I. On the Mnemonic Origin and Nature of Affective Tendencies	1
II. Attention. Part I : Affective Conflict and Unity of Consciousness	30
III. Attention. Part II : Vividness and Connection . .	54
IV. What is Reasoning ?	71
V. The Evolution of Reasoning. Part I : From Concrete Reasoning to Abstract Reasoning	97
VI. The Evolution of Reasoning. Part II : From Intuition to Deduction .	121
VII. The Higher Forms of Reasoning. Part I : Mathematical Reasoning in its Phases of Direct and Indirect Symbolism . .	141
VIII. The Higher Forms of Reasoning. Part II : Mathematical Reasoning in its Phases of symbolic condensation and symbolic inversion	169
IX. The Higher Forms of Reasoning. Part III : Mathematics and Mathematical Logic	188
X. " Intentional " Reasoning. Part I : Dialectic Reasoning . . .	209

vii

viii THE PSYCHOLOGY OF REASONING

CHAPTER PAGE

XI. " Intentional " Reasoning.

Part II : Metaphysical Reasoning . . 229

XII. The Different Logical Types of Mind . 262

XIII. The Pathology of Reasoning.

Part I : The Incoherence and Illogicality of
Dreams 291

XIV. The Pathology of Reasoning.

Part II : Coherent but Illogical Insanity due
to Mono-affectivism 319

XV. The Pathology of Reasoning.

Part III : Incoherent Insanity due to Instability, Impotence or Absence of the Affective Tendencies 338

XVI. Conscious and Unconscious Reasoning . 359

Conclusion.

Reasoning in Relation to Vital Finalism . 388

Index 393

CHAPTER I

ON THE MNEMONIC ORIGIN AND NATURE OF AFFECTIVE TENDENCIES

I

Observation of the behaviour of the various organisms from the unicellular up to man, shows that a large number of their movements or acts, and especially the most important ones, may be interpreted as manifestations of a tendency of the organism to maintain or to restore its "stationary" physiological state (to use Ostwald's terminology).

In other words, if we reserve the term "affective" for that particular class of organic tendencies which appear subjectively in man as "desires" or "appetites" or "needs" and are objectively translated in both man and animals as "non-mechanised movements," completed or incipient, then a whole series of the principal "affective tendencies" thus defined may be at once reduced to the single fundamental tendency of each organism towards its "physiological invariability".

We see, for instance, that hunger, the most fundamental of all affective tendencies, is in reality nothing but the tendency to maintain or to restore that qualitative and quantitative condition of the nutritive circulating medium of the body which will make possible a continuation of the stationary metabolic state. This tendency of an organism towards the invariability of its own metabolism has become, in the course of its phylogenetic evolution, an inherent propensity to perform all acts that have nourishment for their object; yet in doing this it has never lost its original character. This is proved by the fact that all inclination on the part of the animal to procure new food ceases *ipso facto* as soon as the internal nutritive system has attained its normal state.

Accordingly, the hydra or sea-anemone does not react positively to food except when its metabolism

2 THE PSYCHOLOGY OF REASONING

reaches a state requiring more nutriment ("unless," says Jennings, "metabolism is in such a state as to require more material"); for instance, when the large sea-anemone, Stoichactis helianthus, does not experience a sensation of hunger, a bit of food placed upon its disk occasions the same characteristic "rejecting reaction" as if it were any other disturbing object. And all other organisms, the higher as well as the lower, behave in exactly the same fashion.[1]

Schiff's experiments on the injection of nutritive substances into the veins of dogs are direct evidence, on the other hand, that the fundamental condition of hunger is the decrease of histogenetic substances in the blood; for these injections resulted not only in nourishing the animal but also in appeasing its hunger.

Moreover the fact that hunger, especially when it is only moderate, assumes in man the form of a particular localized sensation originating in the wall of the stomach, and that this sensation is sufficient to cause the same acts which would be induced by real hunger, is—it is hardly necessary to state—a natural consequence and of but secondary importance. It is only one of many forms in which we find *the substitution of the part for the whole*, a phenomenon characteristic of all mnemonic physiological processes and true similarly for the tendency to physiological invariability, which is also essentially mnemonic, as we shall see more clearly later on. In fact, this peculiar sensation, localized in the gastric mucous membrane and due to its swelling or to some similar change caused by the empty condition of the stomach, usually takes place before or simultaneously with the actual decrease of histogenetic substances in the blood, and so finally becomes a representative and vicarious sign of hunger.

The same is true of thirst and of its apparent localization in the upper part of the alimentary canal.

We might pass on from hunger and thirst to the other more or less fundamental organic "appetites" or "needs". All would show us in their different manifestations that they are directed simply and solely toward the restoration of the stationary physiological state, which has been destroyed or in some way disturbed.

[1] H. S. Jennings, *Behaviour of Lower Organisms*, New York, 1906, pp. 202, 205, etc.

AFFECTIVE TENDENCIES

Thus there exists for every animal species an optimum of environment with reference to the degree of concentration of the solution in which the animal lives, to the temperature or to the intensity of light, etc., above and below which the organism cannot maintain its normal physiological state and in which the animal consequently makes every effort to maintain itself.

The infusorium Paramœcium, for instance, at 28° C. reacts negatively to a rising but not to a falling temperature, whereas at 22° C. it reacts negatively to a falling but not to a rising temperature ; and Euglena in a moderate light reacts negatively to a decrease but not to an increase in the intensity of light, whereas in a stronger light the reaction is reversed.[1]

The tendency of organisms to invariability in their stationary physiological state consequently resolves itself into a tendency to invariability in their external and internal environments. Thus, for instance, oysters and actinians close when exposed to the air ; that is, they behave so as to keep the standard of moisture unaltered within themselves.[2]

Amongst the environmental factors, whose invariability is wanted by the organism, will be found also its position with regard to the direction of the various forces to which it is exposed, especially gravity. Hence the tendency to preserve or restore its normal position. Thus, for instance, the amœba draws in its pseudopodia when they come in contact with solid non-edible bodies ; but if it is lifted off the bottom of the aquarium and is suspended in the water it stretches out its pseudopodia in all directions. As soon as one of these touches a solid object, the amœba takes hold of it, draws its body over to it and resumes its old position on this new support. Likewise a starfish when inverted tries to turn over, that is, to return to its normal environmental conditions with relation to gravity.[3]

All "needs" to throw off substances which have been produced by the general metabolism and which the organism can no longer use, conform to this general rule. For, although the need for eliminating them

---

[1] Jennings, *op. cit.*, pp. 294-295.
[2] H. Piéron, *L'évolution de la mémoire*, Paris, 1910, pp. 29, 74.
[3] K. C. Schneider, *Vorlesungen über Tierpsychologie*, Leipzig, 1909, pp. 5, 57.

4   THE PSYCHOLOGY OF REASONING

may be called forth by certain vicarious local sensations capable of evoking the act of expulsion in advance, yet in reality, whether in the case of the smallest and simplest infusorium or of the most highly developed vertebrates, it is due only to the circumstance that the accumulation of this waste material within the organism would eventually disturb its normal physiological function. To this class of eliminative affective tendencies the sexual "instinct" or "hunger" seems to belong. For we know that certain recent theories are inclined to regard the whole organism rather than any one definite part of the body as the seat of sexual hunger just as in the case of hunger proper, and at the same time to regard it as due to the need of eliminating the germinal substance.[1]

In other words, sexual hunger seems to be nothing but the tendency of the organism to free itself of the physiological disturbance which the germinal substance, in virtue of its nature as a nuclear substance awaiting fertilization, produces by means of its hormonic secretions, or substances of disintegration, and spreads throughout the entire organism.

The brilliant or striking "wedding garments," which nearly all animals assume when in love, are due to an abnormal condition of general hypersecretion occasioned by the hormonic products of the germinal substance. At any rate they show how deep is the physiological disturbance caused in all somatic cells by the germinal substance.

The tendency to expel so disturbing an element then becomes a tendency to copulation as the means of effecting this expulsion.

Hence the fundamentally selfish character (*nature foncièrement égoiste*) of sexual love which Ribot rightly emphasizes: "In the immense majority of animals, and frequently in men, the sexual instinct is not accompanied by any tender emotion. The act once accomplished, there is separation and oblivion."[2]

This hypothesis which attributes to the sexual

---

[1] See, for instance, though only in certain respects, J. Roux, *L'instinct d'amour*, Paris, 1904, Chap. I, " Base organique de l'instinct sexuel ".

[2] Th. Ribot, *La psychologie des sentiments*, Paris, 1908, p. 258. (English translation, 2nd ed., London, 1911, p. 253) ; and his *Essai sur les passions*, Paris, 1907, pp. 67 ff.

AFFECTIVE TENDENCIES 5

instinct no further significance than a tendency to eliminate a disturbing element, permits us to present this instinct in very different light from that in which it has hitherto appeared. For were this hypothesis to be accepted, the sexual instinct would not have originated and developed for the " good " of the *species*, but of the *individual*. It would therefore not represent the " will of the species " imposing itself upon the individual, as many still maintain with Schopenhauer, but rather, here as always, the " will " of the single individual ; that is, the usual tendency to keep unchanged its stationary physiological condition.

This " elimination " hypothesis, moreover, is sufficient by itself to explain certain peculiarities of this instinct which would be quite incomprehensible from the standpoint of Schopenhauer.

Ribot, for instance, is surprised that an instinct which is so exceedingly important for the continuance of the species is so often exposed to perversions which seem to involve its complete negation.[1]

But we need not consider cases of true pathological perversion, for the very facility with which normal people can adopt neo-malthusian methods accords ill with the hypothesis that the only reason for the existence of such an instinct is the need for the continuance of the race.

Finally, the fact that both animals and man now desire copulation or even certain secondary sexual relations on their own account, *i.e.*, independently of the act of the elimination of the germinal substance, perhaps even in default of any to eliminate—this also, as we shall see better at a later stage, is only the consequence of the mnemonic law already mentioned of the substitution of the part for the whole, and of its derivative, the law of the transference of affective tendencies. According to this law, all phenomena that constantly accompany the satisfaction of certain affectivities become also in their turn objects of desire, and all habits acquired for the satisfaction or in the satisfaction of certain affectivities likewise become affective tendencies.

If the sexual instinct can thus be referred to the class of tendencies which serve to maintain the stationary

---

[1] Ribot, *op. cit.*, *La Psych. des Sent.*, pp. 263, 265. (English translation, pp. 257, 259.)

6   THE PSYCHOLOGY OF REASONING

physiological condition of the organism, then the above law, as regards the fundamental organic tendencies, is open to no exception. Hence we can sum it up as follows :

Every organism is a physiological system in a stationary condition and tends to preserve this condition or to restore it as soon as it is disturbed by any variation occurring within or outside the organism. This property constitutes the foundation and essence of all " needs ", of all "desires ", of all the most important organic "appetites ". All movements of approach or withdrawal, of attack or flight, of seizing or rejecting which animals make are only so many direct or indirect consequences of this very general tendency of every stationary physiological condition *to remain constant.* We shall soon see that this tendency in its turn is only the direct result of the fundamental mnemonic characteristic of all living matter.

This single physiological tendency of a general kind is then sufficient to give rise to a large number of the most diversified particular affective tendencies. Thus every cause of disturbance will produce a corresponding tendency to repulsion with special characteristics determined by the kind of disturbance, by its strength, and by the methods capable of avoiding the disturbing elements ; and for every incidental means of preserving or restoring the normal physiological condition, there will be a quite distinct corresponding tendency such as "longing ", "desire ", "attraction " and so forth.

Even the "instinct of self-preservation " — when understood in the usual narrow sense of *preservation of one's own life*—is only a particular derivative and direct consequence of this very general tendency to preserve physiological invariability. For every condition which would eventually prove fatal first presents itself as a mere disturbance, and it is only as such that the animal tries and learns to avoid it. Jennings' amœba, for instance, which though completely swallowed by another amœba, attempted to escape and succeeded, did not in all probability flee from a phenomenon that endangered its life, but from a condition in its environment which, even though a profound disturbance, was nevertheless nothing but a disturbance.

Quinton, as is well known, was the first to develop

AFFECTIVE TENDENCIES

a theory that organisms tend to maintain in their internal intercellular environment the same chemical and physical conditions that obtained in the primordial environment when life first appeared on earth.[1]

But our theory is clearly limited to a consideration of the tendency to invariability only so far as it manifests itself each moment in the behaviour of each individual. Therefore instead of serving as too one-sided a starting point for the explanation of the evolution of species, it forms the basis upon which all the most important affective tendencies of the animal world may be built up.

As a factor of invariability for the individual, this tendency to preserve the stationary physiological condition is indeed one of the most important factors in the variation and progress of the species, but in quite a different way from that pointed out by Quinton. For from this tendency arose and developed the power of motion which is the greatest, though not an absolute, difference between plants and animals ; and with which the development and perfection of the whole motor apparatus, and of the nervous system, which constitute in themselves so large a part of the fundamental characteristics distinguishing different animal species, have kept pace.

Finally as a factor in individual invariability it has proved by its effect on man to be one of the chief factors in all social evolution ; for we might say that technical inventions and industrial products, from the first cave dwellings, the skins used for clothing, or the discovery of fire to the most complex refinements of our own age, have always had but one single goal, namely the artificial maintenance of the greatest possible invariability in the environment, which is the necessary and sufficient condition for preserving physiological invariability.

II

Closely connected with this fundamental property of every organism to strive to preserve its normal physiological condition or to restore it as soon as it is dis-

---

[1] R. Quinton, *L'eau de mer, milieu organique*, Paris, 1904. Especially Book II, " Loi générale de constance originelle ", pp. 429-456.

8 THE PSYCHOLOGY OF REASONING

turbed, there is yet another which in its turn becomes the source of new affectivities.

For as soon as the previous stationary condition cannot be restored in any way, *i.e.* by any sort of movement or change of position, the organism tends to pass to a new stationary condition consistent with its new external or internal environment. We thus get a large number of new phenomena called "adaptations."

Thus Dallinger's classical experiments on the acclimatization of lower organisms—suggested by the observation that a number of organisms usually living in water of a normal temperature, also exist and flourish in the hottest springs—have proved that infusoria may become accustomed to a constantly rising temperature so that finally after years of continuous slow increase in the degree of heat, they can stand a temperature which would be fatal to another individual not so acclimatized. It is likewise known that the same species of protozoa are found in both fresh and salt water, and that it is possible to accustom fresh-water amœbæ and infusoria to a salinity which would have destroyed them at the start—and many other instances could be cited.[1]

What interests us particularly here is the fact that the new conditions of the environment to which the animal gradually becomes accustomed tend in time to become its optimum. "This individual adaptation (*e.g.* to a different proportion of salt) is affected in accordance with the rule that the conditions of density under which an individual is living, tend to become in time the optimum conditions for that individual."[2]

This takes place even in plant organisms. Plasmodia of the Myxomycetes die when plunged suddenly into 1 or 2 per cent. glucose solutions, and even draw back from $\frac{1}{2}$ or $\frac{1}{4}$ per cent. solutions, and yet they may gradually become accustomed to 2 per cent. solutions so that they finally show by their behaviour that they prefer their new environment to the original one without glucose.[3]

[1] See C. B. Davenport and W. E. Castle, " On the Acclimatisation of Organisms to High Temperatures". *Archiv für. Entw.-Mech. der Organismen*, II, Part 2, July 1895.—C. B. Davenport and H. V. Neal, " On the Acclimatisation of Organisms to Poisonous Chemical Substances," *loc. cit.*, II, Part 4, Jan. 1896.

[2] Davenport and Castle, *art. cit.*, p. 241.

[3] E. Stahl, " Zur Biologie der Myxomyceten," *Botanische Zeitung*, March 7, 14 and 21, 1884, p. 166.

AFFECTIVE TENDENCIES

9

The diatom Navicula brevis ordinarily avoids even the weakest light and tends to retire into the darkest part of the drop of water in which it is being observed. However, if a culture is placed in the bright light of a window for two weeks, it exhibits the opposite tendency and makes for the brightest part of the drop as soon as this is carried back again to its former condition of weaker illumination.[1]

The common actinia (Actinia equina) often found clinging to rocks in every possible position with relation to the force of gravity, sometimes with the axis of the body directed upwards, sometimes downward and sometimes to one side, seems to become so accustomed to its position that it endeavours to resume it when removed to another spot. For instance, if several actinians found in various positions are collected and placed in an aquarium "they show in attaching themselves a distinct tendency to assume the same position they had formerly held."[2]

We might multiply such instances, but we are here chiefly concerned to point out their significance. They show that the new physiological state arising from adaptation to the new environment, when once it has supervened and has lasted for a certain time in the organism, tends to renew itself. This tendency of a past physiological state to "re-activation" or reproduction is merely the tendency inherent in every mnemonic accumulation to "evoke" itself again. Hence it is a tendency of a purely mnemonic nature. But from this it would follow that the tendency to physiological invariability from which originate, as we have seen, the most important organic affective tendencies of all organisms whatever must be equally mnemonic in nature. For if in the above examples an entirely new and recent physiological state is nevertheless able to leave behind a mnemonic accumulation producing a distinct tendency to its own restoration, it is easy to understand that just because the normal physiological state has lasted so much longer it must possess a correspondingly stronger mnemonic tendency toward its restoration whenever it is disturbed.

This implies that the different elementary physio-

---

[1] Davenport and Castle, *art. cit.*, p. 241.
[2] Piéron, *op. cit.*, p. 144.

10 THE PSYCHOLOGY OF REASONING

logical states, each of which is active at one definite point of the organism and which all combine to constitute the general physiological state, possess the faculty of depositing a proper "specific accumulation," in the same manner as appears to happen in the brain, where the nervous currents which constitute the different sensations, leave behind a mnemonic residue capable of being revived or recalled. By "specific accumulations" of the various nervous currents must be understood simply that every accumulation is capable of giving as "discharge" only the particular specificity of the nervous current by which this accumulation has itself been deposited.

The extension of this faculty of "specific accumulation" to all physiological phenomena in general accords with the hypothesis that nervous energy is the basis for all the phenomena of life. If with psycho-mnemonic phenomena properly so called, the action of nervous energy produced by the discharge of the respective stimulated centre appears in the foreground, while the specific physico-chemical phenomena accompanying the discharge remain in the background so that until recently they were almost entirely overlooked, for all the other physiological phenomena we should have—according to the fundamental concept of Claude Bernard on the essential identity of all the different forms of irritability of living matter—a difference of degree only but not of essence, inasmuch as the specific physico-chemical physiological phenomena of each stimulation (muscular contraction, glandular secretion, etc.) would appear with the greatest distinctness, whereas the specific nervous phenomena which also accompany this physiological activity would now pass in their turn into the background. It is in this way that we have tried to explain the fundamental mnemonic property of all living substance which has recently been especially emphasized by Hering, Semon and Francis Darwin, as well as the most essential and characteristic biological phenomena which result from it.[1]

By this extension of the mnemonic faculty to all

---

[1] Eugenio Rignano, *Sur la transmissibilité des caractères acquis. Hypothèse d'une centro-épigénèse*, Paris, 1906 ; Italian Edition, Bologna, 1907 ; English Edition, Chicago, 1911. Especially the chapter on "The Mnemonic Phenomenon and the Vital Phenomenon."

AFFECTIVE TENDENCIES

elementary physiological phenomena we now obtain a *somatic or visceral theory of the fundamental affective tendencies*, in the sense that the tendency toward physiological invariability, or toward the restoration of a previous physiological state corresponding to a previous environment, depends on innumerable elementary specific accumulations, differing at different points of the body and with a total potential energy which would form as it were a force of gravitation toward that environment or those conditions which allow the maintenance or restoration of the whole physiological system represented by all these elementary accumulations.

Naturally in organisms with a nervous system, besides each of these affective tendencies whose origin and seat are purely somatic, there would arise and be gradually developed—in co-operation with it and sometimes as a substitute for it—the affective tendency represented by the corresponding mnemonic accumulations which had been deposited in that particular zone of the nervous system directly connected with the respective points of the body. In man, for instance, this zone would be Flechsig's Körperfühlsphäre to which in certain cases may also be added the frontal zone.[1]

When the cerebral mnemonic accumulations had once arisen phylogenetically under direct somatic action, they would finally have become able to represent by themselves, after all connection with the body had been severed, those former affective somatic tendencies to which they owed their origin. And this would be in virtue of the two fundamental mnemonic laws of (1) *the gradual independence of the part in relation to the whole* and (2) *the substitution of the part for the whole*, which arise directly from the fact that every elementary specific accumulation, when once deposited, is capable of existing on its own account. Hence Sherrington's "spinal" dog, for instance, continued to exhibit the same repugnance to the flesh of other dogs, and other similar affectivities, like those of the normal dog, all of them without doubt phylogenetically of visceral origin.[2]

[1] P. Flechsig, *Gehirn und Seele*, Leipzig, 1896, pp. 19, 21-22, 92, 99-100.

[2] See C. S. Sherrington, *The Integrative Action of the Nervous System*, London, 1906, pp. 260-265. Also the pertinent discussion of these experiments by Lloyd Morgan, *Animal Behaviour*, 2nd ed., London, 1908, p. 292; and Revault d'Allonnes, *Les inclinations*, Paris, 1908, pp. 101 ff.

12 THE PSYCHOLOGY OF REASONING

But this co-operation and this possibility of an eventual substitution of the affective tendency whose seat is in the brain, for the corresponding affective tendency of somatic origin, does not prevent the former from remaining entirely under the control of the latter. Hence the general admission of modern psychology that the affective life "has its cause below in the variations of the cenesthesis, which is itself a resultant of the whole of the vital activities."[1]

Nor does it in the least prevent affective tendencies from keeping all the fundamental properties which they owe to their mnemonic visceral origin, of which the most important are first that they possess a "diffuse" seat, and secondly that they are eminently "subjective".

For every stationary physiological system in equilibrium with regard to its environment permeates the whole organism and consequently all that part of the brain in which this organism is reflected. Accordingly, in contrast to the mnemonic accumulations of sensations each of which to all appearances has a seat distinctly localized at single points or single centres of the cortex of the brain, we have every reason to conclude that each affective tendency is made up of an infinitely large number of different elementary mnemonic accumulations, deposited respectively in every point of the body and in every corresponding point in the brain.

To this mnemonic physiological origin of the affective tendencies is also due their eminently "subjective" character; for the organism is equipped potentially with this or that "idiosyncratic" affective tendency, with this or that "nostalgia", according to the various environments or conditions in which the species and the individual were placed for a longer or shorter time in the past, in other words according to their *individual history*.

Hence the "subjectivity" and infinite variety manifest in the needs, the appetites and desires, and consequently in everything that is an object of "affective evaluation".

[1] Ribot, *op. cit., Psych. des sent.*, p. 10.

AFFECTIVE TENDENCIES

III

The hypothesis outlined above as to the mnemonic nature of affective tendencies in general is supported by other examples of more special affectivities which have also originated by way of " habit."

As a typical instance it will suffice to consider maternal love.

Evidently the habit of having certain relations of parasitism, or of symbiosis in general, with the progeny throughout a long series of generations, has become gradually transformed in a mnemonic way into affective tendencies towards these relations.

"Comparative ethology," says Giard, "shows us most clearly that the relations between the parent organism and its progeny are in principle absolutely the same as those existing between a parasite and the animal it lives upon, and that after a period of unstable equilibrium in which one or other of the two connected organisms suffers to the advantage of its companion, there is a tendency to the establishment of a definite position of mutual equilibrium ".[1]

This applies, for example, to the relations of internal incubation, which though first sought and effected by the embryo itself in some phase of its development for the purpose of nutrition, protection, or some other advantage, and at first simply endured by one of the parents, either father or mother, finally become for his parent actual " needs."

It is equally true of the relations of external incubation which arise at first as the result of some particular circumstance and in this way become a habit. For instance, the attachment manifested by the female spider, Chiracanthium carnifex, for her nest, whether it be her own or one of which she has taken possession, *grows with time*, that is with the length of her occupation of it. Hence " mother love " seems in her case to be really nothing but her attachment to a home to which she has become accustomed.[2]

---

[1] A. Giard, " Les origines de l'amour maternel ", *Revue des idées*, April 15, 1905, p. 256.

[2] A. Lécaillon, " Sur la biologie et la psychologie d'une araignée ", *Année psychologique*, X, Paris, 1904, pp. 63-83.

14 THE PSYCHOLOGY OF REASONING

Similarly the brooding of birds and some reptiles, which owes its origin to the pleasant sensation arising from contact with the fresh eggs, in the feverish condition accompanying the egg-laying process, has become by habit an independent instinctive affectivity.[1]

Finally as regards lactation, the young have gradually transformed the sudoriferous glands on the breast of the mother brooding over them into lactiferous, by sucking their secretions; and thus they have at the same time so accustomed the mother to this process that finally *lactation becomes an actual need:* "With mammals we must look for the origin of the mutually symbiotic relations which unite mother and child in the phenomenon of lactation. The physiological disorders of pregnancy and parturition lead, among other very curious trophic effects, to an excessive secretion of the mammary glands which, as we know, are only a special localization of the sebaceous glands of the skin. The young animal, by licking and sucking the secretion whence it draws its first nourishment, alleviates the discomfort of the female. It thus becomes a means toward the well-being of its mother."[2]

That the need for lactation is the origin of maternal love is shown by the fact that the mother who is deprived of her young tries to replace them by foster-nurslings: "The necessity of getting rid of a troublesome secretion is powerful enough sometimes to cause the female deprived of her young to steal the progeny of another, and these robberies have been observed even in the case of females still suckling their own young, the satisfaction of a need leading them, as is generally the case, to seek a still greater satisfaction, and possibly even leading to excess."[3]

In the cases observed by Lloyd Morgan, this need of the mother takes the form of maternal love solicitous for the nourishment of her young: "I have seen both bitches and cats get up and again lie down so as to bring the teats into closer proximity to the mouth of any young which failed to find them. It has been noticed by a man who is a remarkably good observer and has had much to do with animals, and also by myself, that

[1] Giard, *art. cit.*, p. 266.
[2] Giard, *art. cit.*, pp. 269-270.
[3] Giard, *art. cit.*, p. 270.

AFFECTIVE TENDENCIES   15

when a lamb is weakly and fails to find the teat, the mother not infrequently uses its shoulders, head and neck as a lever to place the lamb on its legs ; and, having accomplished this, straddles over the lamb, and brings the teats against its lips ; and these efforts are continued until the little animal sucks."[1]

This is a characteristic example showing clearly how the necessity for the elimination of the milk must end in arousing an attachment for the nursling as the customary means for attaining this end, just as we have seen that the need for the elimination of the germinal substance must lead to an affectivity for the other sex, here again as the customary means to effect this elimination.

Just as "sexual attraction" ceases after the elimination of the germinal substance, so also, with the majority of mammals, does "mother love" disappear as soon as the need for lactation is no longer felt: "Maternal affection does not generally survive the causes which produced it and only vague traces of it are noticeable after lactation has ceased."[2]

Finally, the fact that the mother's affection is stronger than that of the father, and that the parents' love for their children is stronger than that of the children for their parents confirms the hypothesis that all these affectivities have arisen exclusively by way of habit, for it shows that affection for those with whom we have certain relations is the more intense the more numerous and continuous these relations are. "Among animals as a whole," remarks Ribot, "paternal love is rare and inconstant, and among the lower representatives of mankind it is a feeble sentiment and forms but a slight bond."[3] It is only found in cases of stable union, where the common life "creates a current of affection as a result of services rendered."[4]

"Every one recognizes," says Pillon in his turn, "that the love of parents for their children exceeds in intensity the children's love for the parents, and that of the two parents it is the mother whose love for her child is greater. . . . The reason is that in the mother's case, in virtue of her special functions, much more than

---

[1] Lloyd Morgan, *Habit and Instinct*, London, 1896, p. 115.
[2] Giard, *art. cit.*, p. 273.
[3] Ribot, *op. cit., Psych. des sent.*, p. 285.
[4] Ribot, *op. cit., Psychol. des sent.*, p. 286.

16 THE PSYCHOLOGY OF REASONING

with the father, the love for the child is nourished and increased by the frequent actions which it causes ".[1]

But mother-love, and mutual love within the family in general, owing its origin to certain relations which become habitual, represents only one particular case of a universal law. For every other relation to persons or things, however special, which becomes in the slightest degree a habit, finally appears for this very reason as something "desired." In other words, for every environmental relation, whether general or particular, we can verify Lehmann's law of the "indispensability of the customary," which this investigator established for every stimulus to which one becomes accustomed and whose cessation generates a " need ".[2]

"I have in my room a small clock," wrote a friend to G. E. Müller, " which will not run quite twenty-four hours with one winding. It often happens therefore that it stops. Whenever this occurs I notice it at once, whereas, of course, I do not hear it at all when it is running. The first time this occurred the sensation was somewhat as follows : it happened that I was suddenly aware of an *indefinite unrest*, a sort of emptiness, without being able to discover the cause. It was only after some reflection that I discovered the cause in the stopping of my clock ".[3]

Moreover we have all doubtless had opportunity to observe how things which are disagreeable at first finally become attractive from custom ; and how such habits assumed in the course of man's life become "need" as peremptory as those which we call natural needs : "Smokers, snuff-takers, and those who chew tobacco, furnish familiar instances of the way in which long persistence in a sensation not originally pleasurable, makes it pleasurable—the sensation itself remaining unchanged. The like happens with various foods and drinks, which, at first distasteful, are afterwards greatly relished if frequently taken ".[4]

---

[1] F. Pillon, " Sur la mémoire et l'imagination affective ", *Année philosophique*, XVII, 1906, Paris, 1907, pp. 69-70.

[2] A. Lehmann, *Die Hauptgesetze des menschlichen Gefühlslebens*, Leipzig, 1892, pp. 194 ff.

[3] G. E. Müller, *Zur Theorie der sinnlichen Aufmerksamkeit*, Leipzig, N.D., p. 128.

[4] Herbert Spencer, *The Principles of Psychology*, London, 1899, 4th ed., Vol. I, p. 287.

AFFECTIVE TENDENCIES   17

Thence arises the hankering after certain customary things which we suddenly miss: "In some animals there is produced a condition resembling nostalgia, expressing itself in a violent desire to return to former haunts, or in a pining away resulting from the absence of accustomed persons and things ".[1]

Mere habit, therefore, is enough, as we have seen in the case of family love, to cause other similar affectivities also to originate and take root. Such are gregariousness, sociability, friendship, and so forth: "The perception of kindred beings, perpetually seen, heard, and smelt, will come to form a predominant part of consciousness — so predominant a part that absence will inevitably cause discomfort ".[2]

Finally we are all well aware of the powerful influence of the habits of life current in any family circle during the earliest years of a child's life—of "nurture" in the broad sense, as Galton would call it—whence there arise and develop the feelings and moral tendencies which leave an indelible trace upon the whole life as though they were "innate ".[3]

In short from these few instances adduced simply by way of illustrating our contention, we see how profound is the truth contained in the saying that habit is a "second nature".

But if to a certain extent we can see the most diverse affective tendencies originate by habit before our very eyes, then we may also attribute a similar mnemonic origin to all affective tendencies, since the nature of "innate" differs in no wise from that of "acquired" tendencies. Similarly in the case of morphological evolution we may consider that Lamarckianism is quite justified in drawing, from the few observable cases of adaptation acquired during life, the conclusion that the entire structure of the organism owes its existence to an indefinite number of similar functional adaptations.

Hence we may complete the saying quoted above with the phrase that on the other hand "nature" is nothing but a "first habit".

---

[1] Th. Ribot, *Essay on the Creative Imagination*, Chicago, 1906, p. 95.
[2] Spencer, *op. cit.*, Vol. II, p. 627.
[3] Francis Galton, *Inquiries into Human Faculty and Its Development*, London, 1883, pp. 208-216.

18 THE PSYCHOLOGY OF REASONING

IV

Further confirmation of the hypothesis of the mnemonic origin and nature of all affective tendencies is to be found in a property which is inherent in all of them, namely their "transference" (Ribot). This property is itself essentially mnemonic and through it all other affectivities are derived from those of direct mnemonic origin and thus come to have an indirect mnemonic origin.

For in consequence of the "substitution of a part for the whole," the fundamental mnemonic principle mentioned above, it happens that mere parts or fragments of certain environmental relations, striven for originally in their totality, or that "analogous," *i.e.* only partly similar to those desired, or environmental relations constituting the "means" suited to the attainment of an "end" and therefore its necessary antecedents, or, in fine, that environmental relations which always accompany this "end," evoke the same affectivity as the original "end" itself. Hence this affectivity is "transferred" from the whole to the part, and this attachment for the part, then becomes so much stronger that this partial relation, which is first desired as a substitute for the whole, finally becomes in its turn an habitual environmental relation, and henceforward is consequently desired or sought for its own sake, quite apart from the real and original affective "transference".

This is the case, for example, as was pointed out above, with regard to copulation, the customary means for the elimination of germinal substance, and also with regard to the secondary sexual relations as phenomena usually accompanying copulation. The "conquest" of the other sex, although only a necessary means for the satisfaction of sexual appetite, may likewise become with certain individuals an end in itself. The pleasure of seduction for its own sake, the "sexual vanity" of both male and female and other similar affectivities, are further developments.

The same is the case with the tearing to pieces of prey, the customary means for satisfying hunger, which has ultimately given place to cruelty for cruelty's sake : "One half of the animal race live upon prey ; and as it

AFFECTIVE TENDENCIES

is delightful to eat so it must be delightful to kill. Pleasurable also must be all the signs of discomfiture, the helpless struggles and agonized gestures of the victim ".[1]

The love of victory for its own sake, ambition, thirst for power, desire for fame and glory, the endeavour to surpass his fellows, are all derived in man as consequences of further " transference."

In these and all similar cases of affective transferences to environmental relations constantly becoming less material and more moral, besides the true and proper affective transference which transforms the part into a new " end," there is always involved in man and in the higher animals the co-operation of their own intellectual development.

By increasing the power of predicting external events, the intellect succeeds constantly in devising new means more indirect and more complex for attaining certain ends, and offers thereby a wider sphere of action for " affective transference". Weapons, for instance, invented by man as means for self-preservation have rendered possible that affective transference to themselves which is characteristic of the warrior and the hunter ; and the earth which the agriculturist has utilized to provide his own nourishment has made possible that intense love for the soil frequent among peasants.

Furthermore, since the intellect also constantly increases the power of predicting internal (psychical) processes, it calls into being a large number of new affectivities destined to prevent future affective tendencies from remaining unsatisfied. For instance the anticipation of future hunger becomes, even in the satiated man, a direct inclination to conserve food laid by, and to keep it in his possession ; and thence arises in general the sense of ownership. In the same way the anticipation of the innumerable other desires which civilized man cherishes to-day excites in him an intense longing for wealth, covetousness and other similar passions.[2]

Finally, the intellect renders possible that infinite

---

[1] Alexander Bain, *The Emotions and the Will*, London, 1899, 4th ed., p. 65.

[2] Spencer, *op. cit., Principles of Psychology*, Vol. I, pp. 488 ff. Ribot, *op. cit., Psychol. des sent.*, pp. 110, 269-270.

20 THE PSYCHOLOGY OF REASONING

variety of "nuances" which affective tendencies can assume in man. For since it is able to observe from different points of view, simultaneously or nearly so, each complex environmental relation, it is capable of evoking diverse affectivities at the same time; and these by association, combination, confluence, interference and mutual partial inhibition, as Bain would have said, finally produce an exceedingly complex affectivity which is therefore capable of showing the finest possible gradations from one case to another, according to the number and character of its component parts.

Thus fear, anxiety and kindred feelings had already developed in animals from the instinct of self-preservation in its purely defensive form; but in man it gives rise to all the propitiatory affectivities in innumerable varieties and shades, such as prostration, humility, hypocrisy, flattery and the like. Even the religious sentiment in its lowest forms derives from this propitiatory affectivity, while the higher religious sentiment and the analogous feeling experienced in the presence of the sublime are its further and more highly developed forms.[1]

Similarly from the instinct of self-preservation in its double aspect, offensive and defensive at the same time, had already developed in the higher animals the instinct to attack and all the different varieties of counter-attack; but in man this instinct has assumed the most varied forms and shades from deepest hatred to a scarcely perceptible antipathy, from violent rapacity to the merest envy, and from the most ferocious desire for revenge to the slightest resentment. The noblest sentiment of justice is a very remote and hardly recognisable derivative of the same instinct.[2]

How high may be the degree of complexity which can thus be attained is shown, for instance, by maternal love, which has grown from the purely bodily necessity for lactation to the tenderest feelings of the noblest altruism; and especially by conjugal affection, which has been transformed from coarse brutal sexual appetite

---

[1] Cf., for instance, Ribot, *op. cit., Psych. des sent.*, p. 100. Also E. Rignano, "The religious phenomenon", in *Essays of Scientific Synthesis*, London, 1918.

[2] See Bain, *op. cit., The Emotions and the Will*, pp. 117 f. Ribot, *op. cit., Psych. des sentiments*, pp. 229 f., 271 f. Ribot, *Problèmes de psychologie affective*, Paris, 1910, Chap. III, " L'antipathie ".

AFFECTIVE TENDENCIES 21

to an harmonious co-operation of the gentlest and most delicate moral affectivities.[1]

Yet it would clearly be useless and impossible to investigate here all of the affectivities and their nuances which have ultimately arisen and developed in this way in the higher animals and especially in man. These very summary indications must suffice to render intelligible the fact that as soon as the organism has acquired in the direct mnemonic way a stock of affective tendencies and the intellect has attained its proper development, the number of affectivities which may be derived by "transference" and by "combination", that is to say, by indirect mnemonic means, is infinite.

V

It does not require many words to show the place of affective tendencies among those fundamental psychical phenomena which are most closely connected with them, such as the emotions, the will, and the states of pleasure and pain.

Emotions are only sudden and violent modes of activation of those very accumulations of energy of which the affective tendencies consist.

It is not always possible, of course, to distinguish accurately affective tendencies from emotions, since the former are perceptible neither objectively nor subjectively as long as they remain in a potential state, but become so at their activation which, when sudden and violent, constitutes the corresponding emotion. But the importance and necessity of making this distinction —which the majority of psychologists usually entirely neglect—lies in the fact that one and the same affective tendency may, according to external circumstances, give rise to the most diverse emotions, to the most diverse degrees of their intensity, or even to no emotion at all properly so called. Thus if we see a vehicle approaching at a distance we quietly step aside out of the way ; but if it appears suddenly before us at an abrupt turn in the street we feel a strong emotional shock. And the same affective tendency of the dog

[1] Spencer, *op. cit.*, Vol. I, p. 487 f.

22 THE PSYCHOLOGY OF REASONING

towards a piece of meat can give rise to flight, anger, or the careful, coolly calculated search for a hiding place, according to the circumstances which threaten danger to his succulent repast.

In short, every emotion, as Stout rightly emphasizes, presupposes an affective tendency, but the reverse does not follow; for an affective tendency, even when in course of realisation, may not always imply an emotion.[1]

Every affective tendency "impels" to action, that is, it not only "starts" but really "impinges" upon the organs of motion, either directly as in the lower organisms or through the medium of the nervous system as in the higher. Therefore from the first moment of its activation it has the appearance of a "motion in the nascent state" (Ribot).

If its activation is sudden and intense the resulting activity of the motor muscles is accompanied by that of all the viscera. This "visceral co-operation" which thus takes place in connection with the emotions properly so called, is not, as Sherrington believes, due to the fact that the rapidity and intensity with which the muscles are set in motion induces the immediate action of the viscera which furnish the muscles with the material for their energy; but it occurs because there is an overflow of nervous energy, which when suddenly released in great quantities acts like a flood, and pours forth in numerous other tracts in addition to those closely connected with the locomotor apparatus.[2]

It is this visceral commotion produced as a result of the sudden intense impulse, which, according to the well-known theory of James, Lange and Sergi, finds its centripetal echo in the brain in the form of an emotion.[3]

Hence it is the *affective tendency* which impels us and not the *emotion*, as Sherrington still maintains in accordance with the prevalent confusion between affective tendency and emotion which cannot be too greatly

---

[1] See G. F. Stout, *A Manual of Psychology*, London, 1907, 2nd ed., p. 305 ff.

[2] See Sherrington, *op. cit., The Integrative Action of the Nervous System*, pp. 265 f.

[3] See the famous article of W. James, "What is an Emotion?" *Mind*, April 1884, pp. 188-205. Revault d'Allonnes, *op. cit., Les inclinations*, p. 108 f.

AFFECTIVE TENDENCIES 23

deplored; the emotion is only the reaction of a too rapid and intense realisation of this tendency.

On the other hand if on account of external conditions or the psychical disposition of the individual the activation of the affective tendency takes place neither too suddenly nor with too great intensity, then only are the requisite muscles called into play, without any emotion. Thus the amount of useful work accomplished by the discharge of the affective tendency is greater in proportion as the amount lost in unco-ordinated and useless movements of a purely emotional character is smaller. This is the reason why it is precisely the most unemotional individuals who are often endowed with the most persistent, the most intense and the most productive activity.[1]

As regards the will, there is an act of volition whenever an affective tendency directed towards a future object triumphs over an affective tendency whose aim is in the present; in other words, whenever a far-sighted affectivity is victorious over a short-sighted one. The man who after a long run rushes sweating and panting to drink from a spring, does not exercise an "act of volition"; it is rather to the behaviour of one who forbears to slake his burning thirst for fear of a greater future evil that the term applies. Likewise no act of volition is exerted when an exhausted wanderer throws himself down to sleep, but rather when a mountaineer overcomes his exhaustion in order to reach some particular peak. And the act of a man who on a momentary impulse falls upon his opponent at the slightest provocation with hard words and blows does not demand any will power, as does the conduct of the man who is master of himself and restrains his just wrath, in order coolly to estimate in its remotest consequences the most appropriate course to adopt against the offender.[2]

Essentially then the "will" is nothing else than a true and proper affective tendency which inhibits other affective tendencies because it is more far-sighted, and which in its turn impels to action like all affective tendencies. "There is present in the action of will some desire of a good to be obtained or of an evil to be shunned, which imparts its driving force".[3]

---

[1] See Revault d'Allonnes, *op. cit.*, *Les inclinations*, pp. 207 f.
[2] Cf. E. Meumann, *Intelligenz und Wille*, Leipzig, 1908, pp. 181 f.
[3] Maudsley, *The Physiology of Mind*, London, 1876, p. 339.

24 THE PSYCHOLOGY OF REASONING

Two extreme instances deserve special mention, for they include all the others. The first of these may again be divided into two.

Sometimes one of the affective tendencies is so strong and persistent that it constantly outweighs all others; it checks them if it is contrary to them and strengthens them if it is in harmony with them. Such an "hypertrophied" affective tendency is called "passion" (Ribot, Renda). If it is directed towards some present aim we say that it "annihilates the will," because it successfully withstands the inhibitive effect of every affective tendency directed towards the future; if on the other hand its own aim is in the distant future, an "ideal" whose attainment may require the work of a lifetime, then we say that the individual is persevering, stubborn, unyielding, endowed with an iron will, because every opposed affective tendency directed toward an immediate end dashes in vain against it.

On the other hand it sometimes happens that the two conflicting affective tendencies are evenly balanced. At one moment the far-sighted tendency gains greater force and seems to prevail by calling before the mind new consequences in the future, but the next instant the short-sighted tendency discovers new or more clearly recognised aspects in the object desired at the moment, and becomes more intense, threatening to gain the upper hand. The individual then falls into the state called "indecision." When a philosopher discovers by introspection that he is in this situation, he will readily realize that both affectivities exist together within him, that both are "flesh of his flesh," and that the slightest and most insignificant psychical occurrence is enough to make one stronger than the other. He can then easily succumb to the illusion that *a mere nothing, an entirely arbitrary fiat on his part, is enough* to give one the preponderance over the other. This is the subjective illusion of "free will" which for many centuries has constituted the greatest and most difficult problem that philosophy has been called upon to solve.

Finally to come to the consideration of "pleasure" and "pain", it is the merit of the modern psychological school to have shown the fallacy of Bain's theory that the fundamental fact of animal life is the pursuit of "pleasure", in other words, the search for everything

AFFECTIVE TENDENCIES

pleasant and the avoidance of everything unpleasant; and, on the other hand, to have clearly emphasized that pleasure and pain represent only the superficial part of the affective life, "of which the deep element consists in tendencies, appetites, needs, desires. . . . The basis, the root of the affective life is in them, not in the consciousness of pleasure and pain which accompanies them according as they are satisfied or opposed."[1]

Since to every "satisfaction" of any affective tendency there corresponds an activation of nervous energy, and every "disappointment" is constituted by a suspension or cessation of this energy, pleasure really accompanies every state of discharge or activation of the nervous or vital energy, and pain every state of arrest or suppression of it.

In fact "painful" is every act inhibitive of certain nervous activities; "unpleasant" every too perceptible change of surrounding conditions which renders impossible the continuance of the hitherto stationary physiological state; "agonizing" every sudden and violent change of environment which brings about the complete arrest or entire destruction of life in one or another part of the organism; and "sad" is the individual when there is a general diminution of vital functions in his organism.

Inversely, it is "agreeable" to exercise one's muscles in play and sport; the cessation of any strained condition of the soul procures "relief"; the return to an accustomed environment and the resumption of habits are accompanied by "pleasure"; and in general every state is full of "joy" and "light-heartedness" in which the organism experiences a greater activity of nervous energy.[2]

It is sufficient here to note that the theory of the mnemonic origin of all affective tendencies which we have endeavoured to develop and to defend in these pages, offers a new argument in support of these modern psychological views with regard to the essential nature of pleasure and pain. For in assigning to these affective tendencies the nature of mnemonic accumula-

---

[1] Ribot, *Psychol. des sent.*, p. 2. *Probl. de psych. aff.*, p. 16.
[2] See Ribot, *op. cit.*, *Psych. des sent.*, Part I, Chaps. I-III, especially pp. 52 f. and 83 f. W. Ostwald, *Vorlesungen über Naturphilosophie*, Leipzig, 1905, pp. 388 ff.

26 THE PSYCHOLOGY OF REASONING

tions it implies that the fundamental principle of affective life can be nothing but the tendency to activation inherent in these accumulations, as is the case with every other reserve of potential energy ; and that therefore pain and pleasure, pleasant and painful states, can be nothing but the superficial and subjective side of this activation or of its inhibition.

VI

We may conclude these notes upon the nature of affective tendencies by adding a few remarks, which seem to us indispensable, on the fundamental character of these tendencies, viz. that they constitute a force determining, so to speak, a definite end to be attained but leaving undetermined the path to be followed.

Affective tendencies owe the property of gravitating towards an end, without any preference as regards the means, to the fact that they depend on the potential existence of a certain general or local physiological system or state, which was determined in the past by the outside world as a whole or by particular relations to this outside world, and which now,—as soon as it is released by the persistence or recurrence of even a small part of that environment or those relations— tends, like every other kind of potential energy, simply to resume its activity. Indeed, the existence of this tendency only results in the gravitation of the organism towards the environment or the environmental relations which render possible the activity of the corresponding physiological state ; but it does not imply any preferential "impulse" towards any one or other of those series of passing physiological states constituting the movements which, even if they were capable of eventually bringing the organism back to the desired environment, *yet have nothing in common with the definitive physiological state itself.*

It is only when one series of movements happens to bring the organism back to the desired environmental relations earlier than another, that it will *from that moment* be "preferred" above the others ; and this may

AFFECTIVE TENDENCIES 27

be expressed by saying that the affective tendency has exercised a "choice" (James, Baldwin and the American school in general).

Hence it is only from that moment that the affective tendency will by mnemonic association constitute a force which "impels" these movements towards the end, just as certain reflex movements impinge on one another (Sherrington). And only from that moment will these movements (so long as they have not become mechanical in the form of reflexes) be determined exclusively under the influence of the corresponding affectivity or the equivalent "act of the will".

Until this takes place, however, the affectivity has no tendency at all to discharge in one path rather than in another. Hence the great difference between the affective tendency or act of will on the one hand, and the reflex movement on the other. The reflex movement—in which by mnemonic accumulation the act so chosen becomes, when often repeated, gradually transformed and rendered quite independent of the whole—represents, that is to say, a tendency to discharge along one single path determined in advance. It is a force whose point of application and direction are known beforehand, and might therefore be indicated graphically by the arrow generally used to represent the forces of mechanics. On the other hand the affective tendency constitutes a force of which neither the point of application nor the direction are predetermined, but only the point towards which it tends. It is a "disposable" energy to be applied indifferently to this or that act so long as it leads to the desired end. Therefore it can be represented quite indefinitely by any of the infinite number of arrows which fill the entire volume of a cone and converge at its apex.

The reflex movement admits therefore of *only one solution*. On the other hand, the affective tendency admits of *an indefinitely large number of solutions*, so long as none of the possible movements have been performed by chance and given rise to a choice ; or when there are numerous equivalent paths to the goal.

This possibility of many solutions constitutes the "unforeseen", or "anti-mechanical" aspect in affective or volitional behaviour, in contrast to the predetermined mechanical behaviour of reflex movements or of any

28 THE PSYCHOLOGY OF REASONING

such complex combinations of reflex movements as certain of the "instincts".

Finally, it is this fundamental property possessed by the affective tendency of constituting in some degree a force gravitating towards the environment, or towards the particular environmental relations that permit the reactivation of certain mnemonic accumulations forming this very tendency, which lends that environment or those environmental relations the appearance of a *vis a fronte* or "ultimate cause" differing very essentially from the *vis a tergo* or "actual cause" which alone is operative in inorganic nature.[1]

"The organism," writes Jennings, "seems to work toward a definite purpose. In other words, *the final result of its action seems to be present in some way at the beginning*, determining what the action shall be. In this the action of living things appears to contrast with that of things inorganic".[2]

Now this "final result of its action" really exists from the beginning in the form of mnemonic accumulation. For that environment or those special environmental conditions to which the animal is gravitating, now play the part of *vis a fronte*, inasmuch as they were formerly *vis a tergo* and in so far as the physiological activities then determined by them in the organism have left behind a mnemonic accumulation which now in its turn constitutes the real and active *vis a tergo*, moving the living being.[3]

Thus it is clear that one and the same explanation applies to all the "finalism" of life.

For from the ontogenetic development which creates organs that can only perform their functions in the adult state, to the property possessed by all physiological states determined in the past, by certain environmental conditions, of remanifesting themselves at the first appearance of phenomena usually preceding these conditions but in no wise constituting them ; from the perfect way in which the organism in its entirety is morphologically adapted to its environment even before the latter can exercise its formative influence, to all the wonderful

---

[1] See W. James, *Principles of Psychology*, London, 1901, Vol. I, pp. 7 f.

[2] Jennings, *op. cit., Behaviour of Lower Organisms*, p. 338.

[3] E. Mach, *Die Analyse der Empfindungen*, Jena, 1906, 5th ed., pp. 70, 78 ; English edition, Chicago, 1914.

AFFECTIVE TENDENCIES 29

formations and special structures so exactly adapted to all the most probable conditions to which this organism might later be exposed; from the simplest reflex acts that are already so mechanically adapted for the preservation and welfare of the individual, to the most complex instincts by means of which animals prepare in advance for future conditions of which they themselves are ignorant—all these "finalistic" aspects of life, identical in their nature, can be explained as so many manifestations of a purely mnemonic nature, as we have shown in earlier works mentioned above.

And now, in what has preceded, we see that affective tendencies, which are even more conspicuously "finalistic" manifestations, are likewise based upon the mnemonic property of living substance, and hence ultimately upon the faculty of "specific accumulation," a faculty belonging exclusively to the nervous energy which underlies all life.

This mnemonic property, this faculty of "specific accumulation", whose absence leaves inorganic nature exclusively in the power of forces *a tergo* and deprives it of every finalistic aspect, is on the other hand everywhere present in organic nature and because of its presence makes the world of life a world apart, a world whose most essential features the physico-chemical laws alone, in the limited sense assigned to them to-day, are quite incapable of explaining.

CHAPTER II

ATTENTION

Part I : Affective Conflict and Unity of Consciousness

ALTHOUGH attention rejoices in a more abundant literature than perhaps any other psychical phenomenon, yet it is still far from being fully "explained"; that is to say, it has not been brought in any way into relation with other psychical phenomena, especially with those with which it has the greatest affinity. And although attention, as Titchener has well said, forms the pivot of all psychology, yet to-day the question as to its essential nature is, to the great detriment of this branch of the science, still very far from solution.

The cause of this backwardness is the same as is found to be responsible in the case of all other psychical activities, namely, that the investigation of all these phenomena has been begun at the point where they are most complex and intricate instead of with the simplest forms. The question of attention has usually been studied by means of introspection and in the act of philosophical reflection, instead of by observing, for instance, the beast of prey, waiting for an opportunity to fall upon its quarry, or the child who hesitates before putting a white pellet in his mouth, in doubt whether it is a sweet as usual, or may turn out to be a bitter pill as was the case yesterday.

The expediency of beginning the investigation with the simplest forms involves the expediency of pursuing the phylogenetic method and following the course of evolution back as far as possible in order to reveal the phenomenon in the very moment of its first appearance. This is the course we pursued in the preceding chapter, when investigating the nature of another psychical phenomenon no less important and fundamental, namely that of affective tendencies; and the phylogenetic method, which showed us their mnemonic origin and nature,

ATTENTION

at once threw light upon that hitherto equally obscure class of phenomena.

This procedure may, it seems to us, be equally successful with attention, which is, as we shall see, only a secondary phenomenon directly derived from affective tendencies.

In the preceding chapter we have seen that the affective tendencies are originally only expressions of one and the same intrinsic tendency of the organism to preserve or restore the state of its normal physiological equilibrium, or to re-establish a previous physiological state, general or local, which had been determined in the past by certain environmental relations. As soon as these relations are even partially repeated, they set loose and bring about the discharge, *in the nascent state*, of the mnemonic accumulation which this former physiological system had left behind.

But we must here emphasize the fact that when a physiological system has been disturbed by altered environmental conditions and reduced to a potential state in the form of a mnemonic accumulation, it can become fully re-activated and continue active in a stable physiological state only when its internal and external relations are, not only partially, but entirely and exactly the same as when they induced this physiological state. Thus the physiological system of an infusorian which has previously lived in a certain temperature or in a salt solution of a certain degree will produce an affective tendency towards its former habitat as soon as it is removed to other environmental relations; and this tendency will be expressed by negative reactions to every other change of its environmental relations which tends to remove it still further from its original habitat, and by positive reactions to every change which brings it nearer thereto (Jennings). But the original physiological state cannot be perfectly re-established and made to persist in normal activity until the animal by its own movements has succeeded in getting again into an environment identical with the old one. Likewise the diminution of histogenetic substance in the blood which prevents the continuance of the normal metabolic state hitherto active and stable, will provoke the affective tendency of hunger and all its derivative acts of seeking and absorbing nourishment. But the normal metabolic

32 THE PSYCHOLOGY OF REASONING

state cannot be completely re-established until hunger is "satisfied"; that is to say, until the acts carried on for the purpose of seeking and absorbing nourishment and the processes of digestion have endowed the blood with the same proportion of histogenetic substance, as formerly.

And yet, as with all mnemonic evocations, here also a small part of a certain former complex environmental state is sufficient, we repeat, if not to "satisfy" the relative affective tendency and to re-activate entirely and lastingly the corresponding physiological state, at least to set it free in the nascent state. That is why the sensations in so far as they represent parts of environmental conditions, become the "starters" *par excellence* of affective tendencies. But in this respect there is an essential difference between the " non-distance receptors " and the "distance-receptors" which Sherrington rightly emphasizes, so that a very significant phylogenetic advance was made when the latter gradually developed from the former.

The "non-distance receptors" (senses with direct contact) usually permit the immediate or almost immediate satisfaction of the affective tendencies which they "start." Frequently the sensation evoking a certain affective tendency has in itself the requisites to satisfy this latter. On the other hand, the "distance-receptors" usually produce that particular state in which an affective tendency is *evoked and held in suspense*, and which we must next analyse with care.

"Between touch and assimilation," says Spencer, "there exists, in the lowest creatures, an intimate connexion. In many Rhizopods the tactual surface and the absorbing surface are co-extensive. The amœba, a speck of jelly having no constant form, sends out, in this or that direction, prolongations of its substance. One of these meeting with, and attaching itself to, some relatively fixed object, becomes a temporary limb by which the body of the creature is drawn forward ; but if this prolongation meets with some relatively small portion of organic matter it slowly expands its extremity around this, slowly contracts, and slowly draws the nutritive morsel into the mass of the body, which collapses around it and presently dissolves it. That is to say, the same portion of tissue is at once arm,

ATTENTION

hand, mouth, and intestine—shows us the tactual and absorbent function united in one."[1]

Sherrington in his turn says: "Animal behaviour shows clearly that in regard to these two groups of receptors the one subserves differentiation of reaction, *i.e.* swallowing or rejection, of material already found and acquired, *e.g.* within the mouth. The other, the distance-receptor, smell, initiates and subserves far-reaching complex reactions of the animal anticipatory to swallowing, namely, all that train of reaction which may be comprehensively termed the quest for food. The latter foreruns and leads up to the former. This precurrent relation of the reaction of the distance-receptor to the non-distance receptor (as well as the ' conative feeling' which the distance-receptor induces) are typical."[2]

Non-distance receptors, then, occasion no "suspended" affective tendencies, no "conative feeling," but instead they bring about the immediate satisfaction of affective tendencies at the moment they are evoked, or the immediate accomplishment of the acts contributing to their satisfaction ("final or consummatory reactions," as Sherrington expresses it). Distance-receptors, on the other hand, evoke the relative affective tendency and keep it awake during the entire time of expectation and during the whole series of acts required before the animal can carry out the last consummatory act, which is to satisfy this affective tendency. It follows that in general only the distance-receptors but not the non-distance receptors can bring about a more or less lasting condition of unfulfilled desire: "If all motive impulses could be at once followed up desire would have no place."[3]

The question now arises how can we explain the fact that the affective tendencies evoked by the distance-receptors, nevertheless remain "suspended"; in other words, how is that although they persist in this state of excitation, yet for some time they occasion no actual performance of any of those consummatory acts which indeed would not now have any result, but to which

[1] Herbert Spencer, *op. cit., The Principles of Psychology,* 4th ed., Vol. I, p. 307.

[2] C. S. Sherrington, *op. cit., The Integrative Action of the Nervous System,* page 326 ff.

[3] A. Bain, *op. cit., The Emotions and the Will,* 1899, 4th ed., p. 423.

C

34 THE PSYCHOLOGY OF REASONING

they nevertheless impel, as is shown by the incipient performance of these acts? The beast of prey, for instance, whose appetite is aroused from afar by the scent and sight of his victim coming towards him without presentiment of danger, nevertheless does not bound forward at once, but waits motionless with all the muscles tense, until the poor creature has come within springing distance. What then prevents the affective tendency so evoked from being at once completely discharged in the consummatory act of springing upon the prey and tearing it to pieces?

This can only be the counteraction of a conflicting tendency by which the first tendency is prevented from accomplishing its consummatory act. And the conflicting tendency in this case can only be the consequence of all consummatory acts which were actually performed in the past at the first awakening of the affective tendency, but every time without result. So we may say it was the "deception", occurring at each premature activation of the affective tendency called forth by the distance-receptor, that called into being the opposite tendency by which the first is now held in suspense.

Möbius' experiment with the pike is well known. By means of a pane of glass he divided a large glass bowl full of water into two parts. In one side he placed the pike and in the other he put tiny whitings which provide the pike's customary food, with the result that whenever the pike dived after one of the small fishes it fell against the obstructing pane of glass. After making these vain attempts for a week, it gave up entirely the pursuit of its unattainable prey and did not change its behaviour even when the obstructing pane of glass had been taken away.

Now the constantly repeated deceptions which resulted when the affective tendency released by a distance-receptor produced immediately the complete performance of a consummatory act which was necessarily unsuccessful, must have had a very similar effect on all animals provided with these senses. And so it has come to pass that the evocation by the distance-receptors of any affective tendency and the premature beginning of the movement connected with it, now, thanks to the memory of former unsuccessful attempts, provoke the antagonistic tendency, similar in every respect to that which pre-

ATTENTION

vented the pike from falling upon its prey. *And this conflict produces that state of affective tendency " held in suspense " which constitutes the state of attention.*

Accordingly we may say that phylogenetically *attention originated with the distance-receptors*, and that it consists in the conflict of two affective tendencies, the second of which is released by the first, prevents it for a time from complete activation, and hence keeps it " in suspense."

The state of attention therefore does not consist of a *single affective state*, but of the conflict arising from *the coexistence of two affective states.* It is because this fact has been overlooked that it has not been possible hitherto to understand in what this state of an affective tendency "in suspense", characteristic of attention, really consisted, and why all those movements which the first of the two affective tendencies would itself have provoked, are arrested "in the nascent state" whereas had this affectivity alone been active they would have been completed.

But also under countless other circumstances, beside this case of the unsuccessful performance of a premature "consummatory act", the distance-receptors arouse, in conflict with the first, a second affectivity which for some time prevents the activation of the former, as a consequence of the unexpected, unpleasant results which had some time previously been associated with this activation. And whenever such an affective conflict occurs, a corresponding state of attention arises at the same time ; and vice versa, there is no state of attention without such a conflict of tendencies. For we need only consider carefully a few of the most significant cases, selected so as to be as different as possible from one another, in order at once to see this conflict of tendencies in operation.

" A young chick two days old," says Lloyd Morgan, "had learned to pick out pieces of yolk from others of white of egg. I cut little bits of orange-peel of the same size as the pieces of yolk, and one of these was soon seized but at once relinquished, the chick shaking its head. Seizing another he held it for a moment in the bill, but then dropped it and scratched at the base of his beak. That was enough. He could not again be induced to seize a piece of orange-peel. The

36 THE PSYCHOLOGY OF REASONING

obnoxious material was now removed and pieces of yolk of egg substituted but they were left untouched, being probably taken for orange-peel. Subsequently, *he looked at the yolk with hesitation, but presently pecked doubtfully, not seizing but merely touching.* Then he pecked again, seized, and swallowed it ".[1]

We see here how the first act of attention of the newly hatched chicken was due to the conflict between its first tendency to seize the yolk of the egg and the conflicting tendency aroused by the memory of the unpleasant experience produced by picking up the orange-peel. The "effective guidance and control of consciousness," which Lloyd Morgan mentions as one of the factors modifying the instinctive pecking of the chicken, was thus only the appearance of a new affectivity, repugnance, inhibiting the first affectivity, hunger, which impelled toward the completion of the instinctive act.[2]

A little girl is taken out for a walk by a maid, and suddenly catches sight of her mother on the other side of the street and wishes to run over to her at once. But the maid suddenly calls out, "Mind the carriage!" and the infant at once stops. The carriage has hardly passed and she has almost taken a step forward when another approaching vehicle forces her to draw back again. The conflict of the two tendencies of desire and fear, kept alive in the child by the sight of her mother and the repeated passing of vehicles is shown very clearly by the direction of her steps first forward and then backward. It is faithfully reflected in the expression of the small bright eyes which shine with anticipation and joy as soon as they are turned upon her mother and the child takes a step nearer to her, but look distressed and anxious when they observe one of the tiresome wagons of which there seems to be no end. Finally, however, the street is unobstructed. The state of fear and the "state of attention", have both entirely disappeared, so that the little girl may at last satisfy her wish and throw herself into her mother's arms.

The conflict of tendencies is likewise exhibited with great distinctness in certain typical states of attention where it is expressed in the exceedingly subtle "choice" between almost imperceptible modalities of a certain act.

[1] Lloyd Morgan, *op. cit., Habit and Instinct*, p. 40 f.
[2] Lloyd Morgan, *op. cit.*, pp. 129-131, 135, 139 f.

ATTENTION 37

A billiard player, for instance, who has already directed his cue at the ball, is anxious primarily to make a successful stroke. He is ready to strike but the extreme tension of the muscles in his arm causes him to fear that he may hit too hard, as he did shortly before. In consequence of this conflicting affectivity his muscles are somewhat relaxed. But the weaker tension he now feels reawakens in him the memory of another earlier unsuccessful stroke when the movement of the ball had not been fast enough, and now he finds himself distressed by the opposite fear lest the stroke may be too weak. From the swing of his arm, now longer and now shorter, which precedes the stroke and brings the point of the cue nearer to the ball or farther from it, a spectator can discern the rapid alternation of conflicting affectivities which respectively exaggerate or moderate the tension of the muscles in order finally to bring about the result of giving to the ball the precise force required.

The same is true when a person who is writing attempts to remove a tiny hair from his pen with his fingers. This rarely succeeds at the first attempt because the fear of inking his finger-tips causes him to press them together before they are near enough to the nib and the hair. The first failure gives rise to care lest the second attempt may also fail, and this opposite fear partly suppresses and moderates the fear of soiling the fingers, so that the wish to remove the hair gives this time to the arm and fingers exactly the degree of muscular contraction necessary to get hold of the projecting end of the hair without touching the wet nib.

From this conflict of tendencies, inevitably occurring as soon as we attempt to perform an act "carefully", arises the well-known fact that attention, when directed to actions which by long practice have become mechanical, makes their execution less rapid and perfect than if they had taken place automatically. "An automatic connection of contents or movements has nothing to gain from the intervention of attention— nay, suffers a very positive loss in accuracy and rapidity of realization, if the attention be directed upon it."[1]

Thus the recitation of a poem, which has been learned so well by heart that it can be repeated mechanically, becomes hesitating and uncertain when

[1] O. Külpe, " The Problem of Attention ", *Monist*, Oct. 1902, p. 61.

38 THE PSYCHOLOGY OF REASONING

the speaker gives it his whole attention. Again, a person who writes his name with the greatest facility when he gives no thought to it, is pretty sure to do it clumsily and somewhat disconnectedly when some one asks for his autograph. For in this case every stroke of the pen needs a short preparation and requires a certain application of the will to begin and complete it, so that the passage from one stroke to another becomes studied and awkward instead of easy and flowing as usual.[1]

But there are some cases, even where the attention is very intense, in which the conflict of tendencies is less obvious. For instance, in Sardou's drama, we have the scene where Tosca's lover is tortured, which arouses the keenest sympathy and attention of all the spectators. Is there any conflict of tendencies in this case? We shall find it if we reflect a little. On the one hand there is the tendency, according to the character of the spectator, to fall upon the cruel Scarpia and slay him, to fall at his feet and with Tosca beg his mercy for her lover, or to hasten to the aid of the victim and liberate him after driving away or killing the agents of the torturer. On the other hand the cultured man has acquired the tendency by education or custom to do nothing which convention does not permit, and not to make himself ridiculous, as would obviously be the case where every one knows that the scenes enacted are not reality but mere invention. This is proved at popular theatres, where the actor who plays the part of the villain is often hissed by the public, and sometimes even becomes the target of more or less harmless missiles thrown by the more unsophisticated spectators. I once attended such a spectacle. Behind a curtain some conspirators were lying in wait to kill the king, who had succeeded in winning the favour of the public by his generosity and fearlessness. He had hardly appeared when a voice was heard to call out at the first movement of the curtain, "Look out, they are going to murder you!" The whole audience laughed uproariously, and the simple spectator was overcome with confusion. He will doubtless succeed another time in repressing his magnanimous outburst, thanks to the conflicting

[1] H. Maudsley, *op. cit.*, *The Physiology of Mind*, pp. 520-21. *The Pathology of Mind*, London, 1895, p. 143.

ATTENTION 39

tendency not to make himself again the object of derision.

Attention which is aroused by novelty is likewise the result of a conflict of tendencies due to the fact that just because the object is new, it has not yet been "affectively classified", and therefore arouses both hope and fear at the same time.

We shall see in a later chapter that any "classification" whatever is based either directly or indirectly upon an affective tendency. This is due to the fact that no sensation or perception of the distance-receptor has any value for the organism except as a symbol of a possible environmental state, near or remote, to be striven after or avoided. As long as this symbol has not been placed in either category, the conflicting affectivities of hope and fear oppose each other and hold each other in suspense. This opposition is seen distinctly, for instance, in a child who hesitates whether to drink a beverage of an unusual colour offered him by his mother for the first time, because he is not sure whether it is a sweet or bitter draught; or in a beast of prey that sees a 'strange' looking animal and is in doubt whether it is a dangerous enemy or perhaps a suitable quarry and therefore makes tense both the muscles of attack and those required for flight.

"Curiosity" is only one of the minor forms of this conflict of tendencies or of this particular state of attention produced by novelty. "The craving for knowledge in its instinctive form is called curiosity. It exists in all degrees, from that of the animal which touches or smells a known object, to the all-examining, all-embracing scrutiny of a Goethe." "Curiosity consists of two questions expressed or implied: What is it? What use is it? . . . The dog brought face to face with an unknown object, looks at it, smells it, approaches, withdraws, ventures to touch it, returns, and begins again; he is pursuing this investigation after his own fashion; he is solving a double problem of nature and utility ".[1]

On the other hand the "not new"—and this also may be any particular object even when we see it for the first time—comprises everything we know how to

---

[1] Th. Ribot, *op. cit., Psychologie des sentiments*, pp. 369, 371. E.T., pp. 368, 370.

40 THE PSYCHOLOGY OF REASONING

classify in one of our various affective categories. Three different cases can then be distinguished : It either brings about the evocation and the immediate satisfaction of the affectivity concerned, like the mountain spring which awakens the desire to drink from it ; or it gives rise to a state of attention, that is it evokes the affective tendency but holds it in suspense for fear, as we have already seen, lest its immediate complete activation might involve some unpleasant result ; or finally it may at that moment be unable to evoke any tendency at all, like the sight or odour of a familiar dish when we have had enough. In this case the affective activity is reduced to a *minimum*, the state of attention entirely ceases, and we experience " monotony " or " tedium." If this state of minimum affective activity is reduced to zero, we have the condition of 'sleep.' "To sleep," as Bergson very truly says, " means to disinterest oneself. We sleep in direct proportion to our disinterestedness."[1]

Finally there is only a very slight difference between "curiosity" and the state of attention of the investigator who observes a certain object or phenomenon in order to convince himself whether it really possesses certain properties whose presence has been asserted by others, or which in his opinion should exist. The presence or absence of these properties is of exceedingly great value to the observer, as is apparent from the fact that he applies himself with such great care to observe them, for they may, for instance, confirm certain of his theories or constitute a highly important scientific discovery. Hence on the one hand he cherishes a lively desire that the supposed properties may really be found to exist. On the other hand he is restrained from rashly announcing a discovery whose accuracy may later be contested by other inquirers to the great injury of his own scientific prestige. Think for instance with what great attention —that is to say, with what great fear of being the victim of an optical illusion—Schiaparelli must have conducted his observations before he decided to make known his discovery of the " canals " of Mars. This hope and this fear furnish the conflict of two affectivities without which, here as elsewhere, no actual state of attention would or could be present.

[1] H. Bergson, " Le rêve ", *Bulletin de l'Institut Psychologique International*, Paris, May 1901, p. 118.

ATTENTION 41

When once we recognise the inmost nature of the affective conflict which, as appears from the few examples here adduced, is characteristic of every state of attention, all other properties which always accompany this state are also seen to be so many simple and direct consequences of its nature.

In particular are we able to perceive at once the inadequateness of Ribot's definition of attention as the state of "relative mono-ideism". We might rather call it a state of "mono-affectivity held in suspense", but, as we have seen, it is still better to define it as a state of "double conflicting affectivity".[1]

Ribot's motor or peripheral theory proves to be equally erroneous: "Are the movements of the face, the body and the limbs, and the respiratory modifications that accompany attention, simply effects, outward marks as is usually supposed? Or are they, on the contrary, *the necessary conditions, the consistent elements, the indispensable factors* of attention? Without hesitation we accept the second thesis".[2]

On the other hand the so-called theories of "central origin" seem to be perfectly correct.[3]

Attention is indeed a "central", psychological phenomenon; for the awakening of the primary affectivity and the counter-awakening of the secondary affectivity which holds the other in suspense, are phenomena of this nature. Attention therefore is first of all an essentially affective phenomenon and only indirectly and in a subordinate manner does it become a motor phenomenon, by the fact that the awakening of any affectivity whatever always produces motor and peripheral phenomena, which are therefore only accompanying or derived.

Ribot's error is entirely due to the fact that he has not succeeded in correctly comprehending the nature of affective tendencies, for he sees very well that "attention always depends upon affective states", but he adds soon after: "How are we to represent to ourselves these affective tendencies? The only positive idea that we

---

[1] See Th. Ribot, *Psychologie de l'attention*, 6th edition, Paris, 1902, pp. 6-8; English edition, p. 10.

[2] Ribot, *op. cit.*, p. 32. English edition, p. 25.

[3] See, e.g., J. Sully, "The Psycho-Physical Process in Attention", *Brain*, July 1890, especially pp. 155-157; and Vaschide and Meunier, *La Psychologie de l'attention*, Paris, 1910, pp. 196 ff.

42 THE PSYCHOLOGY OF REASONING

can get of them is to consider them as movements (or as inhibitions of movements), be they real or in the nascent state ".[1]

Accordingly, for him the motor elements would by themselves constitute the entire essence of affective tendencies. But it is the affective tendencies which are the cause of the motor elements, and not the reverse.

As we have seen in the previous chapter, an affective tendency is only a gravitation, so to speak, toward that environment or those environmental relations which permit the reactivation of the mnemonic accumulation constituting this affective tendency. But of itself, it does not produce any preferential impulse towards one rather than towards another series of movements. For even if these movements were such as could eventually bring the organism back into the desired environmental conditions, yet in themselves they have nothing to do with the ultimate satisfaction of this affective tendency. It is only when one series of movements happens to succeed in bringing the organism back to the requisite environmental conditions sooner or better than the others, and only from this moment, that it becomes preferred to the others. Only then will the awakening of the affective tendency give rise to definite motor elements.

But before this occurs, that is to say before the affective tendency has caused any "choice" of the movements capable of leading to the desired end, the affective tendency towards that end will already exist. The very fact of this affective choice proves that in point of time the choosing factor precedes the element chosen. It follows that there can be an affective tendency even in the absence of any motor element. For instance a new and unusual indisposition arouses the affective tendency to be freed from it, but this does not and cannot initiate any motion whatever.

Hence if affective tendencies and motor elements are two different things, and if the latter are caused by the former and not the reverse, then this is also true with regard to attention, for which, consequently, the motor elements are not an indispensable condition but merely quite secondary phenomena.

Since every conflict of affective tendencies is expressed

[1] Ribot, *op. cit.*, *Psychology of Attention*, pp. 166, 172. English Edition, pp. 112, 116.

ATTENTION 43

in a conflict of the motor elements induced by them, a clear explanation is afforded by our theory of attention, though it belongs to the theories of "central origin", for the fact that "muscular tension", "motor innervation", "tonic contraction", and the "elevation of the entire psychic life", characterize every state of attention, as so many psychologists have observed.[1]

Affective choice determines not only the particular movements of locomotion, of seizing, etc., which make for the desired object, but also the adjustment of the sense-organs, itself a muscular-motor phenomenon, on which depends the more or less successful result of the movements, of whatever kind they may be, and for which, therefore, both of the two conflicting affectivities co-operate. When, for instance, we are surprised by a sudden noise and rapidly direct our glance to the distant object from which it seems to come, the state of attention is alert during the whole interval preceding the moment in which the eyes have become adjusted to the new distance, which requires a certain length of time when the object is some way off. Thus attention is awakened (here too in conformity with the theory of central origin) before and not after the adjustment of the organ concerned.[2]

Moreover, even if the peripheral sensory conditions remain the same, the attention may be directed now to some sensations and now to others; as when, confined within our room, we give more heed to certain noises in the street than to others which come from the same direction; for instance, to the hoof-beat of the horses belonging to a vehicle that stops before our door, in order to determine by the sound which of our friends has come to call; or to the roll of the wheels in order to find out whether the friend who has come to take us out driving has brought an open or closed carriage. Attention may even be directed at different times to different properties of a sensation, for instance to the intensity or pitch of a musical note or again to its *timbre*. No other examples could demonstrate better than these how completely attention is independent of the adjust-

---

[1] Maudsley, *op. cit.*, *The Physiology of Mind*, p. 313; Ch. Féré, "Physiologie de l'attention", *Revue philosophique*, Oct. 1890, pp. 401, 404; K. B. R. Aars, "Notes sur l'attention", *Année psychologique*, Paris, 1902, Vol. VIII, p. 216.

[2] See W. B. Pillsbury, *Attention*, London, 1908, p. 13.

44 THE PSYCHOLOGY OF REASONING

ment of the sense, as well as in general of every other "peripheral factor."[1]

From this "central origin" of attention which has been so fully established, and from the fact of its inmost nature being an opposition between two mutually conflicting affectivities as above discussed, a fundamental conclusion may be drawn, whose importance will be seen more clearly in the next chapter, when we come to examine the effects of the affective tendencies on the evocation and vividness of images and sensations; namely, that the object of attention is observed simultaneously *from two quite distinct points of view.* Thus a large number of properties and characteristics, of advantages and disadvantages are perceived, observed, recalled and emphasized, which would by no means be the case if only a single affectivity were operative.

Wundt's well-known metaphorical definition of the *apperception* produced by attention as consisting in the transition of the image "from the internal visual field to the internal visual point of consciousness" (von dem inneren Blickfield in den inneren Blickpunkt des Bewusstseins), might, then, be better replaced by that of *an internal double reflector illuminating the object or the image from several sides at the same time.*[2]

That is why attention prevents the mnemonic supply of sensory evocations, which any affectivity always adds to the first crude elementary sensation at the moment it is aroused, from distorting the "perception" produced by this mnemonic contribution into an "illusion" or "hallucination", which on the contrary is always the case when the affectivity thus aroused remains alone.

Sudden and intense fear, for instance, makes any state of attention quite impossible and may give rise— as in the classical case of the traveller walking at night through a dense forest—to those characteristic hallucinations cited and described in all text-books of psychology and psycho-pathology. On the other hand the "cold-blooded" man is he who does not flee at the sudden rustling of leaves, which at first arouses in him the vision of some dangerous robber lurking behind the

---

[1] O. Külpe, *art. cit.,* " The Problem of attention ", p. 50.

[2] W. Wundt, *Grundzüge der physiologischen Psychologie,* Leipzig, 1903, 5th ed., Vol. III, p. 333. Ostwald, *op. cit., Vorlesungen über Natur-philosophie,* pp. 400, 403.

ATTENTION 45

trees, but who, restrained by his dislike of behaving like a coward, looks around "with attention" to see whether there really is a living creature there, and of what sort it is, or whether the sound was not due rather to the wind.

Similarly in a state of passion any attention to what is connected with this passion becomes impossible, and the passionate man is therefore exposed to all the auto-suggestions and hallucinations of an Othello, because of the existence of a unique hypertrophic affective tendency, not held in suspense by any other.

In monomaniacs also, as for instance those suffering from chronic persecution-mania and similar psychical diseases, the thing lacking is the counter-affectivity which would tend to make them fear that they may be mistaken. They are mono-affective in the proper sense of the word, and are therefore likewise incapable of a real and proper state of attention.

The absence of any counter-affectivity produces in all these cases a total absence of "antagonistic reductives", as Taine would say, which could check the auto-suggestions and hallucinations produced by the one existing affectivity, which reign undisturbed. On the other hand, great attention always protects from suggestion practised by others, just because the opposite affectivity, the fear of being deceived, becomes very strong, as is proved for instance by Binet's experiments on the susceptibility of school children to suggestion.[1]

Passing now to the relations existing between attention and consciousness we must first anticipate the theory which will be developed in our last chapter with regard to the conditions which determine the consciousness and unconsciousness of the different psychical states.

According to this theory, a given psychical state is neither conscious nor unconscious in itself, but seems to possess either one or the other of these properties only when, having been previously active, it is now referred to another psychical state at present existing. And the necessary and sufficient condition permitting

---

[1] H. Taine, *De l'intelligence*, Paris, 1897, 8th ed., Vol. I, pp. 95 ff. A. Binet, *La suggestibilité*, Paris, 1900, pp. 166, 177 f., 186, 191, 196, 200 etc.

46 THE PSYCHOLOGY OF REASONING

a complex past psychical state to present itself again as "conscious" in relation to a complex present psychical state is that there shall be co-existence and superposition or fusion, at any rate in part, between the affective portion of the mnemonic evocation of the first and the affective portion of the second.

Since, as we have seen in the previous chapter, the possession of a "diffuse seat" is characteristic of *affective tendencies*—which in this respect are so different from *sensations* and their *images* whose seat is localised at single points or centres and which therefore may exist and be active simultaneously in great numbers at the same time in the same brain—it is difficult even for only two affective tendencies to have their seats in localities which shall not coincide more or less, so that when these tendencies strive to be operative at the same time, they either inhibit one another or hold each other in suspense, or partially coalesce.

If the awakening of one does not depend on the awakening of the other, and if the respective nervous activities in the part of their seats common to both differ specifically from each other and are incompatible with each other, then—as will be more obvious in the next chapter which treats of inhibition—the activation of one tendency will of itself imply the exclusion of the other and *vice versa*. If the awakening of the one is caused by the awakening of the other and the two tendencies are antagonistic, we will then have the state in which the primary affective tendency is held in suspense by the secondary ; and this condition, as we have seen above, is characteristic of the state of attention. If, on the other hand, the respective nervous activities in that portion of their seats common to both are specifically similar, then their blending together will make the complex psychical state, to which one of the tendencies belongs, "conscious" with reference to the psychical state to which the other belongs.

Finally, a fourth case will occur, though much more rarely for the reasons already stated, in which the two affective tendencies have no part of their seats in common, and accordingly both can be present and operative at the same time without hindering each other or bearing any relation whatever to one another. This case comprises all the phenomena of so-called

ATTENTION 47

double personality. These phenomena nevertheless, as we shall see better in our last chapter, are by no means always of a pathological character, like the typical cases studied especially by Janet, but they may appear also in normal persons in so-called instances of "absent-mindedness". When, for instance, I was climbing down into the valley from Ca' di Janzo by a very steep mule path, leaping from one stone to another constantly demanded the whole attention in order to measure exactly the distance of the leap and lest a foot should slip or dislodge a stone. Yet the descent sometimes proceeded "unconsciously" with reference to some other very different affectivity which produced at the same time quite another train of thought.

In the first of these four cases, the exclusion of all other tendencies with independent awakening, as soon as one of them becomes active,—an exclusion which persists throughout the whole time during which the primary affective tendency of the state of attention remains held in suspense—forms the so-called "unity of consciousness".

In other words, the impossibility for more than one primary affective tendency to be active at any one time results in the impossibility of giving heed to more than one object at a time. "A plurality of stimulations of the nerves may coexist, but they affect the consciousness only by turns, or one at a time. The reason is that the bodily organs are collectively engaged with each distinct conscious state, and they cannot be doing two things at the same instant ".[1]

Consequently, attention ordinarily is never "divided" or "dispersed". If it is sufficiently intense, it will continue to be directed toward any given object for a while, and hence cannot be directed to any others during this entire period. If it is less intense, it can pass from one object to another in quick succession and accordingly seems to be divided among many objects at the same time; but in reality even in this case it is directed at each moment to one object only, that is, to the one which corresponds to the momentary affective tendency. Accordingly, the speaker who passes judgment upon his own speech, the actor who has command over himself, the chess player who plays

[1] Bain, *The Emotions and the Will*, p. 5.

48 THE PSYCHOLOGY OF REASONING

several games at one time, Julius Cæsar who dictated several letters at once, do not prove the simultaneous presence of several states of attention, but rather their rapid succession and the alternating predominance of first one and then another.[1]

For this reason the attention directed by self-contemplation upon any affective state brings about the end and disappearance of that state. "It is impossible to direct one's attention upon an affectivity. If the attempt is made that particular mood ceases at once, and we are turned aside by a compelling sensation or idea which we have not the slightest desire to observe".[2]

For the attention which is directed upon an affectivity within ourselves is a newly originated affectivity, namely, the one that impels us to this observation and analysis, and therefore it displaces the other we wished to observe.

The primary affective tendency of the state of attention, which excludes, as we have now seen, every other affectivity with independent awakening and in this way protects the "unity" of our consciousness, is also what makes it possible for every past state of attention to appear "conscious" to us, if we now think back to it and to the object which at that time roused our interest. For this object will now be recalled by a more or less similar affective tendency, which therefore will partially blend with the recollection of the former.

Every state of attention, accordingly, contains all elements within itself in order later to seem to us to be conscious; but not all past psychical states which now appear conscious were states of attention, as is maintained by Kohn, for whom the state of attention and the conscious state are the same thing. For an affectivity which discharges at once completely and therefore does not give rise to any state of attention—like a hurried flight caused by sudden terror—is nevertheless able to make the complex psychical state involved appear subsequently as a conscious one.[3]

In other words, the state of attention is a sufficient but not a necessary condition of consciousness. The

---

[1] E. Meumann, *op. cit., Intelligenz und Wille*, pp. 22 ff.

[2] E. B. Titchener, *The Psychology of Feeling and Attention*, New York, 1908, p. 69.

[3] See H. E. Kohn, *Zur Theorie der Aufmerksamkeit*, Halle, 1895, pp. 19, 27.

ATTENTION 49

only condition which is at the same time necessary and sufficient is the presence of some affective tendency, no matter whether it be in the state of suspense or of full activation.

The automatic acts, for instance, which originated through affective choice as conscious movements and which were perfected later by means of attention under the affective conflict of the tendencies impelling the performance of the act and striving at the same time to avoid its many imperfections, have finally succeeded after frequent repetition—according to the mnemonic law that the part gradually becomes independent of the whole—in performing themselves without requiring either any affective impulsion or any state of attention whatever. For this reason we are accustomed to say that rendering acts automatic liberates the attention so that it may be directed to other objects.[1]

And just because acts which have become automatic do not require attention on our part and take place without the assistance of any affective element, they always seem to us to be unconscious. "Consciousness", as Maudsley says, "attends the process of adaptation, tentative endeavours, the practice of means to ends, the steps of organisation ; it lapses when skill is perfect."[2]

"Habit," writes James, "diminishes the conscious attention with which our acts are performed. One may state this abstractly thus: If an act require for its execution a chain of successive nervous events, then in the first performances of the action the conscious will must choose each of these events from a number of wrong alternatives that tend to present themselves ; for consciousness is always and chiefly a selective agency. But habit soon brings it about that each event calls up its own appropriate successor without any alternative offering itself and without any reference to the conscious will, until at last the whole chain rattles itself off as soon as the first event occurs, just as if this and the rest of the chain were fused into a continuous stream ".[3]

Just as an act that has become automatic represents a nervous activity which in the absence of any

---

[1] Meumann, *op. cit., Intelligenz und Wille*, p. 23.
[2] Maudsley, *op. cit., The Pathology of Mind*, p. 9.
[3] Wm. James, *op. cit., The Principles of Psychology*, Vol. I, pp. 114, 139.

D

50 THE PSYCHOLOGY OF REASONING

accompanying affective tendency remains unconscious, so will every stimulation of our senses remain unconscious even when it reaches its sensory seat, if it cannot arouse any affectivity in us. On the other hand every stimulation of our senses which succeeds in awakening any one of the many affective tendencies potentially present in the brain, may afterwards appear conscious to us; and this may also be expressed by saying that the "stimulation has succeeded in taking possession of the sensorium."[1]

It follows that if all objective and peripheral-sensory conditions remain the same, it will depend on whether our attention is or is not directed upon something else and on the degree of strength and of persistence of the respective primary affectivity—for it is from these qualities that it will derive its power to exclude every other affective tendency which differs from it—whether certain stimuli remain quite unobserved or whether they will afterwards appear to us as conscious sensations.[2]

Says James: "Millions of items of the outward order are present to my senses which never properly enter into my experience. Why? Because they have no *interest* for me. *My experience is what I agree to attend to.* Only those items which I *notice* shape my mind. Without selective interest experience is an utter chaos. Interest alone gives accent and emphasis, light and shade, background and foreground—intelligible perspective, in a word."[3]

The primary affectivity of a state of attention turned away may be so strong that it can prevent even the most intense irritations, which at other times would seem very painful and arouse within us the most strenuous effort to remove them, from reaching our consciousness. Classic, for instance, is the case of the Christian martyr whose entranced attention was to such a degree absorbed by the beatific visions presented to his eyes, that it prevented him from feeling the pain of the horrible tortures to which his body was subjected. No less significant is the case of Robert

---

[1] G. E. Müller, *op. cit.*, *Zur Theorie der sinnlichen Aufmerksamkeit*, p. 77.

[2] Müller, *op. cit.*, p. 1; Külpe, *art. cit.*, pp. 40-41. Ostwald, *op. cit.*, *Vorlesungen über Naturphilosophie*, p. 400 ff.

[3] James, *op. cit.*, Vol. I, p. 402.

ATTENTION 51

Hall, some of whose "most eloquent discourses were poured forth whilst he was suffering under a bodily disorder which caused him to roll in agony on the floor when he descended from the pulpit; yet he was entirely unconscious of the irritation of his nerves by the calculus which shot forth its jagged points through the whole substance of his kidney, so long as his soul continued to be 'possessed' by the great subjects on which a powerful effort of his will originally fixed it."[1]

Yet a large number of facts go to prove that those nervous excitations which do not discharge any affectivity or are not capable of arousing our attention and therefore remain unconscious, nevertheless likewise succeed in reaching their sensory seats. "The fact that we sometimes become conscious of many sensuous impressions, such as for instance the stroke of a bell, not at once but only some little time after the stimulus has made itself felt in our sense-organ, tends to show that the excitation reaches its destination rightly enough (dass die Erregung bis zu ihrem Endziele richtig eindringe) but that the sensorium happens at the moment to be in a state not suited for the reception of the afferent stimulus."[2]

The conflict itself between the different states of attention which the varied stimuli from the outside world would tend to arouse—a conflict deriving from the fact that only one single primary affective tendency can ever be active at any one moment—indicates that, whatever the relation of the stimulations to consciousness may be, these nervous stimulations always reach their habitual psychical centre; for otherwise they could not tend to awaken their respective affectivities. "When one of the various stimuli succeeds in the struggle to obtain possession of consciousness we say that we are attentive to it according to the intensity of the corresponding process of consciousness." "But we can not maintain that excitations which do not enter our consciousness because of averted attention do not enter at all into the organ of consciousness, the cortex of the brain."[3]

---

[1] W. B. Carpenter, *Principles of Mental Physiology*, London, 1896, 7th ed., p. 138.

[2] Müller, *op. cit.*, *Zur Theorie der sinnl. Aufm.*, p. 105.

[3] Kohn, *art. cit.*, p. 19; and Sigmund Exner, *Entwurf zu einer physiologischen Erklärung der psychischen Erscheinungen*, Vienna and Leipzig, 1894, Part I, p. 72.

52 THE PSYCHOLOGY OF REASONING

It often happens in my own case, for instance, that I am reading a newspaper while the other members of the family are chatting together in the same room or perhaps while one of them reads aloud from a book or a different paper. Sometimes I do not succeed in limiting my attention to what I myself am reading because my interest is aroused by what I hear read aloud. In other cases, however, I succeed very well, and then I no longer hear the words of those in the room. Nevertheless, one word pronounced by the reader in exactly the same tone as all the other words—for he is reading right along in the same monotonous voice—suddenly draws me completely away from what I am reading and turns my attention to what he is reading aloud. Thus my attention oscillates constantly between what I am reading and what I am hearing read. The fact of this conflict between the two states of attention accordingly proves most positively, I repeat, that the nervous excitations produced by the spoken words of another reach their sensory centre, their sensory basis in me, even in moments when I am not attending to them ; otherwise they would not be able from time to time to arouse my interest or to " seize " my attention.

The same is obviously true for all so-called states of absent-mindedness which in essence, as we have already seen, are only the first physiological indications of that dual state of personality which hitherto has been investigated almost exclusively in its pathological forms. This explains the fact that we can often lock a drawer while attention was directed elsewhere ; which proves that all visual, nervous stimulations proceeding from the key-hole and the key placed in it reached their goal although they remained entirely unconscious. Everyone has the experience of walking absent-mindedly through the streets and yet without running into people, vehicles, or any other obstructing objects on the way. Our previously mentioned " unconscious " descent from the Ca' di Janzo proves how perfectly in every respect the perception of all the difficulties of the way must have been—the stones, their form, their position, their state of equilibrium—for me to succeed in leaping from one stone to another without falling or knocking down a stone.

ATTENTION 53

The primary affective tendency which constitutes that state of attention which is directed on a definite object, by no means excludes the intrusion of sensations which at the time "have no interest"; in other words, it does not prevent excitations of a sensory character from reaching their goal, their normal destination, even when we are unconscious of them; but it only *opposes and inhibits the affective tendency which these sensations tend to arouse*.

"The entrance of a stimulus into consciousness"— as it is expressed by Kohn and others—does not rest upon the possible intrusion of the stimulus at any particular part of the brain, or "sensorium", whose specific function would be that of consciousness. Still less does it depend on the excitation of a single "centre of apperception" as Wundt assumes. But *it consists solely in the fact that this stimulus evokes some affective tendency relating to the object which it represents.* When this evocation takes place the stimulus reaches consciousness; if it does not take place, perhaps because at this moment another affective tendency referring to other sensations is active, then, *although the stimulus may penetrate physiologically to the same point as usual*, it cannot reach consciousness and hence remains unobserved and "unconscious". We shall see, however, in the next chapter, that the persistence of the mnemonic accumulations of those sensations which remain outside of consciousness, and the possibility of evoking them again in the future, are at a great disadvantage from the circumstance that they have not been able to excite any affective state peculiar to themselves with which they could be associated.

Having thus elucidated in broad outline the essential nature of an affective conflict peculiar to attention, and having seen wherein consists that unity of consciousness which so many inquirers declare to be one of its most fundamental properties, we may now pass on to the study of the effects on sensations and ideas, and in general on the whole process of intelligence which derive from this essential nature and from this fundamental property of attention. These effects, which can be summed up in two words, *vividness* and *connection*, will be considered in the next chapter.

CHAPTER III

ATTENTION

Part II : Vividness and Connection

IN the preceding chapter we saw that any state of attention whatever may be considered as the result of an affective conflict, and that this is due to the fact that there is a secondary affectivity, which is opposed to some primary affectivity, aroused by a distance-receptor and tending at once to provoke the movements designed to satisfy it. This secondary affectivity is evoked by the primary itself on account of some disagreeable effect produced in the past through having given to these movements a too prompt and complete execution, and tends to prevent the repetition of the unpleasant effect. We saw at the same time that "the unity of consciousness", a fundamental characteristic of the state of attention, is due to the fact that, so long as the primary affectivity is held "in suspense" by the secondary, no other affective tendency can arise ; for each having a "diffuse seat", the new one would be obliged to encroach on the territory of the primary affectivity already aroused.

As we said at the end of the preceding chapter, we must now examine the effects on the sensations, images and ideas and on the whole intellectual process in general, which result from the nature of affective conflict and the fundamental characteristic of unity of consciousness which are peculiar to attention ; effects that may be summed up by the two words *vividness* and *connection*.

Before passing on to this inquiry, however, it is important to understand the word "vividness", to which psychologists have only recently endeavoured to attach a definite meaning.

Everyone in fact, by means of introspection, has had a sufficiently clear idea of a sensation of great or small "intensity", distinct from that of a sensation or a

VIVIDNESS AND CONNECTION 55

memory more or less "vivid." All of us, for example, will have occasionally experienced in the silence of the night, a "very vivid" sensation of a very light noise, as if someone were furtively gliding into our bedroom. The thought of a dead friend can evoke "very vividly" the memory of his last words, pronounced in an almost inaudible voice. On the other hand one may retain a very faint memory of an intense noise that was produced in the past without arousing particular interest.

But it is only lately that the psychologists have expressly emphasised the essential difference that exists between "intensity" and "vividness."[1]

Semon in particular has recently insisted that "the 'vividness' of a sensation is a property quite distinct from the 'intensity' determined by the quantity of the stimulus." And he observes nicely : "The memory of a 'fortissimo', however attenuated the actual evocation may be, always remains a 'fortissimo,' and has not the slightest resemblance to the sensation of a 'pianissimo'. But how is it possible, in comparing the actual sensations with those revived, to measure respectively the smallest differences of intensity, if the latter, in its mnemonic phase, does not remain constant, or at least does not contain a constant element?"[2]

From these and similar facts, one is led to conclude that the "intensity" of a sensation is included in its "specificity", that is to say, constitutes one of the elements of the latter and accordingly is, as such, susceptible of mnemonic accumulation. Thus, for example, as regards the visual sensations, the three elements, colour, saturation and luminous intensity are considered as so many kinds of specificity (Farbenton, Sättigung, und Helligkeit).[3]

On the other hand, as regards the greater or lesser "vividness" of a sensation or memory, one is rather

---

[1] *Cf.*, for example, W. Wundt, *op. cit.*, *Grundzüge der physiologischen Psychologie*, Vol. I, p. 323, Vol. III, p. 339, and : E. B. Titchener, *op. cit.*, *Psychology of Feeling and Attention*, pp. 182, 219.

[2] R. Semon, *Die mnemischen Empfindungen*, Leipzig, 1909, pp. 241, 330-331, 385.

[3] *Cf.*, for example, H. von Helmholtz, *Vorträge und Reden*, 5th Edition, Vol. I, Braunschweig, 1903 : "Die Gesichtsempfindungen," in particular p. 307 ff. ; and W. Wundt, *Grundrisse der Psychologie*, Leipzig, 1907, pp. 33-75.

56 THE PSYCHOLOGY OF REASONING

inclined to admit, in accordance with a number of facts some of which will be examined later, that it is due only to an increase or diminution in the *active quantity* of specific nervous energy constituting such a sensation or memory.

Having said this, it will be easy to understand, first of all, how the state of attention can succeed in increasing the vividness of sensations and perceptions.

Since the "adaptation" of the sense organ has as a result the exposure of the organ and the corresponding nerve to the action of the stimulus in such a way as to bring to the maximum the stimulating effect of the latter, the vividness of a sensation will become the greater, the more perfect the adaptation in question has been. Now the fact that the primary affectivity of the state of attention is held "in suspense" by the secondary, gives more time for the corresponding sense organ to make its appropriate adaptation. Further, in certain more delicate cases, it allows it the necessary time in which still more to perfect its adaptation by an "affective choice" of this or that supplementary detail of the process of adaptation itself. At the same time as it holds the sense organ fixed in the direction of the object, it allows of what is called the "summation of stimuli" and this permits the strongest to increase still more the vividness of their effects, and many of the weaker, whose action would otherwise not be sufficiently vivid, to cross also the threshold of perception.

But this is not sufficient. The stereoscopic experiments of Helmholtz in which, while excluding all possibility of movement or adaptation of the eyes, he succeeded in perceiving one or other of the two different images which were disputing the field of vision, by the sole fact of fixing his attention on one or the other; the work of the same scientist on the perception of the harmonics which constitute the timbre of a given fundamental note; and many other facts of the same kind where an increase of vividness is produced in certain sensations at the expense of certain others without either the length of exposure or the adaptation of the corresponding organ being able to affect the matter in any way—all this is absolutely opposed to the hypothesis that every increase of vividness due to attention can always be attributed to the simple fact

VIVIDNESS AND CONNECTION 57

of the action of the stimulus being more complete or more prolonged.[1]

It is necessary then, in such cases, to have recourse to some further process, more or less analogous in certain respects to the well-known one of an increase of vividness produced by binocular vision and by binaural hearing. Exner, for example, quotes the familiar experience of sportsmen, who, in a certain degree of obscurity, still see the game with both eyes open, but no longer perceive it when they close one in order to take aim: "The central paths which transmit the respective sensations", so he explains the phenomenon, "are the same for both eyes; as a result the stimulation of a certain cone of the retina of the left eye has the same effect as an increase of stimulation of the corresponding cone of the right eye".—"In other words, both the stimulations, after reaching a certain point, of course, turn into the same cerebral paths, and the result of their addition is a stimulation strong enough to be perceived ".[2]

Now in the aforesaid cases of increase of vividness that attention suffices to produce of itself, it might have been that there was a similar addition of two equal excitations, but that one of them was due to a mnemonic evocation produced by attention, instead of it too being the effect of an actual stimulus. In short, we should then have something exactly analogous to the "anticipated perception", in which mnemonic elements, evoked at the moment by the sudden appearance of an object, immediately coalesce, if they are of equal specificity, with the weaker and more slowly produced sensory elements, whose vividness they augment, so hastening the perception of the object itself.

In fact, an affective tendency when aroused implies of itself the sensation or the image of the object that is desired or avoided, and accordingly it implies also its mnemonic association with everything that bears

---

[1] Cf., for example, H. von Helmholtz, *Handbuch der physiologischen Optik*, 3rd edition, Vol. III, Hamburg and Leipzig, 1910, § 32 : "Wettstreit der Sehfelder," particularly pp. 402-410 ; The same, *op. cit.*, *Vortr. u. Reden*, Vol. I, "Vorlesung über die physiologischen Ursachen der musikalischen Harmonie ", particularly p. 146 ff.

[2] S. Exner, *Entwurf zu einer physiologischen Erklärung der psychischen Erscheinungen*, Part I, Leipzig and Vienna, 1894, pp. 181-182, 183.

58 THE PSYCHOLOGY OF REASONING

directly or indirectly upon this object: "The sexual instinct, hunger, thirst, fear, and other more or less analogous organic affective tendencies act like a magic ring to re-awaken the images which are agreeable to, or have any connection whatever with, them."[1]

Thus hunger, evoking in the carnivorous animal the memory of the sour odour of some victim already torn to pieces and devoured, will sharpen the sensibility for this odour, while rendering a herbivorous animal more sensible only to the delicate aroma of pastures.

For this reason too the state of attention should tend to provoke, in anticipation of the real sensations, a number of mnemonic elements relative to all that constitutes the object of attention. And if these successive actual sensations happen to coincide in their respective specificities with the mnemonic elements thus evoked in anticipation, there would result in this case again the "fusion" of the mnemonic elements with the sensory, whence the corresponding increase in the vividness of the latter.

Such is the theory, one may say, of Helmholtz and Müller: "There is perhaps"—writes the former, for instance, *à propos* of his stereoscopic experiments quoted above—"no other phenomenon as suitable as this (the struggle between the two fields of vision) for the study of the modes of attracting the attention. It is not sufficient merely to intend to see now with one eye and now with the other, *but it is necessary to force ourselves to recall as accurately as possible the sensory image of what we desire to see*".[2]

In the same way the practised musician who attends to a fundamental tone of a certain timbre in order to distinguish the harmonics, only imagines to himself in anticipation, by way of affective evocation, "how the tones that he is seeking should sound".[3]

"When the mind directs its proper attention on a certain sensation, for example on a certain tone," writes Müller in his turn, "it is only seeking to reproduce in itself the state which it experienced, when it happened to perceive this tone formerly". "The stimulus towards which our attention voluntary turns, then finds means

---

[1] P. Flechsig, *Gehirn und Seele*, Leipzig, 1896, p. 29.

[2] H. von Helmholtz, *op. cit.*, *Vortr. und Reden*, Vol. I, p. 348.

[3] H. von Helmholtz, *Die Lehre von den Tonempfindungen*, quoted by Müller, pp. 49-50.

VIVIDNESS AND CONNECTION 59

of acting more easily on the mind than if it had to impose itself, after overcoming by its own energy greater resistance; and there is reason to expect that a notably stronger sensation is produced in the first case than in the second, *in so much as the effects of the intention of the mind are added to those of the external stimulus* ".[1]

Nevertheless this anticipated evocation of certain mnemonic elements, which immediately coalesce with those of the senses and give greater relief to the latter, is still not sufficient to explain the exactly similar effects of increase of vividness which the state of attention produces even in simple remembrances. For evidently we are concerned here only with mnemonic elements.

In the case of the perception of an object, the greater vividness of certain characters or attributes in relation to certain others has been found to be due, as we have seen, to the fusion of certain mnemonic elements with the sensory elements of the same specificity corresponding to these characters or attributes. So too, in the case of pure mnemonic images, the first idea that suggests itself is to regard the analogous greater vividness of such and such a mnemonic element in relation to certain others, according as the attention is directed towards it or towards the others, as due to a *greater number of simultaneous evocations* of the element that attracts attention: so that these, coalescing with each other, would form a single evocation rendered thereby so much the more vivid.

The simultaneity of several evocations will in its turn be rendered possible by the property possessed by each mnemonic association of tending to reproduce in its integrity the complex system that has left a mnemonic accumulation of itself. It would then suffice if a certain element were common to two or more associations and the respective systems to which it belongs were evoked, for there to be as many simultaneous evocations and a corresponding increase of vividness: "It is astonishing," Galton remarks, "how the vividness of a memory is increased when two or more links of association are stimulated at the same time ".[2]

This is precisely the theory held by Semon, although

[1] G. E. Müller, *op. cit., Zur Theorie der sinnlichen Aufmerksamkeit,* pp. 5, 47.

[2] F. Galton, *op. cit., Inquiries into Human Faculty,* p. 108.

60 THE PSYCHOLOGY OF REASONING

his not too happy terminology and his adherence to the old view that considers the mnemonic phenomenon as a *trace* or *impression* rather than as a *specific accumulation*, obscures its whole development.[1]

This explanation may certainly be applicable in many cases; when, for example, the memory of some character of a certain object tends to evoke, by sensory association, all the other characters of the same object, while a certain interest, aroused in one of these characters in particular, tends to recall the latter also by affective evocation.

But the fact that the vividness of a sensory mnemonic evocation increases with what is called the "intensity", or more correctly here again with the "vividness" of the corresponding affective tendency, indicates that not even this multiple evocation is sufficient to account for all the processes of augmentation of vividness produced by attention; for in these cases we have only a single evocative agent that is always the same, represented by the more or less vivid affectivity.

In order to explain this "crescendo" of vividness of sensory evocations produced by the increase of vividness of the corresponding affective tendency, it is necessary to have recourse to another hypothesis, and to suppose, for example, that the discharged part of the sensory accumulation can be increased or diminished according to the vividness of the corresponding evoking affectivity. To use the expression of Exner, the action of "clearing the road" (Bahnung) with regard to the sensory evocation exercised by a given affectivity, might be supposed to increase at the same time as the quantity of active energy constituting that affectivity.[2]

All accumulation of energy in fact implies the possibility of a total discharge as much as a more or less partial one. And this should apply to accumulations of nervous energy of any kind whatever. Whence a "graduation of discharge" suggested even by Sherrington, for example as regards the intensity of the reaction of such and such a reflex, in relation to the degree of intensity of the releasing stimulus.[3]

[1] Semon, *op. cit., Die mn. Empf.*, e.g. pp. 286 ff.
[2] Cf., Exner, *op. cit., Entwurf zu einer physiol. Erklär. der psych. Ersch.*, pp. 76 ff.
[3] Cf. C. S. Sherrington, *op. cit., The integrative Action of the Nervous System*, for example, pp. 5, 74-76 etc.

VIVIDNESS AND CONNECTION 61

Ostwald notes likewise that all the "discharges" of nervous energy always also imply a process of graduation of the quantity of energy discharged, and that consequently the quantity of discharged energy always depends, on the one hand, on the quantity of the releasing energy (einerseits, von dem Betrage der auslösende Nervenenergie) and, on the other, on the quantity of the stored-up energy capable of being discharged (andererseits, von dem Energie-vorrath, der zur Auslösung bereit liegt).[1]

Nevertheless certain very remarkable cases of increase of vividness of sensory evocation, even of those which can only have a feeble mnemonic accumulation, and whose very great vividness is thus obviously due to the fact of the exceptional vividness of the evoking affectivity, make it doubtful whether even such a graduation of discharge is sufficient to explain them.

To what a degree the vividness of certain sensory evocations strengthened by a very intense affective tendency can attain, is proved, as we know, by " hallucinations," particularly if they are persistent. In these, the sensory mnemonic part, which does not correspond to reality (*i.e.* which does not coincide in the respective specificities with the actual sensations that the external world would tend to provoke) this part, after having been evoked by the corresponding affective tendency, is at the same time revived by it to the point of acquiring an active energy capable of resisting that of the sensory elements which would tend to inhibit the specifically different mnemonic evocations, and which remain on the contrary inhibited by them.

Such hallucinations, of which fear and the persecution mania on the one hand, and ecstatic visions on the other, afford us the most familiar examples, and all analogous cases in which, under the action of an intense affectivity the vividness of the mnemonic evocation noticeably and persistently surpasses that of the actual sensation, seem to reveal a genuine and actual "reinforcement" of the mnemonic evocation, caused by the affective tendency ; a reinforcement so much the greater as the intensity or vividness of the latter is stronger.

[1] W. Ostwald, *op. cit., Vorlesungen über Naturphilosophie,* pp, 355-356, 426 ff.

62 THE PSYCHOLOGY OF REASONING

And the fact appears to be by no means inadmissible. It may rather be considered as very probable that the specific accumulations belonging to any mnemonic association whatever reinforce each other at the moment of their evocation, in the sense that a part of the energy discharged by those that are better endowed, could contribute to increase the energy of those that are less well furnished, owing to the transformation of the specific energy of the former into the specifically different energy of the latter. This is the only possible interpretation of what is called the "excitation" or "impingement" of a certain nervous centre, or in general of a certain physiological activity, by another centre or another activity ; when the words "excitation" and "impingement" signify something more than the simple fact of "discharging" or "releasing" potential energy.

And as an affective tendency in fact more often represents a reserve of energy much greater than that of each sensory mnemonic accumulation, so the increase of vividness which it causes in the evocation of the latter would only be the consequence of the great quantity of energy that its awakening would set free.

Such is the hypothesis which probably commands the greater number of supporters to-day, although it is generally expressed in the vaguest and most ambiguous forms.

Thus, for example, Pillsbury supposes that the impingement exercised by attention on the sensory centres, in their perceptive as much as in their evocative state, is quite analogous to that which certain reflexes exercise on each other.[1]

According to Ladd there would be "a focussing of psychical energy on certain phases or certain factors or objects of consciousness, and a corresponding retreat of this energy from other phases or other factors or objects".[2]

Claparède draws attention to the "dynamogenic action" exercised by interest on the sensations and evocations that arouse this interest.[3]

[1] W. B. Pillsbury, *op. cit., Attention ;* Chapter XV, " The Physiology of Attention."

[2] G. E. Ladd, *Psychology, Descriptive and Explanatory,* London, 1894, p. 66.

[3] E. Claparède, *L'association des Idées,* Paris, 1903, pp. 138 ff.

VIVIDNESS AND CONNECTION 63

Semon, in addition to the hypothesis of the increase of vividness caused by the multiple simultaneous evocations of the same element, referred to above, is obliged to have recourse also to that of a certain quantity of "disposable vividness" which would be focussed now on these elements of a certain sensory or mnemonic complex, and now on those.[1]

Instances need not be further multiplied. Suffice it thus to have summed up in their essentials the different possible processes—capable, of course, in many cases of working in conjunction—by which an affective tendency, aroused by certain internal physiological conditions or by certain sensory sensations or evocations, can succeed, not only in rendering "conscious", but in "reviving" the sensations or the evocations that have discharged it or at all events concern it directly, and in evoking at the same time a number of other memories which have only some sort of indirect connection with it; such memories being also revived in proportion as they afford "interest". Although brief, this exposition serves to show much better than the simple mention made in the preceding chapter, the importance acquired, for the accuracy of our observations, for the exactness of our judgments and for the validity and consistency of the whole process of knowledge in general, by the fact that what constitutes attention is the conflict of two opposing affectivities.

We have already seen above how, owing to this conflict, which holds the primary affectivity for a long while in suspense, the "adaptation" of the sensory organ has time to complete itself, and in certain cases to perfect itself still more; and how, besides, the prolonged exposure of the sensory organ to the stimulating source, facilitating the "addition of the stimuli", results in giving, to those that are already strong enough, a greater vividness, and allowing many of the weaker to cross what we call the threshold of perception.

But this is not all; for the presence of the two affectivities, simultaneously aroused and opposed, causes the observation of such and such an object, to bring before our eyes, by the affective evocation reviving the sensory element, not only the characters and attributes that interest the primary affectivity, but those that the

[1] Semon, *op. cit.*, *Die mn Empf.*, pp. 341-342, 352, 386.

64 THE PSYCHOLOGY OF REASONING

secondary evokes also. And these are more numerous even than the former, because the fear of being deceived evokes all the characters and attributes which successively can be thought of as equally possible. Hence the positive perception of the object is more accurate in proportion as the attention, *i.e.*, the affective conflict under which it is observed, is intense and prolonged.

Finally as regards the sensory evocations—the images or ideas—relative to some intellectual process followed with attention, the fact that one and the same primary affectivity is held a long while in suspense by the secondary, gives a continuity of action to a single evocative process, and thus succeeds in maintaining the "connection of ideas," about which we have yet to speak. At the same time, it causes the evocative process, which serves as a basis for the intellectual process pursued and which is provoked especially by the primary affectivity, to remain none the less continuously under the corrective control of the secondary affectivity. Hence the guarantee, which would otherwise be completely lacking—a guarantee stronger in proportion as the state of attention is intense—that all the images and ideas evoked, all the memories to which the intellectual process has recourse, instead of being mere fantasies, correspond accurately to the reality.

As for the "connection" of ideas which is manifested in every state of attention, it is more often attributed to a process of inhibition which would exclude all "foreign" sensations or sensory evocations, otherwise capable of being presented also. Many psychologists have accordingly considered attention as essentially or largely a process of inhibition.[1]

"If we approach the psycho-physiologists for their view of the material side of attention, their answer will be almost unanimous : the principal function of attention is a nervous inhibition".[2]

[1] *Cf.* for example, among many others, Wundt, *op. cit.*, *Grundz. d. physiol. Psych.*, Vol. I, pp. 323 ff. ; Vol. III, p. 341 ; Exner, *op. cit.*, *Entw. zu einer physiol. Erklär. d. psych. Ersch.*, p. 165 and following ; Sherrington, *op. cit.*, *The Integrative Action of the Nervous System*, p. 234 ; Pillsbury, *op. cit.*, *Attention*, Chapter XV : "The physiology of attention " ; R. Oddi, *L'inibizione*, Turin, 1898, p. 123.

[2] K. B.-R. Aars, *art. cit.*, " Notes sur l'attention ", p. 217.

VIVIDNESS AND CONNECTION 65

It is necessary to make a distinction, however. In the state of attention, we have the inhibition of a number of affective tendencies by certain others, and this leads to the *failure of the evocation* of all the images that the inhibited affectivities could have evoked. But there is no direct inhibition of sensory evocations.

We have already proved in the preceding chapter that, as far as actual sensations are concerned, attention directed towards certain sensations, does not physiologically check those towards which it is not directed, and which on that account remain unperceived and unconscious. Now what applies to the sensations is true also of evocations of sensations, which differ in no essential way from the sensations themselves. We find a proof in the unexpected appearance of certain ideas, which draw our attention to them when scarcely formed : a sign that the idea is produced even if we are not paying attention to it, otherwise it would not have been able to arise and *subsequently* to call our attention to it.

The direct inhibition of sensations or sensory evocations by the attention would, moreover, be incompatible with the nature of the phenomenon of inhibition. There can only be an inhibition of one physiological activity by another, if either directly, or indirectly, by means of other activities intimately associated with the first, there happen to be two nervous activities specifically different which tend to arise at the same point or in the same tract of the organism. Thus it is that one affectivity can inhibit another different from it if both have a part of their seat in common ; and a sensation or sensory evocation can inhibit another specifically different, if it tends to produce itself in the same part of a nervous conduction (as for example in the "Wettstreit der Sehfelder"). But an affectivity cannot inhibit a sensation or sensory evocation *directly*, nor can a sensation or sensory evocation inhibit an affectivity *directly*, for their respective seats are totally distinct.

An affective tendency will only be able to inhibit a sensation or sensory evocation *by indirect means*, every time that the sensations it revives or the images it evokes and keeps awake, are "incompatible" or "in contradiction" with this sensation or evocation, that is have a seat or tract in common with the latter and a different specificity. And a sensation or sensory

E

66 THE PSYCHOLOGY OF REASONING

evocation will be able to inhibit an affective tendency *equally by indirect means*, if it arouses another affectivity which drives the first from its seat. But, we repeat, direct reciprocal inhibition between affective elements and sensorial elements is not possible, on account of their having no part of their seat in common, nor any point of meeting or conflict.

But though the primary affective tendency of the state of attention can inhibit neither " foreign " sensations nor " foreign " sensory evocations directly, and though indirectly it can inhibit only those which are incompatible with its own, yet practically it succeeds equally in excluding more or less completely the sensorial elements that do not interest it, and it does this whilst inhibiting all the other affectivities on which depend either the intrusion into consciousness or the direct evocation of these foreign elements.

In other words, it is not by direct physiological inhibition of sensorial or intellectual facts that the " connection of ideas " peculiar to the state of attention is produced, but by the *exclusion from consciousness* of all foreign sensations or sensory evocations not inhibited physiologically; and by the *physiological inhibition* of all other possible affective tendencies which would have the immediate effect either of recalling to consciousness the unconscious sensory evocations or of evoking, reviving and sustaining an infinite number of other sensations and ideas. Nevertheless we can continue to speak in the following pages of affective tendencies that inhibit or exclude sensations or sensory evocations that do not interest them, provided that we always understand this exclusion in the sense that we have defined.

By the side of this double result of a purely *negative* or *exclusive* nature—viz. the failure of a great number of extraneous intellectual elements to rise into consciousness or to be evoked—we have also the *positive* double result, still more important, derived from the simultaneous and concordant action of an *affective choice* and a *direct evocation*.

Indeed, in the mass of intellectual elements which are capable of arising through the fortuitous association among the sensory evocations, and which the state of attention directed elsewhere cannot inhibit physiologically but only exclude from consciousness, there are

VIVIDNESS AND CONNECTION 67

some from time to time which have some connection with the object of such a state of attention, or as means to an end towards which the primary affectivity of the state of attention is directed. And suddenly they are brought into consciousness, revived and "sustained"—held, that is to say, for a long period in a state of evocation—by the respective affectivity.

There is thus an "affective choice" between unconscious sensory evocations, quite analogous to that which we have already found among sensory stimulations, a minimum fraction among all those which are simultaneously alive being chosen to form part of the state of attention of the moment. What is called a "happy thought" appearing unexpectedly and in quite an involuntary way, is only the most typical example of the affective choice between unconscious evocations.

Parallel with this "choice" which thus succeeds in giving a common affective link to intellectual material slightly or not at all connected of itself, we have also the direct evocation of other sensory elements, by means of the primary affectivity, under the constant corrective control of the secondary affectivity by which the primary affectivity itself is held in suspense.

And it is precisely this process of evocation—thus guided and "urged" by the primary affective tendency that always remains invariable during the whole correlative state of attention—which creates directly mnemonic intellectual matter already connected of itself with the object of attention.

Whence the great difference between the fortuitous association of ideas as develops in the absence of any durable element of an affective nature, and that which has this affective substratum.

The purely mechanical association of ideas—produced by simple and casual contiguity or resemblance, often very partial and particular, of a merely sensory order, between the evocative element and the element evoked—proceeds quite chaotically, since every evocative element of momentary duration is immediately succeeded by another quite different element, which as soon as it is evoked becomes in its turn evocative, only to give place immediately to a third; so that there is usually no relation of any kind between any two links of the chain that are not contiguous. The

68   THE PSYCHOLOGY OF REASONING

flow of a coherent association of ideas, on the contrary —provoked and canalised by a single evocative element, of an affective order, which remains invariable for a long period and thus serves as a common base and link —possesses a definite direction and tends towards a single end already pre-determined by the evocative affectivity itself.

It is precisely this essential difference between the two kinds of association, one "connected" and the other "non-connected", that the classical English school quite failed to explain.

It is equally clear how important for the recall of the sensory excitations in the future, and their entry into the intellectual capital of the individual, must be their success in rousing some interest.   Those, on the contrary, which succeed physiologically in arriving at their normal point, but remain unconscious because they are not associated with any affectivity whatever, should be considered, if not all, at any rate for the most part, as lost for the intellect; for they would with great difficulty find occasion to be evoked before their over long "inaction" caused them to disappear also as mere mnemonic accumulations.

It may be noted, nevertheless, that the connection which the state of attention succeeds in giving to the whole intellectual process, would lose all value if the psychical factor which produced it were of short duration. It is the long persistence of the connecting psychical factor which brings the phenomenon into prominence. If the most diverse affective tendencies succeeded each other rapidly, each only lasting a moment as happens for example with maniacs, every aspect of connection between successive psychical events would immediately vanish.   It is because the primary affective tendency is held in suspense by the secondary, and thus remains invariable for a long period, that a development of a complete series of consecutive intellectual states presents the appearance of a single connected one.

In other words, it is the primary affective tendency thus held in suspense, that constitutes the "invariable" psychical fact, the one unique link of connection in the whole intellectual process.   And it is on the greater or less strength of resistance of such a primary affective tendency that the "coherence" or "incoherence" of

VIVIDNESS AND CONNECTION 69

the intellectual process itself depends, when the latter requires a long time to reach its full development.

But what ultimately is this "intellectual process", followed and at the same time guided and "urged" by the primary affectivity of the state of attention, which it is the function of the primary affectivity itself to render "coherent"?

In its most typical and fundamental form it is nothing else, as we shall try to prove in the next chapter, than the pursuit, on the part of the primary affectivity, of a number of events or changes, actually observed or simply imagined, relative to the object of the primary affectivity.

Thus the hunter who follows the game with his eye and sees it disappear into a bush, turns his whole attention on the bush; and the almost imperceptible movement of the latter assumes the greatest importance in his eyes, because he knows from experience, that it is "connected" with some interesting fact concerning the game, *i.e.* the movement of the latter inside the bush, and its expected exit.

In the same way the chemist who follows the different occurrences or transformations of a certain substance, and who sees it dissolve in the liquid prepared and heated for the purpose, fixes thenceforward his whole attention on the solution and on every subsequent physical or chemical phenomenon that it subsequently presents, because he knows that it is "connected" with the substance which is for him the object of interest and which he continues to follow even while it remains hidden from sight.

Similarly the thinker who pursues only mentally the different events or changes that he simply imagines as taking place in a given object which interests him, continues to follow the latter in thought even if one of the imagined events or changes has completely transformed it, and has caused it momentarily to disappear as such; for he still hopes to find it again or recover it in its desired primitive state, as a consequence of other subsequent events or changes.

And it is precisely the primary affectivity directed towards the object, under the constant control of the secondary, that urges the thinker to imagine all these events and changes by which the object that has dis-

70 THE PSYCHOLOGY OF REASONING

appeared or been transformed may again be found or recovered ; and this primary affectivity, owing to the double negative process and the double positive process mentioned above, causes the whole process of thought to be directed towards this single and earnestly pursued end.

But here we reach the supreme psychological phenomenon, *reasoning*, which will be the special object of the following chapter.

CHAPTER IV

WHAT IS REASONING?

IN enquiring into the origin and nature of those fundamental psychical phenomena which form the affective tendencies and the attention, we have followed, in our preceding chapters, the phylogenetic method ; that is to say, we have attempted to discover the first signs of these phenomena in animals, even in the lowest, so that the phenomenon itself could be presented to us in the most elementary manner possible. But it would be difficult to employ the same method in the study of the higher psychical phenomenon, reasoning. It is true, as we shall see later, that the simplest forms of reasoning appear even in animals. But an affective tendency or a state of attention, owing to its "literal translation," so to speak, in the way in which the animal behaves, is capable of being studied even from the outside at every moment of its development and in all its phases. Reasoning, on the contrary, does not "exteriorise" itself in the behaviour of the animal, phase by phase, according as it develops, but only when, considered as an internal psychic phenomenon, it is an accomplished fact ; the animal's attitude being only the final, or so to speak, posthumous consequence.

We must then, while endeavouring always to observe reasoning in its simplest possible forms, investigate it first in man, as it is revealed in introspection of ourselves, or in language, which is like an instrument of introspection as regards the thought of others. Once its true nature has been discovered, it will doubtless be possible to investigate its probable manifestation in animals also, and to proceed to the study of its gradual evolution to the highest forms attained in the most developed human minds.

In the present chapter we shall confine ourselves to the analysis of certain of the simplest forms of the most common reasoning, deferring the investigation of its

72 THE PSYCHOLOGY OF REASONING

evolution and that of its higher forms to the following chapters.

I

An old peasant woman of the hills of Fauglia, near Pisa, where I often used to stay, owed me twelve francs that had been given her the previous day to hand to me; I owed her seven francs for expenses she had incurred for me in the morning. "So you owe me only five francs", I remarked. But she was not very convinced. She began to count on the table twelve franc pieces: "There are your twelve franc pieces", she said to me, "now give me my seven francs". I counted her seven francs, and it was only then that she was convinced that our accounts were completely in order.

Totally different as these two methods of procedure appear at first sight, they only differ in that the poor woman found it necessary actually to perform all the operations of counting whereas I had performed them mentally, because I knew the final result experimentally.

I mislay my umbrella, and ask myself whether I have not left it in one of the places where I had to stop this morning. But I recollect that it has not ceased raining the whole morning, so at once reason thus: it is impossible that I returned home without my umbrella; otherwise I should have been drenched; which did not happen, as I had no need to change my clothes.

Here my reasoning consists solely in the fact that I imagine myself running through the street in the rain without an umbrella. This experience, occurring in thought alone, results, as I already know, in a certain state of my clothes (drenched clothes), which is different from what was actually the case.

We can state with certainty that in London, which possesses a population larger than the greatest total number of hairs a man can have, people are to be found who have just the same number of hairs.

The first time the writer heard this statement it surprised him a little, owing to the infinitely small probability that this case will be verified in two men chosen at random. But as he happens to be a strong visualiser, almost as soon as the first moment of surprise

WHAT IS REASONING ? 73

was over, reasoning very rapidly confirmed the conclusion and developed in him in the following way. I began by mentally placing the inhabitants of London beside one another, starting with the one having the least number of hairs, and putting on his left the one with the next smallest number and so on. I remember too that I *saw* all these individuals lined up in front of me in single file, like so many soldiers that I might have reviewed ; while behind them, in the background of the picture there appeared in confusion the "doubles", that is to say, those that I had left outside the file, because I *eventually* found that they had the same number of hairs as one of the preceding. Having thus arrived at the one who possessed the greatest number of hairs of all, I imagined myself counting all those and only those who were in line. Supposing also that the first individual had only one hair and that any two immediately following each other, differed only by one hair, I verified immediately that among these lined up, all the inhabitants of London could not have found place, precisely because the number of persons in line should, according to this hypothesis which allows us to suppose the greatest possible number of individuals in line, be equal to the number of hairs of the last, and thus inferior to the total population of London. I thus found myself with a certain number of individuals remaining outside the file, a surplus formed in fact by the "doubles", whose existence *thus verified mentally* constituted the fact to be "proved". The rapidity with which all these mental operations developed was such that I could say that I had convinced myself of the fact, the bare affirmation of which had at first surprised me, by *intuition* rather than by *reasoning*. My intuition was then in this case a very rapid reasoning, almost instantaneous ; and this reasoning was nothing else than a series of experiments carried out in the mind alone.

In the same way, in order to solve "riddles", it is only necessary to think with the imagination, and perform mentally an appropriate series of experiments. It is sufficient to recall here the elaborate problem N.9 of the *Thaumaturgus mathematicus* (Coloniae, 1651), where, given three receptacles with a capacity equal respectively to 3, 5, and 8 units of measure, the two first being empty, the third filled to the brim with a

74 THE PSYCHOLOGY OF REASONING

liquid, this quantity of liquid must be divided, with the help of the other two receptacles, into two perfectly equal parts.[1]

In this case, the whole reasoning consists in accomplishing mentally a number of transfusions, each successive transfusion having for its point of departure the results of the preceding transfusion or transfusions.

The same applies to the other famous riddle of the goat, the wolf and the cabbage, that have to be transported from one bank to the other in a little boat. The boat can only carry one of the three objects at once, not counting the shepherd. It is a condition that the wolf shall never remain alone with the goat, nor the goat without the shepherd. The riddle is easily solved, as everyone knows, by means of a series of transhipments and a re-transhipment in an inverse sense, which can be actually performed, but which the person invited to solve the riddle merely accomplishes in imagination.

Let us pass from riddles to games which demand considerable "reflection", for example the game of chess. "Reasoning" in this game evidently consists only in the act of performing, always mentally, in advance, a complete series of moves, of one's own pieces as well as those of one's adversary and determining, always in imagination, the respective results, which in this case consist in such and such a grouping of the pieces themselves.[2]

But someone may object that the examples which have so far been given still do not constitute true reasoning. Let us take then a form of reasoning about which there cannot be the slightest doubt :

I have observed in the past with my own eyes the two following facts : 1. That any metal rod transferred from cold to heat becomes longer ; 2. That a long pendulum swings more slowly than a short one. I ask myself what would happen if I transferred a wall clock with a simple pendulum, from a very cold to a very hot room. "Reasoning" tells me immediately that the clock transferred to the hot room will henceforth go

---

[1] E. Mach, *Erkenntnis und Irrtum*, Leipzig, 1906, p. 171.
[2] Cf., for example, A. A. Cleveland, "The Psychology of Chess and of Learning to play it", *The American Journal of Psychology*, July 1907, pp. 288, 290-291.

WHAT IS REASONING ? 75

slower than any other clock remaining in the cold room, though at first they agreed exactly, owing to the length of their pendulums being the same. In what does my reasoning consist here?

Evidently only in this : I imagine that I transfer the clock from the cold to the hot room. It is useless actually to perform this experiment when once I know the result. Simply thinking of it calls up the " vision " of the result already observed before, of the elongation of the pendulum transferred to the hot, as compared with the one left in the cold room. I should now compare the behaviour of the two clocks ; but there is no need actually to perform even this second experiment, because I already know the result of it, and it is sufficient simply to imagine to perform it in order to "see" at once mentally what I have actually seen in the past, viz. that the clock with the longer pendulum which is that transported to the hot room, goes more slowly than the other.

Thus in this case again my reasoning has only been in substance a series of observations or experiments that I could have performed actually, but that I confined myself to doing in imagination only, because I already knew the result of each in advance.

It was a similar process of reasoning that led Galileo, before he had recourse to experimental verification, to "prove" that the velocities of two falling bodies, contrary to the Aristotelian doctrine which prevailed up till then, do not depend on the respective weights of these bodies at all. This reasoning was essentially the performance in thought only of *the experiment which served him afterwards for an actual verification*. The experiment consisted in finding a body double the weight of another and dropping these two bodies together from the same height. " *I pictured to myself*", he tells, "two bodies of equal mass and weight *such as two bricks,* falling from the same height at the same moment. It is obvious that these two bodies will descend with the same velocity, that is to say with the velocity assigned to them by nature. If this velocity had to be increased by some other body, the latter must necessarily move with a greater velocity. But, *if the bricks are imagined falling united and attached to each other*, which of the two will it be that, by adding its impetus

76 THE PSYCHOLOGY OF REASONING

to the other, is able to double the velocity of the other, since this velocity cannot be increased by the supervention of another body if the latter does not move with a greater velocity? From this it must be granted that the union of the two bricks does not alter their primitive velocity ".[1]

The reasoning of the great economist Ricardo is equally typical in this respect : We have as experimental data : the co-existence of soils of a different natural fertility ; the continuous increase of the population which had rendered necessary the cultivation of the less fertile soils after that of the more fertile ; a single price in force on the market for all commodities of the same kind even if they were produced on soils of a different fertility, and consequently, with different quantities of work. Starting with these experimental data Ricardo was led by reasoning, as we know, to his celebrated theory of rent.[2]

Now if we follow the reasoning of Ricardo, as it is set forth at length in his great work, it is evident that each stage is 'only one more experiment, in thought alone, which is connected with the results of previous experiments, also conducted merely in imagination.

Ricardo could have carried out these experiments in actuality, by going to one of the English colonies still in their infancy ; proving that on a limitless stretch of ground only the most fertile parts would be cultivated ; waiting afterwards for the moment when the increase of the population would have forced some farmers to cultivate the less fertile soils also; comparing the quantity of work necessary to produce, in fields of different fertility, the same quantity of grain ; visiting the market in order to see if the two equal quantities of grain were sold at different prices, or at one and the same price, and if the single price was henceforth greater than the former ; verifying the larger remuneration for the same amount of work that the cultivator of the more fertile soils received ; being present when a piece of ground belonging to one of the cultivators of the more fertile soils, who was tired of working, was

---

[1] G. Vailati, " Il metodo deduttivo come strumento di ricerca," in *Scritti di G. Vailati*, Firenze, 1911, p. 127.

[2] Ricardo, *Principles of Political Economy and Taxation* (3rd edition 1821), London, 1903, Chapter II : On Rent, pp. 44-61.

WHAT IS REASONING? 77

rented to one of the others, who up till now had worked on the less fertile soils; and so on. But Ricardo considered it, with good reason, useless to perform in person this whole series of experiments, because he already knew in advance the result of each separately. Consequently he confined himself merely to *executing them in thought* one after the other, and it is in the substitution thus made of *actual experiments* by *experiments thought of* that his whole reasoning consists.

Consider now as another example the reasoning used in demonstrating that the sum of the angles of a triangle is equal to two right angles.

We could measure them one after the other separately with the help of a goniometer and then add them up. Or still better, we could cut with scissors two of the three angles of a triangle out of paper, transfer and turn them round so that they are placed against the two sides of the third angle, with their respective vertices coinciding with the vertex of the third angle, and then measure with a goniometer the total angle resulting.

Now the ordinary demonstration of the theorem in question *is simply a mental execution of the same series of experiments.*

The "proof" of the theorem, in fact, consists simply in this: namely, first the actual performance of operations or geometrical experiments which make it possible to transfer in thought the angles and then the execution of this transfer mentally in such a way as to place the three angles side by side with the apex in common. The operation actually accomplished consists in drawing a line from the vertex parallel to the base. This operation, while adding two new angles to the sides of the angle at the vertex, angles that did not exist previously, provides at the same time the future goniometer, furnished with an aperture equal already to two right-angles, and designed to serve later for the measurement of the sum of the angles. This having been done, it is useless to proceed with the actual execution of the subsequent operations or experiments which still remain to be performed; it is sufficient to perform them mentally.

Indeed, by previous experiments, relative to the superposition, by suitable rotation, of the two parts into which a figure formed by two parallel lines is divided

78 THE PSYCHOLOGY OF REASONING

by a transversal, we have already verified that the two new angles that we have constructed are such that the two angles at the base can coincide with them each to each exactly. Then, we say, *let us transport in thought* these two angles at the base. The experiment of the transfer and the placing of the two angles beside the third is thus performed, not actually but only mentally ; and the result of the experiment, thus carried out only in thought, is that the sides of the angle which is the sum of the three angles fall exactly on the line parallel to the base, which so serves as goniometer.

Once the fact becomes clear that the reasoning followed in the geometrical demonstration consists substantially in the mental performance of just these operations of cutting out, transferring, and placing together of the three angles of the triangle, operations that could be performed actually with the paper triangle, then a certain momentary surprise and astonishment — experienced the first time both by the writer of these lines and by some of his mathematical friends whom he questioned, on seeing with his own eyes that the three angles cut out of a paper triangle and actually juxtaposed really form two right-angles, on seeing, that is, the exact agreement between the results of the experimental proof and those of reasoning—would disappear ; because experimental verification and reasoning appear then to be really *one and the same process*, in the sense that the second is only the experimental proof itself, imagined instead of actually performed.

The demonstration of the theorem relative to the sum of the internal angles of a polygon is also a good illustration of the fact that geometrical reasoning is usually a mixture of mental experiments and experiments actually performed. "When a polygon is presented to us", observes Taine with his usual perspicacity, "the portions of surface which form its elements are not yet distinct and separate ; we are compelled then to create them, and for this, to effect divisions, and trace lines ; a construction must precede the analysis. We take any point in the interior of the polygon ; from this point we draw straight lines to all its angles ; we thus replace the polygon by a group of triangles whose number is equal to that of its sides". All this is the empirical result of a geometrical experiment actually

WHAT IS REASONING ? 79

performed ; so far there has been no trace of reasoning, because all the geometrical experiments have really been performed, and lead of themselves to a tangible result which can be proved actually—the division of the polygon into as many triangles as there are sides, the apices of which all meet at one point, their sides coinciding likewise two by two.

" Now in each of these triangles ", Taine continues, " the two angles at the base, together with the angle at the vertex, are equal to two right-angles ; therefore, if we take all the triangles, and if, adding together all the angles at their bases, we further add all the angles at their vertices, we shall have as many times two right-angles as there are triangles, that is to say sides, in the polygon." As can be seen, it is just here that reasoning begins ; for instead of actually performing new geometrical experiments, it is sufficient to do them mentally, owing to the circumstance that we already know in advance the result of each experiment thus thought of. So it is useless to perform actually in each triangle the operation of adding the angles together, because we have proved previously that this gives, in every triangle, a sum of two right-angles. Hence the result of this operation which has only· been performed mentally is " to put before us " as many pairs of right-angles as there are triangles. It is equally useless to count all the right-angles " before us " ; just as it would be useless, for example, to count all the apples contained in twenty or thirty baskets one by one, if one knew that each basket contained only two. The result of this counting is, in fact, already known ; *i.e.* we know that it results in as many times two right-angles as there are triangles, and consequently, as there are bases to these triangles since every triangle has only one base.

"But these angles at the base are also the angles of the polygon ". Here again there is no reasoning, but only another empirical verification of one of the results obtained by the geometrical operations or experiments which were actually accomplished at first.

" So that the angles of the polygon, if added to the angles at the vertex, are equal to twice as many right angles as the polygon has sides." Here we mentally perform the experiment which consists in substituting, in a given sum of a certain number of magnitudes, for

80 THE PSYCHOLOGY OF REASONING

certain magnitudes of a given sum (the angles at the base of the triangles) others of an equal sum (the angles of the polygon). The expression "so that" indicates the precise moment when such an experiment of substitution is performed mentally, the result of which, known already, is that the total sum remains the same as before; *i.e.* as many times two right angles as the figure has sides.

"Now we know further that the angles at the vertices together equal four right angles". A fresh empirical verification of another of the results obtained by the geometrical operations performed at first actually.

"From which it follows that the polygon contains a sum of angles which, if four right-angles be added, is equal to twice as many right-angles as the figure has sides." Another mental operation of the same kind as before, consisting in the substitution, in a sum of several magnitudes (angles of the polygon plus angles at the vertices) for certain magnitudes of a given total (the angles at the vertex) of others with an equal sum (the four right-angles). Here again, the expression "from which it follows" indicates the moment when this second experiment of substitution is performed mentally, the result of which, also known already, is likewise, that the total sum remains the same as before, that is to say, still equal to as many times two right-angles as the polygon has sides.[1]

It should be especially noticed here how, during the whole course of this reasoning, our attention simply follows the successive transformations, partly performed actually and partly in thought, of a single object which is all that interests us : the sum of the angles of the polygon. This sum alone is the magnitude that we wish to "know," that is to say, to prove equal to as many times another magnitude of the same kind, but which is more familiar to our mind (a unit of measure, which, in the present case, is the right-angle). In the series of experiments, certain of which are actually performed, and others simply thought of, we see this magnitude undergoing a number of changes. We first divide each of the angles of the polygon, of which it is composed, into two base angles belonging respec-

---

[1] See Taine, *op. cit., De l'intelligence*, Vol. II, pp. 400-401 ; English Translation, Vol. II, 1871, p. 494.

WHAT IS REASONING? 81

tively to two different triangles; we transform, thereby, the object of our thought from a sum of a certain number of "polygonous" angles into an equivalent sum made up of a different number of base angles. We then insert this sum into another sum made up of the sum of all the angles of a certain number of triangles. Thence we follow it in thought as it passes into a sum of a different sort, composed of as many times two right-angles as the polygon has sides. Finally, we rediscover it anew "in its purity", but under a more familiar aspect when, from this last sum, we take away in thought the four right-angles of the apex. But in all these transformations *we never lose sight of it*, i.e. we do not cease to pursue it in thought for a single instant, in the same way that the sportsman, who had seen the game disappear into the covert, does not cease to follow it with "his mind's eye" in all the smallest movements of the branches and leaves of the bushes; or as the chemist, who has seen the substance of which he is studying, dissolve and disappear in the solution, continues to pursue it in all the successive reactions of the solution itself, until the substance reappears to him under the particular physico-chemical aspect which is for him more familiar.

"The face of a person eagerly pursuing a thought," observes Maudsley, "is that of one trying eagerly to see something which is difficult to be seen, pursuing it, as it were, with his eye".[1]

II

These few examples purposely chosen among the most varied it was possible to find, could be extended indefinitely and multiplied at will, but they suffice to give a clear idea of what this mental process that we call "reasoning" essentially is. It would seem to be nothing else, we repeat again, than a *series of operations or experiments simply thought of*, that is to say, operations or experiments that we imagine performed on one or several objects in which we are particularly interested, and that we do not perform actually because, by a series of similar experiments which have been really accom-

[1] Maudsley, *op. cit.*, *The Physiology of Mind*, p. 381.

F

82 THE PSYCHOLOGY OF REASONING

plished in the past, we already know their respective results. And the final experimental result, "observed with the mind's eye", to which a similarly connected series of mental experiments leads, constitutes precisely the "result of the demonstration", the "conclusion of reasoning".

Mach, it may be mentioned, devotes a whole section of his work on Knowledge and Error to the "Gedanken-experiment", *i.e.* to the mental operation consisting in the imaginative combination by the experimenter of a certain number of experiments before proceeding to their actual performance.[1]

Miller, too, regards the act of thought as the preliminary imagining in advance of all the results of one of our particular modes of procedure, before passing on to the actual act.[2]

The examples which have been analysed above allow us to generalise further and to affirm, at least provisionally and reserving a fuller verification, that not only such and such a particular form of reasoning which precedes any one of our acts, but the entire reasoning process, in whatever form it appears, is, in essence, nothing else than a true and proper "Gedankenexperiment"; or as we have just said, a mental combination of imagined experiments.

In the following chapters we shall see that the essential nature of reasoning, manifested in the simplest forms which have been analysed above, never contradicts itself in the course of its evolution, not even in its highest forms, although the intervention of a symbolism becoming ever more complicated can sometimes completely disguise its inmost essence.

But here we must pass on to certain consequences which result for the logical process in general, postponing the analysis of the elementary mental processes which, given this nature, come into play in a process so complex as that of reasoning.

In particular we at once understand why, when reasoning has once started from certain premises in agreement with facts, it must arrive at results similarly in perfect agreement with other facts. The perfect

---

[1] E. Mach, *op. cit., Erkenntnis u. Irrtum* : pp. 183-200.
[2] I. E. Miller, *The Psychology of Thinking*, New York, 1909, pp. 133-134, 194.

WHAT IS REASONING ? 83

coincidence of the results of logical processes with the results actually observed, can, as we have seen, if the true nature of reasoning is not understood, cause a feeling akin to surprise as well as admiration, or at least raise doubts as to whether there is still a problem to solve. When certain hypotheses are transformed by means of reasoning, we admit as evident, writes Enriques, that the reality of the premises entails that of their consequences. From which, he adds, arises the general problem which consists in considering "how it is possible for the logical process to give us a representation of reality".[1]

But the problem vanishes when we understand that the logical process is nothing else than a series of experiments, all, theoretically at least, capable of being performed, but limited to thought only in order to economise time and energy. The logical process appears then *to be identical with the perceptual reality itself*, operated solely by means of the imagination instead of actually.

It must not, then, be assumed that reasoning, after establishing contact with reality at the moment of taking its flight, hovers outside or above reality into the elevated atmosphere of logic, to regain contact with it only at the end, at the moment of coming once again to earth. On the contrary, far from losing contact with reality for a single instant, it relies on the solid ground of the real *in each phase of its development*.

In other words the intermediate results of any reasoning whatever, even when developed, as we shall see, by means of the most complicated symbolism, have all, without exception, *a concrete significance*. They represent the respective "empirical" results of the different phases that succeed one another in the series of purely mental operations or experiments.

But let us now proceed to consider the advantages and disadvantages, which, in comparison with the actual accomplishment of experiments, accrue to reasoning from the very fact of its accomplishing them only in thought.

It is evident at the outset that there is, in reasoning, an enormous economy of time and energy when compared with actual performance : "We deal more easily and conveniently with the representations of our imagin-

---

[1] F. Enriques, *Problemi della Scienza*, Bologna, 1906, p. 204. English translation, p. 135.

84 THE PSYCHOLOGY OF REASONING

ation than with physical acts. We experiment, so to speak, on our thoughts with smaller cost ".[1]

Moreover an infinite number of experiments that reasoning imagines accomplished may be theoretically possible of execution, but cannot be realised in practice. Thus, as we say above, we were able to accomplish in thought at once and with the greatest ease, the lining up of all the inhabitants of London, according to the number of hairs possessed by each. It would occupy the entire lives of many men if the experiment had to be actually performed. Similarly, if it is theoretically possible for someone flying across the interstellar spaces to measure a celestial distance directly, it is impossible to do this measuring actually, leaving out of consideration the time that it would take. And so on. Reasoning may also execute in imagination a number of experiments infinitely greater than could actually be performed.

Reasoning has, besides, in many cases, the advantage over actual experimentation, that it has a much more general demonstrative power. The instrumental measurement of the three angles of a triangle which establishes that their sum is equal to two right angles, tells us nothing about any other triangles, whereas the following out of the imagined experiment which constitutes the demonstration of the theorem in question yields in addition that the result obtained holds for all triangles. This is because the reasoner is forced, in the first place, by the very nature of the psychological process involved—it not being possible to perform such an experiment in thought if the results of other similar experiments in the past are not attributed to this last experiment—to attribute to these results, when in the course of the reasoning they present themselves to the mind, a significance of a general order, which perhaps was not given to them by him at the moment when he made the empirical observation relative to one case or to a few particular cases ; a process of generalisation well known under the name of induction. A second reason, and one of greater importance, is because in certain cases, as we shall see still better in what follows, to think of making an experiment allows us to perform in imagination, with very great rapidity, not only this

[1] E. Mach, *op. cit., Erkenntnis und Irrtum*, p. 187.

WHAT IS REASONING ? 85

single experiment, but a very great and practically infinite series of experiments, mentally varied in certain of their conditions, and to verify that they all give the same result. For example, we can vary in imagination in all possible ways the inclination of the transversal of two parallel lines and note that the equality of the alternate angles is always verified ; and if we then vary, still in imagination, in all possible ways, the form of a triangle, we can further note that the transposition of the angles of the base so as to make them adjacent to that of the vertex can always be performed and always gives the same results. It is through this possibility of concentrating, so to speak, a whole infinite series of experiments into one single experiment, that the result arrived at through the reasoning acquires in such cases a value of a general order, which the materially executed experiment, only performed upon one single object, cannot possess.

Further the material performance of the experiment —thanks to the fact that any experiment can be performed on its own account, independently of any other, and yet lead equally to the discovery of some new fact —runs the risk of presenting as independent of one another the single results of varied observations and experiments actually performed. Thus the measurement and summation by means of the goniometer of the angles of a triangle says nothing as to its dependence upon that other fact constituted by the empirical observation which is called Euclid's postulate. On the other hand, the reasoning which necessarily reaches its conclusions not through one single imagined experiment (which, if already made in the past, would yield no new result, and of which, if not yet made, the result could not be known), but through a new combination of past experiments, is forced to have recourse to the already noted results of these experiments : so that the final result, thus obtained, appears as dependent upon them, and the connection which unites the different facts to one another is thus brought plainly into evidence.

But against the superiority of reasoning over the actual performance of the experiments must be set the inferiority due to the danger of error to which by its very nature it is liable :

By the fact that it is obliged at every step to

86 THE PSYCHOLOGY OF REASONING

generalise inductively the results of given experiments of the past, it runs the risk of making some erroneous induction which would lead to an entirely erroneous conclusion. At the same time, when the complexity of the experimental combination to be mentally performed passes a given limit, the thinker can no longer keep in mind all the facts which enter into the situation and all their effects upon one another, and thus may overlook some of them, which would once again lead to an erroneous final result.

Or, while knowing each of these reciprocal effects, such as were obtained in previous experiments, when each of these factors acted *separately* on one other only, and bearing them all in mind, the thinker, by combining his own mental construction with these much more simple single experiments of the past, can reach a result different from the real one, through the fact that in the complex case under consideration these factors *all act simultaneously upon each other*.

Or again, the result of one of the experiments which in the process of reasoning are simply thought of, is admitted by the thinker as certain because it has been actually proved in the past, when it is now erroneous because in the meantime it has been modified. Thus, for example, Ricardo supposed that even in the future the continuous increase of the population would lead as in the past to the cultivation of new soils ever less fertile ; whereas this increase has in fact led rather to the introduction of more and more efficient improvements in agricultural methods and to the cultivation, rendered possible by the great progress in the means of transport, of ever new, remote, and very fertile soils. This led him to completely erroneous conclusions regarding the increase of land rent and of the price of edible commodities, which would, according to him, have consequently continued in ever more disturbing proportions.

And so on.

These few indications must suffice to give an idea of the many different causes of error to which experiments performed in imagination can and must necessarily be subject, as compared with their actual performance. And it may be noted that we leave out of account here all the other very numerous causes of error with which, as we shall see, such mental experiments are beset,

WHAT IS REASONING? 87

when, in their performance, we are obliged to have recourse to "symbols", whether they be verbal, such as those of language, or graphic, such as those of the calculus. The conclusion is that we can never have absolute confidence in the results of experiments simply performed mentally, particularly if this performance is complex; and that in consequence it is always necessary to verify these results, or certain among them at least, by means of actual experiment.[1]

From this possibility of error, characteristic of all sorts of reasoning, mathematical reasoning cannot be excluded. The relatively greater certainty of the latter derives from the fact that the entities with which it deals are, if not constructed, at any rate simplified to the greatest possible extent by the mind which has to deal with them, that is, are supposed to have definite properties, very simple and exactly known, whereby the danger of erroneous induction is reduced to a minimum. Moreover the dangers arising from the complexity of the combinations imagined are reduced by this very simplicity of the objects with which mathematical reasoning is concerned. It is, moreover, perhaps too often forgotten that certain mathematical processes, always the same, are the outcome of the work of thousands of generations and that therefore their certainty derives largely from this control repeated an infinite number of times. And in particular it is forgotten that it is not true that mathematical reasoning can never fail; for whoever knows anything of the history of mathematics is aware how often the conclusions of mathematical reasoning—even the achievements of the most eminent mathematicians — have subsequently been shown to be false.

On the other hand, a kind of inferiority that certain authors have wrongly attributed to reasoning as compared with actual experiment consists in its alleged *sterility*. It has been said that reasoning cannot lead to new discoveries since it is always bound to start from certain premises, which consist of facts already known, and since the conclusion is "implicit" in these premises. It would be difficult to find a more erroneous or more astounding statement, in view of the number of *new*

---

[1] *Cf.* J. S. Mill, *Logic*, 7th edition, London, 1868, vol. I, p. 514.

88   THE PSYCHOLOGY OF REASONING

facts discovered by certain sciences by means of reasoning pure and simple.

The question of knowing how reasoning can be actually productive is made much clearer once it is realised that it is nothing else than a series of experiments simply thought of. It can be put thus : How can a combination of experiments already known, lead to the discovery of new results? The answer then appears very easy, or at any rate it can be connected with the more general question of the "productivity" of the imagination, *i.e.* with the question of knowing how the imagination can create *new combinations* with old mnemonic elements.

Let us take, for example, the reasoning that we referred to above, where owing to the elongation observed in a metal bar under the influence of heat, and the slower oscillation, also established, of a longer pendulum as compared with any shorter one, I drew the "conclusion" that a clock with a simple pendulum, removed from a cold to a hot room, would certainly go more slowly.

This conclusion constitutes a true and proper *new fact*, quite distinct from the facts with which I started. It is actually a *new truth* that is thus discovered, and one that is not contained in either of the two experimental results already established taken singly.

How then has reasoning enabled me to reach this conclusion? By means of the simple fact that my imagination, with the old mnemonic fragments of the metal bar which gets longer when heated and the slower oscillation of a longer pendulum as compared with a shorter, constructed mentally a whole series of events, *as a new combination.* It has invented a whole " history " which causes me to recognise the clock that goes slower as the same one that was in the colder room, merely removed into warmer surroundings. It is this *new mental vision*, thus created by my imagination, which constitutes the *new fact*, the conclusion of my reasoning.

Moreover, in this mental operation of combining and connecting in imagination these experiments, I have also taken account of the respective effects that I previously found to result in fact from each of these experiments. So this conclusion of my reasoning is

WHAT IS REASONING ?   89

not confined to being a purely mental new fact, a mere product of my imagination, but represents at the same time an actual fact, a fact whose reality depends only on the actual performance of operations now simply imagined.

That is why a series of mental experiments, combined with each other by means of the imagination, can and does lead to "discoveries," *exactly as a series of experiments actually performed.*

It is true that in certain respects actual experimenting is better off than reasoning for the discovery of new facts. It has, so to speak, only to *observe* all that occurs ; while insufficient *capacity to imagine* all the possible combinations among the experiments whose results are already known, doubtless leads to our deducing from our empirical knowledge only a very small part of what could be deduced from it. Thus, for example, Jevons observes that the fact of aberration, which could have been proved by means of simple reasoning, was, on the contrary, discovered only empirically by Bradley.[1]

Nevertheless the much greater facility and promptitude with which experiments can be thought of as compared with the difficulty and delay in their actual performance, enables reasoning to attempt again and again in rapid succession, the most varied combinations and connections of experiments and thus largely to increase the probability of new discoveries. So that reasoning is eventually *much more fruitful* than actual experimenting pure and simple, as is proved by the far greater number of discoveries in every branch of knowledge, we may now say, made by reasoning alone, or under the guidance and direction of the preventive suggestions of reasoning as compared with the discoveries made solely according to the empirical method proceeding by chance.

III

We have alluded to the part that imagination plays in this combination of mental experiments which

[1] W. S. Jevons, *The Principles of Science*, London, 1874, Vol. II, p. 169.

90 THE PSYCHOLOGY OF REASONING

constitutes reasoning, and it is now easy to add the little we still have to say about the elementary psychological processes which, its nature being as we have described, come into play in reasoning itself.

Above all we insist on the fact that the *fruitfulness* of reasoning depends on the property possessed by the imagination of being not only *reproductive* but *productive* ; that is to say, the property of inventing or creating new "histories", while combining the old mnemonic elements in a different way from all reality yet observed.[1]

In the second place, we may remark that what especially interests our affective tendencies is exactly the connection between two consecutive phenomena, the succession of events, the "history of things." In fact, all phenomena, precursors of a certain environmental condition, which has a direct affective value for us only in its actuality and totality, or all phenomena that lead us to acquire this or that means of satisfying one or other of our affectivities, are important to us only on account of their "history," which should lead us to this end.

Now this connection of consecutive phenomena with each other does not always present itself in the same way in the course of our experience, but by reason of the number and kind of phenomena which interfere with one another in turn, it appears actually in all sorts of different ways.

So that imagination has at its disposal the widest field of evocation and choice, which enables it to construct or to combine, as regards every particular phenomenon or object that interests it, the "history of things" capable of satisfying most completely the affective tendency which is stimulating our fancy at the moment.[2]

Hence the supreme importance, in reasoning also, of the affective *intensity* directed towards the result to be attained, or towards the destiny of the object whose transformations are followed in thought.[3]

Miller then is right when he observes that the

---

[1] Cf., for example, Maudsley, *op. cit.*, *The Physiology of Mind*, pp. 523-524 ; and Miller, *op. cit.*, *The Psychology of Thinking*, p. 285.

[2] Cf., for example, E. Meumann, *op. cit.*, *Intelligenz und Wille*, p. 126.

[3] Cf., for example, Th. Ribot, *op. cit.*, *Essai sur l'imagination créatrice*, pp. 27, 37, etc.

WHAT IS REASONING ? 91

psychology of the thinking process, and consequently of the reasoning process also, as a finished product, ignores the dynamic aspect of the process, which is really the essential thing.[1]

Let us pause to consider this dynamic aspect of reasoning. A careful analysis reveals it as consisting in a continual activity of *exclusion, evocation* and *selection*, at the same time.

We have already seen at the end of our chapter on Attention, that whenever attention follows the changes, even if in thought only, which a certain object that arouses our attention undergoes or is made to undergo, the exclusion of every other affectivity is primarily in operation throughout the whole duration of the interest so aroused ; and therewith the exclusion of the respective memories that the other affectivity would tend to evoke.

As we have also seen in the same chapter, there then occurs the direct evocation of all the memories—facts, experiments, knowledge—associated mnemonically with the affective tendency which remains in play during the whole process of reasoning.

But this direct affective evocation is not always sufficient, particularly if the case is *new*. In order to succeed in proving a particular result for the first time, or, in more general terms, in following the destiny of a certain object which is being subjected mentally to new environmental conditions, we must imagine new series of actions and reactions, and discover which experiments should be thought of and combined with one another and in what order. Now the affectivity which urges us to follow the destiny of the object that interests it, is not apt to evoke directly and straight away all the experiments, in their exact order of execution, which apply in the present case, *precisely because it is new*.

One must then proceed by the " method of trial " (Jennings) which applies to the behaviour of all organisms, and which has been especially demonstrated by James, Baldwin, and other American psychologists in the production of new voluntary acts or movements. Just as a new voluntary movement is " discovered " by means of selection in an over-production of movements, so, in an exactly similar way, new reasoning always

---

[1] I. E. Miller, *op. cit., The Psychology of Thinking*, p. 144.

92 THE PSYCHOLOGY OF REASONING

proceeds by the method of *selection in an overproduction of acts thought of.*

In other words, among the tumultuous and transient evocations and combinations of experiments that can be made mentally—and that are evoked fortuitously by the simple chaotic association of ideas, stimulated and excited by the state of uneasiness and worry which the person who thinks and searches for a solution, experiences—sooner or later one emerges, the result of which, in order to approach in some way the desired end, is directly or indirectly associated with the affectivity which pursues this end. And then, *ipso facto*, this "happy thought", as we saw in the preceding chapter, is brought into consciousness by means of the affectivity, reanimated and held before the mind. It is precisely this which constitutes the "affective choice", that is of such great importance in any and every imaginative process.

It is this triple form of activity—exclusion, evocation, and selection—peculiar to the affective tendency presiding over reasoning, which gives the latter the aspect and substance of a teleological process.[1]

It is this affectivity for the end to be attained or for the object whose behaviour is being followed, which, since it is always active and always the same during the whole course of reasoning, gives the latter the aspect of a *coherent* process : "In a coherent discourse", we find James Mill already writing, "everything tends to the accomplishment of the end". "The idea of the end predominates and controls the association in every part of the process. It is not only the grand suggesting principle, which sets trains of the ideas connected with itself in motion ; but it is the grand selecting principle".[2]

In a word, it is this affectivity, directed towards a certain end, or following the events of a particular object, which alone remains "*invariable*" during the whole course of reasoning. Consequently it is this which *associates, connects, links up,* the different experimental vicissitudes which the object of our desire is

---

[1] Cf., for example, R. Müller-Freinfels, " Beiträge zum Problem des wortlosen Denkens ", *Arch. f. die gesammte Psychologie*, Vol. 23, Parts 3 and 4 (May 21, 1912), p. 311.

[2] J. Mill, *Analysis of the Phenomena of Human Mind*, London, 1878, Vol. II, Ch. 25, pp. 370-371.

WHAT IS REASONING? 93

supposed to undergo: and in this way it constitutes what is called the "thread of reasoning."

The simple "mechanical association" of ideas, in fact, may be able to explain the evocation and the tumultuous succession of the most disconnected ideas, as for example in dreams, but it by no means suffices to account for the guided and canalised association of which the reasoning process consists. There must be something more to enable order, connection, and coherence to be substituted for the associative chaos, the spontaneous and natural incoherence of ideas. And this something more is precisely the affective "invariable", with its triple action analysed above, of exclusion, evocation and choice. James Mill himself, in the passage that we quoted just now, is forced, in order to explain the coherence of a process of thought, to have recourse to the predominance and control, during the whole process, of the *idea of the end*, the only invariable idea among all the other variable ones, which is nothing else, in substance, than the *affectivity for the end*.

Hence the great importance, if coherence is to be maintained during a long process of reasoning, of the capacity for duration and resistance of the affective tendency which follows its particular object in all its merely imagined vicissitudes.

All this however applies only to the principal affective tendency which is in play during the reasoning process. But if it suffices, in virtue of its *intensity*, to provide an abundance of imagined experimental combinations, and in virtue of its *duration*, to guarantee the connection and coherence of all these combinations, it is not sufficient to guarantee of itself, the *logicality* of the process of thought involved.

In the second chapter we saw, in fact, that the phenomenon of attention consists of two affective tendencies, of which the primary *urges* the accomplishment of a certain action in order to satisfy a corresponding need, while the other, the secondary tendency, prevents the action and thus holds the former in suspense for fear of again encountering the same painful or disagreeable consequences which resulted formerly from too rapid an execution of the action itself. And we saw that even in observation pure and

94 THE PSYCHOLOGY OF REASONING

simple, made with great attention, there is always a primary affectivity in play which is anxious to prove the presence or the absence of a certain object or of one of the attributes of the object; and that to this tendency is opposed the secondary affectivity, aiming at the prevention of some error committed under similar conditions in the past, when, in consequence of too great haste to reach a conclusion in accordance with our desire, we saw what did not exist, or failed to see what did exist.

A very similar secondary tendency consisting in the fear of falling into errors is also present in the thinker who *pays great attention* to what he thinks. And it is more necessary here than ever, in order that the process of combining purely mental experiments shall not become a mere flight of imagination, but may constitute an actual expression of reality, and consequently, true and proper reasoning.

"It is exceedingly rare", Jevons also observes, "to find persons who can with perfect fairness estimate and register facts for or against their own peculiar views and theories. Among uncultivated observers the tendency to remark favourable and forget unfavourable events is so great, that no reliance can be placed upon their supposed observations".[1]

In our chapters on attention we have tried to explain accurately this action of disguising or altering reality, to which our affectivities continually tend, and to show how it is that in the state of attention this disadvantage is remedied by the antagonistic affective tendency, which aims at emphasising just what the first tends not to notice or to forget, and *vice versa*.

Now, this corrective action of the secondary affectivity, is, I repeat, especially necessary in reasoning when it is a matter of *remembering* all the actions and reactions, without forgetting a single one, to which the object, exposed hypothetically to certain environmental conditions, is submitted; when it is necessary to secure accurate mental verification, with reference to past experience, of all the multifarious effects of each of the imagined combinations in question. In observation, the external world with the sensations it tends to arouse directly constitutes an obstacle in itself to this

---

[1] Jevons, *op. cit., The Principles of Science*, II, p. 5.

WHAT IS REASONING?

alteration of reality, though not an insurmountable one. In reasoning, on the contrary, we have only to deal with our own internal world, and are entirely at the mercy of the affectivities which actuate it.

If some action or reaction, which would inevitably be produced were the imagined environmental conditions actual, or one of the consequences of these experimental combinations thus supposed, is not evoked ; or if the evocation is not kept long enough and sufficiently forcibly before the mind so that it may be taken account of in the series of subsequent experiments which are connected with the preceding experiment ; or even if, owing to the incompleteness or inaccuracy of an evocation, the result of a somewhat different experiment is attributed to the one imagined :—then the experimental process followed mentally ceases to correspond to what it would be, if it was actually put into execution, and the reasoning thus falls into error, into "*illogicality*".

Illogicality indeed consists simply in forgetting one of the actions and reactions or one of the relative consequences which would inevitably exist in the actual execution of the whole experimental process, or in attributing to certain of these imagined experiments the result previously obtained, not from the same experiments, but from others more or less different.

And as these omissions and erroneous attributions would always be produced if the primary affectivity, aiming solely at reaching step by step the desired result, were alone in play, the continual and incessant control of the secondary affectivity is more than ever indispensable. For this inhibits by its own corrective evocations those which, although desired, do not correspond to the truth ; and vice versa it evokes, recalls and reinforces all the actions and consequences which, though they may displease, are nevertheless those which would really appear in the actual performance of the experimental process.

If therefore the primary affectivity is indispensable for giving to reasoning the necessary abundance of imagined combinations, and the connection and coherence necessary to all thought, *the secondary affectivity for its part is no less necessary in order to keep the whole reasoning process in continuous and actual correspondence with the real, and thus to guarantee its "logicality"*.

96 THE PSYCHOLOGY OF REASONING

These results, barely outlined, to which our analysis of reasoning has led us, as regards the part played by the two affective tendencies of the corresponding state of attention, will be confirmed in the course of our study, when we go on to examine *the pathology of reasoning*, especially in dreams and in different types of insanity. We shall then prove directly and put our finger, so to speak, on the fact that every pronounced and pathological case of incoherence or illogicality is always due either to the lack of one or other of the two affectivities, or merely to a certain disproportion in their respective intensities.

But, now that we have synthetically stated wherein the nature of reasoning consists, and analysed the principal elementary psychic phenomena which come into play, we may pass on to the examination of the evolution of reasoning and afterwards to the investigation of the higher forms of reasoning itself. And to this task the following chapters will be devoted.

CHAPTER V

THE EVOLUTION OF REASONING

Part I: From Concrete Reasoning to Abstract Reasoning

IN the preceding chapter we have seen that in order to discover the "nature" of that higher order of psychical phenomenon which is reasoning—to reveal, that is, the elementary psychological phenomena to whose combination it is due—it was expedient, while making use always of the simplest possible instances, to study it first as it occurs in man. We could in this case investigate it as shown by introspection of our own mental processes or in the speech of our fellows, and thus follow it through the whole succession of its diverse phases; while on the other hand, if we had wished, by the use of the "phylogenetic" method, to study it from its very commencement in the animal world, beginning with the lowest and proceeding upwards to those which are highest in the zoological scale, we should only have been able to examine it through external behaviour, and even so not phase by phase in the very course of its production, but only when it has already become, as an internal psychical phenomenon, a finished product, and thus no longer capable of analysis. We added, however, that once we had discovered its nature through the study of its appearances in ourselves and in our fellow-men, we could then, but then only, investigate its equally indubitable appearances in the animals and at the same time undertake the study of its evolution. We have here the subject of the present chapter and of those which follow.

It will be useful to recall the result of the enquiries made in the last chapter. Reasoning, as it may be observed in ourselves and in our fellow-men, we found to be nothing else in substance than a succession or a combination of merely imagined operations or experiments which put the individual in the very same state of mental "awareness" in which he would ultimately

98 THE PSYCHOLOGY OF REASONING

have found himself, if these operations or experiments had been performed not merely in imagination but actually—a state of awareness in accordance with which he determines his own behaviour. We must now go on to examine in the first place whether the behaviour of animals in certain cases authorises us to recognise it as being due to a similar process of "awareness" produced through internal causes, and not through external circumstances.

I

Jennings tells us that a Stentor infusorian, fixed by its stalk to the floor of the aquarium, when tormented by a persistent jet of carmine powder, bent itself over first to one side as though to avoid the annoyance. This reaction, the "avoiding reaction" was repeated a small number of times; but the infusorian failing to free itself by this means from the cloud of carmine grains surrounding it on all sides, changed its reaction, reversing instead the movement of the cilia of its peristoma so as to drive the polluted water away from the disk and the opening of the buccal cavity. This lasted only for an instant, after which the habitual ciliary movement bringing up water was resumed. Grains of carmine continued, however, with this resumption of the habitual ciliary movement to annoy the animal, and the reversal of the current was repeated two or three times in rapid succession. But these repeated attempts having no better success than the others in relieving the minute organism, his next reaction was to withdraw completely into his mucus tube. By this our infusorian managed to avoid disturbance but at the cost of a complete suspension of activity and thereby of all opportunity to procure nourishment. Thus the animal remained in his tube no more than about half a minute after which he re-emerged from his tube and resumed his habitual ciliary movement. When the carmine began to torment him as before, he did not repeat the two formerly useless reactions, namely bending sideways and reversal of the current, but simply withdrew again into his tube. But having repeated several times over this third reaction

CONCRETE TO ABSTRACT REASONING 99

which consisted in simple contraction into the tube, always without success, the animal finished by making no further attempt to stretch out afresh, but disengaging himself by strong jerks from the floor of the aquarium, he abandoned his tube with no more ado and went away to seek another abiding place.[1]

Although, when it is a question of organisms so low in the zoological scale as this, we cannot be too cautious in interpreting the causes of no matter what feature of their behaviour, it seems to us nevertheless not too rash to suppose that the repetition of annoyance by the carmine on the first re-emergence of the animalcule must have provoked in him the same tendency to perform anew the two earlier reactions, bending sideways followed by reversal of the current, but that this double attitude, being produced in a barely nascent state—being merely imagined, one might say, if a more highly evolved animal were concerned — should, in virtue of the fundamental mnemonic property of all living substance, and thus in virtue of purely internal causes, have provoked in the organism the same continuance of a state of physiological uneasiness, the same distressing "awareness" of the persistence of the annoyance, as had been provoked originally by the surroundings on the occasion of the two attempts which were actually made and which failed. To this the animal's behaviour is due, his renewed withdrawal without more ado into the tube, in the very fashion which would have occurred if these two attempts had been actually made again on this occasion and if the animal had actually recognised their lack of success.

The same interpretation can be applied to the new change of behaviour when the animal, after trying again and again to emerge from the tube and recognising each time the persistence of the disturbing condition, at last ceases to emerge and in the end abandons the tube.

If this interpretation is correct we can say that the physiological process produced in the infusorian, leading it to "profit by experience," already contains in germ all the fundamental elements of the physio-

[1] H. S. Jennings, *op. cit.*, *Behaviour of the lower Organisms*, pp. 174-175.

100 THE PSYCHOLOGY OF REASONING

psychological processes which in higher animals and in man will constitute reasoning itself.[1]

But if the proof that these fundamental elements, which will later constitute reasoning, are present even in infusoria is doubtful—as from the nature of the case it cannot fail to be—there cannot be the least doubt on the other hand that simple forms of reasoning occur in the higher animals as we mount above these very low levels of animal life.

Among the thousands and thousands of instances which have been recorded of intelligent behaviour on the part of animals the few following, chosen merely as examples, will suffice.

In the path of a column of ants there was placed a large dry branch pressed down tightly on the ground so that the ants could not creep underneath. After a few vain attempts to climb over it, the ants were seen to lay down their loads and set to work to dig a tunnel under the branch, a task which required a full half hour. As soon as the tunnel was made, each ant took up its burden again and the march was resumed in the same perfect order.—The trunk of a tree visited by other ants was wrapped round with a cloth soaked in tobacco water. The ants which ascended as soon as they arrived at the obstacle, "first examined the nature of the barrier, then turned back and procured from a distance little pellets of earth, which they carried in their jaws and deposited one after another upon the tobacco cloth till a road of earth was made across it, over which the ants passed to and fro with impunity", both in going up and in coming down again.—A wasp was seen to alight upon a leaf which formed a caterpillar's nest neatly rolled up. "The wasp examined both ends, and finding them closed, it soon clipped a hole in the leaf at one end of the nest about one-eighth of an inch in diameter. It then went to the other end and made a noise which frightened the caterpillar which came rushing out of the hole and was thus immediately seized by the wasp."—Four shells were thrown near the edge of the burrow which a shore-crab was making in the sand, one rolled in and three other shells remained within a few inches of the mouth. "In about five minutes the crab brought out the shell which had

[1] Cf. Jennings, *op. cit.*, pp. 175-179.

CONCRETE TO ABSTRACT REASONING 101

fallen in, and carried it away to the distance of a foot ; it then saw the three other shells lying near, and evidently thinking that they might likewise roll in, carried them to the spot where it had laid the first."— A morsel of food was thrown into an aquarium in which was a skate and fell in the angle formed by the glass front and the bottom. "The skate, a large example, made several vain efforts to seize the food, owing to its mouth being on the underside of its head, and the food being close to the glass. He lay quite still for a while as though thinking, then suddenly raised himself into a slanting posture, the head inclined upwards, and the under surface of the body towards the food, when he waved his broad expanse of fins, thus creating an upward current or wave in the water which lifted the food from its position and carried it straight to his mouth."—A cobra had thrust its head through the bars of its cage and had swallowed a toad. But being no longer able on account of the swelling produced to withdraw his head inside the cage, he disgorged his precious morsel. As this began to move away, he seized it and swallowed it again and tried anew to draw his head inside. Succeeding no better, he disgorged it again, took it by one leg, dragged it inside the cage and swallowed it finally.—" A number of pouter pigeons were feeding on a few oats that had been accidentally let fall while fixing a nose bag on a horse standing at bait. Having finished all the grain at hand, a large 'pouter' rose, and flapping its wings furiously, flew directly at the horse's eyes, causing the animal to toss its head, and in doing so, of course shake out more corn. This was several times repeated,—in fact, whenever the supply on hand had been exhausted."—Two goats coming in opposite directions, met on a ridge of rock with a precipice on each side, and too narrow to admit of their passing one another. "The animals looked at one another for some time, as if they were considering their situation, and deliberating what was best to be done in the emergency. Finally one of the goats knelt down with great caution, and crouched as close as it could lie, when the other walked over its back."—An elephant, tormented by large flies, went, as soon as she was free to go where she liked, to a thicket of well branched young shoots, "and selecting

102 THE PSYCHOLOGY OF REASONING

one raised her trunk and neatly stripped down the stem, taking off all the lower branches and leaving a fine bunch on top. She deliberately cleaned it down several times, and then laying hold at the lower end broke off a beautiful fan or switch about five feet long, handle included. With this she kept the flies at bay flapping them off on each side ".—A cat had the habit of hiding itself near the place where the crumbs from the table were thrown, to leap at the right moment on one of the birds which were attracted by the food. For some days the practice of feeding the birds was discontinued. The cat was then seen " to scatter crumbs on the grass with the obvious intention of enticing the birds afresh ". —A dog, "one morning when the grass was covered with frost, dragged a mat out of his kennel, from which he had got loose, to the lawn beneath the house windows where he was found lying on the mat which thus served to protect him from the frost." [1]

And we could continue in this fashion as long as we pleased. Everybody knows how great a number of similar examples of animal intelligence can be found, either in Romanes' book or in any other good book on zoology or on comparative psychology. The few which have been recorded here have even been chosen from the simplest and most common, from those which are in no way extraordinary, from those which are most easily interpreted.

None the less, even in connection with these very simple cases, which in themselves are disputed by no one, discussions have certainly not been lacking as to whether they are or are not cases of true and authentic "reasoning." But the difficulty has remained because the true nature of reasoning as it is found also in man, has never been clearly understood either by the supporters or by the opponents of animal reason.

Indeed if reasoning is essentially, even in man, only a series of acts, operations or experiments performed merely in thought, then the facts cited above and all similar facts ought without any doubt to be regarded as so many examples of authentic animal reasoning.

There is nothing really astonishing, for example, in

---

[1] G. I. Romanes, *Animal Intelligence*, seventh edition, London, 1898, pp. 95-96, 135, 195-196, 233, 251, 262, 317, 337-338, 409, 418, 466.

CONCRETE TO ABSTRACT REASONING 103

the fact that in an ant who has already in the past burrowed tunnels even under varied circumstances and has afterwards passed through such tunnels carrying loads, there should now come to be produced, under the impulse of a thwarted affectivity tending to carry the precious booty to the nest, the recall of one of these past feats of excavation associated with the recall of such a passing through. The simple mnemonic reproduction of past facts of this kind, combined in such a way that, were they realised, they would satisfy the thwarted affective tendency, is sufficient for this last to promote such an actual realisation. Similarly there is nothing astonishing in the fact that a wasp, who, in his past experience has very often observed on his buzzing approach to caterpillars' nests that the caterpillar itself issues from the nest by some hole and always on the side opposite, should under the impulse of hunger, produce an image of a hole so pierced in the nest, and thus an image of his own act of piercing, an act which he has several times performed in the past, even should the circumstances have been other and the wasp concerned with different things. The image will be that of an act favourable in its outcome and the affective tendency of hunger will in fact drive the wasp to realise it.

The reasoning of animals, understood in this sense, that is, as a very simple form of "Gedankenexperiment" preceding action, involves nothing then in itself which is extraordinary and in particular nothing more extraordinary than is involved by those other mental or psychical faculties of these very animals which no one would venture to deny.

It is, however, very probable that with animals, as after all with many men also, such reasoning never or hardly ever takes the form of a long and complicated succession and combination of acts, imagined step by step under the impulse of a primary affective tendency and corrected and controlled by the secondary affective tendency of the corresponding "attentive state," which tends to avoid fresh failures due in the past to the imagining of incorrect results for given acts. Reasoning in animals, most probably, takes as a rule the form of a spontaneous and instantaneous evocation of some very short and simple mental combination of acts, aroused at one stroke by the powerful impulse of an

104 THE PSYCHOLOGY OF REASONING

intense primary affectivity, without the control of any secondary affectivity.

In other words reasoning in animals and especially in animals of the lower grades will be rather an "intuitive" mental combination of acts than a "reflective."

Further, reasoning in animals will be *particular and concrete*, seeing that it does not easily rise to become *general* and *abstract* even in men. The ant will certainly not think that piercing a tunnel is the most suitable means *in general* of overcoming *this given category* of obstacles. No more will the wasp raise his system of caterpillar hunting into a theory. On the contrary the "Gedankenexperiment" for one as much as for the other will certainly be concerned each time only with the given obstacle which bars the passage at that given moment, and only with this particular caterpillar's nest which, unprovided with any sort of hole, presents itself now.

But apart from this inferiority of degree—as a mental combination dealing only with *particular* and *concrete* experiments—nothing, we repeat, authorises us to doubt the occurrence of reasoning in animals as well as in men, a fact which is in addition confirmed by their whole behaviour ; and nothing authorises us to allow that reasoning in the animals differs *substantially* from reasoning in men.

At the same time it certainly cannot be denied that the general and abstract reasoning to which the *superior man* can rise, differs very much, if not in substance at least in what concerns its degree of superiority, from particular and concrete reasoning, of which alone even those animals, which are the most highly developed intellectually, seem to be capable. And it is in this very capacity for general and abstract reasoning that many people — beginning with Locke himself — have wished to place (and not mistakenly if we are concerned *not so much with ordinary men as with superior minds*) the chief difference which as regards intellect separates man from the brutes : " It seems as evident to me ", says this great philosopher, "that they do, some of them, in certain instances, reason, as that they have sense, but it is only in particular ideas, just as they received them from their senses. They are, the best of them, tied up

CONCRETE TO ABSTRACT REASONING 105

within these narrow bounds, and have not (as I think) the faculty to enlarge them by any kind of abstraction."[1]

We have then at this point to examine what *general abstract concepts* are, how they are developed and what kind and what degree of superiority they bestow upon reasoning which has recourse to them.

In fact it is in the use of more and more general and abstract concepts that the whole evolution of reasoning consists, and this is precisely the problem which we propose to study in this chapter and in that which follows.

II

But before passing to the study of true and genuine concepts, we must very briefly indicate a humbler and more simple psychological phenomenon which is as it were the primitive matrix from which these are derived. We mean affective classification.

Before a newly-hatched chick were put certain caterpillars of approximately the same shape and size but differently coloured ; among the various species there was one with yellow and black stripes which was offensive to the chick in taste. In a very few days the chick acquired the most complete experience in the matter, and while he eagerly seized the other caterpillars, he did not even touch caterpillars of this kind.[2]

This very simple fact supplies us with a clear example of affective classification on the part of the chick ; all caterpillars which were not striped with yellow and black are evidently for him " equivalent " because all eatable ; and opposed to these he places caterpillars striped with yellow and black, in a single group, in a quite distinct class, as being all for him likewise " equivalent," because offensive in taste.

All animals then, from the lowest upwards, are capable of such affective classification, and this in fact constitutes and sums up their "empirical knowledge." It cannot be doubted that in the case of man as well an entirely similar affective classification presided at all his first acquisitions of empirical knowledge.

[1] J. Locke, *An Essay concerning Human Understanding* (1689), Book II, ch. XI, § 11, p. 105.

[2] Lloyd Morgan, *op. cit., Animal Behaviour*, p. 57.

106 THE PSYCHOLOGY OF REASONING

Whatever may have been their origin—emotional-interjectional, through onomatopoeia, or, according to the well known theory of Noiré and Max Müller, through "clamor concomitans"—it is in any case certain that the first names created by language were nothing but *common names*, that is to say phonetic symbols fitted to indicate this or that class of phenomena or objects, *equivalent in relation to a given affectivity, a given need, or a given desire.*[1]

This affective nature of common names was retained later and is still retained, we might say intact, to-day, in spite of the tendency of everyday use to weaken the lively original colours.

Thus in connection with his need for nourishment man still to-day divides all the objects with which he comes into contact in the same fashion as the chick to which we have just referred. He divides them into eatables and uneatables, the eatables into animal and vegetable foods and each of these into their numerous varieties according to the degree and the fashion in which they are capable of satisfying his hunger ; he distinguishes animals which yield milk from those which do not, fruit trees from those whose fruit is not edible, ripe fruit from green. From the point of view of his sexual need he distinguishes the sexes from one another, the virgin from the woman who is such no longer, the little girl from the adult, the young woman from the old. From the point of view of his instinct of self preservation, he distinguishes friend from enemy, the man of honour from the brigand, the fierce carnivore from the peaceful grass eater. And so on and so forth.

But further, the common nouns which stand for the objects of our most ordinary artificial uses appear, to a close examination, to rest, all of them, and in all cases, upon an affective basis, although this goes nowadays entirely unnoticed. Each one of them, that is, serves only as a symbol of this or that class of objects whose members, even when very different from one another in other connections, are none the less equivalent for us in relation to some one or other of our needs or desires. By "house," for example, we understand a group of objects, different as much as one pleases one from another, but all fitted to shelter us from bad weather :

[1] Cf. M. Müller, *The Science of Thought*, Longmans, 1887, p. 433.

CONCRETE TO ABSTRACT REASONING 107

" house " probably meant originally, Max Müller maintains, " whatever covers ", " a covering ". By the word " clothing " we denote the whole group of objects fitted to protect our bodies taken as a whole from the cold ; while stockings, trousers, coats and hats protect different parts of our bodies. Furs, woollen stuffs, cotton fabrics satisfy in varying degrees and in different fashions our need to be covered. Beds, divans, armchairs, chairs, and stools satisfy to a varying extent and in different ways our need for repose.

The common noun " poison " is typical in this respect. It represents a class of objects, such that from the point of view of perception, it would be difficult to find any which are more diverse one from another ; in their mineral, vegetable or animal structures, in their physical states as solids, liquids or gases, in shape, in colour, in taste, in smell, etc., they could not differ more one from another ; none the less, man has made of them a quite distinct class, because they are all for him equivalent in relation to this instinct of self preservation.

Locke acutely asked himself what greater connection or relation there could be in nature between the idea of killing and the idea of a man on the one hand, than between the same idea of killing and the idea of a sheep on the other, to explain why out of the action of killing one of our fellow-men, and thence out of the man who does so, we have created a particular kind of actions and of men denoted by the words murder and murderer, while no such term exists for the corresponding action of killing a sheep. And why in an analogous fashion the term " parricide " exists but not that of " filicide ". And why there is a special way of denoting the shape of that part of a weapon which enters into people's bodies or strikes them, —for example by " dagger " or " poignard "—and none for the rest of the weapon itself.[1]

It will be seen that affective classification explains this diversity in treatment at once. The reason is that for the members of a society it is those only who have killed one of their fellow-men of their own society, and not those who have killed some animal no matter what, who represent for the remaining members a group of individuals who are equivalent through the fear which

[1] J. Locke, *op. cit.*, *An Essay concerning Human Understanding*, Book III, ch. V, § 6.

108 THE PSYCHOLOGY OF REASONING

they inspire. In the same way, in the interests of social order under a patriarchal regime, the murder of a father by his son was a much more serious matter than the murder of a son by his father. And as far as the seriousness of the wound is concerned, all pointed weapons are equivalent, whatever the shape, material, colour or appearance in general of their handle may be.

Even those common nouns, or "concepts," which would seem at first sight to have no affective substratum at all, are found on a close analysis to have an affective substratum as much as the others. The common name or concept "ball" will serve as an example for them all.

"The child," writes Miller, "has a natural impulse to play. Among other things, his play activities bring him into contact with what we call a ball. His reaction to the ball causes it to roll, and this *interests him*. He comes repeatedly into contact with round things, and as a result of reacting towards them, he finds that he gets *this agreeable experience* of causing them to roll." He therefore places all these things, whatever may be their matter, their colour, their size, etc., in a single group, which constitutes for him the concept of ball.

"In the matter of realising certain other needs", our author continues, "or satisfying impulses, we find that among objects having certain characteristics, *one is just as good as another*." "The concept is thus *general* in nature and is relative *to a need*".[1]

It is through not having understood this very affective nature of all concepts that the question of concepts or "general ideas" has given rise among philosophers to interminable discussions and that some have even denied the possibility of their existence in our mind.

The concept of "dog", for instance, is among those which have given philosophers most trouble. "Who ever saw a dog?" Max Müller writes, "We may see a spaniel, or a greyhound, or a dachshund, we may see a black or a white or a brown dog, but a dog no human eye has ever seen." It is the same with the concept "tree". "No one ever saw a tree, but only this or that fir tree, or oak tree, or apple tree. . . . Tree, therefore, is a concept, and, as such, can never be seen or perceived by the senses, can never acquire any phenomenal or intuitive form".[2]

---

[1] I. E. Miller, *op. cit., The Psychology of Thinking*, pp. 190, 213.
[2] M. Müller, *op. cit., The Science of Thought*, pp. 78-79.

CONCRETE TO ABSTRACT REASONING 109

All this is true ; except that Max Müller does not see how all these difficulties disappear immediately as soon as we recognise that a concept is, not a thing of a perceptual order but, purely and simply, a class or group of affectively equivalent things.

And, in fact, some affective substratum, differing perhaps from the original substratum and also differing even from time to time according to the circumstances, is always ready to reappear on the first favourable occasion, even in those common nouns or concepts in which one would least have expected to find traces of this substratum still remaining. This is clearly shown in fact by these concepts of "dog" and "tree". An animal for example dashes out of a thicket barking. The child runs away in fright and hides his head in his mother's lap. "You silly!" she says to him, "don't you see that it is *a dog*". And under the scorching rays of the sun the exhausted traveller joyfully cries to his companion "Look! there is *a tree* under which we can rest".

III

We see then from these few examples, which have been chosen, as is our endeavour throughout, from among those which are simplest and at the same time most typical, that the most familiar common nouns or "concepts" represent nothing but classes of objects, which may, we repeat, differ extremely among themselves from other points of view, but which are all equivalent in relation to some one of our needs or of our affective tendencies.

In other words every common noun, every concept is essentially merely an affective grouping. In a plurality of objects, differing from the point of view of perception even very widely one from another, we discover the same capacity to satisfy some given affectivity, some given need or desire of ours, and through this capacity we reduce this very plurality to a unity. "Whenever we form a class we reduce multiplicity to unity, and detect, as Plato said, the one in the many".[1]

[1] S. Jevons, *op. cit., The Principles of Science*, Vol. II, p. 345.

110 THE PSYCHOLOGY OF REASONING

It results from this as an immediate consequence that there can be as many ways of classing the same number of objects as there are different affective points of view, kinds of desires which the objects can excite and ends or interests which they can serve : "Let it be remarked that there must generally be an unlimited number of modes of classifying any group of objects ".[1]

It should be noted that this affective classification, strictly "subjective" as it is, already includes in itself, in rudimentary form, the scientific classification which is wrongly described as "objective". In fact if the given objects are capable all of satisfying the same affectivity, this can only be due to their actual possession of some common property or characteristic. The things for instance which please us because they are sweet, all contain certain given substances very similar in their chemical properties ; stuffs which satisfy the organism's need to be protected from the cold all have the physical property of being bad conductors of heat ; the fierce beasts that the savage grouped in one category because they were all equally to be feared, have all of them certain zoological characters which are not possessed on the other hand by those herbivorous animals which primitive man classed as animals to be domesticated in order to draw their milk and to eat their flesh. And similarly with other cases.

Only at a later stage however was a much greater "objectivity" reached with *indirectly affective*, that is with utilitarian or technical classifications. These referred to the various animals, plants, forces of nature in general, according to their products and uses, or even to the various tools and the different materials to be transformed by work : to the various means, in short, *fitted to attain this or that end or result*. And with the ceaseless extension of the transforming activity of man, directed always towards modifying his environment more and more to his own advantage, these classifications have been gradually more and more developed and have in part replaced classifications which are strictly and simply affective. They become as a result more "objective" than these latter because, the proper means of attaining given ends being in most cases the same for all individuals concerned, the relevant classi-

[1] S. Jevons, *ibid.*, p. 348.

CONCRETE TO ABSTRACT REASONING 111

fications of these means thus came to be less subject to the accidental affective dispositions of these individuals.

But the principle has remained always the same: objects or phenomena, even when very different from one another in other connections, are found classed together because they show themselves "equivalent" as means fitted to yield the desired result or end. So that these utilitarian or technical classifications have always remained frankly teleological, that is to say always dependent upon the end or good to be reached.

Thus the concept "paper-knife", for instance, includes a number of objects very different among themselves from the perceptual point of view; some are of wood, others of ivory or of silver, some are all blade, others have handles as well as blades, and the handles for these last have the utmost variety of form. Nevertheless all these objects have been grouped in a well defined class, because, thanks to the fact that they possess a blade which is thin at least on one side, they are all "equivalent" among themselves, in relation to their purpose, to cut the pages of a book without tearing them.

The same thing can be said of any other instrument which can be used in technical operations or scientific research. Let us take for instance the concept of triangle. "Does it not require", asks Locke himself, "some pains and skill to form the general idea of a triangle? (which is yet none of the most abstract, comprehensive and difficult); for it must be neither oblique, nor rectangle, neither equilateral, equicrural nor scalenon; but all and none of these at once".[1]

And Berkeley in refuting Locke, simply denied the possibility of having such a general idea of a triangle.[2]

All these difficulties, we see, disappear if it is recognised that the concept triangle is nothing else in substance than a technical classification of a number of geometrical figures which, even when very different in form from one another, are, however, thanks to the fact that they possess only three sides and thus possess certain given geometrical properties the same for all of

---

[1] J. Locke, *op. cit.*, *An Essay concerning Human Understanding*, Book IV, chap. VII, § 9.

[2] G. Berkeley, *A Treatise concerning the Principles of Human Knowledge* (1710). Introduction, in *Berkeley's Complete Works*, Fraser's Edition, Oxford, 1901, Vol. I, pp. 246 ff.

112 THE PSYCHOLOGY OF REASONING

them, "equivalent" among themselves as instruments of research in certain given geometrical investigations: it is, for example, quite indifferent, if the end be to know the sum of the interior angles of a polygon, whether this be divided into one series of triangular portions or another. Similarly it is quite indifferent for a geodesian or surveyor whether, other circumstances being the same, he employs one system of triangulation or another.

The same thing can be said of the most "abstract" utilitarian or technical concepts also.

All quantitative classifications or conceptions, for example, have had at first merely an affective origin, becoming later a utilitarian or technical as well. The redistribution, for instance, of cultivable lands among the agriculturists, when the water from the periodical floodings of the Nile retreated, in such a way that each portion should be "equivalent" to the others—capable, that is, of producing the same quantity of grain, the only thing which mattered in such a redistribution, whatever in other respects might be the geometrical configuration of the field—this gave rise, as we know, to the concept of surface.

The "equivalence" of different goatskin vessels, even when of the most diverse shapes, with regard to the satisfaction of thirst for the same number of days and for the same number of individuals, could not help making the concept of capacity or volume appear very early. While it is from the "equivalence" of the work of one strong man with the work of several youths in relation to the lifting and transporting of some heavy mass, or from some such other similar "equivalence", that the concept of force certainly derives. And so on and so forth.

The concepts of the different quantities, surfaces, volumes, forces, etc., come in this fashion from comparisons of objects or phenomena made from a certain affective or utilitarian point of view, in connection with which, in order that these phenomena or objects should appear "equivalent", it is necessary and sufficient that such or such attributes should not merely be found present in them all, but present to the same extent.[1]

In this way out of these different quantitative con-

---

[1] Cf. E. Mach, *op. cit.*, *Erkenntnis und Irrtum*, pp. 357-59.

CONCRETE TO ABSTRACT REASONING 113

cepts comes the still more abstract concept of number *as a general means or instrument of noting all and any quantitative equivalences whatsoever.*

Finally the concepts even of space, time, and cause, have had, primitively, a quite analogous affective or utilitarian origin. The primitive concept of space came very likely from the comparison of two or more journeys as different as one pleases under other aspects —towards the east or towards the west, through the fields or through the forest, by day or by night, under a clear or under a cloudy sky, with companions or alone, and so on—but equivalent one to another from the point of view of producing, with the same fatigue, represented here by walking, the same result, namely the transporting of the thinker's own body or of some given load from one place to another.

Similarly two periods of our own existence qualitatively as different from one another as we please— spring or autumn, morning or evening, in our own house or outside, before or after a meal, in tranquillity or in the midst of uproar, and so on—but "equivalent" in relation to an end, namely the gaining of the same product with the same working effort, followed through in the same fashion as regards continuity and intensity, would, it cannot be doubted, furnish our primitive ancestors with the very first concept of time.

And again, among all the infinitely numerous phenomena which come together to produce this or that happening—whose antecedence or concomitance, that is, is necessary if the event is to occur—at first only those few were considered as "causes" which, though as different as possible qualitatively, were "equivalent" *as our only means of intervention* in relation to a purpose of letting the event happen or avoiding it; that is, as being the only phenomena which we could control among all the other necessary antecedent or concomitant phenomena; it being indifferent in consequence upon which of them we acted in order to prevent the occurrence of the undesired or dreaded event in question.[1]

It will be enough if we notice here how the formation of all these concepts has been in the first place made

[1] Cf. G. Vailati, "Sull 'applicabilità dei concetti di causa e di effetto nelle scienze storiche," in *op. cit., Scritti di G. Vailati*, pp. 463-464.

114 THE PSYCHOLOGY OF REASONING

possible, and later greatly encouraged, by the ceaseless and unremitting labour of man in transforming his own environment ; because it is only this labour which could make him discover that certain given objects or phenomena, provided only that they had in common such and such characters and attributes, were equivalent in relation to the end to be obtained. Concepts are not due, as Max Müller appears to allege, to the "invention" of language, but language and concepts, even those most general and abstract, have developed together side by side, stimulated both of them, incessantly, by this *technical progress* in the work of mankind, taken in its largest sense.

IV

Together with this activity of man in transforming and adapting the world to his own multiple and varied needs, an activity which stimulates him to pass from purely affective to utilitarian or technical classification, his activity in the direction of gaining knowledge for its own sake was also progressing and developing itself, an activity which stimulated him to pass from this same original affective classification to conceptual scientific classification properly so called.

It is well known, in fact, that science has passed through a primordial phase, in which scientific speculations were turned exclusively towards an affective classification of phenomena.

Thus all celestial phenomena, if slightly exceptional, such as rainbows, comets, eclipses, extraordinary conjunctions of planets and other similar phenomena, were a continual cause of superstitious hopes and fears ; whence the speculations of the first astrologers which tended to class these phenomena into those which brought good and those which brought evil fortune.[1]

Similarly the motive which led the Greeks to find analogies among phenomena was the uneasiness caused by phenomena which had not as yet been affectively classed. "What the Greek investigators understood by the explanation of a given phenomenon," Vailati well observes, "was not so much the analysis and resolution of this phenomenon into its elementary parts or the determination of the laws of its production, as its approximation to or identification with other more

[1] Cf. Jevons, *op. cit.*, *Principles of Science*, vol. II, pp. 322-323.

CONCRETE TO ABSTRACT REASONING 115

common and more familiar phenomena."—"What drove or stimulated them to perform this mental operation, was, as they expressly recorded, *the desire to free themselves from anxiety*, and sometimes also, as for example with the meteorological phenomena, which occupied so great a place in the speculations of the Greeks, *the desire to free themselves from the terrors* caused them by the occurrence of phenomena differing too widely from those which were subject to their own control. An explanation which could satisfy this condition was, for them, by that fact alone, a sufficient explanation." [1]

And also in times nearer our own we may think of the importance possessed by such facts as, for example, the recognition of the comets, which used to be so much feared, as simple planets possessed merely of very much lengthened elliptical orbits, the reduction of the mysterious rainbow to a mere phenomenon of the refraction of light, the explanation of thunder which has allowed it to be classed among electrical discharges and not among manifestations of divine anger, and so on.

It is out of this need for an affective classification of phenomena, that little by little has come the need of knowing their origins. When we did not succeed in directly classing a phenomenon among phenomena more familiar to us, we attempted at least to see whether it were *derived* from some of these more familiar phenomena, differently combined among themselves. *Thus appeared the scientific need for a connected account or "history" of things.*

Experience then has shown that for one and the same phenomenon, with which we are not as yet familiar, to be derived from certain other given phenomena, which are familiar to us, it is not necessary that these phenomena should be always identical in each and every respect, but it is sufficient if they be so merely with respect to some of their attributes or characters. Thus these phenomena though differing each time widely among themselves in all other respects were considered as equivalents *in relation to their result in producing the phenomenon whose explanation was in question.*

---

[1] G. Vailati, " Il metodo deduttivo come strumento di ricerca," in *op. cit., Scritti di G. Vailati*, p. 129.

116 THE PSYCHOLOGY OF REASONING

Thus it is that conceptual or scientific classification properly so called differs in no way essentially from utilitarian or technical classification, for the production of the phenomenon to be explained constitutes the end in virtue of which the classification of its generating phenomena is made.

Every class of phenomena, which includes all these phenomena which are equivalent in respect of their effect in producing this or that phenomenon which is to be explained, constitutes then a scientific concept. And the pointing out of the particular attribute necessary and sufficient to render all these objects or phenomena equivalent among themselves in relation to this effect constitutes a scientific rule or law : " A rule. reached by the observation of facts," writes Mach, "cannot possibly embrace the entire fact in its infinite richness, in all its inexhaustible manifoldness ; on the contrary it can furnish only *a rough outline of the fact, one-sidedly emphasising only the feature that is of importance for the given technical or scientific aim in question.*"[1]

The "schematisation" of phenomena consists indeed only in reducing them to this particular attribute, which is the sole attribute which concerns the production of the desired phenomena. All schematisation has thus an affective or utilitarian substratum. And there could in consequence be as many different schematisations of the same phenomena as there were ends to serve as their bases.

It is in this schematisation, in this reduction of phenomena, these "aggregates of qualities," to the single quality which alone renders them equivalent in relation to such and such an end to be attained, it is in this extraction and retention, among all the sensible elements or attributes of widely varied objects, of that one alone which is necessary and sufficient for the production of the desired object or event, or of the phenomenon which we are concerned to explain ; it is in this, and in this alone, that the process of " generalisation " or of " abstraction " consists.[2]

---

[1] E. Mach, *Die Mechanik in ihrer Entwicklung historisch-kritisch dargestellt*, Leipzig, 1912, pp. 69-70. English Translation, Chicago, 1907. Chap. I, p. 78.

[2] Cf. Th. Ribot, *L'évolution des idées générales*, 2e éd., Paris, 1904, p. 7 sqq. ; E. Mach, *op. cit., Die Analyse der Empfindungen*, p. 266 ; W. Ostwald, *op. cit., Vorlesungen über Naturphilosophie*, p. 41 ; S. Jevons, *op. cit., The Principles of Science*, Vol. I, p. 30.

CONCRETE TO ABSTRACT REASONING 117

And it is through not having noticed this basis of true and genuine affective or utilitarian classification, upon which the formation of all concepts rests, no matter which they be, that neither Locke nor Berkeley, nor Max Müller, nor Stuart Mill himself has succeeded in understanding the intimate nature of what are called general or abstract "ideas".[1]

V

It follows from all that we have said hitherto that to think by means of concepts is to think by means of classes of objects or phenomena—by means of "bundles of things", as Locke said—equivalent among themselves in relation to the end to which the thought is tending.[2]

In other terms, reasoning made through a general or abstract concept is valid for all the objects or phenomena which, though very different one from another from a concrete point of view, have in common, nevertheless, the attribute or quality which renders them equivalent in relation to the end which should be reached by the operations or experiments which the reasoning imagines as performed upon them.

So that in one single and unique experiment which is merely thought of, there come to be summed up the thousand, ten thousand, hundred thousand experiments which, were the concept lacking, would have to be performed by thought upon each one of the objects or phenomena included in the class which constitutes the concept itself.

To this the wider scope, the greater "technical yield" of general and abstract as opposed to particular and concrete reasoning is due. The former is to the latter, we might almost say, as typographical composition is to the handwriting of the old copyists: the first

---

[1] Cf. J. Locke, *op. cit.*, *An Essay concerning Human Understanding*, book III, chap. III, e.g. § 6, p. 328 ; G. Berkeley, *op. cit.*, *A Treatise concerning the Principles of Human Knowledge*, Introduction, pp. 237-256, especially § 10, p. 242, et § 12, p. 245 ; M. Müller, *op. cit.*, *The Science of Thought*, passim. e.g. p. 267 ; J. S. Mill, *op. cit.*, *A System of Logic*, vol. II, book IV, chap. II : Of Abstraction or the Formation of Conceptions, § 1, 2, 3, pp. 193-200.

[2] Cf. J. Locke, *op. cit.*, *An Essay concerning Human Understanding*, Book III, chap. III, §§ 1 and 20, pp. 326, 335.

118 THE PSYCHOLOGY OF REASONING

once done, serves for all the copies which are required to be printed ; while the second had to be repeated for each copy.

To this equally is due the increase of "technical yield" of reasoning with every new concept or principle whereby we are allowed to consider as equivalent, in relation to the result to be reached by a mentally performed operation or experiment, other particular cases, which hitherto appeared to us to be different in every respect from those grouped under the more restricted concept : "The advantage," writes Mach, "which every general principle offers consists in the fact that it saves us in a large measure from the obligation of thinking again over every new and special case ".[1]

The progress of science has consisted in fact in the continual increase of this technical yield of reasoning, in its continual increase in power, "augmenting," by means of ever new and larger concepts, the number and variety of the particular and concrete mental experiments, which are represented by general and abstract reasoning. Through this, science has come to make its account or history of things, the "description" of the manner or production of phenomena, that is to say, their "explanation", as concise as possible (*The Principle of Economy* of Mach).

As regards language, it has merely a subsidiary and secondary part in this ever greater creation and extension of concepts. This part consists, simply, in fixing and conserving the very concepts which affective or utilitarian or technical classification comes little by little to discover and to create, so that there may be no need to reconstitute them anew on every occasion.

In other terms, the word—or, to speak more generally, any symbol whatever, whether mimetic, phonetic or graphic—is like a cabinet wherein we deposit objects classed according to this or that affective or utilitarian or technical point of view. It plays no active or intrinsically fundamental part in the formation of concepts, as Max Müller would have had us suppose, just as the different cases and divisions of a museum play no active or intrinsically fundamental part in the distribution and placing in these cases and divisions of the objects composing the collection.

[1] E. Mach, *op. cit.*, *Die Mechanik*, etc., pp. 57-58.

CONCRETE TO ABSTRACT REASONING 119

This is no reason, however, for saying that the cases and divisions have not very important uses; those, namely, of conserving and keeping in vigour the classification when it has been made once for all, so that there is no occasion to make it over again every time that we have need of it.

As Hastings Berkeley has very well remarked, a mere natural association of ideas, which would suffice, even without the aid of any symbol, to evoke anew, at the sight of a particular object, the other objects which resemble it from the point of view of perception, that is to say which would suffice to keep on its feet a classification based upon resemblances—and would thus suffice for all concrete reasonings, such as those for example which have been studied above as having been performed by animals—such an association does not by itself suffice, on the contrary, to recall all the objects comprised in a very general and abstract concept. And this because, among all the sensible elements which make them differ so much one from another, the concept takes into account only those elements, or that element alone, which make these objects equivalent in relation to the end which is being sought. How, for instance, could the sight alone of a stone evoke directly, by simple resemblance, all the other bodies, solid, liquid and gaseous, which the physicist has grouped none the less in that vast class of *bodies possessing mass*, because they are equivalent in relation to the production of certain phenomena of movement?

Thence the necessity for an artificial link by means of some symbol, whether phonetic or graphic, which is fitted to evoke anew all these objects, each time that the result or end in relation to which they are equivalent, is in view.[1]

And it is for this reason that, while completely rejecting Max Müller's aphorism "no reason without language", the fact remains, however, completely in accord with the observations of Hastings Berkeley which we have just cited, that reasoning so soon as it envelops conceptions of some degree of generality and abstractness, can scarcely be conducted without the use of phonetic or graphic symbols; that is to

---

[1] Cf. Hastings Berkeley, *Mysticism in Modern Mathematics*, Oxford, 1910, pp. 43-49.

120 THE PSYCHOLOGY OF REASONING

say, without the use of these precious coffers which jealously preserve all the infinite objects of nature in those multiple and varied classifications within which human toil and intelligence, ceaselessly testing and re-testing, have little by little come to group them, according to the interests and the ends, technical as much as scientific, of man.

But, we must now speak of the other kind of development which reasoning has followed parallel to, and as a consequence of, this passage from concrete to abstract forms ; that is, we must discuss the ever increasing complexity and the ever wider application which reasoning has come gradually to attain. This is what we shall do in the following chapter where we deal with the passage from simple intuition to the deductive process of science.

CHAPTER VI

THE EVOLUTION OF REASONING

Part II : From Intuition to Deduction

I

In the preceding chapter we have seen how we pass from concrete to abstract reasoning by discovering in varying objects or phenomena, even in those which from a perceptual point of view appear most different one from another, the qualities or attributes which render them equivalent as far as the production of given phenomena is concerned. To this we tend by means of a series of merely imagined operations or experiments which constitute what we call reasoning itself. And we said that, parallel with and as a result of development from concrete forms to ever increasingly abstract forms, reasoning also progresses in acquiring a continually greater complexity and an ever increasing applicability which from the simplest primitive intuitions leads it in the end to the most complicated deductive processes of science. It is under this second aspect that we are going to examine the evolution of reasoning in this chapter.

It will be best, therefore, to pause a moment to examine what exactly we mean by "intuition," this much heard of intuition, which provokes so much discussion both in the philosophic and in the psychological camps, and on which opinions are formed and such disparate doctrines are founded, opinions and doctrines very often quite in contradiction to one another and always more or less confused.

I

If we examine certain of the more typical cases which would universally be included under the heading of intuition, we shall see without difficulty, that, in

122 THE PSYCHOLOGY OF REASONING

essence, we simply mean by this term *any new observation that arises spontaneously and suddenly*, that is to say, which comes without preliminary enquiry or deliberate examination, unpreceded by those repeated attempts at verification which, at first unsuccessful, at last succeed ; without recourse to the continual effort and control which would accompany a corresponding state of attention.

For example intuition is often the simple observation of some fact, or of some attribute of an object, or of some relation between phenomena ; of a fact, attribute or relation which hitherto has been neither observed nor suspected, and this realisation happens suddenly at a given moment, although in the external circumstances nothing has changed. And this as a consequence of the fact that the habitual exterior conditions fortuitously coincide with the awakening of a particular affective state in the observer causing him to perceive that which now interests him for the first time.

This is in substance just what happens, in any and every act of " perception." Out of all the innumerable sensible qualities of the object, we only discover those which interest one or other of our affectivities ; and the more numerous the affective points of view from which the object is examined the more complete, or to be more precise, the less incomplete is the resultant "perception." The unexpected discovery of a new attribute in an object which is already familiar to us, is only an added component of the perception of the same object and due to the fact that the observer finds himself by chance looking at it from some such fresh affective point of view.

Thus Galileo by an intuitive act discovered the isochronism of the pendulum from the sight of the lamp that not only he but so many before him had seen swinging without having noticed anything of interest. An intuition which was evidently due to the accidental coincidence of an ordinary external fact and of a pre-occupation of his mind, an affective preoccupation concerning the measurement of time.

We must notice at all events, that an observer who had *attentively* set himself to observe how the time of oscillation varied with the gradual diminution of the amplitude of the latter,—which would have implied an

FROM INTUITION TO DEDUCTION 123

affective preoccupation of the same kind,—would have come sooner or later to observe the actual peculiarity itself, no longer by mere chance, but inevitably. The nature of this observation due to applied attention would in no wise have differed from the former observation due to intuition.

Into this particular category of intuitions, which we are now examining, enter equally the majority of the observations which constitute the so called axioms or postulates, whose empirical character is no longer, after so much discussion, challenged by anyone.[1]

And also the intuition or the discovery of these axioms or postulates is always provoked by a play of interest : A dog, for example, was in the habit of putting up a rabbit every morning at one of the ends of a shrubbery shaped like a horseshoe and of chasing it right along its concave side. At the end of this the rabbit, being fleeter than the dog, always managed to escape through an old drain. One fine day, however, the rabbit, having been routed out as usual, the dog ran straight to the drain along the chord to the arc instead of along the arc itself, the latter route being on the other hand followed as usual by the rabbit ; the dog reached the drain first, waited for the rabbit and caught it.[2]

Another dog moved by the desire to find his lost master has an intuition of the axiom that if there are only three alternatives and two of them are ruled out, there necessarily only remains the third : " The dog tracking his master along a road came to a place where three roads diverged. Scenting along two of the roads and not finding the trail, he ran off on the third without waiting to smell."[3]

In an analogous way, from the most distant times, the humblest shepherd preoccupied in preventing his flock from running away during his absence could easily have discovered by intuition the impossibility of making a complete enclosure with only two straight pine trunks by laying them at an angle to one another, whatever the angle and however long the two stems.

And so on with other similar axioms or postulates.

[1] Cf., for example, the controversy of J. S. Mill with Whewell : J. S. Mill, *op. cit.*, *A System of Logic*, vol. I, book II, chap. V, §§ 4-6, pp. 258-278.

[2] Romanes, *op. cit.*, *Animal Intelligence*, p. 461.

[3] Romanes, *op. cit.*, p. 457.

124 THE PSYCHOLOGY OF REASONING

From the intuition as a pure and simple observation of some fact or attribute which is so to speak under our very eyes (to which category belong the examples which have already been cited) we pass step by step to the intuition arrived at as a result of a mental combination, usually of a very simple kind, of merely imagined experiments ; a combination which is produced in us spontaneously and in a flash from the impulse of a single affectivity, without any corrective control being exercised by a corresponding state of attention, that is to say without there having been any secondary affectivity to hold in suspense even for an instant the impulse of the first.

To this type of intuition belongs very probably, as we have said in the previous chapter, the greater part of the "Gedankenexperimenten" of animals, and to this type belonged that combination of merely imagined experiments referred to in our chapter on the nature of reasoning, by which the author of these lines was able, at the very first examination of the question, to recognise mentally through the arrangement of all the inhabitants of London in file in the order of the increasing number of their hairs, the existence in that city of several individuals of just the same number of hairs.

On the other hand a little "reflection" was needed for that other mental combination of experiments (which is after all completely analogous to that just quoted) by means of which I realised, the very first time that I saw it stated, the law of radio-active equilibrium, concerning the ratio between the quantities of the various radio-active elements present in a mineral and their corresponding half life periods. This combination consisted in the fact of my representing to myself, with the aim of attaining a material comparison, a series of cylindrical receptacles with equal bases, each cylinder having along a directrix a crack starting from the bottom and of different width from receptacle to receptacle, next to suppose these put in a column one under the other and the top one under a tap with a constant rate of flow in such a way that the water flowing out of the crack of one falls into the one beneath and from this one to the next and so on, and to wait until a "stationary state", or dynamic equilibrium, is established in which the water maintains a constant height in each vessel,

FROM INTUITION TO DEDUCTION 125

differing one from the next according to the width of the crack.

Simple enough as it is, this mental combination required, as we have said, some "reflection", as opposed to the other, perhaps because for a short time there presented itself to my mind no combination of any kind, or perhaps because the first combinations which did present themselves, I realised to be unsuited to lead me to the end I was seeking. But in spite of this, the two combinations are none the less identical in all that concerns the mental elements employed in the recognition which was finally made. The whole difference rests in this, that in the "pondered" combination, the combination which leads to the mental recognition in view, is arrived at only by repeated attempts, of which a large number are rejected before that one arrives which is apt and which is chosen, whereas in the combination which is produced by "intuition" the "happy idea" presents itself by chance first and is then immediately adopted.

It is therefore by means of similar repeated attempts tenaciously followed that our deliberate reasoning ultimately makes the gaining of the desired result in a large measure independent of mere "chance", whereas when recourse is made to simple intuition alone this very result is left to the uncertainty of chance.

In other cases intuition does nothing but conduct us to the recognition of the general validity of a particular demonstration. "Kroman has asked," writes Mach, "how a demonstration performed upon a single special figure, for instance upon a given triangle, can appear to us to have general validity. He grants that this depends upon the fact that, by rapidly varying the figure in thought, we make it take all possible forms and so convince ourselves of the validity of the result for all special cases. History and introspection teach us that this idea is substantially correct. We cannot however agree with Kroman that every person who occupies himself with geometry succeeds in obtaining each time, 'instantaneously,' this complete vision, and in rising to this degree of clearness and force of geometrical conviction."[1]

---

[1] E. Mach, *op. cit., Erkenntnis und Irrtum,* pp. 386-387 ; *cf.* also S. Jevons, *Elementary Lessons in Logic,* (first edition 1870), Macmillan, London, 1909, p. 219 ; and I. Miller, *op. cit., The Psychology of Thinking,* p. 197.

126 THE PSYCHOLOGY OF REASONING

This "instantaneous" vision by which we recognise the general validity of a demonstration consists then in the fact of mentally perceiving in a flash that, were the same series of experiments, which constituted the demonstration itself, to be repeated on each of the figures considered in imagination to be different, *in certain aspects only*, from those under our very eyes, the result would be always the same.

It follows that intuition consists, in this case, in instantaneous mental repetitions of as many series of merely imagined experiments as there are different forms of the figure which present themselves to our thought, each series being extremely similar to the first series of experiments which have been effected on the particular figure drawn on the paper or the slate. So that the difference between this and the preceding intuition consists in the fact : that, in the case of the alignment of the inhabitants of London, according to the increasing number of their hairs, there is a single series, *isolated and fortuitous*, of imagined experiments ; whereas in the generalising intuition, there is an enormous number of similar series, *succeeding* each other very rapidly and all *suggested* by the first. And it is this second sort of intuition which makes us acquire the concept of determinate geometrical figures, equivalent in respect of a given result or any given properties — such as, for example, the concept of a triangle—transforming by that means the concrete reasoning of a child, at the beginning of his elementary study of geometry, into the abstract reasoning of the experienced geometer.

But, as Mach rightly observes in the passage previously quoted, it is not always spontaneously and in a flash, that is to say by simple intuition, that we arrive at this generalising "vision" of a given particular demonstration. Frequently, it requires, while changing nothing of its nature, a certain amount of reflection, which sooner or later succeeds where intuition, not favoured by chance, may fail.

In yet other cases intuition consists in the fact of finding, as we generally say, *analogies* between phenomena till then considered completely different, that is to say, in the fact of discovering that even phenomena extremely different from the point of view of perception, are, so long as they have a particular

FROM INTUITION TO DEDUCTION 127

given attribute, equivalent in relation to some given result to be obtained. The designation of this particular attribute, both necessary and sufficient for such an equivalence, constitutes what we call a scientific law ; a law enabling us to apply to the whole of a much larger group of phenomena or objects a given order of knowledge already acquired in respect to a smaller group. This extended application of all that we know of a given phenomenon to other phenomena, constitutes, as we know, the foundation of *induction*, and, as we shall see at the end of this chapter, it is this which makes the ever increasing application in science of the *deductive method* possible.

In truth, this discovery of new analogies between phenomena is not essentially different from the preceding case, which consisted in the generalisation of a demonstration ; precisely because, let us repeat, it is in essence but the simple observation that certain particular characteristics, and only those, are capable of making certain objects or phenomena, differing from one another in respect of their perception, equivalent in relation to a given result, obtainable by means of determined operations. But a notable difference between the two examples is that, in the second case, there is a much greater diversity between the objects or phenomena which are realised as equivalent and, in particular, that, as opposed to the first case when we had only to generalise a particular demonstration which had already been successfully achieved, *here the result to be obtained is not decided before hand*.

So conspicuous is the difference, particularly owing to this second circumstance, that in discovering analogies between phenomena intuition, here more than ever at the mercy of chance, can only with difficulty be replaced by reflection. Moreover, as we shall see in a moment, in the case of really new discoveries concentration is as a rule an impediment. In this domain intuition and chance are always the reigning powers and the unexpected flash of insight of a genius is of greater value than untiring reflection and pertinacity.

For example, Galileo imagines a body falling along an inclined plane, and then,—in conformity with all the results of similar experiments made in the past,—rising by virtue of the velocity it has acquired, along a second

128   THE PSYCHOLOGY OF REASONING

inclined plane to the same height as that from which it descended. He then imagines a series of planes of constantly decreasing slope along each of which the body in question is thought to rise every time. The more these planes are brought toward the horizontal, the more gradual is the slowing up of these bodies, the further they move and the longer the time before they stop. In a flash Galileo "*sees*", through analogy, that on the horizontal plane, (supposing there to be no friction), all slowing up ceases. Thus did he discover the law of inertia.[1]

In an analogous way Newton imagined himself throwing from a mountain summit a series of stones with successively increasing horizontal velocities. He "sees" the parabola they describe in falling and, eliminating the consideration of air resistance, he "sees" the gradual lengthening of the trajectory till the stone no longer strikes the ground at all. At this point the stone becomes a satellite of our earth and terrestrial gravity or acceleration shows itself as capable of giving rise to the same phenomena of motion as does celestial gravitation or acceleration.[2]

Evidently the principle of continuity, that is the tendency to extend the sphere of applicability of certain properties of a phenomenon which have been verified only in certain circumstances even to cases where these latter have gradually changed—the principle Newton and Galileo followed in these examples—is just that which the geometer follows when he imagines a triangle drawn upon his paper as changing gradually in every way possible. The only difference (we may repeat) is that the geometer knows the result he is aiming at, namely the generalisation of a particular demonstration which has already been made, whereas there is no guiding light to direct the two pioneers we have mentioned in their immortal discoveries.

Besides, not every new "analogy" between phenomena can be discovered by the application of the principle of continuity. And for those which occur to us without our having recourse even to this doubtful method of orientation, the part played by pure chance and the

---

[1] Cf. E. Mach, *op. cit., Die Mechanik in ihrer Entwicklung historisch-kritisch dargestellt,* pp. 131, 266.
[2] Cf. Mach, *ibid.,* pp. 181, 184.

FROM INTUITION TO DEDUCTION 129

importance assumed by the spontaneous intuitions of genius becomes even greater, whereas even the most indefatigably laboured work of the most vigorous attention and of the most prolonged reflection leads to no result at all.

By all this, what we have upheld above is seen to be confirmed, namely, that intuition is nothing more than *a new vision or observation*, wholly improvised and spontaneous, due, either directly and actually to the fortuitous coincidence of ordinary well known actual phenomena with an unwonted affective preoccupation, or indirectly and mentally, as a result of a new mental combination which itself is more or less fortuitous and whose result is, so to speak, "caught on the way" and held in the mind's eye by virtue, here again, of an intense interest of a practical or scientific nature.

What is important to notice here is that intuition by its very nature is very far from being always true. Even if, on the one hand, there are strong probabilities of its truth because either of the very simplicity of the fact observed or of the small number and simple nature of the imagined experiments which enter into the mental combination of which it consists, on the other hand, it is more often liable to error than is attentive observation or reflective reasoning, for the very reason that it lacks every kind of control from the secondary affective tendency present in any state of attention whatsoever. One must remember, for example, the fallacious intuition of the mathematicians that every continuous function must have a derivative, since if we draw a curve on paper it is possible to draw also a tangent to this curve through any point we choose, or the enormous number of intuitions which Faraday tells us were constantly presenting themselves to his mind during his researches, the larger part of which he had subsequently to abandon because they were wrong.

But if we find that intuition, as opposed to "attentive" observation or "pondered" reasoning, has the drawback of being much more subject to danger of error, it has nevertheless a much greater probability of yielding entirely new truths. Clearly what is necessary for these new truths to appear is first "imagination", that is, a mind that is capable of bursting through the boundaries of ordinary associations. An observer, for

130 THE PSYCHOLOGY OF REASONING

instance, not possessed with this power, never would have perceived in a swinging lamp anything but the qualities that are quite ordinarily perceived, the material of which it was made, its shape, the carvings which adorned it and such like things. But even Galileo himself would not have discovered the isochronism of the oscillations if he had not just at this moment luckily been seized by an affective preoccupation concerning the measurement of time. This preoccupation was, as far as it concerned the lamp, of a totally new kind, and it would not have been born if Galileo, stimulated by one of the ordinary affective interests relating to the lamp (an artist's æsthetic interest, or a verger's interest in making sure that it had not gone out, or that it was not too dusty), had been examining it *with attention.* Similarly the playful imagination of a Faraday needs to give itself an entirely free hand, without being checked at every turn by the incessant limitation, exclusion and control, exercised by both the affectivities of a strong state of attention.

Thus we see not only the usefulness, but the absolute necessity of a continual alternation between intuition and reflection. If this latter has need of the former to escape from the grave danger of sterility; intuition in its turn has need of reflection to control and prove the validity of each of the new observations or discoveries that it makes or thinks it makes at each new free flight of imagination.

II

Step by step, however, as the complexity of the mental combination increases, it lends itself less easily to solution in one flash of intuition and comes all the more to demand a certain amount of reflection. To convince ourselves of this, it is convenient to examine, as a valid example of all the rather more complicated processes of reasoning in general, the mental process which led Stevinus to formulate the law of equilibrium along an inclined plane. At the same time this example will serve to demonstrate that certain particular forms of reasoning, which have given philosophers of all time much food for thought—such

FROM INTUITION TO DEDUCTION 131

for example the principle of sufficient reason, or the proof by "reductio ad absurdum"—show also the whole fundamental process of reasoning to be nothing more than a series of merely imagined experiments.

Having imagined an endless chain laid over a triangular prism with two of its faces oblique and one horizontal, Stevinus notes first of all that the hanging part of the chain, by virtue of its symmetry about the vertical axis passing through its lowest point, cannot contribute in any way either to cause or to prevent the motion of the two portions of the chain at rest on the oblique faces of the prism. This observation concerning the hanging part of the chain, is, as one sees, nothing more than the principle of "sufficient reason" of Leibnitz, applied by Archimedes himself to the equilibrium of the equal armed balance loaded with equal weights and then employed for combining two equal forces to yield a resultant acting at the bisector of their angle or for other similar symmetrical phenomena or processes.

This principle rests essentially upon the observation that the symmetry itself implies the possibility of mentally performing two identical experiments upon the same object or phenomenon either by exchange between the symmetrical elements themselves, or by a suitable change in the position of the observer. We notice moreover that it is in this possibility that our knowledge that an object or phenomenon is symmetrical resides. As a result we expect from these two identical experiments results that are also identical. Lastly we mentally verify the fact that there cannot be this identity of result unless it be just this result that we have admitted.[1]

This series of operations and mental observations is, as we see, not yet so complex that it could not be accomplished all at once in a single flash, that is by simple intuition. It is, however, complex enough to demand, with most people, a certain amount of reflection.

We find moreover in the mental process followed by Stevinus an application of demonstration by reductio ad

---

[1] Cf. Jevons, *op. cit.*, *Elementary Lessons in Logic*, p. 125 ; Mach, *op. cit.*, *Die Mechanik*, pp. 10-11 ; F. Enriques, *Il principio della ragion sufficiente nella costruzione scientifica*, ' Scientia,' (1909), No. IX-I.

132 THE PSYCHOLOGY OF REASONING

absurdum. In fact he does not admit that the endless chain placed on the above mentioned prism has no tendency to move in either one direction or the other, but he *observes mentally* that if it had a tendency to move and did actually move, conditions would remain exactly the same after the motion as before and that in consequence the motion should continue indefinitely ; and it is just this perpetual motion that he realises is contradicted by experience.[1]

This is exactly the process followed in every proof by reductio ad absurdum ; when the non-possibility of a fact cannot be easily *established* we then establish instead the more easily recognised impossibility of another fact, which a more or less complex mental combination shows to be the inevitable consequence of the first. The second fact to which this mental combination leads is inhibited by the empirical observation which contradicts it, and thus its inhibition leads also to the inhibition of the whole process of association of which it was the last link and hence also of the imagined fact which is the starting point, the first link, in the chain of associative process.

The discovery of this other fact, which follows from the first and whose non-possibility is either already known by us or readily realisable, requires in most cases a certain consideration, for we must deliberately seek for it and advance by trial. Thus only rarely can a reductio ad absurdum be established in a flash and purely by an intuitive act.

But besides this—that is to say besides the fact of having recourse to elementary forms of reasoning which are somewhat unusual, such as the principle of sufficient reason and the proof by reductio ad absurdum—the mental process of Stevinus consists not in a single and elementary act of reasoning, that is in a single and unique merely imagined experiment, but *in several elementary acts following one after the other and linked together*. It constitutes in other words a mental combination in which one must advance by stages, stop at each relay, and not forget the results achieved at each of these stages in order that these results may be used as starting points for further stages. Thus in the process followed by Stevinus, as we saw just now, we

[1] Cf. Mach, *op. cit., Die Mechanik*, pp. 24 ff.

FROM INTUITION TO DEDUCTION 133

have to begin with a first stage, that which by the principle of sufficient reason leads to the conclusion that the hanging part of the chain can have no influence on either its equilibrium or movement. Then a second step, independent of the first, led Stevinus by the method of reductio ad absurdum to the observation that the chain does not move. He then proceeds by a third stage in which, by combining the results of the two preceding steps, he finds himself left with only the two pieces of chain, which lie on the two oblique faces of the prism and in equilibrium with one another. It is then, from this result, that he sets out to determine the laws of equilibrium on inclined planes.

All this demands attention and prolonged reflection, that is to say, the presence of a primary affectivity long held in suspense, and, at the same time, the presence of a secondary affectivity corresponding but opposed to it. The first, in order to be able to develop for a certain time the actual work of direct evocation and especially of selection of "happy ideas", which may show considerable delay in arriving, and, at the same time, to be able to keep in mind the successive results of different steps, thus being able to reunite these in a single process ; the second, in order to be able, at each stage of the reasoning, to control the material possibility of each of these partial and imagined combinations and the validity of the respective mentally observed results by excluding all those which would not be in conformity with reality.

This need for sustained reflection will appear more and more evident in what we have yet to say concerning the ever wider application which in science the mental process of deduction has come to receive.

III

In the last chapter we saw that the need for an account or history of things has emerged because, when unsuccessful in classing certain phenomena among others which are more familiar to us, it was natural to seek at least to see whether they are derivable from certain of these more familiar phenomena variously combined amongst themselves.

134 THE PSYCHOLOGY OF REASONING

The "how" and the "why" of each phenomenon was thus found to be constituted by the chain of merely imagined experiments, which, starting from certain given facts familiar to us, enabled us to arrive, as a final result, at the phenomenon which had to be "explained" and which thus came in fact to be "explained."

In the infinite variety of phenomena, we seek, then, to discover always the same elementary and familiar facts, whose differing mental combinations are capable of reproducing the immense variety presented by nature.[1]

This need of deriving the most complicated phenomena of nature from the small number of elementary phenomena which are the most familiar to us constitutes what is called the need of a "causal explanation."[2]

It is to this need of a "causal explanation" that the tendency of science to become as far as possible "deductive" is due, the tendency, that is, to try to derive, by means of more or less lengthy series of suitable experimental combinations which are merely imagined, the greatest possible number of natural phenomena from the smallest possible number of other phenomena chosen from those which are simplest and most familiar to us.

And since the phenomena of the movements of bodies are the simplest and the most familiar among all physical phenomena and, at the same time, are the only phenomena which allow the reasoning man to follow with the "mind's eye" the vicissitudes of objects, which remain always self identical through all their successive displacements, so the "deductive" tendency of science itself becomes a tendency to "Kinematism."[3]

But the *tendency* of science to become deductive is a very different thing from the *possibility* it possesses of becoming so. All depends upon the degree in which it is possible for the science to succeed in combining among themselves merely imagined experiments.[4]

Even taking as starting points phenomena which are the simplest and most familiar, the experimental combinations of greater or less complexity which can be imagined with them are infinite and infinitely varied,

---

[1] Cf. Mach, *op. cit.*, *Die Mechanik*, pp. 5-6.
[2] Cf. Mach, *op. cit.*, *Die Analyse der Empfindungen*, p. 273.
[3] Cf. E. Meyerson, *Identité et Réalité*, Paris, 1908, passim, e.g. pp. 83, 84, 87-88.
[4] Cf. J. S. Mill, *op. cit.*, *A System of Logic*, Vol. I, p. 245.

FROM INTUITION TO DEDUCTION 135

in the number, in the quality, and in the quantitative modalities of the respective components. And if such combinations appeared to differ from one another completely and in all respects it would be impossible to perform them by thought alone, since it would be necessary for this purpose to know first of all what the result would be *for each one separately*. If, on the other hand, by the way of intuition and of the more or less hypothetical corresponding inductive generalisation, we discover that those among these combinations which have certain determinate characteristics alone in common, are equivalent in relation to a given result, then this result, if verified experimentally for some single one among them, becomes capable of being at once applied to each of the others, which now become able, but now only, to be dealt with in thought.

It will be sufficient, as an example, to recall the law of movement discovered by Galileo. This law states that if several forces by their combined action give rise to a given movement of a body, these forces in spite of this fact of acting all together continue to produce, each on its own account—contrary to the belief generally entertained until then—the same effects which they would have produced had they been acting in isolation. That is, each of these combining forces is *equivalent*, in relation to the movement which it produces, to an equal force acting alone. "Before this law was discovered and clearly formulated", writes Vailati, "the student of mechanics who proposed to himself to determine deductively the movement produced by the simultaneous action of several forces, even when perfectly well aware of the mode of action of each, found himself faced with the same kind of difficulties as a chemist to-day would encounter who proposed to determine the properties of a compound a priori by using only his knowledge of the properties of components. On the other hand once the law was discovered, it was possible to perform mentally the most varied combinations of forces, even the most complex, because the simultaneous combination was found to be equivalent to as many successive applications of forces, the results of each one of which was known beforehand ".[1]

[1] Cf. Vailati, *art. cit.*, " Il metodo deduttivo, etc.", *op. cit.*, *Scritti di G. Vailati*, p. 421.

136 THE PSYCHOLOGY OF REASONING

A case where the equivalence discovered between several experimental combinations is of a still more general order is that, for example, of recognising that however varied may be the differences in the quantitative modes of certain of their components the result that concerns us is always of the same kind and that its magnitude is given by a single unique formula which in fact determines the result in terms of these quantitative modes of the components. The formula thus obtained represents the schematisation of this very general "conceptual fact". In this case the particular experimental combinations which are included in the concept and whose results we therefore know beforehand, so that we can perform them mentally, will be much more numerous and varied ; and thus the greater will be the number and frequency of the occasions where the deductive method will be able to be applied.

Newton's law, for instance, when substituted for those of Kepler, rendered possible the mental achievement of a much larger number of experiments on the celestial bodies ; for, whatever distribution of these bodies is imagined, even if it be quite different from any to which the laws of Kepler would apply, this law would indicate immediately the result relating to their accelerations and motions. Further, the phenomenon of tides, the form of the earth, its flattening at the poles and other very varied particular phenomena all have become, by virtue of it, equally capable of deduction, that is to say of being obtained by means of more or less complex suitable combinations of determinate initial modes of distribution of elementary masses and determinate initial motions of each of these masses, because for each of these combinations, when imagined, the Newtonian formula was capable every time of yielding the result beforehand.[1]

Every extension of the deductive method implies then in advance a new and corresponding induction, thanks to which the hitherto unknown results of a whole category of experimental combinations—for this reason not capable of being mentally performed—become on the contrary known, because they are assimilated to those of other categories of experimental combinations,

---

[1] Cf. Vailati, *ibid.*, 144 ; J. S. Mill, *op. cit.*, *A System of Logic*, Vol. I, p. 246 ; Mach, *op. cit.*, *Die Mechanik*, pp. 183-184.

FROM INTUITION TO DEDUCTION 137

whose results have already been observed by means of experiments which have been actually made. And the conditions upon which the different applicability and the different fecundity of the deductive method itself depend in the various fields of scientific research, are all summed up in this discovery of concepts, laws and formulas, by which new inductive generalisations are expressed.

But the utility of these concepts, laws and formulas of an ever more general order is not limited to the yielding of this possibility of mentally performing an ever greater quantity of *particular* experimental combinations by supplying the respective result in advance for each one of them. It has much greater value than this, above all in the possibility opened to reasoning itself of mentally performing experimental combinations which are themselves of a *general order*, that is to say *schematised*, in which each combination represents a whole corresponding group of particular combinations, equivalent among themselves from the standpoint of the result in view.

These *schematised* experimental combinations can, in virtue of their greater simplicity, be more easily thought and followed at greater length by the "mind's eye" than can particular combinations which are as a rule more complex; and the more schematised they are the greater the ease with which this can be done and the longer the series of combinations which can be imagined. General and abstract concepts, then, can contribute powerfully from this point of view also, in facilitating the ever wider application of the deductive method. "As we proceed to higher and higher degrees of generality," writes Ribot, "we do not mount into the void, as some have said, but into the simple."— And as James writes: "The reason why physics grows more deductive the more the fundamental properties it assumes are of a mathematical sort, is that the immediate consequences of these notions are so few that we can survey them all at once, and promptly pick out those which concern us."[1]

The formation of abstract concepts and the application of the deductive method advance then hand in hand

---

[1] Th. Ribot, *op. cit.*, *L'evolution des idées générales*, p. 253; W. James, *op. cit.*, *Principles of Psychology*, vol. II, p. 343.

138 THE PSYCHOLOGY OF REASONING

—for the double reason mentioned : through the quantity of results of experimental combinations, whether particular or general, which these concepts make known in advance, thus allowing us to perform these experimental combinations in thought alone ; and through the great simplicity given by these concepts to the respective schematised experimental combinations, thus rendering it more easy to perform them and follow them out in thought.

By means of abstract reasoning, substituted for concrete reasoning, we obtain finally, as we have seen in the preceding chapter, a very notable increase in the "technical yield" of reasoning itself, since any abstract reasoning takes the place of the thousand, ten thousand or hundred thousand concrete reasonings which would be respectively constituted by each of the particular experimental combinations grouped in the category for which the schematised combination stands.

In this way we obtain, not only an "account of things" capable of satisfying our need for a causal explanation, but, in addition, an account of things which is *continually more concise.* (Mach's *Principle of Economy.*)

The choice of concepts, on the one hand, and the choice of elementary phenomena, on the other, whether sensible or hypothetical phenomena, from which we start on the way to this "account of things", are in fact made with the criterion of rendering this account a 'conceptual shorthand' as short and compendious as possible.[1]

But however concise, however "stenographic" this account may be, it represents, however, a process whose complexity and amplitude grow ever more imposing. Precisely because we start from a small or even a very small number of phenomena, as elementary as possible, whether sensible or hypothetical, to pass on later, by mentally combining them among themselves, so as to produce by degrees an ever greater quantity of the most varied phenomena in nature, the process itself comes to be built up from a very great body of experiments which are all merely thought of, breaks up into an infinite number of stages or phases which have to be traversed one after another, and gives rise

---

[1] *Cf.* K. Pearson, *The Grammar of Science*, second edition, London, 1910, pp. 332, 504.

FROM INTUITION TO DEDUCTION 139

to a continual interlinkage and interference of the results of each of these combinations with those of all others. And the "mind's eye" has to follow all these merely imagined experiments, to note the results which they respectively would yield if they were actually performed, to pass from one phase of the process to another, without, however, losing sight of any of the results of the preceding phases, and to hold present at certain moments in the process all the results of earlier phases, though all these are noted by thought alone, in order to re-combine them among themselves in their turn.

It is easy to understand, then, how absolutely impossible it would be for such a complicated whole assemblage of mental facts to be ever thought of in one flash or to be ever caught at one glance by means of an act of intuition, however powerful this last might be. It can be understood, on the contrary, that all this must demand a state of attention or reflection extremely intense and prolonged, in which the primary affectivity, being held in suspense by the secondary affectivity for the whole duration of the process, can mentally follow out all the successive changes of things, can test and re-test the most varied combinations in order to try to approach the desired production of the phenomenon to be "explained", can evoke in prompt fashion the results of the different combinations imagined, revive and maintain those which must later on serve anew, and link all these different and successively imagined experiments together into one single process of consecutive thought. No less necessary must be the incessant action of the secondary affectivity, which is always on the look out to verify that the different imagined combinations are really possible, that the respective results which are attributed to them are veritably the exact results, that in the interlacing of combinations, no phenomena has been forgotten whose intervention could modify the final result of the whole.

But even the most intense and prolonged attention or reflection would certainly not suffice in the majority of cases, if the whole process had to be produced only by thought, without ever being sustained by any sensible and persistent basis. Hence the necessity to imagine and to resort to increasingly complicated *graphic symbols*, in order to have ever ready before the mind

140 THE PSYCHOLOGY OF REASONING

the results of the various experiments to be carried out by pure thought, to consolidate, so to speak, materially, before the mind itself, what has been obtained by the previous mental combinations, to help the imagination to devise and embrace at a single glance the most complicated combinations to be accomplished between the partial results already obtained, in short to evolve *a tangible schemic representation in which the whole mental process is in a fashion projected as it develops.*

All this has made necessary—as a result of the increasingly great complexity and ever widening application which the deductive process has little by little acquired in what are called the "exact sciences"—an increasingly complicated symbolism, which has frequently culminated in completely hiding the true and essential nature of reasoning — to be namely but a series of merely imagined experiments—a nature however which has nevertheless remained entirely intact, even under the dark veil which covers it. This we shall see in the following three chapters which are devoted to the superior forms of reasoning.

CHAPTER VII

THE HIGHER FORMS OF REASONING

Part I : Mathematical Reasoning in its Phases of Direct and Indirect Symbolism

IN the three preceding chapters we have given an analysis of reasoning and we have followed its evolution under each of its two aspects, as a development, that is, from concrete to abstract reasoning, and as a development from the elementary reasoning, which is conceived at a flash by a single act of intuition, to the ever more complicated reasoning, which is built up of a more or less lengthy series of elementary reasonings linked together.

We saw that reasoning in essence consists merely of operations or experiments which we confine ourselves to performing in imagination, since we know already what the result of each of them will be, a result which is now *observed*, so to speak, only mentally.

We saw that "concepts" are nothing but classes or groups of phenomena or objects, which may even be as different one from another as we please in their external or perceptual aspect, but which are *equivalent* among themselves in relation to this or that end, or in relation to the result which is in view in the merely imagined experiments which constitute reasoning. These phenomena or objects being reduced to the single attribute which renders them equivalent in relation to the result sought by the reasoning, the concept in question thus comes in the end to be represented by a unique schematised phenomenon or object, which transforms the reasoning concerned from concrete to abstract. This abstract reasoning—where the merely imagined operations or experiments, which relate to the phenomenon or object so schematised, continue no less than before to present themselves to the mind as "materially

142 THE PSYCHOLOGY OF REASONING

tangible "—thenceforward takes the place of all the particular concrete reasonings which otherwise would have to be performed upon each of the phenomena or objects comprised under the concept.

Finally we saw that the formation of new or the extension of old concepts—by the implied discovery of new categories of objects which are equivalent in relation to the results of certain determined operations —automatically increases the number of experiments whose results are known beforehand, and thus increases, through this beforehand knowledge of the respective effects, the number of experiments which are capable of being performed in thought alone ; and, at the same time, that the schematisation of phenomena or objects which is implicit in such fresh formation or wider extension of concepts, facilitates the mental representation of long series of operations or experiments by making them, linked together in the most varied ways as they are, more simple in performance, since they deal with schematised phenomena or objects. For this twofold cause, therefore, the final result of the passage from concrete to abstract reasoning is the application, made possible to an ever increasing extent in science, of the deductive method.

It now remains for us—we might almost say as a *verification* of these results of our last three chapters which have just been summed up—to proceed to the examination, still from a strictly psychological point of view alone, of the logical process as it is shown in its highest forms, in mathematical reasoning.

We shall choose, with this in view, four phases or moments only from among those which are most characteristic of the evolution of mathematical reasoning. We can call these four, respectively, direct symbolism, indirect symbolism, symbolic condensation and symbolic inversion. This will allow us also to seek for the explanation of the special difficulties which the study of mathematics offers to the majority, and to show at the same time the value and psychological importance of the symbolism therein employed, and thus to make plain the difference between the value and importance of symbolism in mathematics strictly so called, and its value and importance in what is called mathematical logic.

MATHEMATICAL REASONING : PART I 143

Mathematical reasoning in its phase of direct symbolism

It is only little by little that man has passed from pure manipulation to pure reasoning, by means of mixed series, made up of actually performed experiments alternating with others which are merely imagined. And, in the sciences, geometry and arithmetical calculation were the first to take on this mixed character, thus preparing the ground for the unfolding and expansion of pure reasoning.

Geometrical demonstrations, in fact, as we have seen already in our preceding chapters, are real experimental demonstrations, real chains of experiments, in which, if most of the experiments are made merely in thought, others are none the less actually performed. "It is in this simple, fertile and easily accessible field of geometry," writes Mach, "that the method of mental experiment began to be developed."[1]

But the importance of geometry has not lain only in preparing the way from pure manipulation to pure reasoning, but quite as much in training and predisposing the mind towards abstract reasoning. What, in fact, characterises Greek geometry in relation to Babylonian or Egyptian geometry, is just the generalisation of the demonstration, the fact of seeing in the drawn triangle—upon which, in part actually, in part merely mentally, certain given geometrical manipulations, leading to the ocular or imaginary recognition of the given results, have been performed—not one particular triangle but the "schema" which stands for all triangles ; the fact, that is, of recognising the equivalence of all triangles in relation to the results of the demonstration itself, and thus of giving rise to the formation of geometrical concepts, the first concepts, with those of arithmetic, to be developed in the history of science.[2]

If geometrical manipulations in this way did not assume a general and abstract character until a late date, until the Greeks, on the other hand the proportion of merely imagined manipulations to those actually

---

[1] E. Mach, *op. cit., Erkenntnis und Irrtum*, p. 198.
[2] Cf. G. Milhaud, *Les origines des sciences mathématiques dans les civilisations orientales et égyptiennes : L'apport de l'Orient dans la science grecque ;* in : *Nouvelles études sur l'histoire de la pensée mathématique*, Alcan, Paris, 1911, pp. 123-124.

144 THE PSYCHOLOGY OF REASONING

performed thenceforward increased rapidly, but without ever extending to the complete exclusion of actual manipulations (*e.g.* the drawing of auxiliary lines, and the ocular recognition of certain of the results so obtained).

The manipulations of calculation, on the contrary, took on an abstract character at a very much earlier date—as manipulations performed upon the schematised object "unity"—but on the other hand they remained much longer in the stage of being almost all actually performed. It was not until later that they too became mixed series of manipulations partly actual and partly merely imagined ; they then soon passed into the stage of being *all merely imagined manipulations*, a stage which has never been reached by geometry.

Arithmetical calculation indeed began, as is well known, by a series of "countings", each "counting" in turn being nothing but *the material operation of arranging the objects to be counted in correspondence with an already arranged series of other objects;* this latter series (fingers alone, fingers and toes, and other such series) remaining the same for all the "countings."

Countings of a number of objects greater than the number of the objects making up the series used for comparison encountered for this reason very great difficulties in being performed, so long as no recourse was had to the system of first materially sub-dividing the objects to be counted into so many groups, each group containing precisely the greatest number of objects capable of being simply "counted", and then of "counting" these groups themselves. This method of division into so many groups, extended from the objects to the first groups of these objects and then to groups of groups, still forms as we know the basis of decimal numeration.

Additions and subtractions of groups of objects already "counted" had of necessity to be frequently materially performed and the new groups so obtained when subjected to new "countings" allowed the results of these material additions and subtractions to be *ocularly* realised.

To facilitate these manipulations, objects more easily carried and handled can be made to correspond one by one to the objects which have to be dealt with. In this

MATHEMATICAL REASONING: PART I 145

way were produced "calculating tables" or "abaci" (ἄβαξ), from the very earliest in ancient China and Peru to the more improved decimal tables of Egyptians, Greeks and Romans, for whom the rows of pebbles (calculi) represented, according to their order and to the number of pebbles displaced in each row, the number of groups and groups of groups into which the objects to be counted were sub-divided. With these abaci the operations of addition and subtraction, and of renewed consecutive counting, being made more handy, continued to be in part actually performed; but, to an ever greater extent, they could be performed in imagination alone thanks to the already known results which these very operations when actually performed had given in the past; finally, to increase still further the advantage so obtained, previously compiled tables, such as the ancient small table of addition, which went as far as 9+9 and was very extensively known, began to be learned by heart.

Two very remarkable inventions in symbolic representation, both due it seems to the Indians, greatly assisted the transition to the execution in thought alone of the operations of addition and subtraction, which had been hitherto actually performed with the pebbles of the abacus; in the first place, the invention of graphic symbols to denote each the different numbers of pebbles which could be displaced on each row; secondly, the invention of zero which allowed these graphic symbols to be arranged side by side in the order of the different rows of the abacus, even when no displacement of pebbles had taken place in some one of these rows, so allowing any number made up of several figures to represent exactly — without the need for any special indication alongside of each figure—the corresponding state of distribution of the pebbles in the abacus itself.

Even for those particular kinds of additions and subtractions which consist in the addition or subtraction repeated a certain number of times of the same number of objects (multiplication and division), their results also came to be recorded in memory, though much later and with much greater difficulty, and it was thus possible to sum them up in further special tables, of which Pythagoras' table is the classic example. From multiplication and division, when made in this fashion

146 THE PSYCHOLOGY OF REASONING

sufficiently familiar, it was then possible—at first by means of "radical" fractions, those, that is, having unity for the numerator, which, as for instance with the Egyptians, occurred *materially* in the mensuration of the successive "remainders" of lengths not exact multiples of the unit of measurement, by the double or triple folding and so on of the cord, which was used as their unit of measurement—it was then possible, I say, to pass, very slowly however, from the calculus of whole numbers to that of fractional numbers, which correspond, they too, not less than whole numbers, to the physically real divisions of which many natural objects are capable.

Thus arithmetical calculation is henceforth composed solely of a series of operations, all of which have been materially performed in the past, but now on the contrary *all performed in thought alone.* The long and very slow evolution of this transition, the difficulties met with by primitive peoples in reaching the stage of "counting" a number of objects greater than the number of fingers of one hand or two hands, or of fingers and toes together, the slow evolution of the abacus and its persistence even into relatively recent times, the late and for so long excessively imperfect compilation of mnemonic "tables" of addition and later of multiplication, the very slow evolution of the calculus of fractions, all this shows how very great were the difficulties which man had to overcome in empirically discovering, one by one, the different results of certain operations of calculation, before he was able to reach the stage of performing these operations in thought alone.[1]

At the same time all this shows that the "properties of numbers are dependent upon experience in the same precise sense as the geometrical properties of space ".[2]

For our purpose it is important to notice that the objects of the ordered series into correspondence with which the concrete objects to be counted were materially arranged, by the very fact that they were always the same whatever the objects to be counted might be, must

---

[1] Cf., e.g. H.-G. Zeuthen, *Die Mathematik im Altertum und im Mittelalter.*—" Die Kultur der Gegenwart," Part III, Section I, Leipzig, 1912, pp. 6-14.
[2] W. Wundt, *Logik*, 3rd Ed., Vol. I, Stuttgart, 1906, pp. 488-489.

MATHEMATICAL REASONING : PART I 147

have facilitated the realisation that the results of the calculation were the same in all cases, independently of the nature of these objects ; that is to say, in relation to the results of the calculation, any kind of concrete object was *equivalent* to any other. This realisation led very early to the concept of *unity* (and thence to the derivative concept of abstract number), that is, to the schematised object (fingers, pebbles, etc.) indifferently representing these or those other concrete objects (heads of cattle, warriors of the tribe, etc.) : " The extreme term of numerical abstraction is the notion of unity. Each unity is taken as identical with another unity ; the mind, that is, no longer regards any specific determination, any intrinsic character of the thing, it no longer knows anything of the object, except the fact that it is an object ". [1]

But this extreme term of numerical abstraction, *unity*, does not cease for this reason to be an object. It is very general and as schematised as we please, but it is none the less always *materially tangible*, just as were the fingers or the pebbles of the abacus. The operations of arithmetical calculation were thus, throughout a long epoch, *both abstract operations and at the same time materially performed.*

But, as we have seen, the calculating operations which were all originally performed on matter, became subsequently, step by step, mixed series of operations, performed partly upon things, partly in thought alone, finally coming to be, as we find them to-day, series of operations all of which are performed in thought only, without any change having occurred, throughout this transition, in the character which, in spite of their abstractness, they possessed from the beginning, of being all capable of being materially performed. [2]

Let us now consider the transition from arithmetic to the first phase of algebra—the phase, that is, which precedes the introduction of positive and negative numbers. As is well known this occurs through a further process of abstraction, strictly similar to that just considered, which constitutes the transition from

---

[1] L. Brunschvicg, *Les étapes de la philosophie mathématique*, Paris, 1912, p. 479.
[2] Cf. J. S. Mill, *op. cit., A System of Logic*, Vol. I, p. 284.

148 THE PSYCHOLOGY OF REASONING

concrete to abstract numbers. As an example let us take the number 8 and the fraction $\frac{1}{8}$; let us add 1 to each of these; the greater of the two sums thus obtained $(8 + 1 = 9)$ contains the less $(\frac{1}{8} + 1 = \frac{9}{8})$ exactly 8 times. Now this property is possessed by every number, not only by the number 8. If then we let a stand for any number whatever we have in all cases $\dfrac{a + 1}{\dfrac{1}{a} + 1} = a.$[1]

In relation to the result expressed by this formula, as in relation to other similar results in algebra, all the abstract numbers of arithmetic are *equivalent* one to another; and "algebraic number" is the term used to express indifferently any one of them.

Thus the difference between algebraic and arithmetical calculation—before the introduction, we repeat, of positive and negative numbers—consists in the following. While arithmetical calculation is composed of *concrete operations performed upon abstract objects* (such as, for instance, the pebbles of the abacus which represent the schematised unity), in algebraic calculation on the other hand *the operations themselves are abstract*, each, that is, represents, not one single determinate operation, but *an infinite number of operations which are equivalent* in relation to a given result.

The psychological difficulty experienced in rising to this further abstractness is thus of the same kind as that met with in geometry, when we have to see in a given operation performed, say, upon a given triangle, not only this single operation, but all the infinite similar operations to be performed upon an equally infinite number of triangles, which are equivalent one to another in relation to the result obtained by the demonstration performed upon the particular triangle drawn upon the paper.[2]

In this very respect, algebra possesses a great advantage over geometry. *This consists in the fact that, thanks to the use of letters as symbols, algebra succeeds in bringing well into prominence the general properties of the objects operated upon and in eliminating their particular*

---

[1] Cf. P. E. B. Jourdain, *The Nature of Mathematics*, London, 1910, pp. 30, 32-33.

[2] Cf. E. Goblot, "La démonstration mathématique", *Année psychologique*, Paris, 1908, 272, 275-276.

MATHEMATICAL REASONING : PART I 149

properties. The geometer, in fact, in extending the results of a demonstration performed upon a given particular triangle to all triangles in general has to watch at every step of the demonstration to see that they are attained without making use, either of the particular magnitudes of the angles, or the absolute or relative lengths of the sides, or any other such feature. He cannot, to bring this into prominence, have recourse to a *symbol of a triangle*, or of any other geometrical figure, which would of its own accord set aside the particular elements out of which the actual figure may from case to case be formed. The algebraist, on the contrary, thanks to his representation of the numbers through alphabetical symbols, brings into prominence from the beginning that a given result of a given demonstration is independent of the particular values of the numbers operated upon.

We must be careful to notice at this point that each of the infinite particular operations represented by a given algebraic operation, remains in all cases none the less a strictly arithmetical operation. It is, that is to say, an operation which is capable of being materially performed but which is mentally performed instead. Thus algebraic calculation is itself built exclusively of operations of this kind. For this reason algebraic calculation—before the introduction of positive and negative numbers, we repeat again—is nothing but the symbolisation, through convenient formulas, of a long series of these quantitative operations or experiments, actually performable as they are though in fact only mentally performed, linked in chains one to another.

This character which algebraic expressions possess of representing not one single operation expressing the establishment of one quantitative relation only, but an infinite number of such operations which are equivalent in relation to a given result, is exactly why algebra lends itself so marvellously well to the expression of those " natural laws " which regulate quantitative relations between phenomena, and also to the deduction of the most remote consequences which derive from these laws. In fact, just because they are " laws " which regulate quantitative relations between phenomena, they serve, not only for this or that particular value of these

150 THE PSYCHOLOGY OF REASONING

very phenomena, but for a whole infinite series of such particular values.[1]

Every algebraic formula, and every equality between formulas comes to constitute then, as Mach justly observes, a kind of rule of compilation (*eine Herstellungsregel*) for an immense table which records the progress of a given phenomenon in all its particular manifestations ; a rule of compilation which thus furnishes, ready made, with a great saving of time and labour, the particular results of an infinity of physical operations or experiments which can in time be performed by us mentally.[2]

Thus, the algebraic formula, for instance, which expresses Newton's law of attraction, is the translation of the general fact of gravitation into a language, which expresses also all its particular cases.[3]

To this same character of algebraic expressions of representing, not one single operation of arithmetical calculation, but an infinity of operations which are equivalent in relation to a given result, is due the fact that, when the equality of a given complicated expression with another more simple expression is arrived at— —as, for instance, the equation $\dfrac{a^2 - b^2}{a+b} = a - b$—this constitutes, as Mach points out, a great "economy in counting" (Oekonomie des Zählens), in so far as it allows us to avoid all the particular series of arithmetical calculations, each of which would lead us, on its own account, to the verification of the equation for the corresponding particular case.[4]

Finally the fact that algebra, happier in this than geometry, has succeeded through its use of letters as symbols, in bringing into prominence the general and eliminating the particular properties of the objects operated upon, this fact has allowed and encouraged the "mechanisation" of algebraic calculation itself.

By this we do not so much wish to allude to the assistance and "repose" which algebra, as in general any other method of symbolic notation, gives to the

---

[1] Cf. P. E. B. Jourdain, *op. cit., The Nature of Mathematics*, pp. 47-48.

[2] E. Mach, *op. cit., Die Mechanik, etc.*, pp. 137-138, 461.

[3] G. Milhaud, "Descartes et Newton", in *op. cit., Nouv. études sur l'hist. de la pensée scient.*, p. 222.

[4] E. Mach, *op. cit., Die Mechanik, etc.*, p. 462 ; *Erkenntnis u. Irrtum*, p. 328.

MATHEMATICAL REASONING : PART I 151

reasoner, by allowing him to follow the whole history of mentally performed operations which make up any given reasoning. It is well known, in fact, that the use of appropriate symbols, in relation to the different operations and the different results, relieves the mind of the reasoner from the necessity and the effort of continually holding clearly before him the results already attained which will be of service later on, when the "thread of the reasoning" leads him to perform in imagination further operations or experiments linked on to these results. Such a symbolism prevents the otherwise inevitable overlooking of results already obtained, as well as the inevitable *illogical conclusions* due to this forgetfulness.

We allude rather to the fact that, thanks to the very generality of algebraic symbols and of the corresponding operations they represent, recurring as they do in the same way on a very great number of occasions, and so allowing and facilitating the discovery of rules for the *practical manipulation* of these symbols, it is henceforth sufficient simply to follow these rules in order to be certain of arriving at the correct conclusion, without in any way thinking of the significance of the symbols themselves. As a consequence there results a very important economy both of time and of mental fatigue.[1]

"It has often been pointed out", writes Pierre Boutroux, "that mathematics, a work of the active intelligence, tends to make intelligence unnecessary by reducing reasoning to a set of rules which let themselves be passively applied ".[2]

"This manipulation of algebraic symbols which can be called, in the widest sense of the word, *calculation*, presupposes "—as Duhem in his turn writes—"in the inventor and the user, not so much a power of abstraction or skill in conducting ordered trains of thought, as ability in representing to oneself the different complicated combinations which can be made out of certain visible and writable signs, so as to see at a glance

---

[1] Cf. J. S. Mill, *op. cit.*, *A System of Logic*, vol. II, p. 260 ; E. Mach, *op. cit.*, *Erk. u. Irrtum*, p. 182 ; P. E. B. Jourdain, *op. cit.*, *The Nature of Math.*, pp. 20, 53.
[2] P. Boutroux, " L'évolution des mathématiques pures ", *Scientia*, 1909, XI, 3, p. 3-5.

152 THE PSYCHOLOGY OF REASONING

those transformations which allow us to pass from one combination to another ".[1]

To the merely imagined experiments, *represented by the algebraic transformations*, there must thus be added actually performed experiments, *consisting in the algebraic transformations themselves*. This makes possible the ocular recognition or empirical discovery of continually new results of these manipulations of formulas; and these algebraic results resolve themselves, in their turn, into as many new results of the reasoning represented by the algebraic calculation: "In mathematics, the experiment often takes a special sense, as where it is reduced to a matter of recognising the form of an algebraic expression ".[2]

From this derives the great value even in mathematics of that "sense of position" characteristic of chess players, which leads in algebra to the discovery of fundamental analogies between given algebraic expressions, however complicated and diverse they may be in their details.[3]

In this way even very complex algebraic situations become capable of being considered *as wholes* apart from their constitutive elements and of being represented by new special symbols. The rules of analytical transformation of these symbols of higher degree, discovered and fixed by means of the operations of calculation which we already know how to perform upon symbols of lower degree, allow the mathematician to proceed thenceforth to operations upon these symbols of higher degree without further concerning himself with the signification which they would have had if they had been "translated" into the equivalent much longer and more complicated operations, expressed by the symbols of lower degree.

To those who do not succeed in "seeing" the whole group of lower symbols behind the higher symbol, and behind the lower symbols the whole group of actual generalised operations which they represent, mathematics can indeed seem to be altogether emancipated

---

[1] P. Duhem, *La Théorie physique, son objet, et sa structure*, Paris, 1906, pp. 98, 99.

[2] G. Milhaud, " La pensée mathématique, son rôle dans l'histoire des idées "; in *op. cit.*, *Nouvelles études sur l'hist. de la pensée scient.*, p. 24.

[3] A. A. Cleveland, *art. cit.*, " The Psychology of Chess and of Learning to play it ", p. 299.

MATHEMATICAL REASONING: PART I 153

from those ancient operations of material calculation, at first actually performed, and later merely imagined, from which mathematics have taken their bold flight. None the less, it is clear, as is demonstrated even by the short account of the origin and development of algebraic calculation which we have just given, that these ancient experiments or operations actually performed upon matter still continue to be the one and only substratum of all calculation.

But, if this is the state of affairs, then every transition and every intermediate result of algebraic transformation, of whatever nature it be, cannot help having, in a more or less direct or indirect way, a real significance; one, that is to say, which is empirically tangible and empirically precise, as representing the result of this or that step in the series of imagined operations or experiments upon matter making up the mathematical reasoning in question. On the other hand, as is well known, certain intermediate results of algebraic calculation occurring at first as expressions devoid of all "real significance", have seemed in past centuries not to have this character and thus to transgress the fundamental rule of all reasoning whatever.

A study of these expressions, or "imaginary" quantities, and a sketch of the difficulties they have encountered before gaining full and unchallenged rights of citizenship cannot fail to have an interest *from the purely psychological point of view which we take up in this study of reasoning,* and will not be without assistance in our aim of carrying still deeper our analysis of the psychological nature of mathematical reasoning in general.

But in order to proceed to the examination of these "imaginary" quantities we ought properly to say first a few words upon positive and negative numbers, and upon the *indirect symbolism* which they have come to build up.

Mathematical reasoning in its phase of indirect symbolism

We know that a considerable number of quantities, if not all, are capable of occurring under a double aspect that mathematicians have, in fact, called "positive" and "negative." An army of 100,000 men cannot lose 120,000 men in a battle but a possessor of 100,000 francs

154 THE PSYCHOLOGY OF REASONING

can very well lose 120,000 at play. We cannot draw 12 litres of wine from a barrel which only contains 10 litres, yet we can very well lower its initial temperature by 12 degrees, even though this was of no more than 10 degrees. The 20,000 francs lost at play beyond those which the loser could pay and the 2 degrees of temperature lost beyond the 10 at first possessed, represent quantities of the same kind as these, only "with an opposite sense."

For such physical quantities, capable in this fashion of a relation of opposition, arithmetical symbols are clearly no longer adequate, neither are the corresponding algebraic symbols, so far as these confine themselves also to representing merely the number of units of measure which are contained in these quantities. In order to furnish a symbolic representation of such physical facts, capable at once of "quantity" and of "opposition", recourse must be had to a *geometrical symbolism*, by means of segments taken in one and the same straight line, whose lengths provide the symbolic representation of the magnitudes of the physical fact concerned and whose directions do the same for the two mutually opposed senses which the physical fact itself is capable of taking.

Once this symbolic representation *of a geometrical kind* has been established for such physical quantities then all the events concerning them in which they did not substantially alter—events, that is, consisting only in changes either of their absolute magnitude or of their 'sense'—all these events could be represented by means of suitable directions, in one or other of the two opposed senses, given to different segments, and by means of relative *slidings* performed along the straight line containing them. Properties empirically verified as being inherent in these changes of physical quantities thenceforth will determine and fix given rules of sliding, adequate to represent these changes themselves symbolically.

For example, in order to represent symbolically the fact that a moving body now leaving zero with the uniform velocity v along a straight line, will be found, after a time t, at the same point on the straight line occupied t seconds ago by another moving body which, moving with the same velocity but in the opposed

MATHEMATICAL REASONING: PART I 155

sense, is now found at the point zero, it is necessary to represent the movement of the first body by carrying, from zero, the segment representing in quantity and in direction the velocity v, as many times *forward*, that is in the segment's own direction, as there are units of *future* time expressed by the number t; and it is necessary to represent the movement of the other body on the contrary, by shifting, always from zero, the same segment, representing the same quantity of velocity whose direction is now opposed to that in the former case, as many times *backwards*, that is in the direction opposite to the segment's actual direction, as there are units of *past* time expressed by the same number t.

When this and similar rules become in this way established for such slidings of segments, all to be performed upon one and the same axis, so as to constitute a symbolic representation of those physical magnitudes which are capable of "opposition" and of events in which they are concerned, the question arises of whether it is possible to *represent in their turn symbolically these slidings of segments on an axis, by means of suitable algebraic signs*. This has been done, as we know, by indicating the absolute lengths of segments by ordinary letters of the alphabet, and allocating the signs $+$ and $-$ to these letters, according as the directions of the respective segments are turned to the right or to the left. In a parallel fashion by the same signs $+$ and $-$ are also indicated the geometrico-kinematic operations of sliding, according to whether they are operations of *advance* or *retrogression*, that is, according to whether they are to be made in the same sense as the direction of the segment to be moved, or in the contrary sense.

In this fashion the double sliding just mentioned, which serves to represent geometrically the double physical fact of the movements of the two bodies and the final result, becomes capable, in its turn, of the well known algebraic symbolisation : $(-t)(-v) = vt$, which gives rise to the general rule of signs that the product of two negative numbers is a positive number.

This "rule of signs," as well as the others which have to be observed in the manipulation of algebraic figures, is what it is only in order to make these manipulations capable of symbolically representing those slidings of segments which have been verified in their

156 THE PSYCHOLOGY OF REASONING

turn as capable of representing physical experiments. It follows that while the retrogressions and advancements of segments, all sliding upon one and the same axis, constitute the *direct* or *first order* symbolic representation of physical experiments, either actually performed or to be mentally performed upon the quantities represented by these segments, the algebraic operations on the other hand, to be performed in conformity with the established rules of signs upon letters representing these segments, are clearly in their turn direct or first order symbolic representations of these operations of shifting the segments, but for this very reason only indirect or second order symbolic representations of the physical experiments themselves.

In other words, the admission granted by mathematics to physical quantities capable of opposition has made it necessary to have recourse to *an intermediate geometrical symbolism*, thanks to which algebra is in fact transformed into a symbolic representation which is merely an indirect or second order representation of the physical fact.

In virtue of the subsequent realisation that the ordinary arithmetical numbers, or letters capable of representing them, although they do not themselves, as direct symbols adequate for all quantities not capable of opposition, need this intermediary geometrical symbolism, yet could none the less be replaced by such a symbolism composed of segments all turned to the right, mathematicians were led to the adoption of this intermediary geometrical symbolism for them also and so to the second order algebraic symbolism which is the consequence. It thus came about that the rules of algebraic calculation, discovered for quantities capable of opposition, became valid even for quantities not capable of opposition, or arithmetical quantities properly so called, provided these latter—which so far as purely arithmetical are neither positive nor negative—were considered as positive. By this means, all quantities, those capable as much as those not capable of opposition, came to be equivalent from the point of view of the respective formal operations of calculation for which the same laws or rules were applicable. And it is in this equivalence, verified in this fashion, that the new enlarged concept of "number" consists after the tran-

MATHEMATICAL REASONING : PART I 157

sition from the purely arithmetical to the algebraic concept.

It is important at this point to bring into prominence that all the difficulties in being understood which were encountered by positive and negative numbers at their birth, in particular the difficulties relative to the rules of signs to be observed in their manipulation, have depended upon the fact that their true nature as merely indirect symbolic representations was not seen from the beginning : "The negative numbers have always given rise to preoccupations". "In particular the rule that the product of two negative numbers is a positive number has always met with difficulties, which could very well be hidden, but not overcome. People came even to think, as for instance the Jesuit Clavius (1612), of all these rules as correct in reality, but at the same time as absolutely incomprehensible".[1]

This difficulty of comprehension, and the resultant hostility, sometimes very lively hostility indeed, which these new numbers encountered in early days, is explainable if we notice that mathematical symbolism in becoming in these cases indirect, that is a symbolism of a symbolism, has made the relation uniting the symbolism to the physical fact a mediate and more complicated relation, so that it is more difficult to "see" this physical fact behind the transformations of the symbolism itself.

At the same time, this hostility shows how the mind instinctively revolts against any symbolic manipulation, even though it should be governed by precise rules which show themselves to be able to lead to results verified in due course by experience as correct, if behind the manipulation and for each of its phases there cannot be seen the actual, that is the empirically tangible and empirically exact, operation or experiment which the symbolic manipulation itself represents.

This, however, will appear in a still more evident manner if we pass now, even though in an equally summary fashion, to the consideration of the so called "imaginary" numbers.

We have seen how, in virtue of the very rules established to govern the geometrically symbolic repre-

---

[1] A. Voss, *Ueber das Wesen der Mathematik*, 2nd Edition, Leipzig, 1913, pp. 36-37.

158 THE PSYCHOLOGY OF REASONING

sentation of physical quantities which are capable of opposition and of events in which these are concerned, and in virtue of the fixed correspondence between this geometric, first order representation and the algebraic, second order representation by means of positive and negative numbers, it follows that the product of two negative numbers is always a positive number. This plainly excludes the possibility that algebraic calculation, while it remains an indirect symbolic representation of real physical facts, should ever lead to expressions built up of square roots of negative numbers.

And yet these expressions did not fail to appear. Moreover, it is well known that, in early days, algebraists instead of halting continued to make use of them, subjecting them to certain given axiomatic rules of manipulation, which were made such as never to lead to any contradiction and to guarantee the permanence of the formal laws of algebraic calculations.

At the same time, as a guide to light up the path to be followed in these "meaningless" algebraic manipulations—without which they would have inevitably degenerated into a childish game of combining graphic signs—there remained the end which every algebraist throughout implicitly sets himself, namely the attainment in one way or another of the elimination of these "meaningless" expressions in order to arrive anew at real expressions alone.[1]

This autonomy of which the mathematical algorithm has been capable in relation to the reality which it should represent, this introduction and application of given modes of symbolic procedure before their meaning had yet been understood, this fact which appears so paradoxical from the psychological point of view, is explained by the process discussed above of the mechanisation of algebraic calculation. The familiarity, in fact, with the handling of a highly developed symbolism removes in the long run the necessity of keeping the attention fixed upon the reality which the symbolism represents ; and this makes possible, because they pass almost unnoticed, the introduction and manipulation even of "meaningless" symbols.

---

[1] Cf., e.g., D. Gigli, " Dei numeri complessi a due e a più unità ", in : *Questioni riguardanti le matematiche elementari*, collected and arranged by F. Enriques, Vol. I, Bologna, 1912, pp. 515-516.

MATHEMATICAL REASONING : PART I 159

We can even say that thanks to this mechanisation of calculation, the symbol, which, as we have seen in the preceding chapters, usually has a merely passive function of "registering" concepts independently discovered, has had here an active function also in so far as new concepts, capable of giving a meaning to algorithmic terms obtained we might say almost accidentally through a mere mechanical prolongation of calculation (the square roots, for example, of expressions which are *eventually* negative), did not begin to be formed or to be elucidated until after the development of a large part of the consequences due to the introduction of the new algorithmic term while still deprived of significance.

But this does not in any way imply that we can in the final analysis do without a real significance for such symbols, or that it is sufficient to fix for them certain axiomatic rules of union and manipulation in order to be able, thanks to these "implicit definitions" of the symbols themselves, to construct the whole of mathematics upon them. That this opinion, which is shared by a very great number of mathematicians, is psychologically altogether erroneous is precisely what these "meaningless" algorithmic terms show.

In the first theories concerning these terms, in fact, the conditions for the implicit definition of symbols by means of given rules of calculations are completely satisfied. But the welcome which these "entia rationis" received so long as they remained at this stage of purely formal definition is well known.

The endless conflicts and discussions which they have provoked, their rejection by the greatest mathematicians of the time, the almost, we might say, injurious epithets which have been addressed to them ("imaginary" numbers, "false" solutions, "impossible" quantities, "amphibious" or "monstrous" entities, and so on) indicate the energetic refusal of sound common sense to deal with relations between graphic signs governed by conventionally fixed rules, if their significance be not first apprehended. In other words, these epithets indicate the pressing need of the human mind, due directly to the fundamental nature of all reasoning whatsoever, of considering a symbol as such, that is, as representing always some physical reality, and thus

160 THE PSYCHOLOGY OF REASONING

of considering further every operation made upon the symbol as likewise representing symbolically some real physical operation.

For these reasons imaginary numbers did not gain their full rights of citizenship until mathematicians were successful in giving them a *real* significance, namely, as is well known that of the *analytic representation of direction*.[1]

Thanks to Argand's conception—Hoüel writes in his preface to Argand's "Essay"—"symbols of the form $a+b\sqrt{-1}$, to which mathematicians had succeeded in reducing the results of all analytic operations, no longer show any impossibility or incomprehensibility"; they can "be translated *by geometrical constructions which address themselves to the eye.*"[2]

In Argand's Essay the symbol $i=\sqrt{-1}$, expresses *the relation of perpendicularity*, that is to say, a and ia are merely symbols of vectors perpendicular to one another. To multiply a vector by i means then merely to turn it through a right angle about its origin. Every complex algebraic expression, every expression, that is, composed of real numbers and of imaginary numbers, comes in this way to represent determinate geometrical relations between segments situated in a plane, and every operation between complex numbers acquires the significance of *a geometrical construction*, by which in a plane we obtain from certain given vectors other vectors. Algebra thus becomes an immense system of *translation* which allows the most varied geometrical operations of slidings and turnings of segments in a plane to be expressed by means of corresponding algorithmic manipulations.

As examples let us take two expressions, the first real and the second 'imaginary': $a^2-b^2=(a+b)(a-b)$; $a^2+b^2=(a+ib)(a-ib)$. Like any other mathematical equations or equalities, these only express the fact that a given number which has been reached in a certain way is equal to another number reached by a different way. But here the first tells us that the point at which we arrive in the axis of the segments a and b, by means

---

[1] Cf. A. Voss, *op. cit.*, *Ueber das Wesen der Math.*, pp. 38-41.
[2] J. Hoüel, preface to the second edition of R. Argand, *Essai sur une manière de représenter les quantités imaginaires dans les constructions géométriques* (1806), Paris, 1874, p. XIII.

MATHEMATICAL REASONING: PART I 161

of the three slidings represented respectively by $a \times a$, $b \times b$, and $a^2 - b^2$, can be reached equally by means of three other slidings, analogous to the former, represented respectively by $a+b$, $a-b$, and $(a+b)(a-b)$. The second expression on the other hand, tells us that for the point $a^2 + b^2$ there is no such second way of reaching it, *without leaving the axis on which the segments* a *and* b *are situated*, but that there is a corresponding way if we do leave this axis. Indeed with the significance of operations of sliding and rotating segments, which algebraic formula containing 'imaginary' expressions now come to have, the formula $(a+ib)(a-ib)$ comes to represent the construction of two perpendiculars such that the respective right-angled triangle has for hypotenuse the segment $a^2 + b^2$; so that with this construction we end by reaching the axis of the segments at the same extreme point of the segment $a^2 + b^2$.

The geometrico-kinematic operations represented by complex numbers, those, that is to say, constituted by real and imaginary numbers together, are, therefore, *infinitely more numerous and more varied* than those which are represented by "real" numbers only, in so far as these last, since they consist only in *slidings* of segments along an axis, do not allow of the axis being left, while the former, which add rotations to slidings, allow extension over the whole of a plane and thus make possible the discovery, even among the very segments of the axis from which the operations to be performed in the plane begin, of a great number of relations which it would not have been possible to discover if we were confined to slidings alone.[1]

The geometrico-kinematic operations represented by complex numbers are, further, *of a more general order*, in so far as they include, as a particular case, the operations of simple sliding of segments along one single axis. At the same time, the algebraic symbolism constituted by complex "numbers", and fitted to give an analytic representation of these geometrico-kinematic operations, completely satisfies the principle which has been already mentioned above, that of the *permanence* of formal laws, or of the *immutability of symbolic properties*; the principle, that is, that all the properties and rules which hold for the symbolism and the manipulations

[1] Cf. A. Voss, *op. cit.*, *Ueber das Wesen der Math.*, p. 58.

L

162　THE PSYCHOLOGY OF REASONING

which concern real numbers, continue to hold also for the symbolism and the manipulations which concern complex numbers, in spite of the changed and enlarged significance of these last. In this way, in relation to the formal result of any manipulation whatsoever of algebraic symbols—and algebra, as Goblot has well said, "has no other object than the *form* of algebraic expressions"—the "numbers" imaginary or complex are equivalent to real numbers. It is in this equivalence in relation to the formal results of calculation, and exclusively in this, that here too the corresponding enlargement of the concept "number" consists.[1]

This is so true that a further enlargement of the concept of number to new symbols, as analytic translations of analogous geometrico-kinematic vectorial operations extended to the whole of space, has not been found possible, precisely because these symbols being no longer able to satisfy completely the above mentioned principle of the permanence of formal laws, could not for that reason appear equivalent to real and complex numbers in respect of all the formal results of the respective operations of calculation.

Finally it is evident that the geometrico-kinematic operations of sliding and rotation, represented by the "imaginary" and complex numbers, are *not less empirically tangible* than those of simple sliding along one single axis, which are represented by the "real" numbers. There is however this difference : while these operations of sliding along one single axis, thanks to established conventions, form the symbolic representation of quantitative events or of changes of direction relative to physical quantities which are capable of opposition, those of sliding and rotation in a plane are not, on the contrary, capable of forming such a symbolic representation. But this is so solely because the very fact that a given system of geometrical symbolic representation has been fixed by convention implies the suppression of this representative property in any other system ; even though this other system should, by the use of different conventions, have been eventually capable, it too, of forming another mode of symbolic representation.

It follows that, while algebraic expressions, composed

[1] E. Goblot, *art. cit., La démonstr. math.*, pp. 275-276.

MATHEMATICAL REASONING: PART I 163

of "real" numbers, as being direct or first degree symbolic representations of slidings of segments along one unique axis, are thus also indirect or second degree symbolic representations of events involving physical quantities which are capable of opposition; on the contrary, algebraic expressions containing "imaginary" and complex numbers, although they have, as a direct symbolic representation of geometrico-kinematic operations of sliding and rotation of segments, a signification no less real than that of the former expressions, cannot be at the same time an indirect symbolic representation of events involving physical quantities. It is in this and this alone that what may be called their "imaginaryness" consists.

Nevertheless they can equally serve to discover new relations between these physical quantities. For as soon as these are represented by given segments of an axis, whatever may be the ways in which we later come to discover new relations between these segments, these relations thus discovered between the segments will represent as many corresponding relations between the physical quantities which were represented by these segments.

That there is, after all, the possibility of reaching these very relations, once they are discovered in this way, by means of symbolic operations which have, all of them, a physical significance, is shown by the possibility of conceiving complex numbers without having recourse to any geometrical representation on a plane, as simple combinations of real numbers.

This analytic theory of complex numbers is founded, as is well known, on the definition of a complex number as an ordered couple of real numbers, and thus all the operations of calculation which little by little are defined, —and whose rules agree with those which hold for complex numbers with a geometrico-kinematic significance—come to be each, in fact, constituted of several common algebraic operations made upon real numbers, *cumulatively represented in the symbol of this single operation between complex numbers.*[1]

---

[1] Cf., e.g., D. Gigli, *op. cit.*, *Dei numeri complessi a due e a più unità*, pp. 528 ff. 531 ff.; and Ch. Meray, *Leçons nouvelles sur l'analyse infinitésimale et ses applications géometriques*, 1st Part, " Principes généraux," Paris, 1894, chap. III, pp. 37-58.

164 THE PSYCHOLOGY OF REASONING

Thus every analytic transformation through complex numbers leading to the discovery of certain relations between the segments of the axis of real numbers, becomes, thanks to this, reducible to a series, it may be much longer and far more complicated, of algebraic operations performed exclusively on real numbers, which thus will as a whole come to represent exactly that method, so much desired by the physicist, of reaching, throughout by means of real significations, the very relations which have already been discovered by the shortest route.[1]

We believe that even this short account is sufficient to bring into evidence the special further difficulties which the symbolism of a symbolism, already introduced with positive and negative numbers, occasions when it is further complicated by the introduction of these so called imaginary numbers.

Indeed the difficulty of always keeping before the mind the distinction between the process of actual reasoning based upon imagined physical and tangible operations, and the process of its symbolisation, increases the more the relations which connect the first to the second become indirect and complicated. And, consequently, a great confusion of ideas arises when the second degree symbolic process, while remaining a first degree symbolic representation of another category of empirically tangible and empirically exact operations, ceases at the same time, in certain determinate moments of its development, any longer to constitute a second degree representation of that physical world, which symbolic operations, whether of the first or of the second degree, were intended to represent.

Further, certain generalisations or extensions of concepts which, precisely because they are generalisations, include the former concept as a particular case, modify the concept so much, that they end by representing, essentially, something quite different ; and if the symbol for the earlier concept to whose external form the concept itself has come to be indissolubly associated, is used without some modification of its external form to stand for the new concept also—as

---

[1] Cf. P. Duhem, *op. cit.*, *La Théorie Physique* etc., pp. 27 ff. ; and P. Boutroux, " La théorie physique " de M. Duhem et les mathématiques, *Rev. de Métaph. et de Morale*, May 1907, p. 364 ff.

MATHEMATICAL REASONING: PART I   165

has happened for instance with the symbol for the square root of negative quantities—it is difficult for this immutability of the symbol not to be for many a serious obstacle to the complete assimilation of the new concept.

Thirdly, imaginary numbers have been invented— and are also for the most part still introduced to-day in teaching—*after* encounter with the obstacle of expressions already implicitly denounced by previous teaching as void of meaning, and, we might say, as a *subterfuge* whose purpose is to avoid the obstacle itself. Hence the kind of sentiment of mistrust felt with regard to these imaginary numbers, which puts the mind in a state not favourable to their understanding or their clear and precise acceptance ; a sentiment of mistrust, which would not be felt if they had been invented, or at least if they were now introduced in teaching, *at the same time as positive and negative numbers*, starting from the beginning from the 'plane of numbers' in order at once to proceed to the analytic representation of all the operations of the sliding and rotation of segments which are capable of being performed respectively along given axes of the plane and upon the plane.

Finally, analytic geometry itself has on its side come to augment these psychological difficulties of clear understanding and hearty acceptance, encountered by imaginary numbers. In fact as a system of translation allowing questions of geometry to be reduced to the solving of algebraic equations, and thus as a system of "parallelism" or continual correspondence between algebraic expressions and geometrical figures, it has led to geometrical figures being looked for to correspond even to imaginary algebraic expressions. Hence certain paradoxical metaphorical expressions, that, for instance, of the "imaginary points" of intersection of two circles in a plane, which do not meet, and others, which, through the mental habit of forming blind associations between phonetic symbol and corresponding object, have led many to fall into nothing less than a state of "mysticism", that is a state of belief in the existence of something, we do not know what, which appears to us to be wrapped in mystery, because not capable of being known through any of our senses nor of being imagined

166 THE PSYCHOLOGY OF REASONING

through any combination whatever of sensible elements.[1]

In analytic geometry, the physical quantities capable of opposition for whose representation it is agreed to adopt segments taken on one single and unique axis, are, in fact, the co-ordinates; consequently, to "imaginary" algebraic expressions there correspond no actual co-ordinates, and no point which these expressions could determine. This is why the use of such metaphysical expressions, fitted as they are to excite the opposed belief, would be in this connection simply to be condemned.

But the usefulness of such expressions which has led mathematicians to introduce them and to retain them, consists, as is well known, in the analogy with certain geometrical constructions which they bring out, and in other advantages which they secure in mental economy and in the fixing of wider concepts, whose importance certainly cannot be sufficiently estimated.

Thus, for example, if we are given any two circular arcs which do not meet one another, belonging to two circles in a plane, a certain construction leads us to find a certain straight line. If completing the two arcs, the two circles which result intersect, it is found that the straight line in question passes through their two points of intersection; if on the other hand the circles do not meet, the straight line does not meet either of them; but since the construction is the same, in order to bring into relief this analogy of construction, we continue to say that the straight line passes through the two points of intersection of the two circles, adding only that these points of intersection are now imaginary.[2]

The property of this straight line, or 'radical axis', of being the common chord to the two circles is thus, to borrow the words of Chasles, one of its *contingent* or *accidental* properties, while other properties of this radical axis—for example, that which consists in the fact that the tangents to the two circles drawn from any one of its points are equal to one another, so that every point on the axis is the centre of a circle which cuts the two given circles orthogonally—are *permanent*,

---

[1] Cf. Hastings Berkeley, *op. cit., Mysticism in Modern Mathematics,* pp. 70-72, 131, etc.

[2] A. Cayley, " Presidential Address to the British Association in Sept. 1883 ", in *Collected Mathematical Papers,* Cambridge, 1896, vol. XI, n. 784, p. 438.

MATHEMATICAL REASONING : PART I   167

that is they hold whether the two circles intersect or whether they do not.[1]

Thus the imaginary solutions of equations which supply us with the co-ordinates of the two eventual points of intersection of the two circles are there to indicate that actually these circles do not meet and that, in consequence, the *contingent* property of the radical axis, which consists in being their common chord, is not verified. None the less these imaginary solutions represent *permanent* properties no less than the real solutions, although in an indirect way. Indeed if, by the same system by which we construct the algebraic equation of a straight line passing through two real points whose co-ordinates are known to us, we now construct the analogous algebraic equation, using instead these imaginary expressions, and if through suitable transformations, we then eliminate the imaginary quantities from the equation—which in this case is in fact always possible — the real equation so obtained gives us at once the equation of the radical axis. On the other hand, the establishment of this equation would be much longer and much more difficult, if we had to deduce it by analytically translating the permanent properties of the radical axis itself.

Further, not only were the contingent properties in fact discovered *before* the permanent, thus becoming more familiar to us, but these permanent properties in their turn were discovered *at first only in the figures which showed also the contingent properties*. The discovery of these permanent properties, *even* in other figures which no longer showed the contingent properties, took place only *posteriorly*. Thus a widening of the concept was produced, in so far as in relation to these permanent properties, the equivalence has been verified of diverse figures, which had not appeared equivalent in relation to contingent properties. And the " imaginary points ", the algebraic expressions of which represent these permanent properties, as we have just seen, in an indirect way, and which appear to us as an extension of the concept of point, thus serve very well to fix this

---

[1] M. Chasles, *Aperçu historique sur l'origine et le développement des méthodes en géométrie*, Paris, 1889, pp. 205-206, and his Note XXVI : " Sur les imaginaires en géométrie ", *ibid*, pp. 368-370.

168 THE PSYCHOLOGY OF REASONING

new wider concept of figures equivalent in respect of their permanent properties.

To sum up :—the bringing out of certain analogies between geometrical constructions, greater facility in the analytic transcription of certain figures, the fixing of new widened concepts, these are the advantages which militate in favour of these paradoxical metaphorical modes of expression. In face of these advantages is always to be found, however, the serious drawback mentioned above, the danger of the human mind not being able to support the tension necessary for grasping the indirect and complicated reality which is hidden behind each of these expressions and of its yielding instead to its natural inclination towards simplicity, by attributing to such expressions the immediate significance of representing directly some real object, falling in this way into a most fantastic and cloudy mysticism.

In all that we have just said we believe that there can be seen clearly appearing the psychological causes through which mathematical reasoning, while remaining even in its phase of indirect symbolism, actually unchanged in its fundamental nature, has inevitably given rise, in comparison with its earlier phase of direct symbolism, to special difficulties, through its having recourse to a symbolism of a symbolism. These difficulties have enabled us, however, to penetrate still more deeply into the analysis of the mental process of which mathematical reasoning consists. We shall see in what follows that mathematical reasoning has encountered difficulties of another kind, but not less serious, in its phases of symbolic condensation and symbolic inversion. With these we shall be concerned in the following chapter.

CHAPTER VIII

THE HIGHER FORMS OF REASONING

Part II: Mathematical Reasoning in its phases of symbolic condensation and symbolic inversion

AFTER having passed in review in the last chapter the first two phases in the evolution of mathematics, those of direct and indirect symbolism as we have called them, we propose in the present chapter to sketch very rapidly the other two phases which we consider must still be examined. When this has been done a brief summary, in the chapter which follows this, of all that we have said concerning mathematical reasoning and the function which symbolism has performed in this kind of reasoning, will enable us, by way of conclusion, to make certain comparisons between mathematics and mathematical logic.

Mathematical reasoning in its phase of symbolic condensation

It is in the infinitesimal calculus, before the practice was extended in general to other parts of mathematics, that the origin and first development of the particular phase of mathematics, which, for lack of a better term, we can call symbolic "condensation", is to be found. Symbolic condensation it is, in the sense that to an algorithmic expression there no longer corresponds one single operation, not even one which in its generality includes an infinite number of particular and similar operations, but instead many diverse simultaneous or successive operations all represented "in a condensed fashion" by a single symbol.

It is then in the field of the infinitesimal calculus that we should study, *still from our peculiar and purely psychological point of view*, this new phase of symbolic evolution to see what consequences and what repercussions have occurred in the mental process of reasoning concerned. A few remarks only will, we trust, be sufficient for this purpose.

170 THE PSYCHOLOGY OF REASONING

It is to be noted before everything else, that the mathematical operation of 'passing to the limit' in no way destroys the fundamental nature of reasoning as a series of imagined operations.

We know indeed how the notion of the limit is introduced into mathematics, for example that of a finite limit: *Taking at choice* a number *as small as we please* if, by the indefinite approach of the variable to a given quantity, the difference between another given quantity and the function of this variable *ends by becoming and thereafter remains* less in absolute value than the small number arbitrarily chosen, this second quantity which the function continually approaches is said to be the limit of the values of the function.

Now, this number, "taken at choice" and "as small as we please", implies the repetition of very numerous experiments of calculation in which, taking first a given small number we go on to take a smaller, and then a third smaller still and so on, each time verifying for each of these values the fact that there is a value for the variable sufficiently near to the quantity to which it indefinitely approaches to satisfy the above mentioned conditions, necessary and sufficient if we are to say that the function of the variable tends to such and such a given limit. It is these experiments in calculation that a beginner has actually to perform, before becoming convinced of this tendency to a limit, and that the most distinguished masters of the infinitesimal calculus, as the present writer recalls, do actually perform, with a view to making this tendency of a quantity to a limit clearly tangible to their audience.

As to the fact that we can acquire this feeling of belief in the tendency of a quantity toward a certain limit, while confining ourselves to the performance, whether actual or in imagination, of a small number only of calculations, we have here a psychological phenomenon which is quite similar to the acquisition of the same feeling of certainty as to the absolute generality of a given geometrical demonstration, performed, say, upon a particular triangle, through the mental repetition of the same demonstration upon a very small number only of other triangles, different in form from that which is drawn upon the paper.

That once the tendency of a given quantity towards

MATHEMATICAL REASONING : PART II 171

a given limit is recognised, we can imagine this last as already attained by the quantity itself and take the limit simply in place of this latter—this rests upon the general psychological fact which holds for all reasoning whatever, that *the fact of seeing in imagination the possibility of performing certain operations or experiments leads naturally to their being imagined as already performed.* This takes place because essentially the one thing is identical with the other. Thus the fact of recognising, as I did in the example which has several times been cited in the preceding chapters, the possibility of ranging all the inhabitants of London one after another in the order of the increasing number of their hairs, made me that very instant imagine that I had already performed all the very many acts of arranging them. This mental act was nothing else, psychologically speaking, than a real and proper passing to a limit.

As we know, the fundamental conception of the differential calculus does in fact consist in taking advantage of certain passings to the limit of relations between minute quantities, which are supposed to tend to diminish ever more and more, with a view to obtaining finally quantitative relations which are more simple than those which hold between the finite quantities from which we start. And by this we are enabled, inversely, once these dependencies between certain more simple and certain other more complex quantitative relations have been in this way discovered, to return, in many cases, by an inverse procedure which constitutes the integral calculus, from simpler quantitative relations either discovered by chance or more easy to discover between given phenomena, to more complex relations between these same phenomena or between other phenomena quantitatively connected in some way with these last.

The quantitative relations which are obtained by these passings to the limit—" differential " relations as they are called—are for the most part more simple than those which hold between finite quantities, because they are concerned with quantitative elements whose effects later accumulate and develop in the finite quantities themselves, and so make them more complex.

A heavy body, for instance, starting with a velocity equal to zero and subject to a constant acceleration g,

172 THE PSYCHOLOGY OF REASONING

accumulates and develops in its velocity $v = gt$ the effects of this constant acceleration g; and then accumulates and develops the effects of this velocity v in the space $s = \frac{1}{2} gt^2$ traversed in the time t. Thus it is because the phenomenon of the fall is allowed to accumulate and develop these successive characteristics, each the immediate effect of that which precedes, that the corresponding quantitative expressions become more and more complicated.

For the same reason, inversely, the less the number of successive characteristics that a given phenomenon is allowed to accumulate and develop during the time it lasts, the more elementary are these characteristics themselves, and consequently the simpler are the quantitative relations which represent them.

To neglect then in the passings to the limit of differential relations, quantities said to be " infinitely small ", that is to say tending to zero, which are found in the second member of the equation in connection with the finite quantity which thus comes to represent the limit sought—and more generally to neglect " infinitesimals " of any degree whatever with regard to all those of a lower degree—is equivalent to removing from our consideration, from their very earliest occurrence, these most complex phenomenal characteristics which would result from the accumulation and development of the effects of the most elementary characteristics, represented by the finite quantities or by the "infinitesimals" of a lower degree : It is equivalent, in other words, to stopping the respective process of development at the point where it would in fact have begun to produce those more complex characteristics, which are quantitatively represented by the infinitesimals neglected.

Given that this is the nature of the differential calculus, namely that it consists only in passings to the limit of relations between minute quantities, which are supposed to tend to diminish ever more and more, the reasoner must in all cases see very clearly that these minute quantities upon which he imagines himself to be operating, though they tend to become ever more minute, are in all cases, at the moment of every operation, whatever it be, which is mentally performed upon them, always *finite* quantities, the only quantities — as Berkeley long ago rightly pointed out—which the

MATHEMATICAL REASONING : PART II 173

human mind can conceive of as matter for operations of calculation.[1]

It is precisely through this finite nature of infinitely small quantities before their passage to the limit not having been quite clearly seen, that they encountered, as is well known, at the first appearance of the infinitesimal calculus, so much and such vigorous opposition, and later so many difficulties in gaining full and complete standing. "During the first phases of the development of the infinitesimal calculus of Leibnitz, there arose the difficulty of forming a logically satisfactory representation of infinitely small magnitudes. Some interpreted them as quantities which were entirely null, others mystically pictured them as magnitudes which although smaller than any other imaginable magnitude whatever, yet contained in all cases the germ capable of producing a finite quantity."[2]

During certain phases of their manipulations they appeared as finite quantities, in certain other phases, as entirely null quantities. "There are great difficulties in trying to determine what infinitesimals are: at one time they are treated like finite numbers, and at another time like zeros."[3]

All this was due to the difficulties in conceiving infinitesimals now as finite quantities and now as quantities tending to a limit, that is sometimes as static quantities sometimes as dynamic quantities.

The excellence and the "economy" of the symbolism of Leibnitz, which succeeded in expressing both significations by means of one and the same single symbol, formed at first, for this very reason, a further aggravation of their difficulties. With the algorithms dy and dx of Leibnitz, indeed, the relation $\frac{dy}{dx}$ already constitutes in itself the symbol of a passing to the limit, without its being necessary to indicate this passage to the limit by an additional special symbol, as did Newton. At the same time, so long as dy and dx are separate the idea of a passage to a limit remains completely suspended ; dy and dx are then only simple symbols of

---

[1] G. Berkeley, *op. cit.*, *A Treatise concerning the Principles of Human Knowledge* (1710), § 132, p. 332.

[2] A. Voss, *op. cit.*, *Ueber das Wesen der Mathematik*, p. 47.

[3] P. E. B. Jourdain, *op. cit.*, *The Nature of Mathematics*, p. 70.

174 THE PSYCHOLOGY OF REASONING

ordinary algebraic quantities, static, that is to say small, but finite and fixed in their value, on which all the ordinary algebraic operations may be performed. As soon, on the other hand, as even a single dy and a single dx occur in the form of a relation, they are transformed, and with them every other unconnected dy and dx in the same algebraic expression or equation, from static into dynamic quantities, for which and for whose relations it is a question of finding the limit.

Thus, for example, in the expression $y = ax^2$, by substituting $x + dx$ for x and $y + dy$ for y we deduce by means of simple ordinary algebraic transformations performed upon dy and dx as finite quantities, the other expression $\frac{dy}{dx} = 2ax + ax \ (dx)$. But when we reach this point the algorithms dx and dy, *although unchanged in their outward aspect*, change their significance in so far as they henceforth represent quantities which tend to approach indefinitely near to zero, and thus give as the limit of their relation the quantity $2\ ax$.

The expression then $\frac{dy}{dx} = 2ax$ is not less rigorous than the other $\frac{dy}{dx} = 2ax + ax \ (dx)$, *because the algorithms* dy *and* dx *have in one expression a different signification from that which they have in the other*. On the other hand the first expression would cease to be as rigorous as the second if in it the algorithms continued to represent static quantities as before.

It is this double and very different signification, which is in this way attributed at different moments to one and the same symbol, that has constituted the greatest difficulty in rightly understanding the method of Leibnitz ; a difficulty which consisted not only in gaining a clear view of this double signification of the symbol, but in seeing now one now the other of the two significations at the proper moment, but never both at once, otherwise this double signification would have been actually inconceivable, as it would be impossible to conceive an object which should be at the same time at rest and in movement.

It is the exclusive or preponderant relief given to the *static* character which did in fact at first occasion so

MATHEMATICAL REASONING : PART II 175

many doubts as to the rigorous exactitude of the procedure followed. Indeed those who maintained for the algorithms dy and dx, even when they occurred in the form of a relation, the static character which they actually possessed while they were subject to the ordinary algebraic operations—and Leibnitz himself set them a fine game when he said that he neglected the infinitely smalls in comparison with finite quantities "as the grains of sand in comparison with the sea"—these, I say, were reluctant to attribute to Leibnitz, method, in comparison with that of Newton, who distinguished the static from the dynamic phase by different algorithms, more than the value of an approximate calculus, or at most a calculus of "compensated errors".[1]

Cavalieri's indivisibles, on the other hand, instead of putting the static character of infinitely smalls more in evidence at the expense of the dynamic aspect, leapt with a bound over the first to consider only the term already reached by these infinitely smalls themselves regarded in their dynamic aspect. By this, they made quite inconceivable the ordinary algebraic operations to be performed upon these infinitely smalls, operations which have no signification unless these latter are considered under their static aspect, *prior to their movement toward the limit.*

All these difficulties encountered in this way by the infinitesimal calculus at its commencement, and those which belong on its own account to every passage to the limit, implying as it does the "vision" of the result towards which we indefinitely approach by a given series of merely imagined operations of algebraic calculation, explain the special psychological difficulties which still to-day act to make this further phase of mathematical reasoning difficult of access for very many persons. The reasoner is forced, in fact, never to lose sight of the double and sometimes multiple signification which this or that symbol has at different times, *although it remains always the same in its outward aspect.* This requires that at the right moment certain operations must be now held in suspense, now performed, or that he proceed now to such and such operations, now on

---

[1] Cf. A. Comte, *Cours de philosophie positive* (1830), 5th Edition, Vol. I, Paris, 1892, pp. 200-220 ; also, A. Voss, *op. cit.*, pp. 30-31.

176 THE PSYCHOLOGY OF REASONING

the other hand to others, *without any indication to this effect being provided on the part of the symbol, which meanwhile remains unchanged.* At the same time the reasoner should be able to embrace in one glance, at this right moment, all the very great complication and multiplicity of whole series or chains of operations, such as those necessary in performing a passage to the limit, these being all the while expressed by this one, single, impassive symbol. This multiplicity and variety of significance at different times, and this multiplicity of operations at single given moments, the whole expressed in bulk by one single graphic sign, this, which constitutes the " symbolic condensation ", demands from the reasoner a continual and powerful intellectual tension to hold in mind, to distinguish, now to perform and now to hold in suspense, then to follow out at length, *and without any support from as many distinct evocative and fixative symbols*, a whole infinity of operations to be mentally performed, each of which is possibly by itself very simple, but which are, taken as a whole, as complex as it is possible to imagine.

This complexity increases the further we proceed in the infinitesimal calculus, as we pass, for example, from the derivatives of a function of one variable to the partial derivatives of a function of several variables, from the calculus of the derivatives to the calculus of variations, from the differential calculus to the integral calculus, from definite integrals to indefinite integrals, and so on. The quantity and the variety of things expressed by each of the symbols, that is the " symbolic condensation," increases continually : it will suffice to consider, for instance, how many and varied are the simultaneous and successive operations represented by the symbol, not by any means amongst the most condensed, of a partial derivative of the second order, or by that of an indefinite integral. Hence the support and repose which the mind found in algebra through the fact that each of the operations of any process whatever of calculation was always represented by its special symbol, comes on the contrary to be more and more lacking through this increasing symbolic condensation ; and in consequence the mental tension necessary to supplement this absence of intermediate points of support and of rest goes on increasing.

MATHEMATICAL REASONING : PART II 177

The difficulties, then, experienced by many people in the understanding and the employment of mathematics, difficulties which we have already seen to begin in the phase of direct symbolism and to occur already in a striking fashion in the phase of indirect symbolism, again grow still greater in the phase of symbolic condensation which we have just been examining. And this because condensation from its own side contributes towards making the contact between the representing symbol and the reality represented ever less and less immediate and the relation of their correspondence ever more and more complicated, each symbol concentrating and condensing an ever more ample and ever more complex reality.

Difficulties of another kind, which also deserve our attention, occur in the fourth evolutionary phase which we propose to examine, that of symbolic inversion, which we go on to discuss, as far as possible even more briefly than the preceding phases.

Mathematical reasoning in its phase of symbolic inversion

We have already seen in the preceding chapter that analytical geometry, as a system of translation allowing questions of geometry to be reduced to the solution of algebraic equations, has come to constitute a system of "parallelism" or correspondence between analytic expressions and geometrical figures. Since every geometrical figure, corresponding as it does to a given analytical expression, often very complicated, constitutes a *concrete signification*, we almost say a *synthetic objectification*, for the expression, every such figure became, for the reasoner lost in the confusion of a thousand other such algebraic expressions, a ray of light and a basis for repose, allowing him afterwards to resume the series of successive algebraic transformations with more vigour and with a more certain orientation.[1]

But obviously this correspondence between algebraic expressions and geometrical figures or phenomena cannot always hold. The former as purely quantitative relations are, in fact, of a more general order than the geometrical relations. It can well be understood, then,

---

[1] Cf. e.g. A. Comte, *op. cit.*, *Cours de philosophie positive*, Vol. I, pp. 357-358, and, for the similar concrete significations offered by mechanics, pp. 502, 581-584.

M

178 THE PSYCHOLOGY OF REASONING

that there may be infinite systems of quantitative properties for which, whether through the number of elements involved, or whether through the kind of relations between them, any geometrical correspondence whatsoever, comes to be lacking. For instance the many algebraic equations of more than three variables can no longer find, like equations of two or three variables, correspondences in geometrical figures, because in analytic geometry only two or three co-ordinates are required to determine each point.

Employing anew the terminology of Chasles with which we have already been concerned in our preceding chapter in connection with "imaginary points", we can say that the property of analytical expressions to represent purely quantitative relations is their *permanent* property, whereas that of representing certain geometrical figures is one of their *contingent* properties, that is to say, a property which in many cases can fail.

But the mathematician, by means of *symbolic inversion* has found how to retain the most important advantages of the system of "parallelism" or of reciprocal correspondences between geometry and algebra, even when this contingent property of algebraic expressions no longer holds. This *symbolic inversion* consists in this, that the geometrical figure which was symbolically represented by a given algebraic expression becomes a symbol in its turn of other algebraic expressions, which are *analytical analogues*, though no longer capable of representing any geometrical fact. In other words the object which, in addition to the corresponding direct properties of a geometrical order, presents indirect determinate properties of a quantitative order furnished by its analytical representation, is taken as a symbol of any analytic system whatsoever which only possesses these latter.[1]

In this way, for example, geometries of four or more "dimensions" can be obtained, by introducing into systems of four or more variables restrictions and definitions analogous to those which hold for three dimensional geometry ; but such systems do not cease, for that, to be plainly, in spite of their geometrical terminology, only so many "chapters of pure algebra". (Exception must be made for the case in which for the

---

[1] Cf. W. Wundt, *op. cit., Logik*, I, p. 484.

MATHEMATICAL REASONING : PART II 179

consideration of geometrical figures as wholes composed of simple points, there is substituted the consideration of "geometrical figures" as wholes composed of geometrical objects of a certain type, such as curves or surfaces of a certain order ; in which cases even equations of more than three variables can become capable of concrete geometrical representations, though very complicated representations.)[1]

Recourse to this symbolic inversion offers the great advantage of allowing quantitative treatment of a more general order, *while serving as a very valuable guide*, almost as valuable as is the actual geometrical parallelism in the cases in which it holds. And these quantitative operations of a more general order that are so greatly facilitated, since they contain as particular instances the cases of actual geometrical parallelism, lead in this fashion often by a shorter way to the discovery of new properties even in these latter. Against this advantage there is, however, to be set, as may easily be imagined, the danger of "mysticism" to which we are exposed, if by losing sight in the course of the treatment of the signification and the aims of this symbolic inversion, we end by attributing an actual existence to the geometrical symbol of an algebraic expression for which on the contrary no geometrical correspondence any longer holds. A danger of mysticism which, as we know, occurs especially in the analytic treatment of non-euclidean geometries.

The origin of non-euclidean geometries is well known. From attempts, which did not succeed, by Saccheri and many others, to establish through a demonstratio ad absurdum Euclid's postulate of parallels, there was reached, with Gauss, Lobatschewski and Bolyai, the construction of a new planimetric geometry, which starting from the negation of this postulate, ended in results which were naturally altogether different.[2]

Up to this point no modification in the nature of

---

[1] J. Tannery, *Science et philosophie*, Paris, 1912, Chap. II, Le rôle du nombre dans les sciences, p. 22.

[2] Cf. e.g. R. Bonola, " Sulla teoria delle parallele e sulle geometrie non-euclidee ", in *op. cit. : Questioni riguardanti le matematiche elementari*, collected and arranged by F. Enriques, Vol. I, pp. 248-268 ; and G. Fano, " La geometria non-euclidea ", *Scientia*, 1908, VIII-4, pp. 257-265.

180 THE PSYCHOLOGY OF REASONING

reasoning as a series of merely imagined operations, and no impossibility in a still tangible conception of our space, were implicit in these constructions. The fact that they gave rise to no logical contradiction (that is, did not lead to the mental establishment of any geometrical fact incompatible with other facts either already admitted or already established), which had at the time very great philosophical importance, because it made the purely empirical nature of Euclid's postulate stand out, and by ricochet that of all postulates and axioms in general, to-day appears to us very natural, seeing that the impossibility of demonstrating this postulate meant that it is not the necessary consequence of the preceding postulates and axioms ; just as, for the same reason, it appears to us quite natural that *e.g.* celestial mechanics starting from a different hypothesis than that of Newton should lead to no logical contradiction. There is this difference, however : as regards the non-correspondence of a non-newtonian hypothesis with the facts of reality, this could only be perceived by the results which would follow from that hypothesis ; but on the contrary as regards Lobatschewski's hypothesis, if it is not taken with a very close approximation to Euclid's, it is not necessary, in order to perceive that it does not conform to the truth, to wait and verify that this or that result to which it leads, for instance the result relative to the sum of the angles of a triangle, fails to be in accordance with the result obtained by direct measurement of these angles. The direct recognition of the hypothesis itself by the eye, or by eye and touch together, is sufficient.

That Lobatschewski's hypothesis, if it is made to approximate very closely to that of Euclid, is not capable even of empirical rejection, need not surprise us, because any hypothesis whatever which is verified by the facts (and none is so verified to such a high degree of approximation as Euclid's hypothesis) can always be replaced by an infinity of other diverse hypothesis, sufficiently close to it to satisfy in equal measure the same empirical verification, which can only be more or less approximate.[1]

With Beltrami's demonstration that the planimetric

[1] Cf. e.g. F. Enriques, *op. cit., Problemi della scienza*, p. 290 ; and A. Voss, *op. cit., Ueber das Wesen d. Math.*, pp. 92-94.

MATHEMATICAL REASONING : PART II 181

geometry of Lobatschewski is not anything else essentially than the Euclidean geometry of the pseudo-sphere, provided that by "straight lines in the plane" we understand the geodetics of this surface, the matter completely changes its aspect. The geometry of Lobatschewski, until then considered to be a geometry of the plane, excluding Euclid's geometry and not in contradiction with the data of experience for the case only in which it is very near Euclid's geometry, becomes through this demonstration a simple branch of the Euclidean geometry relative to a certain surface, the theorems of which then entirely cease to seem strange. The concept of "plane," as a surface whose curvature is constant and null, is thus extended so as to include also surfaces whose curvature is constant, but with value different from zero and negative, such as that of the pseudo-sphere. A result which leads on, with Riemann, to the inclusion thereunder of surfaces of constant and positive curvature, that is of spherical surfaces. Remembering still that by "straight lines in the plane" we must now understand geodetics of the surface, this comes to be the concrete interpretation of a second non-euclidean "planimetry" in which no parallel lines at all exist (that is two straight lines on the same plane always meet) and in which even the postulate of the uniqueness of the straight line shows exceptions, in the sense that two straight lines having two points in common may, with certain particular positions of these points, not coincide, and on the contrary enclose a space between them (as happens in fact for the great circles passing through the two extremities of a diameter of the sphere). These "planimetries" of Euclid, Lobatschewski and Riemann, do not then, let us repeat, imply three different systems of geometry, but merely three different branches of ordinary geometry.[1]

We can say then that with Lobatschewski there began the logical methods of *isolation*, which consist in isolating and rejecting now one now another of the mutually independent axioms and postulates of ordinary geometry, thus giving rise to as many abstract geometrical systems differing from the ordinary system.

[1] Cf. Hastings Berkeley, *op. cit.*, *Mysticism in Modern Mathematics*, pp. 208-209.

182 THE PSYCHOLOGY OF REASONING

On the other hand with Beltrami the methods of *substitution*, we will not say began, but received a new and fruitful impulse, methods in which through interpreting and translating geometrical terms by as many corresponding objects, different from those ordinarily understood, but such that the reasonings made for these last remain formally valid, we pass directly from the geometry of certain given figures to the geometry of other figures. The logical methods of isolation and substitution have, as is well known, in recent times very greatly enriched the mathematical sciences.[1]

All this can be obtained without any real analytic treatment of the question, and merely by means of geometrical operations or experiments very clearly imagined, whether we attribute to these operations supposed to be performed upon the plane results deliberately admitted to be by hypothesis different from the results supplied by direct observation, or whether it is established later on that these results so admitted are really empirically exact, provided that they are interpreted as being connected with other determinate surfaces different from the plane. And the final result of all this is to place before us three kinds of surfaces ; all of them of constant curvature — null, positive, or negative respectively— showing themselves as very different in certain fundamental properties (the postulate of parallels, holding for the plane, but not for the pseudo-sphere, or the sphere ; the postulate of the uniqueness of the straight line, holding for the plane and for the pseudo-sphere, but not, in certain cases, for the sphere), and having other no less fundamental properties in common, consisting in "elementary planarity" and in "congruence" (that is in the fact that each of their parts if taken as infinitely small can be considered as plane, and in the free transportability upon them of any figure whatsoever, at the most by simple flexions without extensions).[2]

If we wish to translate these common fundamental

---

[1] Cf. e.g. W. Wundt, *op. cit., Logik*, Vol. I, p. 494 ; and R. Bonola, the essay already quoted : "Sulla teoria delle parallele", etc., pp. 274-280.

[2] Cf., e.g., W. K. Clifford, *The Philosophy of the Pure Sciences*, Lecture III : "The Postulates of the Science of Space", in *Lectures and Essays*, Vol. I, London, 1901, pp. 369-381 ; and : H. von Helmholtz, "Ueber den Ursprung und die Bedeutung der geometrischen Axiome," in *op. cit., Vorträge und Reden*, Vol. II, pp. 10-11, 14-15.

MATHEMATICAL REASONING : PART II 183

properties analytically, it is sufficient to consider any three surfaces belonging respectively to the kinds above described and to take upon each of them the same system of two co-ordinates; then the analytic expression of the first property which all three have in common will consist in the equality of the square of the distance between any point on the surface and any other point infinitely near to it with a certain homogeneous differential expression of the second degree; while that of the second property equally in common will be given by our fixing as constant, that is as independent of the variable co-ordinates of the point considered, a certain algebraic expression, which is found later to correspond to the measure of the curvature of the surface in question.

It is clear, however, that these two analytic relations are not sufficient, owing to their too great generality, to define particularly either one or another of these three surfaces and that for such an analytical system to be capable of a geometrical interpretation in terms of one of them, say of the plane, the realisation of some further analytical condition is necessary, that in fact which expresses that the curvature, beyond being constant, is null.

If we now desire to pass by analytic analogy from the treatment of two variables only to that of three variables it will be understood that the possibility of such an analytic treatment in no way implies that the three corresponding systems of analytic relations which are thus obtained are capable, as much as the others, of geometrical interpretation.

Riemann, we know, went still further. Starting with the very general concept of continuous " multiplicities " (stetige Mannigfaltigkeiten) n times "extended" he confines himself later to those for which he established analytic relations corresponding to those of elementary planarity and congruence which hold for the surfaces above described, and he went on to deduce the possibility of a constant "curvature" different from zero even for continuous multiplicities of three dimensions.[1]

But evidently the general notion of multiplicity n times, or even only three times, extended, which he

---

[1] B. Riemann, "Ueber die Hypothesen welche der Geometrie zu Grunde liegen", in Bernhard Riemann's *Gesammelte Mathematische Werke*, 2nd Ed., Leipzig, 1892, Vol. XIII, pp. 272-287.

184 THE PSYCHOLOGY OF REASONING

subjected to mathematical analysis, is nothing but a purely algebraic conception, which implies nothing more than simple quantitative notions much more general than those which spatial relations properly so called would have been able to provide.

The names "point", "place", "dimension", "line" and "length of line", "elementary planarity" (Ebenheit in den kleinsten Teilen), "curvature", and others similarly used in connection with a multiplicity n times extended, imply purely analytic expressions only; although they represent a very happy symbolic inversion, which has served admirably as a means of orientation and as a guide in the handling of calculation pure and simple (applied to the analysis and separation of some among the various axioms and postulates of geometry), they ought not however to deceive us. The question of deciding whether all the three analytic cases with three variables, here also analytically possible and corresponding to the cases with two variables which find a geometrical interpretation in the three surfaces of constant curvature above described, are capable they also of a geometrical interpretation, or whether none of the three are, or whether some only of the three are, this question still remains open, in spite of these conventional denominations. No analytic consideration can settle it, but only the comparison of these expressions with the representation which we make of space on the basis of our daily geometrical experience. This comparison, as we know, tells us that only one of these three analytical cases, that of "curvature" zero, is capable of this geometrical interpretation.[1]

The recourse to the celebrated two dimensional animalcules of Clifford and Helmholtz, which, while living on surfaces or on bounded portions of surfaces whose curvature was constant, could never come to suspect the existence, or form any idea of this curvature of their space although it actually subsisted, only obscured the question.[2]

It was a question in fact of knowing whether certain

[1] Cf. W. Wundt, *op. cit.*, *Logik* I, Section III Chapter iii, 2b.: "Der Mathematische Raumbegriffe", pp. 480-494, especially pp. 481, 483, 486.

[2] Cf. W. K. Clifford, *The Common Sense of the Exact Sciences,* London, 1907, Chap. IV, § 19: On the Bending of Space, pp. 214-226; and Helmholtz, Essay already cited: "Ueber den Urspr. u. die Bedeut. d. geom. Axiome", pp. 8 ff.

MATHEMATICAL REASONING : PART II 185

analytical expressions, to which geometrical denominations have been conventionally given by symbolic inversion, were or were not capable of some actual geometrical interpretation. Recourse to these two dimensional animalcules does not answer this question, it answers it in the affirmative still less, since Helmholtz himself "to avoid misunderstandings" hastens to add "that this so called measure of the curvature of space is an algebraic magnitude found by analysis, and its introduction is in no way based upon the presupposition of circumstances which would have a significance only for sensible intuition ".[1]

Recourse to these animalcules has as its goal, to predispose us, even through purely geometrical considerations, to admit as *not impossible*, the actual existence of a geometrical "something" which no geometrical fact in any way authorises us to suspect, and of which we cannot, it must be insisted, even form the least idea, but whose possibility would be demonstrated by purely analytic considerations. All this is in order to exalt the power of the calculus itself, which thus would show itself to be capable even of "transcendental" results, true "empirical extrapolations ".

But all this "transcendentalism ", as we have seen, consists only in the merely conventional denomination by geometrical terms of purely algebraic expressions. Whoever will may certainly believe in the existence or the possibility of existence of such "noumena"— whether it is a question of this curvature of our space, or of spaces of four dimensions or more—of which no phenomena and no combination of phenomena can give us the least idea, but in doing this he falls into the purest mysticism, since any act of mysticism does just consist in admitting the existence of something mysterious which is not capable either of coming under the observation of any of our senses or of being imagined by means of sensible elements combined together in any fashion whatever.

This mathematical mysticism recently has reappeared with renewed vigour in Einstein's Theory of Relativity, in which mention is made, as though it really had some correspondence with reality, of a "space" of four dimensions in which the fourth dimension is of a

[1] Helmholtz, *ibid.*, p. 18.

186 THE PSYCHOLOGY OF REASONING

temporal nature, of a "curvature" of our tridimensional space, of "tensors" in this quadridimensional space, and so on.

So far as relativists insist upon giving substance to such shadows, by affirming the physical reality of these purely algebraical entities, they certainly cannot boast that they have succeeded in explaining the phenomena for which this theory has been constructed. "Explanation", in fact, as we have shown in the preceding chapters, consists, from the psychological point of view, merely in the process of deducing, of obtaining certain facts from the imagined combination of other facts which are simpler and more familiar to us. To have recourse then in the explanation of certain phenomena of physics or of celestial mechanics to conceptions, which not only are not familiar to us, but which our mind, formed as it now is by our three dimensional Euclidean space, can in no way, even in the most distant fashion, represent, certainly does not constitute any explanation whatever. The theory of relativity is up to the present nothing but a purely mathematical construction, to which no doubt there must correspond some physical reality, seeing that certain of its results are confirmed by observation. But the task of the relativists is now to seek to discover in what this physical reality consists, so as to make it accessible to our imagination. Only then can they rightly claim to have "explained" those facts for whose explanation their theory has been constructed.

Finally, as for the projective interpretation which, thanks to the new conceptions due to Cayley and to Klein, it has been possible to give for the non-euclidean "spaces" just spoken of, this plainly represents quite another matter and forms part of those methods of substitution mentioned above, which have proved themselves so fruitful in the field of geometrical reasoning.

We can also conclude that the introduction and employment of symbolic inversion in mathematics, which has been of a very great fecundity in promoting the development of new and the analysis of old branches of this science, has at the same time demonstrated all its dangerousness in predisposing mathematicians to mystical conceptions, very prejudicial to the clear understanding of the real state of affairs.

MATHEMATICAL REASONING : PART II 187

Having thus passed in review, in the first part which forms the preceding chapter, and in the present second part, the four phases in the evolution of mathematical reasoning—direct symbolism, indirect symbolism, symbolic condensation and symbolic inversion—which for our purposes have the most importance, it now remains for us to recapitulate our thought and draw our conclusions upon mathematics in general. At the same time, the evaluation of the importance which symbolism has thus possessed will lead us, as we have already indicated, to make certain comparisons between mathematics and mathematical logic, which also has attempted to utilise an analogous system of symbolic representation. This task will occupy us in a third and last part of this study of the higher forms of reasoning.

CHAPTER IX

THE HIGHER FORMS OF REASONING

Part III : Mathematics and Mathematical Logic

THE brief space to which we have restricted ourselves in this study of the higher forms of reasoning represented by mathematical reasoning, has forced us to confine our treatment to four special phases only of mathematical reasoning, those considered in the two preceding chapters. We chose these four phases rather than any others, because from our point of view, they seemed to us to be the most important of all. The first of these phases, that of direct symbolism, appeared to us the best fitted to show that the transition from primitive material counting to arithmetical calculation and thence to algebraic calculation, has in no way changed the nature of the operations or experiments of primitive, material, counting itself, operations or experiments which, in arithmetical calculation, are merely imagined, and, in algebraic calculation, imagined as united in groups, instead of being actually performed. At the same time, the examination, although very brief it is true, which we have made of the other three phases appeared necessary in order to show that the nature of mathematical reasoning, as a mental combination of materially tangible operations or experiments, remains the same in those cases also in which perhaps more than in others it seems on the contrary to be contradicted by certain results having, at first sight, no longer any " real " substratum, or seems to vanish behind pronounced symbolic condensation which no longer brings the particular operations to be performed one by one into evidence, or seems to give rise to the paradox of apparently leading to empirical extrapolations which its very nature renders completely inadmissible.

We can now sum up the conclusions, which these two chapters authorise us to draw as regards mathematics in general and upon the function of symbolism

MATHEMATICAL LOGIC 189

in mathematics. We shall then pass on to compare mathematics themselves both in nature and in value with the other great branch of advanced reasoning, namely mathematical logic.

Mathematics : Summary and Conclusion

The first question which arises in connection with mathematics is to explain, given that the nature of reasoning as a series of merely imagined operations or experiments remains, as we have seen, without alteration in all procedures of calculation whatsoever, how it comes about that we find certain special difficulties in mathematical reasoning much greater than those in ordinary reasoning. This, as we have seen, is in fact due to the very improvements themselves which have made mathematics so powerful a logical instrument.

The first of these improvements which helps to make mathematical reasoning difficult for most people is *the great abstractness of its concepts*. This implies that we have to imagine all the operations or experiments as performed upon materials of such a high degree of generality that they seem almost to be emptied of all content capable of being grasped in intuition. Thus it becomes for many people more difficult to "see", at the necessary moment, behind every operation of this very general order, all the infinite particular operations or even only those particular operations which may at this moment have a special importance for the reasoner. So that, through the absence of any vision of the real signification of these very operations, all interest is taken away from the procedure of the reasoning. While it is this interest which alone maintains the "logical thread" of the reasoning.

But the great abstractness of the concepts is not sufficient by itself to explain why so many people are so recalcitrant to mathematics ; this is so true that among the most refractory of these people may often be counted even consummate philosophers capable of the greatest feats of abstraction.

The enormous development of its symbolism, a development entirely peculiar to mathematics, certainly plays a very great part in this. Symbolism, in fact, now almost completely usurps the place of ordinary language in mathematical reasoning, so that the mind can no

190 THE PSYCHOLOGY OF REASONING

longer, save very rarely, rest upon facts or results expressed in terms which are familiar to it. Later on with the phases of indirect symbolism, symbolic condensation and symbolic inversion, as we have seen, and with other phases to a still greater degree, the representing symbol becomes more and more removed from the reality represented, and the relation of correspondence between them becomes ever more complicated and less easy to grasp. So much so that a severe mental tension, of which few people are capable, is required, each time the need arises, in order to see behind a given symbol all that it represents and no more than it represents.

The prolongation and complication of reasoning made possible by the very deductive power of mathematical calculation, produce, the first, great fatigue which often makes it impossible to follow the development of the procedure out to the end, and, the second, a kind of loss of orientation amid the swarm of formulæ which express the linking and dovetailing at a single moment of so many imagined quantitative operations or experiments. Analytic geometry, as we have seen, as well as mechanics and mathematical physics in general, greatly contribute, by the *concrete significations* or *synthetic objectifications* which they provide for certain expressions and certain analytic developments, to diminish in many cases these difficulties due to the prolongation and complication of calculation. We have seen also that symbolic inversion aims, and with success in spite of its dangers, at the same result. But all this does not suffice to remove this order of difficulties entirely. In this connection we may recall that Poincaré when he asked himself why it is, since mathematical reasoning rests upon the same principles as common reasoning, that there are so many people who do not succeed in it, attributed this fact to the absence in many people of that "feeling of mathematical order" which enables the general trend of certain even very long and complicated processes of calculation to be grasped at a single glance, and so enables the diverse algebraic elements which will make it up to be placed with ease in their proper places in the picture of the process as a whole thus glimpsed.[1]

[1] H. Poincaré, " L'invention mathématique ", in *Revue du Mois*, 10 July 1908, pp. 9-12, 18-19 ; and in *Science et Méthode*, Book I, Chap. III, p. 44 ff. ; see also by the same author " L'avenir des mathématiques ", *Scientia*, 1908, VIII-3, p. 5.

MATHEMATICAL LOGIC 191

All these special psychological difficulties in mathematics do not in any way change, we repeat once more, its essential nature, which remains the same for all reasoning. And since it has in no way undergone any essential change, mathematical reasoning retains all the fundamental properties and characteristics of reasoning in general.

Thus, for instance, although it is purely and simply a deduction of, one might say, an infinite series of results from a few, a very few premises, it is none the less very far from being an empty tautology, since, like all reasoning in general, it forms *an imagined account* or *a devised history* of quantitative operations or experiments, combined and linked together in the most varied ways, a combination of experiments which produced *new facts*, *new situations*, which we recognise or establish in the conclusions of our reasoning.

The new quantitative situations to which every operation or experiment of calculation gives rise, *are in no way implicit in the premises from which the calculation itself starts*, no more than—to recall an example already used in one of our earlier chapters—the lengthening of metal bars under the action of heat and the slowness of oscillation of a longer pendulum compared with that of a shorter, *in any way contain as implicit the operation or experiment of carrying a given pendulum from a cold room into a warmer room.* This transportation gave rise *to a new historical succession of events freely created by my imagination*, at the end of which I was able mentally to "recognise" that the pendulum now oscillating more slowly in the warmer room *was the same which oscillated more rapidly in the colder room.* This is, we repeat, *a new fact*, which we now recognise for the first time and which was in no way implicit in the premises by themselves, because, in order to produce it, a mentally performed *material operation of transportation* was necessary, and of this the premises made no mention.

In an entirely analogous fashion the premises from which mathematical calculation sets out do not at all implicitly contain the operations of this calculation ; *our imagination on the contrary is left entirely free to contrive them as we please*, and these "historical successions" of quantitative operations or experiments thus freely imagined and combined together in the most varied

192   THE PSYCHOLOGY OF REASONING

ways, lead, even in this case, *to new quantitative facts for whose production it is first necessary to create in imagination this succession of events:* It will perhaps be said—writes Milhaud in this connection—that the mathematician only "brings out from the initial data all that they implicitly contain? This could only be a way of speaking. Who does not feel all the activity, the ingenuity, the creative power necessary to make all that was hidden in the initial ideas appear, or more precisely, *to construct upon them as bases, the greatest edifices?*"—" Who does not feel that mathematics effects the miracle of securing the clearest of its successes less through a docile submission to reality which presents itself to us, than by the spontaneity of the impulses of our mind, by the richness and power of its creative activity?"[1]

To this is due the spontaneity and all the irregularity of the evolution of mathematics, characteristics which belong to every combinatory process of whatever kind which takes place in the imagination.[2]

It is then not necessary to have recourse, as Poincaré did—in order to understand why mathematical reasoning is not a tautology—to what is called the "principle of complete induction" or "reasoning by recurrence", a principle which is essentially but a process of generalising demonstration like any other (like that, for instance, which in geometry leads a demonstration made upon a particular triangle to be generalised for all the infinite triangles possible) and which is based like any other process of generalisation upon an ordinary passage to the limit, in the sense that we suppose as great a number of a certain kind of operations as we please to be performed.[3]

Similarly, the capacity to perform in imagination infinite successions and infinite combinations of new quantitative operations or experiments, whose single results are already known in advance, which mathematical calculation possesses to a far greater degree

---

[1] G. Milhaud, essay quoted : " La pensée mathématique, son rôle dans l'histoire des idées ", in *op. cit., Nouvelles études sur l'histoire de la pensée scientifique*, pp. 22-23, 24-25.

[2] Cf. L. Brunschvicg, *op. cit., Les étapes de la philosophie mathématique*, p. 9.

[3] Cf. H. Poincaré, "On the Nature of Mathematical Reasoning" in *Science and Hypothesis*, Part I, Chap. I.

MATHEMATICAL LOGIC

than all the other forms of reasoning, comes to it from no essential difference, but from the property which, as we have already seen, is common to all reasoning whatsoever, and which consists in the increase in deductive capacity in proportion to the increase in degree of abstractness.

It is because the concept "unity", from which mathematical calculation starts and on which it is based, represents the most schematised object which is possible—in so far as every particular attribute, except that of plurality, is removed from it—in other terms, it is because mathematics is the science of the utmost degree of abstractness that it has been able to carry to the highest degree the number, variety and complexity of the operations or experiments which are imagined as performed upon this object "unity" so schematised.

It is further assisted in this by the continual process of further generalisation relative to the different quantitative operations and their combinations or modes of combination, which as far as determinate groups of them show themselves to be equivalent with regard to certain results, whether formal or substantial, give rise to the formation of corresponding new concepts which thus still further increase, on their own side even, the possibility and capacity of deduction of further quantitative combinations.[1]

Hence, in the evolution of mathematics—as for that matter in the evolution of all the sciences which are to a large extent based upon reasoning—the continual oscillation between the two opposed forms of the activity of thought: between the synthetic tendency, on the one hand, and the analytic tendency on the other. In other words, at one time a movement towards the discovery and formation of new concepts, at another towards drawing and developing the greatest possible number of deductions from these new concepts when so acquired.[2]

It is thanks to this same extremely abstract concept "unity", capable as it is of representing indifferently all special unities of measure, that calculation has come

---

[1] Cf. G. Milhaud, *Essay cit.*, *La pensée math.*, *etc.*, p. 24.
[2] Cf., e.g. L. Brunschvicg, *op. cit.*, *Les étapes de la philos. math.*, p. 537.

194 THE PSYCHOLOGY OF REASONING

to form, for all the physical sciences—beginning with geometry, through representation by means of co-ordinates—an immense system of 'translation' into one single language for all the quantitative relations which occur between their phenomena.[1]

Thus mathematics can be defined by saying that it is the science in which the merely imagined experiments, which constitute reasoning, are of a very general quantitative nature, capable of making the most varied physical phenomena equivalent in regard to the quantitative relations thus discovered.[2]

As to the symbolism—if exception be made of a few very special cases, *e.g.* the indirect rôle which, as we have seen, it has had in the formation of the most general concept of number, when extended even to imaginary and complex expressions—we can say that it has never in general played a truly *active* rôle in the development of mathematics. Indeed it has been most often limited to the modest function of a docile and passive instrument of thought, now appearing as a well arranged cabinet for all the new concepts which little by little have been formed, now as representing and summing up in a more and more concise fashion the long and complicated series of analytic operations in ever greater quantity which laborious and persevering deduction has come to draw from these new always wider concepts.[3]

But its function as simple "registrant of thought" has not been less useful. It is, in fact, just thanks to its marvellous symbolism that mathematics has been able to increase the number, variety and complexity of new imagined quantitative combinations indefinitely. The imagination of the mathematician would never have been able to form them if the symbolism had not always held open before him a complete inventory of the materials—initial facts and results little by little acquired —upon which his imagination could exercise itself further, and if the symbolism had not also furnished him at each step with a concrete and concise representa-

---

[1] Cf., e.g., A. Voss, *op. cit.*, *Ueber das Wesen der Mathematik*, p. 13.
[2] Cf. the different definitions of mathematics, quoted in A. Voss, *ibid.*, pp. 26-29.
[3] Cf. A. Comte, *op. cit.*, *Cours de philosophie positive*, Vol. I, pp. 120-121.

MATHEMATICAL LOGIC 195

tion of the path which the imagination was in the act of following.

The imagination has been able to make use of this symbolism because, *thanks to the homogeneity of all the operations or experiments which the symbolism represented*, it could always see, behind this, the content of quantitative, we should almost say tangible, operations or experiments, thus symbolised.

Doubtless, in the swarm of quantitative combinations which can be imagined, the imagination even of the most experienced mathematician, has often had need of some still more concrete signification which would objectify synthetically this or that analytic result and set him straight whether with regard to the path already traversed or that which still remained to be followed. Hence, as we have seen, the powerful assistance that the system of "parallelism" between analytic expressions and geometrical figures begun by analytic geometry has given to pure calculation, and the usefulness of having recourse, in spite of its dangers, to symbolic inversion in order to take advantage of this valuable guide even when the parallelism no longer holds. Hence also the help which the development of calculation has equally received from mechanics and mathematical physics in general which, like analytic geometry, has on its side assisted in providing new and more varied points of departure, secure foundations on which to rest, and valuable indications by which to steer in the fierce toil of the combining imagination.[1]

But the chief and most solid reason for the powerful aid which mathematical symbolism has given to this combining in imagination of more and more new quantitative relations, derives from the *homogeneity* of the operations or experiments, always of a quantitative order, which it represents. This, we repeat, enabled the imagination, even in the absence of a more concrete and synthetic signification, to form none the less a sufficiently tangible idea of the facts which the symbolism presented and on which the imagination had to operate.

We must now consider whether as much can be said for the symbolism employed in what is called mathematical logic, and whether we can from an equal

[1] Cf., e.g. V. Volterra, *Sur quelques progrès récents de la physique mathématique*, in Clark University Lectures, Worcester (Mass.), 1912, p. 2.

196 THE PSYCHOLOGY OF REASONING

extension of symbolism in this field expect the same marvellous fertility, which the corresponding symbolism has yielded in mathematics strictly so called. This enquiry will supply us with an occasion for making a few brief remarks of a general nature upon this latest new branch of logic, with which we shall close this study of the higher forms of reasoning.

Mathematical Logic

Any reasoning whatsoever, as a connected series of imagined experiments, implies in itself for each experiment a corresponding process of induction, a more or less unnoticed induction perhaps, by means of which the result obtained by a given experiment or by several like experiments actually performed in the past, is generalised so that the result is attributed to the present merely imagined experiment, which itself is similar to those which preceded it. When this linking together of merely imagined experiments, through which we follow the various vicissitudes of the object which interests us at the moment, has been performed by the work of the combining imagination, the attention of the reasoner, hitherto wholly engaged in the creative act, can then go over the route, which has been rapidly followed in this creative act, and stop at each step to check and verify, on the basis of the reasoner's own very carefully evoked memories, whether the result attributed to each experiment is really correct, that is to say, whether each of the inductions on which the reasoning is founded is really legitimate. There is thus involved *another mode of distribution of attention* which aims at making 'explicit' each such induction, at bringing it clearly into relief in the form of the membership of a certain object to a certain class, or the inclusion of one class of objects in another class : such and such an object or all the objects of such and such a class, when subjected to a certain experiment show such and such attributes, that is come to belong to such and such another class.

It follows that reasoning, in addition to being a true thought experiment ("Gedankenexperiment"), takes further the form of determinate *classificatory operations* (comprising inclusions, adjunctions, intersections, etc. of classes) *performed upon materials already produced and*

MATHEMATICAL LOGIC 197

presented to the mind by the preceding creative act of the combining imagination. For instance, the imagined experiment which we have several times mentioned of the metal pendulum which is carried from a cold room into a warm room, takes the syllogistic form :—the pendulum thus transported belongs to the class of metallic bars which are heated ; the class of metallic bars which are heated is included in that of bars which are lengthened ; the class of bars which are lengthened is included in that of bars which oscillate more slowly ; thence, etc.

The form of deduction by means of operations performed upon classes to which any reasoning whatever can be thus reduced, is nothing else than a kind of "cataloguing" of the results of determinate experiments *after these have been mentally performed by the combining imagination.* It is like the *anatomical dissection* of an organ after the function concerned has determined and created its complicated structure. In other words, it is a *static* mode of regarding the products of a *dynamic* process.

The possibility of transforming any piece of reasoning, thanks to the induction on which it is based, into corresponding operations of inclusions, adjunctions, intersections, etc. of classes makes these operations, representing as they do experiments of a very general order, valid for all reasoning. At the same time, thanks to their great generality and to our resulting familiar hourly experience of them, they are such—for example that of a class or recipient containing some object and contained in its turn in another class or recipient, into which we have just transformed our reasoning on the pendulum—that we know the result of each of them beforehand, and so they can be performed merely in imagination.

These merely imagined operations, of inclusions, adjunctions, intersections, etc. of classes, give rise equally, for this reason, to results of a very general order, in relation to which all reasonings, considered in their *static* mode, are equivalent to one another. They sum up therefore the "fundamental principles of reasoning" and thus constitute "pure logic", a manner of reasoning, that is, which is applicable universally to all possible cases, these becoming so many applications.

198 THE PSYCHOLOGY OF REASONING

Language with its propositions and syllogistic processes, on the one hand, and mathematical logic or logistic with its special symbols and its algorithmic transformations, on the other, being applied one as much as the other to giving the expression or adequate translation of these operations performed upon classes, constitute in their turn the corresponding "formal logic", in other words, the form in verbal or algorithmic symbols which pure logic puts on.

The rules which are empirically observed to hold for the processes of pure logic, rules which but record the above mentioned operations performed upon classes and the results yielded by each, have as pendants the "laws" or "axioms" which regulate the corresponding processes of formal logic.

These axioms or laws of formal logic, these so called "laws of thought" are thus nothing else than the expression of "actual properties of collections of things"; "they merely express the properties of all possible classification"; they, no less than geometrical axioms, are in short nothing but mere empirical observations, mere empirically observed data, only of a still more general order. They have a normative character precisely because they represent "the quintessence of our experience in its largest sense".[1]

So that it is not geometry, it is not arithmetic, but logic, the purest and most formal logic, the logic described by Couturat as "the collection of formal implications independent of all content", the logic described by Russell as a science in which we never know what we are talking about, nor if what we say is true—it is this purest and most formal logic, we say, which is the first of the experimental sciences. And reasoning—naturally before it was capable of being transformed into a mechanical process through the symbolism employed and the long established habit of making use of it—never for a moment ceases, even in the purest and most formal logic, to be a succession of *intuitive acts*, since it represents always a succession of operations, of a very general order it is true, but none

---

[1] Cf. F. Enriques, *op. cit.*, *Problemi della scienza*, pp. 218-220 ; H. Poincaré, " Les derniers efforts des logisticiens ", in *op. cit.*, *Science et Méthode*, p. 212 ; C. Mineo, " Logica e matematica ", in *Riv. di Filosofia*, 1911, p. 50.

MATHEMATICAL LOGIC 199

the less always quite 'tangible', like that operation of double inclusion we have mentioned (that is, of a class or recipient containing some object and contained in its turn in another class or recipient), or other similar inclusions, adjunctions, intersections etc. of classes, imagined by the mind as performed upon given groups or collections of things.

It follows that the pretension of being able, thanks to the symbolism introduced, to eliminate from " pure logic" all trace of intuition ("intuition ought", writes Couturat, "to have no part in rigorous reasonings ; to be such these ought to be purely logical "), amounts to believing that we can in fact renounce that very psychic activity which alone allows us to deduce consequences or establish new "logical relations" from given premises ; but this belief is quite erroneous just because all deduction, even in the purest and most formal logic, is nothing else, we repeat, than a combination of merely imagined operations or experiments.[1]

Now, mathematical logic has contrived to express these operations of a very general order upon classes, which classical logic expressed by propositions in ordinary language and by connecting them in the forms of the syllogism, by means of special algorithms and corresponding symbolic transformations.

For this it was sufficient to designate the different classes by letters and to employ a very few signs invented for this purpose, to indicate first of all : the *equality* between objects (already distinct one from another through having been hitherto considered each from a different point of view), or between classes of objects (distinct from one another from the point of view of comprehension, of the properties, that is, which characterise them, and identical in extension, in the number, that is, of their members) ; the *membership* of objects in classes and the *inclusion* of classes in other classes ; the *adjunction* and *intersection* of classes (operations also called logical "addition" and "multiplication" on account of certain properties which they have

---

[1] Cf. on this pretension put forward by some mathematicians and many mathematical logicians, A. Voss, *op. cit., Ueber das Wesen d. Math.*, pp. 83, 87 ; L. Couturat, *Les principes des mathématiques*, Paris, 1905, p. 288 ; H. Poincaré "Les mathématiques et la logique ", *Revue de Metaph. et de Mor.*, Nov. 1905, pp. 825, 829-830 ; L. Brunschvicg, *op. cit., Les étapes de la philos. math.* p. 400.

200 THE PSYCHOLOGY OF REASONING

in common with the algebraic operations so named, the second of which, consisting essentially in choosing from a given class of objects a special given sub-class of these objects, was named by Boole "election") ; and later to choose signs to indicate the four principal cases of membership or inclusion, whether initial or derived from given operations, namely those consisting in the fact that a class contains *a single object*, or *all the objects which do not belong to another given class*, or *no object* or *all the objects of which one is speaking*. So that, by means of these few signs indicating only relations and operations between objects and classes and between classes and classes, mathematical logic has come to represent all the possible logical connections.[1]

Afterwards, profiting from the results already furnished, as we have mentioned above, by our most familiar daily experience, concerning inclusions, adjunctions, intersections, etc., of classes—experience of double inclusion and other similar experiences—or helping itself by the concrete representation of classes themselves by means of regions of space or circles in a plane, mathematical logic has found out, in the same way as the mathematicians in algebraic calculation, the properties of symbols and the consequent laws of logical calculation, in other words the rules which ought to govern the transformation of given formulæ into other equivalent formulæ, in order to express these operations performed upon classes and their results.[2]

It has thus been discovered, for example, that commutative, associative and distributive properties, analogous to those which hold for algebraic addition and multiplication, hold also for the logical operations of adjunction and intersection of classes, while certain other properties hold for logic but not for algebra, which greatly simplify logical calculation in comparison with algebraic calculation. It has been found further, that other properties, such as reflexiveness, symmetry, transi-

---

[1] Cf., e.g., A. Padoa, *La logique déductive dans sa dernière phase de développement.* Paris, 1912, pp. 21-41 ; G. Peano, *Notations de logique mathématique, Introduction au formulaire de mathématique,* Turin, 1894, esp. pp. 4, 7 ff. ; G. Vailati, " La logique mathématique et sa nouvelle phase de développement dans les Écrits de G. Peano ", in *op. cit., Scritti de G. Vailati,* pp. 230 ff.

[2] Cf., e.g., A. N. Whitehead, *A Treatise on Universal Algebra,* Cambridge, 1898, Vol. I, pp. 38 ff.

MATHEMATICAL LOGIC 201

tiveness, which are also analogous to the corresponding properties in algebra, hold for certain logical relations but not for others ; and so on. The rules in short have been in this way fixed for logical calculation, rules which, *once thus established by empirical methods*, enable other logical truths to be later demonstrated in a fashion analogous to that of algebraic calculation, by way of pure transformations of calculation.[1]

None the less these are pure transformations of calculation, which, so far as they satisfy the rules, do not cease—unconsciously for the calculator who employs them henceforth mechanically—always to represent very general‧experiments of inclusions, adjunctions, intersections, etc., of classes.

From relations and operations concerning classes it was easy to pass to those concerning propositions, which, in a more or less direct way, only indicate essentially the same relations or operations, each "predication" expressing in fact merely the membership of objects in classes or the inclusion of classes in other classes. All the grammatical relations can then be expressed by means of the signs of mathematical logic, signs which but represent *ideographically* relations and operations concerning classes. Logical ideography and mathematical logic thus come to provide respectively the vocabulary and the syntax which are common to all the deductive sciences.[2]

The first advantage gained by this "logical ideography" is that it constitutes a system, the most concise system possible, of *universal writing*, independent of any language whatsoever. In other words it supplies, with a view to economy of space and international comprehensibility, an instrument of symbolic-stenographic translation or transcription for given already constructed deductive theories, in particular for mathematical theories. For this it is sufficient to make use, in addition to logical symbols properly so called, of symbols to represent the

---

[1] Cf., e.g., A. Padoa, *op. cit., La log. déd.*, etc. pp. 62-73, 95-96 ; L. Couturat, *op. cit., Princ. des Math.*, pp. 10 ff., and *L'algèbre de la logique*, Paris, 1905, pp. 1-25, English translation, pp. 4-30.
[2] Cf., e.g., G. Peano, *op. cit., Notations de la log. math.*, pp. 18 ff., 42 ff. ; G. Vailati, *ıss. cit., La log. math. et sa nouv. ph. de dev.*, p. 236 ; L. Couturat, *op. cit., Princ. des math.*, pp. 2 ff., 16 ff. ; and *L'algèbre de la logique*, pp. 3 ff. (Eng. trans., pp. 5 ff.) ; A. Padoa, *op. cit., La log. déd.*, etc., pp. 19 ff., 45 ff.

202 THE PSYCHOLOGY OF REASONING

fundamental elements concerned in the given deductive theory which it is wished to transcribe. The most typical application of this is Peano's well known " Formulaire ", which thus forms a *reconstruction* pure and simple and a condensed *repertory* of mathematical theorems and their principal results, theorems already constructed and results already found by the methods of ordinary mathematics.[1]

A second advantage which logisticians have expected from their symbolism is that of remedying the imprecision of ordinary language and of thus obtaining a more delicate and more perfect means of scientific analysis and expression. Certain grammatical terms, for instance, such as the expression "some", can, through their doubtful extension, give rise to ambiguity. Other terms in common language have often different meanings according to the different whole phrases in which they occur and according to the place they occupy in the phrase, while in the interests of scientific rigour it would be desirable that to every term there should correspond always only one meaning. The "predications" of spoken language do not for the most part indicate whether the subject of the proposition is an individual or a class, in other words whether the proposition expresses a membership or an inclusion, and in the first case they do not say clearly whether the subject is or is not the only individual in the class constituted by the attribute. Similarly the verbal expression of this attribute sometimes does not make sufficiently precise what the class it represents actually is ; and so on. By substituting then, for verbal expressions which often present these and similar ambiguities, rigorously defined symbols, logic acquires —its adherents maintain—a much greater precision, which enables it to submit all deductive theories to a more precise and more methodical analysis.[2]

That mathematical logic possesses an advantage in its greater precision of expression and its greater delicacy of analysis, certainly cannot be denied ; but this advantage has been much exaggerated. It has been over-estimated both because ordinary language itself has its

---

[1] Cf., e.g., G. Peano, *op. cit., Notations de log. math. ; Introduction au formulaire de math. ;* and M. Winter, *La méthode dans la philosophie des mathématiques,* Paris, 1911, pp. 60-65.

[2] Cf. A. Padoa, *op. cit., La log. déd.,* etc., pp. 11-12, 60 ; F. Enriques, *op. cit., Probl. della Sc.,* pp. 159-161 ; L. Couturat, *op. cit., Princ. de Math.,* p. VI.

MATHEMATICAL LOGIC 203

own means of remedying by happy circumlocutions the ambiguity of certain of its forms, and because ordinary reflection applied *less to the verbal expressions which translate the reasoning than, independently of these, to the essential reasoning itself as a series of imagined "tangible" experiments*, i.e. as a process imagined and followed by the "mind's eye"—applied, in short, to the actual reasoning based on *things* and not at all to its enunciation by means of *words*—remains and always will remain, in the majority of cases, the best way, although a less methodical way, of avoiding erroneous conclusions. In this way, in fact, we avoid from the outset, the dangers which always arise, in judging of the validity of mental combinations and conclusions, from losing sight of these combinations, which it should be the function of language merely to recall to the memory, and thus from having to trust exclusively to language itself, or to any other process whatever of formal expression, which may be all the while nothing but a clumsy and more or less untrustworthy translation of these mental processes : "There is ", writes Jevons, "no worse habit for a student or reader to acquire than that of accepting words instead of knowledge of things. On this account we should lose no opportunity of acquainting ourselves, by means of our senses, with the forms, properties, and changes of things, in order that the language we employ may, as far as possible, be employed *intuitively*, and we may be saved from the absurdities and fallacies into which we might otherwise fall ".[1]

A third advantage, sought by Leibnitz himself, is that of arriving, with a view to the economy of mental labour, at the "mechanisation" of reasoning, by reducing it to simple transformations of formulæ, performable according to fixed and so to speak automatic rules as in algebra. It was hoped at the same time that by thus facilitating all the possible combinations between symbols it would be possible to attain, here too, to the discovery of continual new results, a great part of which would on the contrary have escaped ordinary reasoning limited as this is to the mental combination of operations and experiments which are tangible to the imagination. In other words, it was hoped that logistic, as an instrument of analysis, by discovering and bringing into

[1] S. Jevons, *op. cit., Elementary Lessons in Logic*, pp. 59-60.

204 THE PSYCHOLOGY OF REASONING

evidence the constitutive elements of all possible reasonings, would go on to reach, as for instance has in fact happened in chemistry, new syntheses and new complex results by associating these elements one with another in the most varied ways.[1]

But it follows from our whole exposition that it is idle to hope that logical symbolism can, as regards fecundity, ever be compared even distantly with algebraic symbolism. Logical calculation in fact by its very nature is and can only be a means of verification never of discovery. It can be like the microscope, like the eyepiece of the watchmaker, which enables the absence or presence of some slight imperfection in the minute and complicated cog-wheels of the mechanism to be observed when this has *already been constructed*, but can be of no assistance *in imagining* this mechanism. It has been said with justice that logistic can produce experts in controlling reason, but not inventive reasoners; that it can be a support preventing falls, for one who is not sure of himself, but that it cannot give wings to the constructive imagination required for a new reasoning; that it is to true fecund reasoning what metrical knowledge and harmony are to the creations of poetic and musical genius; and that the facts demonstrate that it has never by itself solved a single problem or ever even in part contributed to the creation of any new theory.[2]

This *aridity* or *sterility* of logistic, so markedly opposed to the great fertility of algebra, resides, we repeat, in its very nature. And this for two reasons of a fundamental kind.

In the first place, the fact that logic does but consist essentially of operations of *cataloguing* products, already obtained by means of creative reasoning, necessarily implies the prior work of this last in order to supply logistic itself, in all its applications, with matter upon which it can be exercised. Not until inventive reasoning

---

[1] Cf., e.g., G. Vailati, "Sul carattere del contributo apportato dal Leibniz allo sviluppo della logica formale", in *op. cit.*, *Scritti di G. Vailati*, pp. 619 ff.; L. Brunschvicg, *op. cit.*, *Les étapes de la philos. math.*, pp. 375, 402; A. Padoa, *op. cit.*, *La log. déd., etc.*, p. 839.

[2] Cf., e.g., L. Couturat, *op. cit.*, *Princ. des math.*, pp. 34-35; A. Padoa, *op. cit.*, *La log. ded., etc.*, pp. 15-16; H. Poincaré, "Les mathématiques et la logique", *Rev. de Métaph. et de Mor.*, May 1906, p. 295; L. Couturat, "Pour la logistique", *Rev. de Métaph. et de Mor.*, March 1906, p. 215; M. Winter, *op. cit.*, *La méth. dans la philos. des math.*, pp. 60-65.

MATHEMATICAL LOGIC 205

urged by the free play of imagination has led to fresh results, can one set to work to put these results patiently and methodically in order. Deduction, whether syllogistic, or still more logistic, can proceed step by step and methodically only in the ordering phase of reasoning, not in the creative phase where the imagination rules and should rule as sovereign power.[1]

In the second place, if we renounce any descent to some application, then the too great *indeterminateness* in the very nature of the phenomena with which the merely imagined operations which constitute logistic are concerned, removes all possibility of the combining imagination being exercised in these merely imagined operations. In fact, whereas in algebra, as we have seen, algebraic symbolism enables the combining imagination, even in the absence of a more concrete and synthetic signification, to form none the less in all cases a sufficiently tangible idea of the facts upon which it has to operate, and this thanks to the *homogeneity* of the phenomena that the symbolism itself represents, which are all of quantitative nature ; in logistic, on the contrary, the great indeterminateness of the symbols causes them indistinctly and simultaneously to represent *the most heterogeneous phenomena possible*, so that all possibility comes to be lost of any concrete interpretation whatsoever, even the most remote interpretation, which can awaken in the reasoner *an interest in his own reasoning* and at the same time open to him *a synthetic view of this last as a whole*. Without this interest, he loses all incitement to imagine combinations capable of leading to the desired goal, or, in any case, to any result which can seem of importance ; while without this synthetic view of the whole of the reasoning, he lacks even a criterion of any sort by which to evaluate and choose between the infinity of symbolic combinations, which can indifferently be obtained by the accidental play of mechanical calculation.[2]

In other words, when abstraction passes a certain limit and reaches the point of including under its concepts things as heterogeneous as possible, that is

---

[1] Cf., e.g., E. Mach, *op. cit., Erkenntnis und Irrtum*, p. 318.

[2] Cf. H. Poincaré, " Les math. et la log." in *op. cit., Science et Méthode*, p. 158, " Les définitions mathématiques et l'enseignement ", *ibid.*, pp. 133-134, 137 ; A. Voss, *op. cit., Ueber das Wesen d. Math.* p. 28.

206 THE PSYCHOLOGY OF REASONING

to say when *abstraction* becomes *complete indetermination*, then all the advantages which are always gained by passing from a concrete and particular reasoning to one which is more abstract and more general—and Russell claims that we ought to gain them in their highest degree in logistic—all these advantages on the contrary cease; precisely because the incitement *to new imagined experimental researches* is by this made impossible. The incitement, that is, to try new combinations in the most varied directions, an incitement which comes from the use of images, of concrete representations, into which any concept, however abstract, which contains things capable from some point of view at least of being considered as homogeneous, can always be translated.[1]

Further, whereas algebra, although operating by its symbolism upon phenomena already in themselves sufficiently tangible to the imagination because homogeneous in nature, is in spite of this continually driven, as we have seen—and analytic geometry, mechanics, mathematical physics in general and symbolic inversion itself are cases in point—to "make concrete" and "synthetically objectify" its symbols and formulæ as much as possible, and this precisely with a view to exciting and stimulating the combining "imagination", logisticians, on the contrary, have made it a point of honour to render their symbols as little concrete as possible, emptying them with the most scrupulous and meticulous care of all contents of intuitive evidence, in any case of everything capable of giving the imagination a point of support. By this, logistic, already sterile by its very nature, came deliberately to increase this sterility still further.[2]

Finally, we shall not linger over the last, the most exaggerated pretension of certain logisticians, Russell and Couturat for example, that logistic can serve by itself for the construction of the whole of mathematics without needing the help of further inductions. The fact alone that logistic is in itself merely a method of cataloguing, capable of serving for all possible kinds of imagined operations or experiments and for their

---

[1] Cf. B. Russell, " L'importance philosophique de la logistique ", *Rev. de Métaph. et de Mor.*, 1911, p. 286 ; E. Mach, *op. cit., Erk. u. Irrt.*, p. 249.
[2] Cf., e.g., L. Couturat, *op. cit., Princ. des Math.*, pp. 7-8.

MATHEMATICAL LOGIC 207

results, implies that, in order to descend from this very general order of cataloguing to particular cataloguings, holding only for given categories of operations or experiments, it is necessary further to know the particular properties which differentiate these given categories from all others. We know, indeed, that in their definitions, those for instance of the arithmetical elements and of the operations to be performed upon them, logisticians do nothing but express the fundamental properties of arithmetical operations, which arithmetic and algebra themselves have shown to be sufficient to serve them as a basis from which to deduce their whole admirable edifice.[1]

Thus we can conclude that if logistic, as a system of international steno-ideographic transcription, has attained the goal which was proposed for it, and if, as a system of controlling logical rigour, it can at times be useful, it is on the other hand, condemned, as a means of discovery, to the most complete sterility ; and still less can it pretend to be by itself the fertile source of the whole of mathematical science.

Psychologically then, we should be completely mistaken if we hoped from the symbolism of logistic, even in the remotest degree, the truly immense advantages that its own symbolism has yielded in mathematics properly so called.

With this we have completed this rapid, but at the same time perhaps too lengthy excursion into the field of the higher forms of reasoning. It appeared to us necessary, in order to bring clearly into evidence that the fundamental nature of reasoning, as a series of merely imagined operations or experiments, remains without change even in cases where an abstractness pushed to its extremest limit and an excessively complex symbolic form might at first sight succeed in concealing or even disguising this fact.

The very name of "calculus", after all, still retained

---

[1] Cf., e.g., L. Couturat, *op. cit.*, *Princ. des Math.*, pp. 5, 25-26 ; H. Poincaré, "Les Math. et la logique", in *op. cit.*, *Science et Méthode*, pp. 164-170 ; M. Winter, *op. cit.*, *La méth. dans la philos. des math.*, pp. 48, 72, 98-100 ; G. L. de Pesloüan, *Les systèmes logiques et la logistique*, Paris, 1909, p. 269.

208 THE PSYCHOLOGY OF REASONING

by the operations of mathematics, would have sufficed alone to testify in an indelible manner that the present day splendour of the supreme forms of reasoning derives its humble origin from the very first painful and material operations of counting, which our distant ancestors performed at first upon heaps and later upon rows of pebbles. It is from such modest and practical beginnings that the creative imagination, through the genius of infinite generations of chosen spirits, has boldly set out to construct the rich and marvellous edifice which present day mathematics presents.

By this, then, mathematics supplies us with the typical example and the supreme crown of true or "constructive" reasoning, the form to which we have until now confined our study, the form, that is to say, which *creates new accounts or histories of things*, by the mental combination of merely imagined experiments, and so arrives at the discovery of *new facts, new connections between phenomena*, exactly as does the scientist in the laboratory, who actually performs his experiments which lead him to new results.

But by the side of this "constructive" reasoning, another form of reasoning has appeared and been developed which represents *psychologically*, we may say, a deviation, an aberration from true and proper reasoning. Instead of constructing new combinations of experiments and thus tending to the discovery of new facts, this derived and debased form seeks *to classify, to present* facts already known, in one fashion rather than another.

This is the "intentional" reasoning, which we will examine in the next two chapters.

CHAPTER X

"INTENTIONAL" REASONING

I: Dialectic Reasoning

IN our previous enquiries into the nature, evolution and higher forms of reasoning, we found that it was always the object of the reasoner to foresee, by means of suitable series of experiments only mentally performed and certain imagined "histories of things", the result to which the performance of a given action would lead him ; or, more generally, to discover truths yet unknown, that is to say new derivations of one group of phenomena from another.

In such reasoning, the reasoner has at the outset no intention or desire to maintain certain points at the expense of certain others. He wishes only to discover *the truth*, whatever it may be. The "intentional" reasoner, with whom we must now occupy ourselves, starts reasoning in order to try to demonstrate the accuracy of definite assertions in which he has a particular interest. In the one case the reasoner does not know in advance the final result of the new series of imagined experiments, any more than the experimentalist knows the result of certain experiments which he sets himself to perform for the first time. The second, on the other hand, already knows the result of his reasoning *because he desires it*.

Further, the reasoner who creates, by his own imagination, new combinations of mental experiments, "constructs" new histories of things, "produces", if only mentally, new facts in the true and proper sense of the word, which enrich the inheritance of human knowledge, exactly as does the scientist by experiments actually performed. The "intentional" reasoner is inclined, as we shall see, rather to "classify", to "present", objects and phenomena already known,

210 THE PSYCHOLOGY OF REASONING

in some particular way, than to endeavour to discover new facts.

It is clear that such "intentional" reasoning must, on account of this different function, present aspects and peculiarities very different from "constructive" reasoning with which we have been exclusively occupied up till now. We must therefore make a rapid examination of its fundamental characteristics, in order to complete our psychological analysis of reasoning in general.

It will be sufficient to confine ourselves here to the study of the two principal varieties of "intentional" reasoning, the dialectic and the metaphysical, beginning with the former.

Dialectic Reasoning

The nature of intentional reasoning in general, as of dialectic in particular, is, as we said, "classificatory", whether it takes the classical form of the explicit syllogism, or assumes other forms, more or less similar, which do not alter the substance of it. These syllogistic forms do not, however, belong exclusively to intentional reasoning in general, and dialectic in particular. Indeed, in the preceding chapter, we saw that they may serve to express all constructive reasoning also. But while in the latter they have quite a secondary or subsidiary function of simple control, and can only be used when constructive reasoning has accomplished its work and already produced, mentally, the new material on which this function of control can be exercised, in intentional reasoning, on the other hand, and in dialectic in particular, they come into the foreground. Their function becomes primary instead of secondary, which is possible since they work on material which exists already and need not be created.

It is then necessary to examine afresh as briefly as possible the *psychological* nature of the syllogism and other similar forms, so as to understand the great importance of these forms in intentional reasoning in general, and in dialectic in particular.

At the beginning of our remarks on mathematical logic, we saw that any reasoning, *qua* connected series of imagined experiments, implies of itself, as regards each of these experiments, a corresponding process of induction, unobserved perhaps, by means of which we

DIALECTIC REASONING 211

infer that the result obtained by a certain experiment or experiments, actually performed in the past, can also be attributed to the similar experiment now simply thought of. This is spontaneous inference from particulars to particulars, as J. S. Mill has so well remarked; an inference which does not involve our having passed through the corresponding definite general proposition, represented by the major premise of the syllogism. The particular series of imagined experiments by means of which the different transformations of the object which excites our interest at the moment succeed each other, having been thus accomplished, the attention of the reasoner, at first turned wholly towards the creative act, can then retrace the road at first traversed rapidly. It can stop at each step in order to control and verify, on the basis of his own memories evoked with greater care, whether each result attributed to each mental experiment is really correct ; whether, that is to say, each of the inductions on which the reasoning is based is legitimate. We have thus— as we have already remarked—*a different mode of distribution of attention* which aims at rendering explicit each of these inductions.

This process of rendering explicit each induction gives rise to operations of *classification* and *cataloguing*, for it consists in showing that all the objects of such and such a class, once submitted to such and such an experiment, present such and such attributes, that is to say, are contained in such and such another class. It is just in this classification and cataloguing that what is called the syllogism consists. For example, our mental experiment, of which we have already spoken, with the metal pendulum transferred from a cold to a hot room, *once it has been imagined and performed mentally*, can give rise, as we saw in our preceding chapter, to operations of classification expressed in the following syllogistic formulæ. The pendulum thus transferred belongs to the class of elongated bars ; the class of elongated bars is included in that of bars that oscillate more slowly ; therefore the pendulum transferred from a cold to a hot room belongs to the class of bars that oscillate more slowly.

The major premise of the syllogism, "rendering explicit" the spontaneous inference from particulars to

212 THE PSYCHOLOGY OF REASONING

other particulars which has served as a basis for the dynamic or creative phase of reasoning, has therefore no other use than to give a greater guarantee that the spontaneous inference is correct. The greater guarantee thus obtained depends on the fact of inferring, from certain particulars, not only another particular but all the particulars of a certain class. In this way, the attention is obliged to concentrate more particularly on this process of generalising, rather than on the act of combining the imagined experiments, which itself at first absorbs the whole attention.[1]

But these operations of *classification* and *cataloguing* represented by the syllogism, may concern not only new facts, produced by our creative imagination, but old facts also, which have already existed for a long time, so to speak, before us, and which are the result, now old, of past observations and experiments, perhaps even of our everyday life. The chief function of the syllogism in the first case is, as we said above, to control and verify, by rendering each of the inferences from particular cases to particular cases explicit, the accuracy of the constructive reasoning based on them. In the second case, it is rather to impel us, when we are in the presence of a certain object that we usually observe from a particular affective point of view, to regard it from a different one, or to remind us of the observations and experiments already performed on it in the past, the results of which are again of importance from this point of view which now interests us in a particular way. The nature of the syllogism, which is that of an actual act of *classification* and *cataloguing*, is more accentuated in this case, *in so far as its aim now becomes principally or exclusively to recall the attention to the attributes of the phenomenon which render it capable of being placed in the class in which we desire to place it.*

Let us take, for example, the famous syllogism which "proves" that the king is mortal. Let us examine the *psychological* function that it may actually have in certain cases. Let us suppose, for this purpose, the passing of a royal procession. The proud mien of the king, the gorgeous procession which follows him and all the other external signs of his power set up in the spectator an affective-emotive state of fear and

[1] *Cf.* J. S. Mill, *op. cit., A System of Logic,* Vol. I, p. 219.

DIALECTIC REASONING 213

admiration together, very different from that of pity which is aroused by the image of one of our fellows in a dying condition, of his impotence to do harm, and even his need of help. In ancient times, the impression of power that the king thus succeeded in giving was such that it could never spontaneously occur to his loyal subjects that some day he also must die. But a good logician, animated by hostile feelings towards the monarch, would have been able to recall them to the reality of things by the syllogism : All men are mortal, the king is a man, therefore the king is mortal.

In this case the syllogism has evidently the *psychological* function of impelling the observer to notice, among all the king's attributes, solely that which interests a new affective point of view, and which makes the king equivalent, from this new affective point of view, to the objects of another class, so different from that in which he had been placed by the feeling of fear and admiration of his faithful subjects.

Of the numerous sensible properties of an object, we discover, indeed, in any act of perception, whether material or mental, only those things which interest some affectivity ; and the more numerous the different affective points of view from which an object is considered, the more complete becomes the perception, material or mental, that is gained of it in this way. So that the syllogism appears to us, when it has a true psychological function, *as a guided mental perception, as a perceptive completion caused by a new point of view, from which follows a new cataloguing also of the object itself.*

It is just in this action of the syllogism of impelling consideration of an object from a well determined point of view, in such a way that certain of its attributes do not pass unobserved and certain results of observations or experiments made on the object in the past do not remain forgotten, that the whole rôle and importance of the syllogism in such cases consist. If this particular attribute does not pass unobserved, or if the result of a past observation or experiment does not remain forgotten—as in the example quoted by Mill of the child who, having once been burnt by a candle, has no need of the explicit generalisation " flames burn " in order to keep him from attempting the painful experiment again—the syllogism is completely useless. But if

214 THE PSYCHOLOGY OF REASONING

this particular attribute tended to pass unobserved, or if the result of an observation or experiment in the past threatened not to be evoked, without the express recall of the attention to it, as in the case of the subject impressed too vividly by the gorgeous display of the power of the king, then the function of the syllogism may become not only useful but necessary ; just as it is also necessary, even in direct observation, to place oneself at different affective points of view, if we do not wish certain sensible qualities that we have before our eyes to escape us.

This psychological function of guiding, or completing the mental perception of a certain object or phenomenon in a new direction, in order to present it as belonging to the class in which we desire it should be placed, is also exercised by all the other forms of *dialectic arguments*.

Let us consider, for example, what is called the *principle of contradiction*, of which the *reductio ad absurdum* is only a particular case. Such a principle rests psychologically wholly on the reciprocal inhibition of antagonistic images. Two contradictory assertions always represent two images which never having been presented together in our past experience, or, better still, one of them having always disappeared at the moment when the other appeared, are inhibited reciprocally— just as, in stereoscopic experiments on the struggle of visual fields (Wettstreit der Sehfelder), the two different sensations or images which tend to be produced at the same instant, the one in one eye and the other in the other eye, inhibit each other. Consequently, the dialectician who desires to prove the non-existence of a certain attribute in an object, and so to show that it does not belong to a certain class, will try to emphasise some other attribute of the object itself which contradicts, *i.e.* inhibits, the antagonistic image of the attribute which is to be excluded. Thus Dante makes the good logician of the "black cherubim," who disputed the soul of Guido da Montefeltro with Saint Francis, say, "He who does not repent cannot be absolved, nor can one repent and wish at the same time, because of the contradiction which does not allow of it". The image of a man who is about to sin, emphasised by the reference to the villainous advice given by Guido da

DIALECTIC REASONING 215

Montefeltro to Boniface VIII, inhibits that of a man who was repentant at the same moment, an image which St Francis tried to make prevail; and it is by the successful negation of the latter attribute that the devil succeeds in persuading St Francis also that the disputed soul should be classed, not among those which are pardonable, but rather among the damned.

The *dilemma* or *reasoning by exclusion* also rests entirely on the eliminatory principle of contradictory ideas, which here too succeeds in completing the mental perception of an object in a certain direction. A man, for example, is found dead in a room, killed by a pistol shot, the pistol being found on the floor of the room. The man has either killed himself, or been killed; but the ball has penetrated at a certain point of the body which shows that he could not have killed himself; therefore he has been killed. Here reasoning consists in a double series of evocations, with the addition of the inhibition of one of these series. The sight of the body and the weapon evokes, as an integration of the fact before our eyes, the image of a man killing another man as much as that of a man killing himself, and it evokes only these two images. The mental perception of the suicide, thus completed, includes the gesture of the man directing the weapon against himself, and, consequently, the possible point or points of the body towards which the weapon could be directed. But the actual proof that the point at which the ball entered is none of these points, but rather such that the imagination cannot possibly construct an image of a man directing the weapon towards himself at such a point, inhibits the idea of a suicide. So the only evocation not inhibited is the homicide. The emphasis given to one of the attributes of the body, viz. the point where it was struck, thus guides and fixes the completion of the mental perception of the fact before us in the direction which may interest us at the moment, by the indirect means of inhibiting the other concurrent and antagonistic image.

Even the familiar argument, "*a farthing is a farthing*", is no exception to the rule. For example, to the reproach of having given only a farthing to a beggar, the niggard may reply: "*a farthing is always a farthing*", thus drawing attention to the fact that even a farthing possesses a

216 THE PSYCHOLOGY OF REASONING

certain exchange value, not to be disdained by one for whom a piece of bread is enough to live on. In Zola's *Pot-Bouille*, occurs the following dialogue : " 'Leave your papers alone ; they get on my nerves '—' But, my good woman, I am addressing wrappers '. ' Oh yes ! your wrappers at three francs a thousand ! As if you could marry your daughter off with those three francs ! ' —' *Three francs are three francs* ', he replied, in his slow weary voice. ' Those three francs allow you to buy ribbons for your dresses '." Berthelot himself begins one of his official reports on the methods of preventing explosions of powder-magazines with these words : " *an explosive is an explosive* ; it should be surrounded with constant precautions ". Which means : an explosive, that is to say this substance which has the essential property of exploding at the right moment, has also the capacity of exploding with facility, even when an explosion is not desired. The argument "a farthing is a farthing " then consists in drawing attention to a new attribute of the object referred to, and it does this by the repetition of the name. By this means the speaker is notified that in introducing such an object into the discussion for the defence of his own views, he has overlooked some of its attributes which are contrary to his thesis.[1]

The function of the syllogism and other dialectic forms being only that of *guided mental perceptions* of a given object or phenomenon, that is to say of *mental perceptions completed in the particular direction which especially interests us*, we can well understand the importance that they acquire in "intentional" reasoning. Such reasoning aims, as we have said, less at seeking new combinations of experiments simply thought of, and constructing new "histories of things" so as to succeed in discovering new facts or new relations between phenomena, than at classifying or cataloguing already existing material, in one manner rather than another.

That the work of classification or cataloguing is the true and proper function of all dialectic reasoning, may be proved by the analysis, however brief, of *legal dialectic*, the prototype of dialectic in general.

Mill himself observes that when the major premise of the syllogism, instead of rendering explicit a certain

[1] Cf. J. Paulhan, " L'argument ' un sou est un sou '," in *Le Spectateur*, Feb. 1912.

DIALECTIC REASONING 217

inference, *i.e.* being a formula which sums up particular cases, is a legal enaction, then the only thing to determine is whether the authority which declared this general proposition intended to include in it the particular case in question or not; and certainty is arrived at by inquiring whether the case possesses certain marks or not.[1]

Every code, civil or penal, is only a large set of pigeon-holes in which the different social facts which give rise to disputes are distributed. According as a certain fact is catalogued as belonging to one class rather than to another, the advantage or loss for the disputant is greater or less. Consequently, all the efforts of legal dialectic aim at classifying the facts under one article of the code rather than another.

The vagueness of most of the terms of every code makes debate possible, and such debate is really only *a conflict of classification:* "A number of legal terms and ideas", writes Maillieux, "do not receive any direct or indirect definition from the law. It is tradition, education, jurisprudence, which give them a significance." "The code of Napoleon, for example, does not explain, when it speaks of obligations of parents towards children, what is meant by 'maintenance'. In the case of dissolution of marriage, the woman is entitled to 'recompense'; what is meant by this, the code does not say."[2]

The dialectician may attempt to attain the desired classification of a fact under some particular article of the code in two ways: either by "interpretation" in the sense desired, of certain legal conceptions, or, when the latter are beyond dispute, by emphasising among all the marks or characteristics of the fact in question, only those which are likely to bring it under the convenient conception.

We have an example of the first case when the dialectician, by appealing to certain other facts of the past, which were already classified by the term under which he desires the new fact to fall, or from which he wishes to see it excluded—and by evoking these facts alone—tries to determine the attributes that any fact should possess in order to be able to enter this class.

---

[1] Mill, *op. cit., Logic,* Vol. I, pp. 215-216.

[2] F. Maillieux, "Le rôle de l'expérience dans les raisonnements des jurisconsultes", *R. de Métaph. et de Morale,* Nov. 1907, pp. 757-758.

218 THE PSYCHOLOGY OF REASONING

"Tradition", "past experience"—that is the citation, for example, of cases of prestations of "maintenance" that fathers of families were obliged to make to their sons—is intentionally submitted to a "selection", so that it helps to determine in the desired sense the attributes that the new phenomenon should present, in order that it can be classified in the same category of "maintenance" as is specified by the law. One of the parties, in consequence of differently guided mental perceptions, will tend to appeal to facts of more important prestations, the other to facts of lesser prestations, all classified equally in the past under the same term of maintenance. Both will be able to develop their dialectic reasoning by the syllogism : In "all" previous cases similar to the present, for example in respect of the economic conditions of the family (that is to say, in all those, *but only in those*, that each dialectician will have recalled), the obligation of the maintenance has consisted in such and such prestations. Here is a case of obligation of maintenance ; therefore it is a case of such and such prestations.

It is, then, in the establishment of such a major premise—which is only the verbal expression of the "mental perception", guided by the objective followed, of the *schematic* phenomenon representing the legal conception of prestation of maintenance—that the whole reasoning may in this case be said to consist : "The solution of legal problems," writes Maillieux again, "depends almost entirely *on the evocation suggested by the text.*"[1]

A very large part of legal dialectic consists then in the "interpretation" or "delimitation" of concepts, with the object of classifying the particular phenomenon which is the subject of the trial, under one term rather than another : "It is not because of a determined verbal meaning", writes Erdmann, "that a certain thesis is maintained, but it is because of this thesis that the meaning of a word is artificially restricted or enlarged."[2]

"One may say", remarks the same author again, "that a large part of legal activity is based on the labour of Sisyphus of seeking conceptual limits or creating them. In saying this, I am thinking less of specific

[1] Maillieux, *ibid.*, p. 785.
[2] K. O. Erdmann, *Die Bedeutung des Wortes,* 2nd edit., Leipzig, 1910, p. 49.

DIALECTIC REASONING 219

legal concepts which do not come into common use, such as *dolus eventualis*, *premeditation*, *force majeure*, and so on, although the meaning of these terms may be doubtful; and the layman usually finds, to his great astonishment, according to the accounts given of the trial, that for every interpretation of a concept regarded as correct by some famous jurist, another authority, no less famous, will be found to dispute it. I am thinking rather of the infinite number of words in common use which have found a place in all the enactments of the law. Who is, for example, a *dependant*, who a *servant*? What is a *secret*, what is an *edifice*, what is *personal property*, what is a *business* or a *factory*? What does *at night* mean?"[1]

A burglary, for example, is declared by a law to be more serious if it is performed *during the night*. If therefore it was committed in winter about 7 o'clock in the evening, the dialectician for the defence would maintain that it was not night, while the plaintiff dialectician would affirm the contrary. The first will say, "To determine what constitutes the period of 'night-time', not the actual time of darkness, but only that during which the quietness of night exists, should be taken into account." The second on the other hand will say, "According to common usage, which does not identify the night at all with the period of the time of nocturnal quietness, the *night* constitutes the opposite of the *day*. Consequently the former begins with the arrival of darkness, after sunset and the twilight which follows." And each of them will quote, in favour of his argument, legal articles, opinions of jurists, considerations as to the purpose of the law in making this distinction, sentences in the past, etc. The whole dialectic of either will consist, in other words, in intentionally citing all the facts, and only those, which are suitable for establishing the marks that a particular time is required to possess in order to be called "at night"; and this, with the object of being able to classify the certified time of the burglary in the category of thefts committed "at night" or out of it.

In dialectic reasoning, the rival interpretations or delimitations of concepts have each, as we see, their aim. Each, that is to say, is "intentional"; so that in most

[1] Erdmann, *ibid.*, p. 35.

220 THE PSYCHOLOGY OF REASONING

of the cases in dispute it by no means follows that one of the two affirmations must be the "true" one and the others the "false". The two rival affirmations only represent two different guided evocations of past facts, two different "selections", and it depends solely *on the end pursued* whether preference is given to one rather than to the other. "A delimitation or interpretation of a word", writes Erdmann again, "always rests on a question of greater or lesser conformity to an end (auf einer Zweckmässigkeitsfrage). And so long as several objectives of nearly equal value are opposed to one another, it is an illusion to believe that only one of the two interpretations must be the "true" the "really correct", the "only possible", the "necessary"".[1]

We see then that one of the methods followed by dialectic reasoning in order to succeed in classifying the case in dispute in one particular way rather than in another, consists in the interpretation or delimitation of certain legal conceptions. The other, employed of necessity when the interpretation is beyond discussion, consists rather, as we said above, in emphasising, among all the marks or characteristics of the particular case submitted for judgment, only those which are capable of coming under the convenient concept.

In drawing attention, for example, to certain attributes of the offence or the accused, rather than to others, the accuser aims at classifying the action of the accused among crimes, and especially in a certain class of crimes, and at including the accused among the guilty, and especially in a certain class of these. The defence on the other hand by drawing attention to quite a different series of attributes or circumstances, aims above all at excluding the accused from the number of those responsible for the action under trial or the action itself from the category of crimes ; and if neither is possible, it endeavours at any rate to exclude the action from certain classes of crimes, and consequently the accused from certain classes of criminals.

Certainly the dialecticians on either side should, when it is a matter of reconstructing a fact from a few clues only, proceed by means of hypothesis and constructive reasoning proper. But even in such cases, the latter will be continually interspersed with dialectic

[1] Erdmann, *ibid.*, p. 101.

DIALECTIC REASONING

reasoning designed to present each of the clues on which the constructive reasoning should be based, in such a way as to influence this latter in one direction rather than another.

The defence will try, for example, to draw attention to secondary attributes or facts which make the alleged participation of the accused in the crime improbable. It will emphasise, for example, that it was rather to the interest of the man accused of homicide that the dead man should live, because he was his sole benefactor, and no profit could be derived from his death. The attempt thus made to present the accused as one of those interested in preserving the dead man's life tends to inhibit, by the principle of contradiction referred to above, the conception of the accused as himself the murderer.[1]

Or the defence will try to show by emphasising certain details, perhaps even the slightest, either that the alleged agreement in the evidence of two witnesses, or, more generally, the alleged agreement between the various clues to the crime, is non-existent; or vice versa, from a too close resemblance between two depositions — a resemblance purposely emphasised and exaggerated—will argue so as to create the impression that a previous agreement between the two witnesses had been arrived at, with the object of ruining the accused by collusion.[2]

The dialectician will try to classify as invalid certain depositions, after having first drawn attention to certain of their characteristics, even though the witness may be supposed incapable of perjury. He will do this by disputing, for example, that the witness was in a position to realise the true facts of the case, because, in the place where the witness happened to be and at the time mentioned, he could not have identified the perpetrator of the crime with certainty; or by denying the possibility that he could have remembered accurately all the minute and numerous details involved; or by raising doubts as to his reporting the whole truth, in consequence of threats which alarmed him.[3]

---

[1] See, for example, C. G. A. Mittermaier, *Teoria della prova nel processo penale* (*Théorie de la preuve dans le procès pénal*). Italian translation by Dr Filippo Ambrosoli, Milan, 1858, p. 69.

[2] Cf. Mittermaier, *ibid.*, pp. 72, 81, 82, 83, 160.

[3] Cf. Mittermaier, *ibid.*, pp. 63, 69, 73, 168.

222 THE PSYCHOLOGY OF REASONING

Where by an application, partial though it may be, of the theory of the legal system of proof, the law indicates certain conditions required for the validity of certain forms of proof (no relationship or at least no very close relationship between witnesses and those interested in the trial, age and number of witnesses, formalities to observe in establishing the proofs such as the oaths of witnesses, etc.), the dialectician will exert himself, by drawing attention to certain special attributes of each of the proofs submitted by the adversary, to prove that they cannot be classified among those that the law declares valid.[1]

When it is not absolutely possible to deny the crime, the defence will try at least to classify it in a category of crimes less serious than that in which the opposing dialectician tends to place it. He will try, for example, to prove that the wound was not fatal in itself, or that death did not depend solely on the poison administered. He will attempt this by leading the magistrates or the jury to entertain a conception of the lack of skill of the doctor who was summoned to attend to the injury or the feeble state of health of the poisoned man, in such a way as to present these circumstances as important co-factors in the subsequent death.[2]

If this method fails, the last refuge of dialectic will be to attempt to classify the kind of intention, criminal or not, the degree of seriousness of the criminal intention, or of the responsibility of the accused. He will discuss whether there really was a criminal intention, whether there were extenuating circumstances or not, such as the excited state of the accused man's mind at the time of the crime, and whether he was in full possession of his faculties. For example, by calling attention to the strange demeanour of the accused or recalling episodes in his life which show that in the past he has been subject to repeated mental attacks, the defending dialectician will try to " present " his client to the magistrates or the jury as irresponsible ; while by emphasising the cleverness or the amount of thought implied by his answers, or recalling a very different series of facts from his past life testifying for example to his ability in business, his careful judgment, etc., the accusing

[1] Cf. Mittermaier, *ibid.*, pp. 80, 83, 85.
[2] Cf. Mittermaier, *ibid.*, pp. 166, 167, 261.

DIALECTIC REASONING 223

dialectician will try to "present" him as quite sound in mind.[1]

And so on.

The difference then between the first and second methods employed by dialectic reasoning, in order to classify the object or fact in dispute in one way rather than another, is quite clear. The first, that is to say the method of interpretation or delimitation of concepts consists, by means of the guided evocation of quite a large number of past facts which have already been classified as coming under a certain concept, and with the intentional exclusion of many others, in completing this concept or determining it in the desired sense, so as to make it coincide with the object or fact to be classified. The second, by means of the guided evocation of certain attributes of the object or fact in dispute, and the exclusion of certain others, rather "presents" the object or the fact so as to make it coincide with the concept already established and fixed, under which it is desired to see the particular object or fact in question classified.

In other words, the first method consists in trying to mould the concept on the model of the object or fact to be classified, that is to say to "displace" or "impel" the concept towards the object or fact that remains fixed ; and this is the only possible method when the modalities of the latter are beyond discussion. The second method, which must of necessity be resorted to when it is the juridical concept that happens to be beyond discussion, tends rather to mould the object or fact to be classified on the model of the concept, that is to say, to "displace" or "impel" the object or fact towards the concept which now does not move. When neither the concept nor the modalities of the case to be classified are beyond dispute, the dialectician may naturally use both methods simultaneously, by making the conception and the instance to be classified approach one another, instead of keeping one fixed and moving the other only.

To express it in terms of classical logic, the first method aims at establishing the *major premise* of the classificatory syllogism. For example : "all thefts committed before two hours after sunset should not be considered as having taken place during the night." The second method aims, on the contrary, at establish-

[1] Cf. Mittermaier, *ibid.*, pp. 64, 178, 181, 185, 232.

224 THE PSYCHOLOGY OF REASONING

ing the *minor premise*. For example: "Such a theft was committed before two hours after sunset." But in both cases the function of the dialectic syllogism consists always and only in *guiding certain mental perceptions*, with the sole purpose of arriving at one classification rather than another.

We have seen that this is equally the function of other dialectic forms more or less analogous to the syllogism, of which we have examined above only the chief kinds. So that we can understand how the syllogism and all these other analogous forms, have, in dialectic or classificatory reasoning, a very great importance which they have not got at all in constructive reasoning.

We can therefore also infer the very different mental qualifications that the dialectic reasoner must possess as compared with the constructive. The special gift of the latter consists chiefly in his success in trying new combinations of imagined experiments such as will lead to the fruitful discovery of new results or new facts, and in always attributing, with the greatest precision, to each imagined experiment the exact result that it would give if it was actually performed ; while that of the dialectic reasoner consists rather in the promptitude with which he can *evoke*, the skill with which he can *present*, the cleverness with which he can *select* certain attributes of things rather than others, so as to succeed in the desired classification.

It must not, however, be imagined that the dialectician always tries *consciously* to alter or deform reality, so as to "present it" in conformity with the ends that he follows. It can and often does happen quite honestly, because the great intensity of the primary affective tendency in regard to the end to be attained prevents the controlling action of the secondary affectivity which would tend to raise doubts as to the truth of any assertion, or to evoke facts and attributes unfavourable to the thesis, in addition to those which are favourable. The intentional reasoner is in this respect very different from the constructive one, who does not lack this control, as he is only concerned with discovering the truth, whatever it may be, so that in his case there is no opposition to impede the action of the secondary affective tendency, *the fear of being deceived*.

DIALECTIC REASONING 225

This desire to arrive *at all costs* at a certain classification may even impel the "*intentional*" reasoner to pass from dialectic to *specious* and from specious to *sophistical* reasoning.

Indeed, the efforts of the dialectician which tend to prove—by means of the respective guided evocations represented by the two syllogistic premises—that the particular case to be classified and the concept under which he desires to see it classified are coincident with each other, run the risk of not being successful when the meaning attributed to the concept in ordinary usage is too different from the actual characters of the case in question. The dialectician, for example, will easily be able to present a theft committed at 7 o'clock in the evening, even in winter, as "not having been committed at night"; it will be more difficult for him to present as such a theft committed at 10 o'clock in the evening; and he will fail completely if he wishes so to present one committed at midnight. Even in this case he may try, however, *by quibbling arguments*, to maintain his assertion, by observing, for example, that at midnight, on account of the theatre crowd the streets are nearly as lively as by day. But the argument will become quite *captious* if the theft has been committed in a lonely street where there is not the slightest echo of the brief period of animation produced by the exit from the theatres. The same formal reasoning can, then, by insensible degrees, from being *dialectic* become *specious*, ending by being completely *sophistic*.

The last development occurs when the intentional reasoner, forced by the nature of things prudently to abstain from maintaining any coincidence between the particular case in dispute and cases of the class in which he would like to see it classified, is impelled to exploit, as *ultima ratio*, the natural tendency of the majority to believe that the same term always expresses the same thing. If, in the two premises of the syllogism he succeeds in calling by one and the same middle term the particular case to be classified, as well as the class of objects included in that in which he would like to see this particular case classified, although they are substantially quite different, he may hope to obtain also the support of the listener, by relying on the mental indolence which prevents him thoroughly examining

P

226 THE PSYCHOLOGY OF REASONING

the meaning that the same term has in the major and the minor premise respectively. The middle term of the syllogism then becomes *a really deceptive instrument, a single mask for two different faces*, allowing a spurious appearance of correct reasoning to be given to certain phrases.

The whole skill of the sophist will consist therefore in finding this single term with a double use, such as to conceal its double meaning as far as possible. Thus a reactionary may try even in a modern democracy to persuade the judge of the incriminability of the promoter of the most peaceful meeting by constructing, on the term with the double meaning "agir contre", the following sophistical syllogism : whoever "*agit contra*" the powers of the state commits an incriminable offence ; the promoter of a meeting expressing disapprobation of the policy of the government "*agit contra*" one of the powers of the state ; therefore, he commits an incriminable act.[1]

It is enough to observe here that what renders sophistical reasoning possible is solely language, which makes a single verbal symbol suffice for two objects or concepts which thought conceives as quite distinct and which it could not possibly confuse of its own accord : "If," writes Locke, "we consider in the fallacies men put upon themselves as well as others and the mistakes in men's disputes and notions, how great a part is owing to words and their uncertain or mistaken significations, we shall have reason to think this is no small obstacle in the way to knowledge."[2]

The different kinds of fallacies "of ratiocination" which logical treatises emphasise and analyse in sophistical reasoning, all rest on a basis of "verbal deception" represented by a term with a double meaning, or a double term with a single meaning.[3]

Dissertations on logic abound in rules calculated to preserve us from these fallacies, and relying especially on the correct application of the laws of the syllogism. But the rule par excellence is and always remains that

---

[1] Cf. Mittermaier, *op. cit., Théorie de la preuve dans le procès pénal,* pp. 127-128.

[2] J. Locke, *op. cit., An Essay concerning Human Understanding,* book III : " *Of Words*," chap. X : " *Of the Abuse of Words* ", § 21, p. 396.

[3] Cf., e.g. Mill, *op. cit., Logic,* vol. II, book V : *On Fallacies,* chap. VI : *Fallacies of Ratiocination,* chap. VII : *Fallacies of Confusion.*

DIALECTIC REASONING 227

of reasoning *by images* instead of *by words*, that is to say of having, as Mill puts it, "the things themselves present either to the senses, or to the memory."

To mistrust language continually, always to *translate* the different terms on which a discussion turns into the corresponding images, whether concrete or as abstract as possible, and to continue to reason "inwardly" about them, though afterwards *retranslating* the whole into the corresponding verbal symbols, is the best means of defence against all verbal "deception." It is absolutely indispensable in constructive reasoning where the creative fancy must combine its series of imagined experiments, and it is no less useful in controversy. For it is sufficient in itself to make a breach in all sophistical reasoning; and in dialectic reasoning, it serves at least to determine exactly what are the different conceptual interpretations adopted by each of the dialecticians in view of the respective classification sought for.

We have thus brought our very rapid analysis of dialectic reasoning to a close. It seems, however, to have been sufficient to prove the—*psychologically*, we would almost say *substantial*—difference between dialectic reasoning itself and the constructive reasoning studied in our preceding chapters. If both *can be* put under one and the same *form*, the syllogistic, this is due, as we have seen, to the fact that constructive reasoning, if considered not in its creative phase but in the systematic phase of verification and control, also resolves itself into a kind of "classification" of material obtained in the preceding creative phase by means of the mental combination of imagined experiments. But this classification is neither the essential nor the secondary object of constructive reasoning. It rather endeavours by the creation of new "histories of things", to discover new facts, new relations between phenomena, new truths. In dialectic reasoning, on the other hand, classification is actually the sole and essential aim, and is exactly what intentionally guides the evocation of certain past observations in preference to others, intentionally emphasises certain attributes at the cost of others, intentionally determines the interpretation and de-

228 THE PSYCHOLOGY OF REASONING

limitation of certain concepts, always keeping in view the classification to be attained.

It is this *possibility* that they can assume one and the same *form* which has led classical logic into error ; the difference—which from the *psychological point of view*, we insist on calling *substantial*—between dialectic and constructive reasoning having been completely neglected. Logicians have consequently believed that they have discovered in the syllogism, as Mill writes, "a universal type of the process of reasoning". Our examination has shown adequately, as it seems to us, that the syllogism is, on the contrary, merely the *sole form* that can be assumed by *two reasoning processes which, whether as regards the ends pursued or the means employed, are quite different from each other*, the one assuming it in a somewhat constrained manner, the other in conformity with its very nature.

In the following chapter we shall see that metaphysical reasoning, the other fundamental form of "intentional" reasoning still to be studied, pursues an end similar to that of dialectic reasoning and adopts an analogous method of procedure.

CHAPTER XI

"INTENTIONAL" REASONING

II: Metaphysical Reasoning

In the last chapter we saw that in dialectic reasoning the reasoner sets out to *classify* or *present* certain objects or facts in one way rather than another, in accordance with his aims or desires. We shall now see that metaphysical reasoning is analogous to dialectic in that the reasoner sets out to classify or present the whole phenomenal world in accordance with his inmost and deepest aspirations. In other words, metaphysical reasoning is also a process of *classification* or *intentional presentation ;* but instead of considering, as does dialectic reasoning, certain determined phenomena, it has in view rather the whole universe or large portions of it, which, directly or indirectly, may be related to the destinies or supreme purposes of human beings.

A strong and *irrepressible sentiment*, religious or akin to that of religion, leading irresistibly to its end and inhibiting every mental phenomenon, perceptive or evocative, which is opposed to it, is what chiefly characterises metaphysical reasoning in general. It may be said of the metaphysician, as of the religious man, that what matters to him most of all is not the truth but rather the object of his faith.

Without this powerful and predominant desire, his tendency to go beyond and to deny reality, to imagine and support systems in spite of reality itself, could not be explained.

Guastella's work on metaphysics, which may in some respects be called classic—a work which tries to solve the psychological problem of man's tendency to go beyond the world of experience—suffers from the fundamental error of attributing an excessive importance

230 THE PSYCHOLOGY OF REASONING

to the purely intellectual factors whereas the affective indisputably preponderate.[1]

The tendency to make the most familiar phenomena the explanatory medium of all the others, on which Guastella so rightly insists, is characteristic not only of metaphysics but also and above all of science. Purely intellectual factors therefore may no doubt have given rise in pre-scientific times to the anthropomorphic explanation of reality, that is to say to the comparison of all the other causes productive of phenomena with the act of volition so familiar to us through introspection, as well as to the mechanical conception of the world, which reduces all phenomena to those, also very familiar, of movement and transmission of movement by collision.

Purely intellectual factors are still sufficient to-day to explain the ever greater persistence, development, and diffusion of the mechanical conception, on account of the confirmation that this hypothesis has constantly received from fact and experiment. But these factors by no means suffice to account for the persistence of the anthropomorphic or volitional explanation, which is continually and completely contradicted by experience.

The persistence of the anthropomorphic or volitional explanation, which fails to satisfy intellectual needs and even aggravates their non-gratification owing to the continual disappointments inflicted upon it by the reality of everyday life and the flagrant logical contradictions which result, can only be due to motives of an affective order. It is easy to discover the origin of these affective motives in the religious sentiment, which, consciously or not, forms the basis of all metaphysical speculation.

Theological Metaphysics

Religion, whose fundamental importance, as we have shown elsewhere, dates from the earliest beginnings of human societies, has always endeavoured with complete success, by means of a continual and admirable work of collective suggestion, to connect with religious beliefs, that is to say with the theological-anthropomorphic conception of the world, all the deepest sentiments of man, such as the need of protection, and

---

[1] C. Guastella, *Filosofia della Metafisica*, 2 vols., Palermo, 1905.

METAPHYSICAL REASONING 231

afterwards that of justice which is a derivative of and a substitute for it, the aspiration after happiness, the love of life, and so on.[1]

Hence the great interest that man has in retaining such a theologico - anthropomorphic conception, on which the preservation of the supreme human values also depends. Hence too the fundamental task of metaphysical reasoning—that of saving this theological anthropomorphic conception at all costs from the destructive blows that reality deals it by continual contradiction. Such reasoning constitutes therefore a *work of defence* by the affective part of man against the conclusions at which the intellectual part would arrive spontaneously in its relations with the external world.

How has metaphysical reasoning proceeded in this work of defence? Principally by the continual *dematerialisation* or *disintelligibilisation* of the theological-anthropomorphic conception itself, for it is necessary to save this conception less for itself, than as a support to the supreme values that we have just enumerated.

"The basis of theological philosophy", writes Guastella, "is an inductive process which consists essentially in likening the causes of phenomena and their manner of acting to man and human activity. This process is afterwards masked by another, in a certain sense contrary, to which the theological concepts conform in their evolution, and which consists in assuming that God and his way of acting differ progressively from man and human action. It is, therefore, a process, which may be called, as in fact it has been, the *disanthropomorphisation* of Divinity." "The person, the physical substratum of the Divinity is gradually dematerialised, and ends by becoming a *spiritual substance*, that is to say a *quid* inaccessible to the senses and the imagination."[2]

This *dematerialisation* or *dephenomenisation* of Divinity has proceeded in correspondence with constant contradictions by reality and under their continual pressure. Indeed, every discovery of reality has been an intellectual fact antagonistic to some fact or attribute

---

[1] See E. Rignano, Essay quoted : "Le phénomène religieux", in *op. cit.*, *Essais de synthèse scientifique* (E.T. *Essays of Scientific Synthesis*).

[2] Guastella, *op. cit.*, *Fil. d. Met.*, Vol. I, p. 129.

232 THE PSYCHOLOGY OF REASONING

supposed until then to belong to Divinity, and tending in consequence to inhibit it, and has thus dealt a formidable blow not against the Divinity, that had to be saved at all costs, but against such and such a material residue, still attached to the conception of God, which in its origins was completely anthropomorphic and material. By thus making the latter ever more unintelligible and unimaginable, it was sheltered from the destructive and inhibitive action of reality.

At the same time it was necessary to save the supreme human values connected with the idea of Divinity. This was done by attributing arbitrarily and intentionally to the latter a series of attributes, themselves also dematerialised as far as possible and perhaps even incompatible with each other, but of such a nature as to ensure the desired preservation of these supreme values. The idea of the Divinity thus ended by being reduced *to a simple, quite arbitrary and intentional conglomerate of attributes*, purely, or almost purely verbal, a conglomerate which was no longer capable in its ensemble of any intellectual representation :

"The ensemble of the metaphysical attributes imagined by the theologian", writes James,—(God, being *First Cause*, possesses an existence *a se;* he is *necessary* and *absolute, absolutely unlimited, infinitely perfect;* he is *One* and *Only, Spiritual, metaphysically simple, immutable, eternal, omnipotent, omniscient, omnipresent,* etc.)—" is but a shuffling and matching of pedantic dictionary adjectives. One feels that in the theologians' hands, they are only a set of titles obtained by a mechanical manipulation of synonyms ; verbality has stepped into the place of vision, professionalism into that of life." [1]

That a divinity thus postulated can no longer satisfy any intellectual need, and consequently have only a purely affective value, is proved above all by the fact of the absolute unintelligibility and unimaginability of this Divinity as of most of his attributes : and in the second place by the irreconcilability either of certain of the attributes with each other, though all are necessary in this ensemble in order to guarantee the desired

---

[1] W. James, *The Varieties of Religious Experience*, London, 1906, pp. 439-446.

METAPHYSICAL REASONING 233

preservation of values, or of attributes insufficiently dematerialised with the facts of reality.

The logical incompatibility of some of these attributes is indicated for example, by Guastella, as follows : —"We can imagine a changeless being", he writes, "but it is then impossible to imagine him as endowed with intelligence, reason and will. A mind, that is to say a complete representation of reality, which is not composed of successive states is a contradiction in terms". The same may be said of the will. In spite of this, the contradictory attributes of immutability, intelligence, and will are assigned to the metaphysical entity of God. In the next place, by attributing to God an "instantaneous eternity," that is to say an eternal duration not composed of successive moments, an indivisible eternity, an immovable and infinite present, "we end with the most flagrant contradiction, the assignation to the same subject of two opposite attributes : the maximum and the minimum, infinite duration and existence which is exhausted in an indivisible moment." No less irreconcilable is the omnipresence of God with his simplicity and indivisibility : "God is present in all things, because he works the whole in everything, and in each thing he is wholly present because he is simple." Similarly the immutability and simplicity of God are logically incompatible with his act of creation, each act implying of itself some modification in its creator.[1]

But the almost complete unintelligibility of these entirely dematerialised attributes, and the great elasticity which they consequently possess, always allow the metaphysical dialectician to try to present them as not incompatible with each other. Thus, for example, as regards the logical incompatibility between the immutability and simplicity of God on the one hand and the act of creation on the other, "the metaphysician will say that God, while modifying himself in order to produce the world, has been neither annihilated, nor has given to the world a part of his substance ; that in spite of this modification, he has not lost his immutability and his simplicity ; and it is thus because the divine substance, although single and very simple, exists simultaneously in two states : in the one without

[1] Guastella, *op. cit.*, *Fil. d. Met.*, Vol. I, pp. 132-136.

234   THE PSYCHOLOGY OF REASONING

modification, when it is God himself, the creator, and in the other modified, when it is the universe, the things created." A pure play of words such as the following thus results : " The nature of God is essentially different from that of the creature that he creates, although the substance of the creature is fundamentally only the substance of God." [1]

Other attributes, instead of being irreconcilable with each other, are, as we noted, irreconcilable with the facts ; they are attached too directly to certain human values that have to be conserved to allow of their dematerialisation so complete as to be no longer exposed to contradictions by reality : " There is no evidence whatever in Nature for Divine Justice ", remarks J. S. Mill, " whatever standard of justice our ethical opinion may lead us to recognise ". " If the motive of the Deity for creating sentient beings was the happiness of the beings he created, his purpose, in our corner of the universe at least, must be pronounced, taking past ages and all countries and races into account, to have been thus far an ignominious failure." [2]

In these cases, the metaphysical theologian attempts either simply to deny the obvious contradiction with reality, as when he asserts that the limitation of human intelligence cannot succeed in understanding the ends pursued and the means employed by the infinite divine intelligence ; or he creates by fantasy a new " reality ", agreeing with the postulated attributes and constituting of itself the realisation of some one of the supreme values sought after, as when he refers the work of divine justice to a supernatural world ; or finally he proceeds to try to reconcile the irreconcilable by dialectic, thus opening the way to a whole series of still more irreconcilable and inconceivable ideas. Perhaps the most typical example of this is the doctrine of free-will, that " mass of inextricable contradictions " as Bain defined it, created purposely in order to reconcile the creation by the work of God of beings who act wickedly, with the infinite goodness and power of this God.

Sometimes it is not a question of attributes in opposition to the facts of reality, or of attributes which

---

[1] Guastella, *ibid.*, vol. I, pp. 188, 189.
[2] J. S. Mill, *Three Essays on Religion*, London, 1885, third essay : " Theism ", pt. II : " Attributes ", pp. 186-187, 192, 194.

METAPHYSICAL REASONING 235

though irreconcilable with each other are united because their ensemble is necessary to the preservation of the supreme values : What in these cases is involved is rather a logical incompatibility due to the union of attributes required for this purpose with others, which, though not of themselves necessary to the purpose, have been handed down and admitted because they were at first kept inoffensive by an old tradition, spontaneous and tenacious. Here also the mode of procedure consists in dematerialising these contradictory attributes as far as possible, by putting in their stead mere verbal envelopes, void of all intelligible content, so as to eliminate the reciprocal contradiction and inhibition to which they would inevitably give rise if they were allowed to furnish matter for the imagination in however small a degree ; and a dialectic method is developed at the same time, in order to dissipate possible doubts concerning the irreconcilability of such attributes. Take as an example of such a process the primitive triads still partly capable, especially in their naïvest forms, of sensible representation, in that they were composed of three quite distinct beings having human attributes. From these we pass little by little as a result of constant disanthropomorphisation, necessary in order to reconcile these same triads, *i.e.* the three divine persons, with the dogma of the unity of God, to the metaphysical trinity which cannot itself be represented at all. Parallel with this dematerialisation, the whole formidable dialectic edifice patristic and scholastic is constructed with the object of convincing human reason of the absence of logical inconsistency in the greatest of absurdities.[1]

In short, while dialectics properly speaking, as considered in the preceding chapter, tends to *delimit* or *interpret* every concept such as those established by law, by means of the guided evocation of attributes of real facts of the past (those facts only being utilised which serve to make the concept, under which we wish to class the particular object or fact that interests us, appear to include that object), theologico-metaphysical dialectics endeavours, rather, simply to *create* or *invent* its own concepts by pure imagination, by intentionally

[1] Cf. Ch. Guignebert, " Le dogme de la Trinité ", *Scientia*, nos. 32, 33, 37 (1913, 1914).

236 THE PSYCHOLOGY OF REASONING

seeking for all the attributes capable of presenting as implicit in Divinity the preservation of the supreme values it is desired to save, and by uniting all these attributes in a single artificial conglomeration—without any care for, or in spite of, their reciprocal inconsistency or incompatibility—and finally by dogmatically postulating the existence of the entities thus arbitrarily constructed. These are the so-called "transcendent concepts" which metaphysics uses and abuses, and which, just because they "transcend", not only experience, but imagination also, are reduced to purely verbal expressions, devoid of all intellectual content and all sensible representation.

These "transcendent concepts" could certainly never serve for any constructive reasoning; for this, in order to be able to proceed to the combination of purely imagined experiments requires that its materials shall all be perceptible to the mind and that its concepts however abstract shall all be capable of presentation to the imagination. On the other hand they serve very well for the desired conservation of values, since they can be loaded with all the attributes necessary for this purpose, and because just in so far as they are "transcendent", that is to say unintelligible, they run no risk of being inhibited and eliminated by the concrete imagination, on account of the incompatibility of certain of the attributes with each other or with reality.

But this is not sufficient; for the theological metaphysician, after having created his concept of Divinity in conformity with the goal at which he wishes to arrive, instead of confining himself to the purely dogmatic assertion of the existence of this creation of his phantasy, often feels obliged to try to prove it. And thus a new and vast field is opened up for the exercise of metaphysical dialectics.

It is sufficient to quote as an example the famous ontological argument that Descartes later converted to his own use, and which starts from the two following propositions: Every very perfect being cannot but exist (that is to say the existence forms part of the perfection); God is very perfect; whence it is immediately inferred that God exists.[1]

---

[1] Cf., e.g., F. Enriques, *Scienza e Razionalismo*, Bologna (undated). Second essay : *Razionalismo e Empirismo*, Chap. II : *La prova ontologica di Dio e i giudizi di esistenza a priori. L'argomento di Anselmo*, pp. 62-64.

METAPHYSICAL REASONING 237

In this argument, the postulation of the minor premiss, *God is very perfect* appears less arbitrary than the other *God exists.* For, since the question is not to know whether God is very perfect, but rather whether he exists, we are led to confuse the assertion *God is very perfect* with the other, which is a mental fact actually verified by introspection, *God is thought of as very perfect.* As regards the postulation of the major premiss *Every very perfect being cannot but exist*, it affords us the typical example of one of the methods most employed by metaphysics in order to achieve the illusion of avoiding the arbitrary character inherent in certain of its assertions. This method consists in asserting the desired fact, not in all its nudity and crudeness, but in another form of a more general order, so that the desired fact may appear as a consequence of this more general assertion, which, just because of its greater generality and greater indetermination, can appear less arbitrary. The metaphysician thus deceives himself by "deducing" the fact that he has at heart, instead of postulating it simply and directly.

It is evident that such general propositions, invoked to constitute the major premises of similar syllogistic "demonstrations" of the desired fact, are not established by any such induction as precedes those on which scientific reasoning is based. They are rather imagined intentionally by the metaphysical reasoner, *who thus goes back from the desired conclusion in search of the premises from which it may be deduced:* "The logical reason of man", writes James, "operates in this field of Divinity exactly as it has always operated in love: it finds arguments for our convictions, for indeed it *has* to find them."[1]

But the too obviously sophistical nature of such ontological arguments leads metaphysical theologians to look for the proof of the existence of God in the facts themselves. Here again, as in ordinary dialectic, the process consists in selecting the facts most suitable to the desired end, in drawing attention to certain attributes in preference to others, and in presenting these emphasised attributes as the immediate consequence of certain attributes of God, and thus as so many proofs

---

[1] W. James, *op. cit., The Varieties of Religious Experience*, p. 436.

238 THE PSYCHOLOGY OF REASONING

of these divine attributes, and, consequently, of the existence itself of God.

Thus according to Malebranche, the simplicity of the laws of mechanics would denote that they have been the object of a choice, and such a choice would directly imply the existence of someone who had presided over it : "Having resolved", for example, he writes, "to produce by the simplest means the infinite variety of creatures that we admire, God has wished that bodies should move in a straight line, because this line is the most simple." It is in just such a way that Descartes derived the law of conservation of the quantity of movement from the immutability of God "who must conserve in the universe, by his permanent action, as much movement and rest as he has put into it in creating it."[1]

As these examples show, the metaphysical hypothesis, which is supposed to be confirmed by the verification of the facts wrongly supposed to be deduced from it and which should serve to demonstrate the existence of God, is chiefly characterised by its great indetermination. This indetermination which would be fatal to constructive reasoning, because it is concerned with determining something not yet known, *i.e.* with establishing what *new facts* are obtained in consequence of a certain combination of imagined experiments, is by no means fatal to classificatory intentional reasoning, because *the phenomena are already there*, i.e. they are already known, and it is only a matter of classifying them in one way rather than another. As regards the hypothesis, for example, which we have quoted, and which attributes to God the intention of producing all things "by the simplest means", it is not a matter of deducing from this hypothesis whether the movements of the planets should be rectilinear, or circular, or elliptical, or whether the movement of the falling body should be uniform or variable, and how variable, and so on (which is what is possible for instance with the hypothesis of Newton), but rather of taking these movements as they are already known and simply placing them in the class of "the most simple" phenomena. Now this classification is

---

[1] C. Guastella, *op. cit.*, *Fil. d. Met.*, Vol. I, 1st pagination, p. 94. 2nd pagination, pp. 449-450 ; G. Milhaud, Les lois du movement et la philosophie de Leibnitz, in *op. cit.*, *Nouvelles études sur l'histoire de la pensée scientifique*, pp. 197-198.

METAPHYSICAL REASONING 239

not only not prevented, but is rendered always possible and easy by the very indeterminateness of the class in which it is desired to place these phenomena.

It is the same with the other argument that we have also quoted, that of Descartes. From the attribute of "immutability" supposed in God, an immutability not only in himself but also in his external action, the metaphysician imagines he can "deduce" the principle that the quantity of movement in the world is unalterable, as well as the law of inertia and the other mechanical principles that he had previously discovered by inductive means. All Descartes' intentional reasoning tends therefore, not to deduce, but quite simply to classify, to present the mechanical laws, that he already knew, in accordance with a certain scheme that he has chosen as regards the attributes of God, so as to be able to prove the laws to be consequences and proofs of those attributes, and accordingly proofs of the existence of God, the possessor of these attributes. Naturally, to assign to the Divinity certain attributes rather than others, is an altogether arbitrary proceeding, so that the metaphysical dialectician has full liberty to choose them in such a way that they will afterwards serve him for classifying certain facts or laws of the real world in the system that the attributes in question are found to constitute. But, here again, the great indetermination of these attributes, thus assumed by hypothesis, facilitates the classification, where a greater precision might render it more difficult. "If there must be a close connection between the divine immutability and the constancy of a sum, why", Milhaud asks in the sequel to the passage quoted above, "choose the sum of the quantity of movement in preference to another?" Moreover the attribute of the immutability of God, if it were better determined, would be of such a kind as to place the metaphysical dialectician in a great difficulty, since the greater determination might lead to the conclusion that everything in the world, and not only the quantity of movement, must be unalterable, the whole phenomenal world and not one only of its aspects being a manifestation of God.

Finally, at other times an inductive truth is expressed so vaguely that one may afterwards present as forming part of it a totally different proposition serving to prove

240 THE PSYCHOLOGY OF REASONING

the desired existence of God. Thus Leibnitz enunciates the truth, more and more confirmed by experience as the knowledge of scientific laws extends, that every phenomenon can be deduced by constructive reasoning from other phenomena which have preceded it, if suitably combined with each other in thought, by the entirely vague proposition that there is no "thing" which has not got its "sufficient reason". From this vague major premiss he passes directly, by means of a simple syllogism, to the conclusion that the "universe" itself, that is to say the *entire series* of successive states of the world, each produced by the state immediately preceding, must have its "sufficient reason" (which will of necessity be outside the series in question, if this is taken in its totality). Now, as it may not be noticed that to say this is equivalent to considering the series of successive states of the world as non-infinite, that is as beginning at a certain moment, it is likewise overlooked that it is equivalent to postulating quite innocently, contrary to all the data of experience, a creative act out of nothing, and consequently a creator.

Even this argument of Leibnitz then proves the advantage that metaphysics derives from the greatest possible imprecision and nebulosity of its concepts. This imprecision allows metaphysicians, as we have seen, in some cases to classify under their own conceptual categories all that is best adapted to their dialectic end; and it allows them in others, as in this example of Leibnitz, to invest in syllogistic forms, apparently strict and resting on empirical bases, fallacious sophisms which would be immediately unmasked by more exact concepts and in consequence rendered impossible.

Metaphysics properly so called

The assertion of a divine being, though dematerialised as much as possible and reduced to a simple unintelligible aggregate of attributes, was, however, still not vague enough to suppress all the contradictions of those attributes amongst themselves and with reality. Moreover, the arguments that were brought forward to prove his existence did not succeed, in the face of the incessant critical work of the reason, in concealing their purely sophistical nature. Hence the necessity of

METAPHYSICAL REASONING 241

passing from theological metaphysics to metaphysics properly so called which substitutes for the Divinity still vaguer entities, more devoid of intelligible or thinkable content, yet preserving a sufficient resemblance to the Divinity for them also to guarantee the preservation of the supreme values, which were exactly what it was most important to save.

It is thus that the concept of "efficient cause" originated ; and while it was assumed that this cause was the only one capable of explaining the "essential manner" of the production of phenomena, it was yet always presented as an occult power generative of these latter. It remained a concept even more nebulous and vague than the most disanthropomorphised Divinity, because, while the anthropomorphic characteristics of intelligence or will, or in general the pursuit of an end were thereby preserved, these attributes were, at the same time, deprived of any "subject" capable of bearing them.

To renounce any "subject" whatever who might serve as a support for these characteristics, had the advantage of dispensing with the obligation of proving the existence of a certain being, whatever it might be. And the intellectual or volitional characteristics so vaguely attributed to the efficient cause, allowed it to be entrusted with the preservation of the supreme values, which were at first guaranteed by Divinity. The strong desire to be able to continue to *present* the world as being the product of an *intelligence* or *will*, which as such can be considered as a guarantee of the preservation of the supreme human values, is therefore responsible, after the overthrow of the theological conception proper, for the introduction and obstinate defence of the concept of efficient cause and all other such concepts.

In this respect, various metaphysical systems commonly regarded as differing widely from each other, all have the same substantial nucleus in common : the Idealism of Plato—and scholastic realism with its "universals" is, as Guastella rightly remarks, only a degenerate form of this, resulting from a traditionalism which leaves out of account the true *raison d'être* of the system—with its presentation of reality as the product of the realisation of the ideas of a creative mind, that is to say, the whole universe as the result of an already

242 THE PSYCHOLOGY OF REASONING

fixed design, imagined by an intelligent being; the Pantheism of Spinoza which treats reality as the immediate manifestation of the immanence in nature of the "unique intelligence of the all"; the Voluntaryism of Schopenhauer who relates to will all the productive forces of nature; the Dialectic of Hegel according to which all ideas, taking effect in reality, are only successive moments of the development of a single idea, and which tends in consequence to exhibit reality and its evolution as due to the development, in the creative mind, of a special dialectic process; and so on. All these systems, which seem to be at opposite poles, are only so many derivatives and varieties of the old divine anthropomorphism, so many different specific forms assumed by the single and constant tendency of metaphysics to make of the universe, as Schopenhauer himself says, a *macranthrope*; to give it, that is to say, a consciousness and personality, always with the intention of presenting it as a guarantee in itself that the supreme human aspirations and finalities shall not, sooner or later, by direct or indirect means, lack complete satisfaction.

There is not indeed a substantial difference in the fact that certain of these systems prefer to compare the efficient cause to the will and human action, while others liken it to the imaginative intelligence or logical process of thought. For what the metaphysician is concerned to obtain, is always and exclusively the presentation of reality as a manifestation of a creative mind tending towards certain ends. "In romantic philosophy", writes Enriques in his study on Hegel, "the traditional God inclines towards the immanentism and pantheism of Spinoza; there is nothing external to the world: it is the creative force that operates in all things." "It does not suffice Hegel that the dialectic process is applied at the same time to the development of thought and to the development of reality. He interprets this intimate agreement in the sense that the nature of the reality underlying phenomena is thought itself. Here enters, or more accurately here is discovered, a new sentimental motive of a religious order, to which the system of absolute idealism attaches itself." "Idealism", writes Guastella in turn, "unlike the other forms of anthropomorphism, takes as the type of its

METAPHYSICAL REASONING 243

explanation not our voluntary action, that is to say the activity that our mind exercises on things, but the purely internal activity of thought, and more precisely, in the systems of Schelling and Hegel, its logical activity. In these systems, there is, however, an element which constitutes a point of contact with volitional philosophy : it is their teleology, because teleology, immanent or transcendent, always involves the resemblance of the actual manner of production of things to our voluntary and external activity."[1]

It is of course in these more advanced metaphysical systems that the vagueness and nebulosity of the concepts are made more and more manifest and still further increased, quite contrary to what happens in science. The progress of science aims, spontaneously or deliberately, at ever greater exactness in its special concepts, so that the logical structures raised on them by constructive reasoning may become progressively more solid ; much as in the technique of construction the materials, from the combination of which the structure must arise, are squared as accurately as possible. But metaphysics, as we have seen, pursues quite another end. It tends towards new presentations of the same reality in conformity to its own aspirations rather than towards new constructions ; and it is therefore impelled, unconsciously or not, to use more and more vague and nebulous concepts, either because the desired classification or presentation of reality under these concepts is thus always facilitated, or because it hopes in this way to protect the intentional presentations of reality from the assaults of reality itself. Such immunity is similar to that enjoyed by the optical images of ghosts on the stage, which resist all the efforts of the real actors in the drama to destroy them by sword or pistol.

The system of Hegel may be quoted as a typical example. The associative connection of ideas by means of contrasts (which he wrongly calls logical), which is afterwards transformed into an ontological link between things, so as to present the evolution of the world as though it were governed by an intelligent

[1] F. Enriques, "La Métaphysique de Hegel", *R. de Métaph. et de Morale*, Jan. 1910, pp. 11-12, 13-14 ; Guastella, *op. cit.*, *Fil. d. Metaf.*, Vol. I, p. 196.

244 THE PSYCHOLOGY OF REASONING

principle, results in the presentation of this evolution as a continual rhythm. In this rhythm an idea is followed by its antithesis, and the latter by a more comprehensive idea, which reconciles the opposing ideas and carries in itself the germ of a new opposition involving in its turn another synthesis, and so on indefinitely. Now it is evident that this classification or "framing" of successive phenomena of reality in thesis, antithesis, and synthesis is always possible, owing precisely to the great vagueness of these concepts. So that, even if the evolution of the world had followed another course, the same classification would still have adapted itself without any difficulty. This great vagueness of concepts, let us repeat once more, would be fatal for constructive reasoning, which starts from a certain actual mode of existence of the real, and endeavours to *construct* mentally, and consequently to foresee, the mode of existence which will follow. But it is of the greatest advantage for metaphysics, because it shelters the intentional *presentation* of the whole of reality, as it already exists, from any possibility of contradiction on the part of reality itself.

We see then with what skill metaphysics properly so called has tried to preserve what is of most importance to it in the theological conception—*i.e.* the production of the world by the work of such and such an "efficient cause", intelligent or volitional—while renouncing its weakest point, the postulation or proof of the existence of any "subject" who would have had to be the support of these attributes of intelligence or will. It succeeded by confining itself to classifying or presenting the phenomena of reality as so many manifestations of these attributes, and resorting, in order to succeed in this classification or presentation, to all the arts of dialectic ; but above all by beginning with the creation of more and more nebulous and vague concepts, designed to represent and replace the attributes of intelligence and will, and capable, in virtue of their vagueness, of containing the whole reality that it was desired to prove to be at the same time the direct manifestation of these attributes and their confirmation.

Finalism, Animism, Vitalism

The efforts of metaphysics in their arduous task of

METAPHYSICAL REASONING 245

saving at all costs the values on which human aspirations converge with so much intensity do not, however, stop here. To admit a mysterious efficient cause is essentially equivalent to postulating a world-soul or will or intelligence, and so involves, owing to the diffusion in the people of the most elementary physio-psychological knowledge, the danger of unduly re-anthropomorphising the "subject" which it was desired to get rid of, and of raising the embarrassing question as to where the brain corresponding to this world-soul resides.

That is why, at first as a reinforcement, and then as a substitution, either of the theological hypothesis of a divine being, or of the metaphysical hypothesis of an efficient cause also characterised by volitional or intellectual attributes, and with the definite object of distracting the attention more and more from the "subject" which would have to support these attributes, metaphysics has very often been induced to present nature as endowed of itself with a special finality ; and this was naturally selected so as to coincide with the aspirations to be satisfied.

As with the theological so too as regards the finalistic hypothesis, there really exist certain facts which might lead at first to imagining and supporting it. The world furnishes us, indeed, in its organic part, with unquestionable examples of adaptation to an end. So the hypothesis that the universe in its entirety is adapted to an end could well claim to have been suggested by some facts and on that account to be called, at the outset at least, scientific.[1]

But this hypothesis was afterwards contradicted by the verification of the remaining facts, proving that nature in its entirety seems neither to be adapted to nor to tend towards any end whatever. Hence it was the function of finalistic metaphysics to try to present the world, in spite of the facts, as endowed with some sort of finality. It did this in two ways, corresponding to the two fundamental dialectic systems examined in the previous chapter : the one consists in looking for concepts of finality which approximate as nearly as possible to the real world as it is, the other in trying

---

[1] Cf., e.g., Mill, *op. cit.*, *Three Essays on Religion*, 3rd essay : "Theism, The Argument from Marks of Design in Nature ", p. 167.

246 THE PSYCHOLOGY OF REASONING

to present the world as corresponding or coinciding exactly with the concept of finality which has been intentionally adopted as the most suitable.

Certain of the concepts of finality thus selected—as, for example, the perpetuity and immutability of the existing order of the universe assumed to be proved by the stability of our planetary system, and others like it —bore, it is true, only distant and indirect relations to the human aspirations to be satisfied. But the end was also attained, for, once having proved a certain finality, one could easily admit or try to deduce, by making use here again of the extreme vagueness of the relative concepts, that it implied also that or those which were of more consequence ; and because, above all, any finality whatever towards which the universe tended was of itself the proof of the world-soul, intellective or volitional, to which all human hopes still remained, in spite of everything, tenaciously attached.

However, the greatest and most frequent efforts were naturally designed to prove directly the finalities that were looked upon as more important. Hence, the attempt to present the real world as the best possible. This was always attained by the usual dialectic method, that is to say, by evoking the only manifestations of the real world capable of giving any impression whatever of perfection, or, which is the same thing, of adjustment to some need or tendency of life in general and of the human race in particular. The manifestations selected were therefore such as to make the world itself appear to enter into the desired concept—a process facilitated by the great vagueness of the concept "the best world possible" which could include all that one wished to put there. At the same time all the manifestations which would have drawn attention to the great imperfections of the world were passed over in silence.

Simultaneously with these attempts of metaphysics to demonstrate a general purpose of the universe, with a view to saving en bloc the totality of supreme values, others, more modest and limited, were made to save at least some of these values, or even only some particularly significant one among them. Thus, for example, parallel with finalistic metaphysics was developed animistic metaphysics.

It has often been said that the ultimate cause of all

METAPHYSICAL REASONING   247

reasoning in favour of the existence and immortality of the soul is the natural desire to live, the spontaneous reaction against the idea of death. But this desire would not have sufficed of itself to create and then to implant so deeply in the human mind a whole legend unsupported by any fact, without the collective suggestion working for thousands of years of religious systems, to which reference has already been made. On the fragile base of the simple interpretation given by the primitive mind to certain physical and psychical events of everyday life, religion, by the exercise of its supreme social function, has raised the whole imposing edifice of divine rewards and punishments, extending further and further beyond the death of the individual.[1]

In any case with the animistic doctrine as with the theological we observe the same progressive dephenomenisation, necessary in order to support the edifice against the contradiction of reality. Starting from the primitive peoples or the savages of to-day who endow the soul with all the material bodily qualities, even going so far as to place in the tombs, food, clothing and weapons for the use of the soul of the dead; starting even from the ancient Hebrews who strewed the places which they supposed were visited by the souls of the dead with cinders or flour, in the belief that they would leave their footprints there :—we can then follow this slow but continuous process of dematerialisation, emphasised also by Spencer, which makes the soul constantly more impalpable and invisible, like some vaporous and ethereal thing, lending itself no longer to any representation whatsoever.

Sometimes this process of dematerialisation of the soul advanced so rapidly, under the spur of the need felt to protect it from the contradictions of reality, that it raised the protests of those who saw all the dangers of pushing such a process too far. "If the soul is not a body, who is this being who descends into hell after death, and remains there till the day of judgment?" asks Tertullian. "The soul? But that is impossible, if the soul is nothing; and that which is not a body is nothing. Moreover an incorporeal being could not suffer imprisonment and would be immune from punish-

---

[1] E. Rignano, essay quoted : " The religious phenomenon ", in *op. cit., Essays of Scientific Synthesis.*

248 THE PSYCHOLOGY OF REASONING

ment. If the soul is capable of feeling torment or pleasure, in the midst of hell-fire or in Abraham's bosom, that proves its corporeality, for an incorporeal thing would be necessarily impassive." But these scruples are soon completely vanquished, and the animistic metaphysics of scholasticism can seal the triumph of the purest spiritualisation of the soul, by even denying that the latter can be found anywhere. "*Non in loco sed ubi*", said the scholastics in speaking of it. " An absurd distinction ", comments Guastella, " for these words simply mean that the soul is, and is not, somewhere." But the object that this verbal nonsense has in view was exactly that of assigning two attributes to the soul, each, it is true, a negation of the other, but both useful because sometimes one, sometimes the other would be recalled according to the momentary need of the dialectician. It was, indeed, necessary to deny that the soul was anywhere in order to parry the question where it was ; and yet it had to be admitted that it was somewhere in order to soothe those who believed in its existence and in the rewards which were accorded to it.[1]

But on the other hand the excessive spiritualisation of the soul raised fresh and greater difficulties, particularly that bearing on the connection between the soul and the body. Hence we find quite a new series of dialectic efforts to solve these difficulties, or more correctly, to attempt to present them as non-existent. There is, for example, Leibnitz' celebrated doctrine of "pre-established harmony", which, while admitting that the material body could not influence the spiritual soul, nor vice versa, explains their perfect agreement by comparing it to that of two clocks independent of each other yet striking the hours simultaneously, because they have been previously regulated by their maker. Or again, there is the theory of "occasional causes" of Malebranche, which, returning to the comparison of the two independent clocks, supposes that God continually intervenes and makes both strike in correspondence every time.

In spite, however, of this continuous process of dematerialisation of the soul designed to save it from

[1] Guastella, *op. cit.*, *Fil. d. Met.*, Vol. II, CLXXI-CLXXII, CXCVI, p. 196 ; 2nd pagination, pp. 42, 49.

METAPHYSICAL REASONING 249

the contradictions of reality, and in spite of all the most ingenious dialectic efforts to parry the fresh difficulties which arose from this excessive spiritualisation, the metaphysicians were unable to set at rest the agonising doubts which continually reappeared, and with increasing insistence, relative to the existence and immortality of this soul. Again and again metaphysical-dialectic reasoning rose promptly to the defence, endeavouring to "prove" the existence of the soul and particularly its immortality, at first simply postulated and blindly admitted, and now, on the contrary, called into question. "When the belief in the immortality of the soul", writes Ribot, "is forced to strengthen itself against the doubt and difficulties proceeding from reflection, then reasoning is no longer an instrument of conjecture for discovering, but an effort to prove; it becomes a justification, a special *pleading*."[1]

This "pleading" proceeds according to the usual methods of dialectics. For example, instead of directly postulating the immortality of the soul, it is assumed, as in the case of the Divinity, to be an arbitrary ensemble of vague and ambiguous attributes, such as can afterwards be presented as implying of themselves the desired immortality. The soul, says St Augustine, is life, and the beginning of life for every living being. Therefore, it cannot die; for if it could be without life, it would not be the soul, but an animated thing (something, that is to say, which has not got life of itself, but which owes it to the presence of the soul). The soul, others maintain, is a substance or an elementary *quid*; it is in short an element; now, every element, as such, that is to say in so far non-composite, cannot cease living; the soul, therefore, is immortal. And so on.

But these "pleadings" and many others like them, in favour either of the existence or the immortality of the soul, could not fail to appear even to the eyes of the most convinced animists, of little value and little or no persuasive efficacy. So many have thought that it was much wiser to confine themselves to showing that in every living being there must be something, a *quid*, which is absent in dead substance and in the whole inorganic world. This *quid*, which so differentiates

[1] Th. Ribot, *La logique des sentiments*, Paris, 1905, pp. 99, 101.

250 THE PSYCHOLOGY OF REASONING

life from brute matter, should be and is the last citadel, still capable certainly of a vigorous defence, in which animistic metaphysics, thereby transformed into vitalistic, has taken refuge.

Here a distinction is necessary. From the scientific point of view, it may, and should be admitted that the laws of the inorganic world known at present are still very far from giving an account of the fundamental properties of living substance. Once this is admitted, it may either be supposed that it is only because the knowledge of these laws is as yet insufficiently extended that they are unable to explain vital phenomena ; or it may be regarded as probable that they will never be able to furnish the desired explanation by themselves. In this case, some may be induced to renounce altogether the idea of " understanding " life, that is to say of referring its phenomena to those of the inorganic world already known ; while others may be led rather to attempt to compare it to some " model ", which, though furnished by the inorganic world, is suitably modified by some new and different property, well defined and belonging, by hypothesis, exclusively to the particular form of energy which serves as the basis of life itself. This particular form of energy, characterized and well defined by the model thus modified and capable of sensible representation, would then furnish the desired " explanation ". It is,. for example, what the author of the present work has tried to do in order to " explain " the fundamental property of living substance, which perhaps alone differentiates it from non-living substance, that is to say the mnemonic property ; of which all the most diverse finalistic manifestations of life — phylogenetic, ontogenetic, morphological, physiological, affective psychical and intellective psychical—are only so many aspects or particular cases.[1]

But in doing this—in attempting to refer life quite simply to already known inorganic phenomena, or rather in trying to compare it to some physical " model ", suitably modified, or even recognising the failure of both methods, at any rate up to the present,—in all these cases, the constructive reasoner, who is moved only by the purely scientific desire to discover new

[1] See E. Rignano, " Biological memory in energetics ", in *Scientia*, 1909, No. 3, republished in *op. cit.*, *Essays of Scientific Synthesis*.

METAPHYSICAL REASONING 251

analogies which may allow him to reconstruct through reasoning the most complex phenomena by means of suitable combinations of more simple ones, does not set out with the preconceived intention of proving either assertion, and has no preference for one or other of the solutions. That is to say there does not exist in him any affectivity strong enough to inhibit the vision or the evocation of such and such other facts, according as they are contrary or favourable to one or other of the hypotheses, *i.e.* to make an actual state of attention impossible, in which the secondary affectivity of control, of the fear of being deceived, is freely exercised : " The most useful investigator, because the most sensitive observer," writes James, " is always he whose eager interest in one side of the question is balanced by an equally keen nervousness lest he become deceived."[1]

Very different is the state of mind of the vitalistic metaphysician. He *desires* and *wills* to prove, above all, the failure of any process that aims at " explaining " life. Nothing exasperates him more or arouses his resentment more strongly than the most objective and calm attempt of the kind which resorts to some " materialistic " hypothesis, that is to say one capable of sensible representation. In the second place, he *desires* and *wills* — and it is on this account that he combats with such vigour any attempt at a materialistic explanation — to prove the necessity of admitting as regards life some *quid*, of which it is impossible to form the least idea ; a mysterious and nebulous entity, which he does not call " soul " deliberately, in order to protect it from the objections raised against the latter, but which in his thought and desire is nothing else than the immediate equivalent for the soul itself.

Further, he often endeavours to prove the existence of this *quid*, the principle of life. And in order to arrive at such a " proof ", he resorts to the usual method of assuming as regards this *quid* an ensemble of attributes, which are really nothing else than those very fundamental properties whose explanation is being sought. He is naturally careful to present this mysterious *quid* and its attributes in the vaguest and most ambiguous way possible, so that the latter may not appear to be identical with the fundamental properties to be explained,

[1] W. James, *The Will to Believe*, London, 1905, p. 21.

252 THE PSYCHOLOGY OF REASONING

and also in order to give them an appearance of greater generality which allows even these fundamental properties to be deduced as so many particular cases. It is enough, for example, to suppose an "entelechy" at the basis of life and to endow it with the attribute consisting in giving to each being a special aim, in order to explain at once the finalism of life, and better still, to present the latter as a proof of the existence of this entelechy.

Let us be content to remark once more that as regards the constructive reasoner the absolute impossibility of all sensible "representations" of these "entities" or "principles", invoked to fill the place of the soul, would render any "explanation" of this kind completely illusory, and any deduction and prevision of new facts impossible. But as regards the intentional reasoner, this nebulosity and mystery in which these "principles" are enveloped, and the extreme vagueness of the respective concepts which result, are to him of great and unquestionable advantage. For these concepts are thus saved from all contradiction by reality, and at the same time are successfully and with the greatest facility made to include all the phenomena that it is desired should be presented as consequences or effects—and therefore as so many proofs—of the principle which is postulated as the basis of life and serves as a substitute for the soul.

The Function of Language in Metaphysical Reasoning

In the preceding pages we have frequently insisted on the great vagueness of the concepts employed by metaphysical reasoning. This indetermination and nebulosity and the consequent unlimited elasticity of the concepts or the "philosophical abstractions", would —it cannot be too often repeated—be fatal to constructive reasoning, which aims at producing mentally and consequently foreseeing new *facts*. But, as we saw, it is actually a very great advantage to the metaphysical reasoner who aims solely at classifying phenomena or objects of reality, *existing and already known*, in some conceptual frame, with the object of presenting the world in conformity to his own desires.

Now a concept, no matter how abstract, provided it be exact and imaginable, can be presented to the mind, and persist and be reproduced several times, even without the help of any corresponding verbal or graphic

METAPHYSICAL REASONING 253

symbol, which serves at most as a simple means of evocation. On the contrary it will be impossible for the mind to keep before it for long, or re-evoke several times in succession, an inexact and nebulous and therefore a continually variable and fluctuating concept without the support of some symbol which substitutes for the incessant fluctuation something which is determined and invariable. This is so true that the use and abuse of the conceptual terms, to which it is felt necessary to resort, increases *pari passu* with the increase of the nebulosity and obscurity of metaphysical speculations ; and it is precisely in mysticism, where the concepts are most confused and fluctuating, that we find a veritable orgy of symbolism, verbal as well as graphic.

Hence one of the fundamental functions of language in metaphysical reasoning is that of furnishing a stable verbal support for inexact, nebulous and fluctuating concepts to be recalled to the mind whenever required, without any prejudice to their elasticity.

Hence too the divergence of direction in the development of scientific and metaphysical language. "Language", writes Couturat, "is a system of signs, and a system of signs is only perfect, and only even useful and reliable if there is univocal and reciprocal correspondence between each sign and the idea that it signifies." Now, this is true only for scientific language, in conformity with the aims of constructive reasoning. But for the quite different aims of intentional classification and presentation pursued by metaphysical reasoning, the ideal of language is just the opposite, because such aims require that to the same verbal symbol there should correspond, according to the dialectical necessities of the moment, now one of the multiple significations that the elastic concept is capable of assuming, and now another, perhaps very different.[1]

It is the same with regard to clarity : for while the ideal of scientific language is to furnish the mind with the clearest and most concrete images of the concepts on which the constructive reasoning should act ; that of metaphysical language, on the contrary, is to use terms as vaporous and mysterious as possible. Hence the so-called terms "written in profundity", referred to

---

[1] L. Couturat, "Sur la structure logique du langage ", *R. de Mét. et de Mor.*, January 1912, p. 12.

254 THE PSYCHOLOGY OF REASONING

by Ribot, and dear to all metaphysicians precisely because they are so admirably suited both to contain everything it is desired they should, and to conceal the contradictions and absurdities of the doctrines based on the respective concepts. "There is no such way," writes Locke, "to gain admittance, or give defence to strange and absurd doctrines, as to guard them round about with legions of obscure, doubtful and undefined words. For, untruth being unacceptable to the mind of man, there is no other defence left for absurdity but obscurity."[1]

At other times, as we have seen, the metaphysical concept is reduced to a simple arbitrary aggregate of attributes which not only escapes in its ensemble all sensible representation, but is even logically inconsistent because of the contradiction that exists between certain of these attributes and certain others. The function of the verbal symbol is therefore to keep these attributes forcibly united, though all of them could not possibly be present to the mind at the same moment, just because they inhibit each other ; it being important that the metaphysician should have them at his disposal in order to deduce from the concept, from their aggregate, sometimes one set of conclusions and sometimes another, according to the presentation of reality desired.

From this arises another difference between the function of scientific and of metaphysical language. The scientific term, once it has evoked the corresponding concept, may be put aside because the concept, capable of sensible representation, remains of itself before the mind and is thus available for the respective combinations of imagined experiments in which it is called on to take part. The metaphysical term, on the contrary, in cases where it represents an arbitrary aggregate of attributes incompatible with each other, may not absent itself, so to speak, for a single moment, precisely because it is the indispensable cement, the "coat-of-mail," without which the artificial compound of attributes corresponding to it would be shattered, under the reciprocal inhibitive action of the elements of which it is composed.

---

[1] Ribot, *op. cit.*, *La logique des sentiments*, pp. 166, 167 ; Locke, *op. cit.*, *An Essay concerning human Understanding*, bk. III : ch. V : *On the Abuse of Words*, § 9, p. 401.

METAPHYSICAL REASONING 255

Moreover, the metaphysical concept, as we have seen, is very often not only something vague and fluctuating, to which the respective term has the function of giving a fixed support, nor yet an arbitrary aggregate of attributes incompatible with each other, which the respective term is invoked to keep forcibly united; but, on account of the process above mentioned of dematerialisation carried to the highest degree, it is sometimes actually reduced to a word completely devoid of all intellectual content. Now, it is precisely on account of this invaluable capacity of the word for being completely substituted for the intellectual content which at first it was meant simply to recall, and the possibility thus provided of following to its extreme limit this process of dematerialisation, so necessary to the ends pursued by the metaphysician, that language renders the greatest service and is absolutely indispensable to him. "Denn eben wo Begriffe fehlen", says Mephistopheles, "da stellt ein Wort zur rechten Zeit sich ein." A valuable property derived by the word from the illusion, acquired from childhood, that to every term there always corresponds some object.

As the old carapace, abandoned by the crustacean after shedding, retains the appearances of the animal which moulded it and which now inhabits it no longer, so the word which continues to represent a quite dematerialised metaphysical concept, is no more than a verbal *carapace*, now completely abandoned by the intellectual content for whose symbolisation it had been originally created. Without this verbal *carapace*, the disappearance of all intellectual content would involve the disappearance of all trace of the past existence of such content. But the *carapace* preserves something which, just because it proves the past existence of a concept which formerly had a real life, may quite well be taken for one still existing. So that this something, although devoid of all intellectual content, always constitutes a valuable point of attachment and support for the corresponding emotion, which is so intense that it does not perceive that the cherished resemblances no longer clothe the beloved object.

So metaphysics is not, as Spencer thinks, a disease of language; but rather metaphysics, being an irresistible reaction of the affective part of the individual

256 THE PSYCHOLOGY OF REASONING

against his intellectual part, makes language diseased, by reducing it to mere sounds deprived of meaning.[1]

This purpose is well served by the *affective colour* or the *emotive value* of the terms which are gradually emptied of all intellectual content. " By the *emotive value* (Gefühlswerth) of a word", writes Erdmann, "we should understand the whole reacting ensemble of emotions and affective tendencies that it provokes." And of many of the terms employed to express metaphysical "concepts" it may be said in general "that they only possess an emotive value, or better still, that their intellectual content is entirely dissolved into emotive value." [2]

That is to say it is a kind of "affective resonance" which remains in the terms, when all intellectual content has disappeared from them : "When language is once grown familiar", writes Berkeley, "the hearing of the sounds or sight of the characters is oft immediately attended with those passions which at first were wont to be produced by the intervention of ideas that are now quite omitted." [3]

This is true not only of the terms which directly express the objects or concepts towards which the most ardent aspirations of the metaphysician are directed, such as *God, soul*, and others like them, but also of all the terms which have even the most indirect and remote connection with these objects or concepts. A typical case is that of the term "absolute", which, because it constitutes an attribute of Divinity, has since acquired all the emotive value of the term God, so that whenever it comes to be denied—even if the natural philosopher denies the possibility of conceiving absolute rest, absolute motion etc.—the feelings of the metaphysician are offended, as they would be by the direct denial of God.

Certain terms thus become in time pure sounds, no longer evoking intellectual representations, but only emotions ; and not certain particular emotions relating to a well-determined object, but "general emotions" similar to those aroused by "a series of musical notes

---

[1] Cf. H. Spencer, *op. cit., The Principles of Psychology*, vol. II, pt. VII, chap. XIV, § 474, p. 502.

[2] K. O. Erdmann, *op. cit., Die Bedeutung des Wortes*, pp. 107, 114.

[3] G. Berkeley, *op. cit., A Treatise concerning the Principles of Human Knowledge*, Introduction, § 20, p. 252.

METAPHYSICAL REASONING 257

in the minor mode." They thus, to use the happy expression of Ribot, represent only "emotional abstractions." It may be said of them what Ribot says of terms employed by symbolist poets : "They no longer act as signs, but as sounds ; they are musical notations at the service of an emotional psychology." The metaphysician who employs them, as Erdmann also remarks, "only sets going the corresponding emotive content, devoid of meaning and thought."[1]

Consequently, though at this extreme limit metaphysical reasoning may be intellectually quite incomprehensible ; though, that is to say, it may actually become "vocem proferre et nihil concipere", it acquires by way of compensation *an emotive signification* which is peculiar to it, *i.e.* it is transformed into a kind of musical language stimulative of sentiments and emotions.

The vague and nebulous imagination of the metaphysician is thus more and more deformed and dissolved, and evaporates finally into "diffluent" imagination, as Ribot calls it, or mystical imagination, which then proceeds only by a harmonious series of emotional abstracts. It is thus, and only thus, that the defensive work of the affective part of the individual against his intellectual part, which, as we have tried to show above, constitutes the whole mission of metaphysical reasoning, completely attains its desired result.

Conclusion : Positivism and Metaphysics

From the pursuit of two ends which diverge from each other more and more as the naïve interpretations of reality attempted by primitive man are left behind, spring the two great speculative categories : the positivist and the metaphysical. Positivist or scientific speculation, by resorting to the simplest and most familiar phenomena, and using constructive reasoning, tends to *reconstruct* reality as it actually is, so as to understand, as it were, its mechanism ; metaphysical speculation, on the other hand, by resorting also to certain analogies between phenomena, which first occurred spontaneously to the mind and have afterwards been contradicted by experi-

[1] Cf. Th. Ribot, *op. cit., La psychologie des sentiments*, pp. 187-189 ; the same, *op. cit., Essai sur l'imagination créatrice*, pp. 163-164 ; the same, *op. cit., La logique des sentiments*, pp. 129 ff., 166 ff. ; Erdmann, *op. cit., Die Bedeutung des Wortes*, pp. 120 150-151.

R

258 THE PSYCHOLOGY OF REASONING

ence, tends to *present* reality in conformity with certain intimate and profound aspirations.

In order to attain his end, the positivist has no need to go beyond phenomena, to penetrate their " essential nature ", or to torment his imagination on the subject of an underlying "noumenal entity " completely imperceptible and unintelligible. He is content to admit the univocal correspondence between what happens outside us, and what happens inside us, between the external world and the sensations, for here is an hypothesis which has never been contradicted. This correspondence, admitted and continually asserted, is more than enough for the purpose he has in view, viz. to obtain the more complex and less familiar facts from the combination of other facts less complex and more familiar, and so to acquire by means of constructive reasoning the power of prevision which has made him master of the forces of nature.

The metaphysician, on the other hand, far from being content with the scientific explanation which in itself does not interest him at all, feels the irresistible need of conceiving the universe in accordance with his own aspirations. These aspirations derive their origin, as we have seen, from the intimate connection that religion, by its constant work of collective suggestion, has succeeded in establishing between the highest human values, such as life, happiness, defence against violence, justice, and so on, on the one hand, and the theological-anthropomorphic conception on the other, to the point of confusing the cause of the former with that of the latter. Hence the irresistible and irrevocable tendency of so many to persevere at all costs, in spite of continual contradictions by experience, in this conception or any other which keeps the substance of the fundamental conception itself intact. For this rescue-work the aid of metaphysical speculation was invoked, and consequently the metaphysician, as contrasted with the positivist, is constrained to penetrate the "essential nature" of phenomena, so as to discover, or at least to have the illusion of discovering, the cause, volitional or intellectual, that he desires to see at the base of all reality.

The positivist perceives clearly, by the use which he makes of it and the results that he obtains, that

METAPHYSICAL REASONING 259

reasoning is merely a combination of imagined experiments and that, in consequence, it can never "transcend" experience. He discovers inductively that certain objects or phenomena, more and more numerous and diverse from the point of view of perception, are yet equivalent as regards the result of some operation or experiment that reasoning is to perform mentally. He therefore reduces all these objects or phenomena to the sole attribute to which they owe this equivalence, so as to obtain a "schematised" object or phenomenon greatly simplified but not thereby rendered less tangible to the imagination which is to make use of it. And he utilises these more and more general and abstract "concepts", thus inductively discovered, in order to enlarge continually the sphere of action and increase the output of his own reasoning a hundredfold. But by all this he can only succeed, as he is well aware, in increasing his own capacity for scientific prevision and satisfying more completely the spontaneous tendency of the mind, a true intellectual need, to "explain" the more complicated and less familiar phenomena, by obtaining them from determined combinations of more simple and familiar phenomena. He thus arrives at a schematic and closely connected, *yet always materially tangible*, representation of reality.

The metaphysician, on the other hand, finding no satisfaction for his peculiar aspirations either in experience or in a similar "material" representation of reality; and regarding experience and each of its representations not without reason as so many negative proofs of everything that he would desire should be ; uses all his efforts to "transcend" the empirical barriers which inexorably arrest the flight of his aspirations. But all that he actually does is, as we have seen, to borrow concepts from reality, merely blotting out their outlines and vaporising their content more and more so as to render them capable of as elastic an interpretation as possible, or to pile up attributes into an ensemble logically inconsistent and unrepresentable to the mind, or, worse still, to continue to use verbal expressions devoid of all intellectual content and reduced to mere sounds evoking emotion. These "concepts" thus dephenomenised and rendered unintelligible, these "ideas" thus dematerialised, give the metaphysician the illusion of actually transcend-

260 THE PSYCHOLOGY OF REASONING

ing experience and matter, and of being thus entitled to claim the name of "idealist", in opposition to the positivist "materialist" who is guilty of considering as impossible and vain all reasoning not based on concepts, which, however abstract, are yet always tangible to the imagination.

Finally, the positivist is *resigned* to what in reality is actually inevitable. But he knows that a part of this reality, however small it may be, is capable of being modified by human action; and towards this part he therefore directs all his efforts, in order to make it as consistent as possible with his own aspirations. For it would be only a gross and vulgar ambiguity, a dishonest play with the terms "materialist" and "idealist", to suppose or insinuate that the positivist, *intellectually materialistic*, could not on that account be no less capable than any one else, as regards the affective part of his mind, of the highest and noblest ideals.

The metaphysician, on the other hand, is a *rebel* who assumes that all reality must be consistent with his aspirations. His intellect, less vigorous than that of the positivist, capitulates to sentiment. It is the rebellion of the affective part against the intellectual which constitutes the "philosophical torment" of the metaphysician, for he cannot admit that reality does not correspond with his aspirations, and he tortures his mind in order to imagine a representation of reality consistent with them and yet immune from the contradictions of experience. It is his rebellious attitude that impels him to react against science, which is most responsible for these contradictions, to combat it, and to try to discredit it; so that when confronted by "reason" he sets a far greater value on "intuition", understanding this term not in the sense of simple and spontaneous intellectual discovery, but in the very different one of belief provoked and nourished by profound personal affectivity. But it is just in this titanic labour that he vainly exhausts all his energy. He is content to dream continually of a better reality, but he does nothing to improve reality as it exists. If he is a rebel against reality in all his thought, he is *inert and passive* as regards his action, though he could in part bend this reality to his will.

But just as in the past it was society which, by means of religion, linked the supreme human values

METAPHYSICAL REASONING 261

indissolubly to the theological anthropomorphic conception of the world, so to-day, it is still society which, on account of the continual tendency of this organ to atrophy, and the consequent progressive alienation of humanity as a whole from faith, tends to make these values as independent of the old conception as of any other which might be opposed to reality, and seeks rather to attach them by other means to other conceptions which will at the same time accord with reality and with its own supreme and better interpreted needs. So that while in the past even the most distinguished minds, dominated as they were by the ideas of their environment, were also obliged to give themselves up to metaphysical speculation, to-day such speculation only attracts mystical minds, in whom the affective part reigns supreme and makes the intellectual its humble servant.

These mystical minds—which will always exist—will always continue to try to realise and systematise their aspirations and their dreams in transcendent constructions, ever new, ever different, ever vain; pale reflections of the great systems of the past, the last gleams of a great human illusion that has vanished. And these metaphysical speculations, old and new, will in their entirety constitute a great epic handing down to posterity the exploits of the tragic revolt, worthy of Prometheus, which the infinitely small microcosm has dared and will dare again to attempt against the infinitely great macrocosm.

CHAPTER XII

THE DIFFERENT LOGICAL TYPES OF MIND

In our previous studies of *constructive* reasoning, we have seen that the evolution of such reasoning presents itself under two different aspects, depending one upon the other—the passage from the concrete phase to a phase which is always more abstract, and that from elementary reasoning, conceived at the outset by a single intuitive act, to the lengthy and complicated process of logical deduction, properly so called. The first passage is due, as we have seen, to the discovery of concepts of an order always more general, that is to say, to the recognition of classes or groups, which are always more extensive, of phenomena or objects, equivalent in relation to a given end or to the result of a given piece of reasoning. This formation of new concepts, or extension of old concepts, increases, as we have shown, the number of operations or experiments, the results of which we know beforehand and which can in consequence be simply imagined. At the same time, thanks to the reduction of all the phenomena comprised in a given concept to the attribute or group of attributes only, which makes them equivalent under such and such an aspect, the operations or experiments to be performed on the schematized phenomenon, which thus come to represent the particular concept, are rendered so much the simpler. The reasoner profits, then, by this ever-increasing number of operations or experiments, of which he knows the outcome in advance, and also by the greater simplicity of the operations or experiments to be conducted mentally, in order to imagine and link together an ever-increasing number of experiences, and to complicate and prolong the process of combination ; which is precisely the application, always in a larger measure, of the deductive method.

LOGICAL TYPES OF MIND 263

I. *Synthetic and Analytic Minds*

To this double aspect assumed by the evolution of reasoning corresponds the fundamental division of logical mentalities into synthetic and analytic. The former are concerned chiefly with the discovery of new concepts or to the extension of old concepts; the latter drawn rather to the reflective, patient, and persevering combination of operations or experiments, capable of being simply imagined, in order that by deductive means they may extract from the extant heritage of concepts all that it is able to give.[1]

Synthetic minds, accordingly, prefer comparison and the pursuit of new analogies (every "analogy", indeed, being essentially no more than the recognition of equivalence with respect to a given end or result); and thus by one mental act—the discovery of a new concept or a new analogy—they greatly increase our knowledge at a single stroke, by extending all that we already knew about one category of phenomena to another category where our knowledge was much more limited. So they seem to advance by leaps, or rather, perhaps, by bold flights. Analytic minds, on the other hand, progress by means of continual trials of imagined experimental combinations, in order to establish the respective results. They prefer lengthy and patient reasoning, long and complicated calculations. Thus they appear to advance prudently and with safety, by taking only one step at a time.

It is of interest to note that in the determination of the one or the other of these two mental characteristics, which might at first sight be thought to be of a purely intellectual order, factors or elements of an affective order play a considerable part.

Every synthetic act, indeed, consisting in the sudden recognition of some analogy or equivalence in relation to a given end or to a given result, demands, at the moment of its performance, an especial and exclusive interest in the question or the problem which this analogy or this equivalence is about to solve. It follows that each synthetic act is, in the ordinary way, eminently *subjective* and is generally achieved under the impulse of a unique

[1] Cf. E. Mach, *op. cit.*, *Erkenntnis und Irrtum*, p. 179.

264 THE PSYCHOLOGY OF REASONING

and powerful affectivity. Each analytical act, on the other hand, or, to be more accurate, each succession of analytical acts, which pursue the research in different directions among the manifold results to which the various purely mental experiments can lead, testifies rather to the *objective* desire on the part of the reasoner to enlarge the field of his knowledge in many directions, than to a pronounced and intense interest in a single problem to the exclusion of all others. Thus synthetic minds imply, as a rule, *a more intense and more concentrated affective nature* than analytic minds. The latter, just because of their less affective intensity, are capable of a more diverse curiosity, *more distributed over many things at the same time.*

The single intense affectivity, present at the moment of each synthetic act, neglects all the sensorial differences of objects or phenomena which would have no relation to the end or the result which is of exclusive interest at the moment, while it accentuates and sets in relief the single attribute, or those attributes only of these phenomena or objects which render the latter equivalent with respect to that end, or that result. On the other hand, the less affective intensity and the greater affective variety of the analytic thinker, that is to say, his more dispersed curiosity, impels him to consider each detail of the object or phenomenon he studies, to break down and dissect every whole into its different parts, to consider each one of the latter separately, on its own account, and to take pleasure in the details, so losing sight of the whole.[1]

In other words, it is affective singleness and intensity in the face of a given problem, which is responsible for the faculty of abstraction, of generalization, of conceptualization, characteristic of synthetic minds. It is this which leads to the discovery, between phenomena or objects, however greatly they may differ sensorially, of the analogy or equivalence which corresponds to the unique affectivity. It thus renders spontaneous, to use the expression of Mach, "the preoccupation of the general in the contemplation of the particular". On the other hand, it is the less affective intensity and the consequent absence, even at the moment of the inquiry, of any marked preponderance

[1] *Cf.*, e.g., W. Wundt, *op. cit., Grundriss der Psychologie*, p. 401.

LOGICAL TYPES OF MIND 265

of one affectivity as compared with others, in other words, it is the very multiplicity of the affective points of view, from which the analytic regards the various phenomena or objects that present themselves to him, which causes him to see the differences rather than the analogies. Whilst "assimilative" minds, writes Maudsley, "discover slight and nice resemblances that remain imperceptible to others", "discriminative" minds are signalized by "the capacity of recognising and recording points of difference which other minds fail to observe." "The analytic", says Meumann, "*distinguishes*, he sees differences; the synthetic prefers *comparison*, the search for resemblances and analogies."[1]

Analytic minds, in short, owing to their greater affective variety, to their more scattered curiosity, can with difficulty detach themselves from particular phenomena, or particular qualities of phenomena, in order to derive from them—as do synthetics, on the contrary, thanks to the single affectivity by which they are stimulated at the time of the inquiry—a generalized or schematic vision. As a compensation for this lack of synthetic capacity, they become for the same reason much richer in particular and exact knowledge, far more "erudite" than synthetics. The too broad views of the latter, on the other hand, are repugnant to them, because, as Poincaré says, "beautiful though a spacious landscape may be, distant horizons are always a little vague; they prefer to limit themselves, so as to see the details better."[2]

Analytics, then, possess the more refined critical sense, which consists in setting in relief even minutiæ, though they may have no importance in relation to the only question upon which all the interest of the synthetic is concentrated. In their reasoning they are therefore more preoccupied than synthetics with "logical strictness", that is, with the necessity of rendering explicit, one by one, all the numerous inductions upon which their reasonings are based. For example, the celebrated algebraist Weierstrass "was a master of the art of detecting errors of reasoning where his pre-

---

[1] E. Mach, *op. cit., Die Mechanik, etc.*, p. 29; Maudsley, *op. cit., The Physiology of Mind*, p. 283; E. Meumann, *op. cit., Intelligenz und Wille*, p. 161.
[2] E. Lebon, *Notice sur Henri Poincaré*, Paris, 1913, p. 9.

266 THE PSYCHOLOGY OF REASONING

decessors believed that they had achieved a deduction of unimpeachable strictness ; with consummate skill, he replaced the faulty parts of the chain by new links in which there was no longer any risk of rupture ". One of his pupils, Hermann Amandus Schwartz, was fond of saying : " I am the only mathematician who never can have made a mistake ". " He purchased this impeccable exactitude at the cost of an extreme minuteness : in the course of his deductions he never left to the reader the responsibility of supplying the smallest intermediate step." Synthetics, on the other hand, derive their sense of security rather from their general view of the course of the reasoning, or from some analogy which serves as a support to the latter (like the old demonstration of the existence, at every point of a continuous function, of the respective derivative, by analogy with the tangent to a curve, a demonstration rightly shown to be inadequate by Weierstrass ; or, like Klein's demonstration of the existence of a certain function upon a certain surface, by analogy with the electric current distributing itself over a metallic surface). Owing to the greater need for analytics to set forth every induction explicitly, and in consequence of the pleasure with which they linger over the various particulars or qualities of phenomena or objects, they have recourse not infrequently to the syllogism, which synthetics, on the other hand, never employ.[1]

The synthetic act, by which new equivalences, previously unsuspected, are brought to light, can only be spontaneous and accidental. For it depends upon the occasional meeting of two intellectual elements with an affective element. It is necessary, in fact, at the outset, that the attribute which renders the two groups of phenomena or objects equivalent with reference to an end, or to a given result, shall present itself to the mind, sensorially or mnemonically, at the same instant both in the first and in the second group. Next, and above all, the simultaneous presentation of this attribute in the two distinct groups must coincide with the fact

---

[1] Cf., e.g., P. Duhem, La science allemande, Paris, 1915, p. 9 ; H. Poincaré, " L'intuition et la logique en mathématiques ", in La valeur de la science, Paris (undated), pp. 11-34, particularly pp. 11-12, 13, 17 ; the same, " Les définitions mathématiques et l'enseignement ", in op. cit., Science et Méthode, pp. 123-151. (English Translation, Book II, Chapter II.)

LOGICAL TYPES OF MIND 267

that the affectivity relative to the end or to the result is already awakened, or awakes precisely at the selfsame moment. Volitional or meditated can only be the deductive activity, applied subsequently to verify more accurately the equivalence thus glimpsed. "What is generally meant by genius", writes Galton, "is the automatic activity of the mind, as distinguished from the effort of the will. In a man of genius, the ideas come as by inspiration; he is driven rather than drives himself." [1]

To facilitate the threefold fortuitous conjunction of which we have just spoken, the mind must not be too fatigued, nor be pursuing at the same moment any process of combination already determined. The imagination instead, rich in an accumulation of nervous energy, and filled with mnemonic materials relating to the problem to be solved, must be free to call up at random those mnemonic materials and to effect with them the most varied and unpremeditated comparisons. A familiar example is the interesting psychological analysis made by Poincaré of the way in which his own most remarkable creations were produced. They all consisted in the discovery of some new class of mathematical objects or of some new equivalence or analogy between these objects (*e.g.* classes of functions, analogies between analytical transformations, etc.). They never took place except after a certain interval, which may be regarded as rest, following long and laborious attempts, made without success, at the solution of some problem, and all presented themselves to him with the same characteristics: "Unexpected enlightenment", "brevity, suddenness and immediate certainty." [2]

Helmholtz, too, in his famous discourse pronounced on the occasion of his seventieth birthday, thus expresses himself: "Happy ideas come unexpectedly, without effort, like an inspiration. So far as I am concerned, they have never come to me when my mind was fatigued, or when I was at my working table".

---

[1] F. Galton, *English Men of Science, their Nature and Nurture*, London, 1874, p. 233; on the spontaneity and instantaneousness of genial conception, see also, e.g., C. Lombroso, *L'uomo di genio*, 6th edition, Turin, 1894, pp. 23 ff. (English Translation, Part I, Chapter II.)

[2] H. Poincaré, "L'invention mathématique", in *op. cit., Science et hypothèse*, p. 50 *et seq.*; Dr Toulouse, *Henri Poincaré*, Paris, 1910, p. 186.

268 THE PSYCHOLOGY OF REASONING

Previous investigations of the problem "in all directions" was nevertheless necessary; but the rest that followed was not less necessary. Frequently brilliant ideas occurred to him in the morning, after the night's rest. "They came particularly readily during the slow ascent of wooded hills, on a sunny day."[1]

The true "genial idea", which opens up new horizons to scientific research and discovers new concepts of which patient deduction will afterwards make use, is, then, always a synthetic act, the recognition of given equivalence or analogies.[2]

Stevin, who discovered the analogy, as regards the result of equilibrium, between all the different cases of heavy bodies situated upon an inclined plane, and the case of an endless chain laid on a prism of triangular section and with a horizontal base; Galileo, who finds out the equivalence, with respect to the modalities of motion, between the rolling of a sphere along a slightly inclined plane, and the vertical fall of a body, or, by continually decreasing the inclination of a second and opposite plane, upon which the sphere, after rolling the length of the first, ascends to the same height whence it started, recognised in uniform motion along a horizontal plain a limited and particular case of uniformly retarded motion, and thus discovered the law of inertia; Newton, who imagined a stone thrown in a horizontal direction from the top of a high mountain with an ever-increasing velocity, until the stone becomes a satellite of the earth, and so came to recognise in the acceleration of planets around the sun, and of satellites around planets, an effect of the same kind of force as that which causes bodies to fall upon the earth; all the other similar generalisations using this "principle of continuity" to discover that certain properties, already manifested in particular given phenomena, are present also in other phenomena, at which we arrive by starting from the first phenomena and by modifying, little by little, this or that of their other properties; Mayer, who had an inkling of the equivalence between given quantities of heat and given quantities of work with respect to the

---

[1] H. von Helmholtz, *op. cit., Vorträge und Reden*, Vol. I : "Erinnerungen, Tischrede gehalten bei der Feier des 70. Geburtstages", Berlin, 1891, pp. 15-16.
[2] *Cf.* Th. Ribot, *op. cit., Essai sur l'imagination créatrice*, p. 32.

LOGICAL TYPES OF MIND 269

amount of food required by the animal organism to produce them, and thus discovered the principle of the conservation of energy ; Faraday, who imagined a given spatial structure (his lines of force), in relation to which, when conceived as a fact of very general order, the most different magnetic and electric phenomena are found to be so many simple particular cases ; Maxwell, who discovered the perfect analogy or identity between electric waves and luminous waves ; Galileo Ferraris, who, by reflecting on the phenomenon of the circular or elliptical polarization of light, obtained by combining two bundles of luminous rays, polarized at a right angle, of equal frequency but of different phase, was enabled unexpectedly to discover, by analogy, that a rotatory magnetic field should be obtained in similar fashion by means of two alternative magnetic fields, also of equal frequency, but of different phase, produced by two coils disposed at a right angle ; Davy and Liebig, who succeeded in reducing a chaotic medley of chemical facts to "simple fundamental lines", in "gathering big groups of these facts into a single whole", *i.e.* in classifying them in given conceptual categories ; Lamarck and Darwin, who saw in the slight transformations of organs as the result of prolonged use, or in small individual hereditary differences, the general cause of organic evolution of organisms ; the mnemonic conception of life, which finds in the reproduction by internal causes of physiological phenomena, produced at first exclusively by external causes, the basic property of living matter, and thus regards functional adaptation, ontogenetic development, transmissibility of acquired characters, animal instincts, affective tendencies, mnemonic phenomena properly so-called, etc., as so many simple particular cases of this very general mnemonic property ; Comte, to whose great and comprehensive mind each separate fact, whether historical or appertaining to his own life, appeared always as a particular case of some general fact or law ; Marx, who in the economic interests of the various social classes and in their consequent economic antagonisms saw the intimate bearing of the most different historical phenomena, which therefore seem to be nothing else than as many particular manifestations of this very general principle : — all these "genial ideas" are so many examples of synthetic

270 THE PSYCHOLOGY OF REASONING

mental acts, consisting in the discovery of equivalences or analogies, from given points of view, among phenomena till then considered as totally different and having nothing in common.

If genius is most frequently synthetic, that does not exclude the possibility of certain analytic minds being also capable of genial creations. In fact, reasoning and deduction being merely mental combinations of experiments, creative genius may consist in imagining completely new combinations that lead to results which are also completely new. Leverrier, for example, who by his calculations *discovered* the existence of a new planet, may perhaps be counted among the analytics of genius. And numerous other analysts, as Poincaré truly remarks, have also been genuine inventors.[1]

Moreover, *technical inventors* themselves, who, particularly for the public (which cannot sufficiently value the genial ideas of synthetic minds), typify genius, and who come upon their discoveries by testing and re-testing mentally the most varied experimental combinations and perfecting in its smallest details each new combination adopted—a Watt, a Stephenson, a Marconi —are as a rule very pronounced analytic mentalities.

But the combination, even when completely original, of purely mental experiences, is a difficulty which can yet often be overcome by patience and tenacity, that is to say, by multiplying and varying the experiments in combination, *because the mental materials to be combined are there before the thinker.* On the other hand, no patience, no tenacity, can cause the synthetic idea to spring forth, the genial idea which, instead of proceeding from combinations of materials already available, creates of itself with the analogy perceived a *matter completely new*, a *matter* whose existence has not yet been conjectured even remotely.

Examples in which the discovery of the same new result is reached both by the synthetic and the analytic method, admirably illustrate the substantial difference between the two kinds of mind. It will suffice to mention here, as a typical instance, the very different attitude of the two brothers Bernouilli in regard to the problem of the Brachystochrone (the curve joining two points in a vertical plane and such that a body sliding

[1] Poincaré, *loc. cit.*, " L'intuition et la log. en math.", 30 *et seq.*

LOGICAL TYPES OF MIND 271

upon it takes the shortest time to fall from the upper to the lower point). Johann, a mind essentially synthetic, solves the problem in one stroke by discovering *the analogy* between this fall of the body and the phenomenon of the transmission of light through a series of parallel strata of suitably diminishing density, because in that case light also travels over the trajectory of shortest duration. His brother Jacob, on the other hand, a mind essentially analytic, starts from general principles of motion which are already known, and by patient trials and analytic developments succeeds *in deducing* the required curve.[1]

To these two great categories of synthetics and analytics, the various peoples, by their thinkers, contribute in different measure. The Anglo-Saxons, the Slavs and the Latins, especially the last, thanks to their greater affective vivacity, provide a larger proportion of synthetics ; the Germans, on the contrary, are for the most part analytics. It is necessary, however, to add the proviso that the true genius, as many observers have shown, entirely escapes from the average characteristics of the race or nation to which he belongs : it is sufficient to recall the genial synthetic powers of a Leibnitz, a Gauss, and a Helmholtz.

It is precisely to the strong predominance of analytic minds among the learned men of Germany, that are due the fundamental characteristics of German science, in which, if genial intuition and wide synthetic views are usually lacking, one finds on the other hand the most rigorous deductive method, minute and patient elaboration in every subject whatever its importance, together with the most extensive, solid and profound erudition. A thoroughly typical characteristic of German science, for example, consists in the reduction to pure algebraic developments, rigorous, but arid (because deliberately pursued to the most complete elimination of all intuitive content), both of geometry and of mechanics and physics ; which constitutes a simple deductive systematization of these sciences, rendered possible by their previous advances, whereof the fundamental share has always been due rather to the intuitive and synthetic minds.[2]

---

[1] E. Mach, *op. cit., Die Mechanik, etc.,* pp. 412-414.

[2] Cf., for example, P. Duhem, *op. cit., La sc. allem.,* passim, e.g. pp. 8-13, 31, 35, 76, 85-86, 119-120, 138-139, etc.

272 THE PSYCHOLOGY OF REASONING

In consequence of this different mental nature of the respective thinkers, the function that science comes to play in the various countries differs correspondingly. Here, it consists in brilliant discoveries of truths, completely new and of a general order, which revolutionize, sometimes to its foundations, the whole of science, and represent so many milestones on its triumphal way. There, in the patient systematization and elaboration, and the fullest utilization of the new truths so discovered. It is thus, thanks to such different racial dispositions, that *an international division of scientific work* is produced spontaneously, with the result that the scientific work of one people is not complete without that of another: a fresh proof, if evidence were still required, of the solidarity which ought indissolubly to bind together the scientists of all countries—as a prelude to the desired fraternity between the peoples themselves.

II. *" Intuitive " minds and " logical " minds*

To the division into synthetic and analytic minds, which we have just examined, there corresponds roughly the distinction drawn between the so-called " intuitive " minds and the so-called " logical " minds, which applies also in the case of ordinary people. And it is said that intuitive minds, endowed with that quality which Pascal called the *esprit de finesse*, ordinarily "judge better", "see more rightly", than drily logical minds.

De Candolle shows very clearly the difference between "to judge" and "to deduce": "the faculty of judging, or what may be called the sound judgment of man, is the ability to weigh well, one against the other, opposite facts or opposite views, so as to form a correct idea of what is probable; but deduction consists in the faculty of following a given series of connected ideas. A mathematician arrives at his deductions satisfactorily, but he may not possess a right criterion, or he may be entirely wanting in the faculty of judgment."[1]

Now, it is precisely the synthetics who possess this faculty in a greater degree than the analytics, because their affective intensity, deeper and more concentrated, confronted with the fact whose greater or less degree of

---

[1] A. de Candolle, *Zur Geschichte der Wissenschaften und der Gelehrten*, Leipzig, 1911, p. 45.

LOGICAL TYPES OF MIND 273

probability is in question, puts the elements on which this probability depends in precisely the correct perspective of high, middle, and low relief. The analytic, on the other hand, succeeds with more difficulty in placing those elements in the due perspective, just because he is incapable of considering them from a single affective point of view. In other words, the perspective vision of multiple elements is, in substance, a prospect of a unique whole, obtained by adopting a single affective point of view; and as such it is by itself a synthetic act: "*The thing must be seen all at once at a single glance*," wrote Pascal very justly in reference to the *esprit de finesse* necessary in these circumstances, "and not by a course of reasoning."

Thus it is, *e.g.*, that the German mentality, which, as we have seen, is primarily analytic or "logical", is also that which most lacks intuition and "esprit de finesse."

The mentality of woman is more intensely affective, at every moment, in relation to certain familiar facts of daily life, than that of man, and at the same time, thanks precisely to a greater affective impulsivity, is less capable of being interested for a long period in one and the same object. Women, therefore, follow with more labour than man a long process of reasoning, which demands the persistence of interest in the object whose vicissitudes are mentally pursued; but with respect to those facts of daily life, they often have a more correct perspective. It is therefore said that woman is less "logical" than man, but that she frequently excels him in intuition.[1]

Naturalists, biologists, historians, etc.—all those, in short, who have to compare many facts at a time, or to judge of the relative importance of simultaneous multiple factors in the causation of a given phenomenon—require the faculty of judging more than the faculty of reasoning: "Naturalists, like historians," writes de Candolle, "are generally distinguished by a sound criterion, that is to say, by the ability to judge well, more than by the strength of their logical faculty. They observe, compare, describe, appraise. It would be possible to name some who have never drawn a really deductive conclusion." "The 'esprit de finesse' alone," Duhem writes in his turn, "can in science find a natural order, establish a

[1] Cf. A. de Candolle, *ibid.*, p. 217.

S

274 THE PSYCHOLOGY OF REASONING

natural classification, because it alone is able to appreciate the degree of importance of various truths."[1]

The same may be said of great statesmen and men of business, of great strategists—of all those, in short, whom J. S. Mill calls practical minds of a high order. They judge a given situation *synthetically* at one glance, *weighing and estimating* rightly the elements related to it. The rapid view of the whole which they form in this way is, as a general rule, never the result of long and considered reasoning.[2]

III. *Romantic and Classic Minds*

To the fundamental classification so far considered of mentalities into synthetic and analytic, which is the classical one, Ostwald opposes another into romantics and classics. The former have a much more rapid mental reaction and a more exuberant imagination ; the latter a slower reaction and a more prolonged meditation.[3]

We hasten to remark that this classification of Ostwald does not coincide with the preceding, because if as we may affirm the romantics are all synthetics, thanks to the very intensity of their affective impulses, and if the analytics can all be regarded as classics, the synthetics are also numerous among these latter. Moreover, it may be stated that the mightiest geniuses are at once synthetics and classics, and it is sufficient to recall that Newton, Mayer, and Helmholtz are justly placed by Ostwald among the classics.

This is quite natural. In the first place, slowness of mental reaction does not in fact exclude affective intensity and concentration, which is the fundamental quality requisite for a synthetic view ; moreover, the very slowness of reaction in the synthetic classics makes their affectivities more tenacious, while these are of shorter duration in the romantics. Robert Mayer, for example, after having perceived the equivalence, as we have mentioned above, between given quantities of heat and given quantities of work with respect to the quantity

---

[1] A. de Candolle, *ibid.*, pp. 241, 248-249 ; P. Duhem, *op. cit.*, *La sc. allem*, p. 85.

[2] Cf. J. S. Mill, *op. cit.*, *Logic*, Vol. I, p. 209.

[3] W. Ostwald, *Grosse Männer*, 2nd edit., Leipzig, 1910, passim, e.g. pp. 45, 47-48, 371-388.

LOGICAL TYPES OF MIND 275

of food required by the organism to produce either, devoted himself *passionately*, for the rest of his life, to the sole problem of seeking out all the various aspects and all the different consequences of the principle of the conservation of energy, which resulted from his discovery. In the second place, it is this greater persistence of the respective affectivity for the problem to be solved, or already solved, that by urging the synthetic-classic to investigate with precision, as did Mayer, all the consequences of the new equivalence, or generalization, or abstraction, of which he has obtained a glimpse, enables him to accomplish the construction of the great new edifice, perfected in all its parts. It is only in this respect that it has been possible to say that genius is merely a capacity for taking pains.

On the other hand, the impulsivity of the romantics with its more brief affective persistence, though it may render them capable at any given moment, when one or other of their intense and concentrated impulses is in play, of the synthetic view, nevertheless prevents them afterwards deriving therefrom through their reasoning all the more remote and more detailed consequences. They leave, as a result, works that are less complete, less finished in their details.

Thus, it was said of Poincaré "that he was more a conqueror than a colonizer, leaving to others the care of organizing his discoveries, and never revising a memoir in order to render the statement more didactic " (Borel). Poincaré, a romantic and synthetic type, has a remarkable antithesis in Zola, a classical and analytic type : " In the one case, that of Zola, there was a voluntary, conscious, logical and methodical intelligence, as though made for mathematical deduction : he produced a whole world of romance. The other mentality, that of Poincaré, was spontaneous, scarcely conscious, nearer to dreaming than to reasoning, and it seemed especially fitted for works of pure imagination, not subordinated to reality : it triumphed in mathematical research." [1]

The mentality of romantics, by reason of their greater impulsivity and their less affective persistence, approaches the mentality of women. in whom we have seen a marked capacity for intuition and a deficiency of

[1] Dr Toulouse, *op. cit., Henri Poincaré*, pp. 194, 200.

276 THE PSYCHOLOGY OF REASONING

logic. It approximates also, at the same time, to the artistic mentality. In fact, it is precisely the rapid succession of the most varied and intense affective impulses, characteristic of the artist, which renders him capable of brilliant synthetic intuitions. But artists are at the same time very poor logicians, because they are wanting in the first condition of logicality, that is to say, in that affective resistance necessary to follow with interest the successive events of the "thought history" which constitutes reasoning. Carlyle and Tolstoi, for example, were artistic mentalities, synthetic and illogical at the same time.

On another side, the great intensity, the very brevity and variability of their successive affective impulses, allow the romantics a greater promptitude, a greater quantity, and a greater richness of synthetic views, though these are less profound than in the classics, who are more "faithful" to any synthetic view acquired by them. We can thus understand that Ostwald's classification, into romantics and classics, coincides nearly with that of Meumann, into rapid and deep intelligences, and with that of Duhem into broad though weak and strong though limited minds.[1]

As for the classification of mentalities adopted by Taine into two basic types, classic and Anglo-Saxon, this would not be, properly speaking, a classification of *logical* mentalities, if the Anglo-Saxon mentality were really distinguished, as he claims that it is, by being simply a "collection of facts", not connected together by any bond of reciprocal dependence. The Anglo-Saxon mentality would then be only an *a - logical* mentality. We can, however, understand the classification of Taine rather as a division of mentalities into more and less synthetic; the more synthetic, by the fact of employing a few concepts, so as successively to draw from them all the deductions possible, would be the "classic" or "systematic" mentalities ; whilst the Anglo-Saxon mentality, incapable of such vast abstractions, would have recourse to a greater number of less general concepts, such that the respective deductions drawn from them would not appear to be connected by

---

[1] Cf. W. Ostwald, *o* '. *cit.*, *Gr. Männer*, p. 374 ; E. Meumann, *op. cit.*, *Intelligenz u. Wille*, pp. 120-121 ; P. Duhem, *op. cit.*, *La théorie physique, son objet et sa structure*, Part I, Chap. IV, §§ 1-5, pp. 85-108.

LOGICAL TYPES OF MIND 277

a single superior principle, so as to constitute a veritable "system".[1]

There is no need to repeat that this classification of Taine, even when thus understood, shows at the most merely the average relative tendencies of two peoples or races and that there is nothing absolute in it. It is sufficient here to recall that Newton is Anglo-Saxon —Newton, pre-eminently the type of the classic and systematic logician, even in the sense of Taine.

But it is useless to linger over these and similar classifications. It is enough to note here that the true "natural" classification remains meanwhile the classical division into synthetic minds and analytic minds. More than all others, it takes count of really fundamental psychic differences, of an affective nature, which divide all mentalities into two great and opposed branches: those who, in the face of a given problem, or a given group of phenomena or of objects, remain mono-affective, and those, on the contrary, who *at the actual moment of each research*, show themselves to be poly-affective. The first spontaneously and intuitively discover new equivalences, the second minutely and patiently observe differences and deduce consequences; the first boldly conquer new lands, the second merely clear those lands. That does not hinder the first great branch from subdividing itself, later on, into unstable and tenacious mono-affectives: the latter only, after the conquest of new lands, apply themselves also to their cultivation.

IV. *Bold and Timid Minds*

Also contributing to favour the synthetic or analytic qualities, which flow directly from the diverse affective nature of which we have spoken, there is another side of the affective character of the thinker, namely, his degree of daring or timidity. Boldness alone leads to a search for new principles, and inspires confidence in the worth of such and such a fresh equivalence which may be perceived, whilst the timid man ventures only

---

[1] Cf. H. Taine, *Notes sur l'Angleterre*, Paris, 1845, Chap. VIII, *De l'esprit anglais;* The same, *Les origines de la France contemporaine, L'ancien régime*, Paris, 1896, Book III, Chap. II, *L'esprit classique.*

278 THE PSYCHOLOGY OF REASONING

upon the safe path of deducing consequences that result from principles or concepts already discovered by others and generally admitted.

The greater boldness of synthetics urges them also to address themselves to the investigation and solution of certain problems, even before taking cognizance of all their predecessors' works on the same question; while the greater timidity of the analytic impels him to store up the utmost amount of every sort of information, and, if he ventures on the study of a given question, never makes him consider it over-prudent to take careful notice of all that has previously been done, said, or written in reference to the matter.[1]

Moreover, daring and courage are the more necessary to develop synthetic dispositions, by reason of the serious impediments and opposition encountered in the social milieu, which resents innovations; and, in particular, in the academic world, which crystallises itself in the way of thinking that has hitherto served as a guide in its own research. These impediments and opposition are aroused only by the synthetics, discoverers of new concepts and new horizons, and never by the analytics, who leave old concepts intact.[2]

At the same time the reliance or diffidence which a people or race feels in regard to themselves and their own destinies, may largely contribute, on their part, to direct their thinkers towards one road rather than the other. Indeed, the high opinion which a nation collectively has of itself, whether by tradition, or as the result of recent good fortune or economic prosperity, or for any other reason — the collective "imperialist" opinion, as one might call it, making use of a word very much in fashion to-day—contributes very much to inspire each of its members with the courage necessary to make a start in the search for new principles, and with confidence in the new principles discovered; a courage and confidence that he would not have possessed at an epoch of national discouragement and depression. Thus it is that great new principles, the grand new hypotheses or theories, which have been so many milestones in the evolution of science, were most often

[1] Cf. A. de Candolle, *op. cit., Zur Gesch. d. Wissensch. u. d. Gelehrten,* p. 168.

[2] *Cf.,* e.g. W. Ostwald, *op. cit., Gr. Männer,* p. 275.

LOGICAL TYPES OF MIND 279

discovered and diffused in countries which at the time were at the apogee of their history.

V. *Imagination and Erudition; Originality and Memory*

Passing now from characteristics of the affective order to those of an intellectual order, we must in the first place remark how a little ignorance, instead of being prejudicial, is favourable to the creative imagination. This is not only because, by diminishing the number of facts to be compared, it facilitates the discovery of equivalences amongst these facts, which would have been impeded by a more considerable number of facts ; but still more because imagination itself is more free and more daring when it is not restrained and frequently stopped by the knowledge of opinions or principles, which impose themselves as dogmas and from which the thinker may believe there is no escape.[1]

On the other hand, too much culture or erudition is a hindrance to originality, not merely because, by increasing beyond measure the facts liable to present themselves to the mind, it fetters comparison and the discovery of new equivalences, but still more because the ideas of others, absorbed and stored up in our minds in too great number, substitute themselves, little by little, for our own more personal and original ideas.[2]

It follows too that an excess of memory is prejudicial, whilst a deficiency of memory is advantageous to originality of thought: "A bad memory," declares Meumann, "nearly always forces him who is endowed with it to form, in each particular case, a personal opinion, just because his knowledge of the matter leaves him without any suggestion."[3]

A limited memory facilitates generalization, that is to say, the discovery of new equivalences or of new concepts, not only because the deficiency is the cause of a certain degree of ignorance in general, but also and especially, because it is the occasion of an ignorance *sui generis*. In fact, the obliteration from the memory of the details by which various given phenomena or objects, equivalent with respect to an end or a result,

---

[1] Cf. Th. Ribot, *op. cit., Essai sur l'imaginat. créatr.*, p. 136.

[2] *Cf.* A. de Candolle, *op. cit., Zur Gesch. etc.*, p. 260 ; W. Ostwald, *op. cit., Gr. Männer*, p. 347, et seq., p. 364, et seq.

[3] E. Meumann, *op. cit., Intell. u. Wille*, p. 115.

280 THE PSYCHOLOGY OF REASONING

are distinguished from one another, facilitates the recognition of their equivalence. Contrariwise, a strong and lasting mnemonic impression of these details hinders the schematization or reduction of the phenomena or objects to the sole attribute or attributes, which make them equivalent with respect to the end or result in question. "An over-ready perception of sharp mental pictures," writes Galton, "is antagonistic to the acquirement of habits of highly - generalised and abstract thought." He relates that a young lady, suddenly asked what the word "boat" recalled to her mind, replied that she had immediately seen the image of a rather large boat, leaving the shore, full of ladies and gentlemen, the ladies dressed in white and sky-blue. "It is obvious," observes this author, "that a tendency to give so specific an interpretation to a general word is absolutely opposed to philosophic thought."[1]

Deficiency of memory may lead to generalization, because the latter, as a connection between things which are otherwise without any link of association, is suited to serve as a technical mnemonic expedient. Those who have not a good memory for particular facts, says Maudsley, should seek to bring them under some grouping principle. Such bonds of "intellectual resemblance" are the most powerful, remarks Piéron, and are those which constitute "useful memory," that is to say, "the certain evocation of memories at the moment when they are necessary." Poincaré was typical in this respect; to remember any fact whatever, he had at the outset to see it embodied in some coherent system, that is to say, "to intellectualize it." Helmholtz himself, in the celebrated discourse cited above, confesses his bad memory for matters which have no bond among themselves; and he declares that "the most efficacious mnemotechnic expedient" was for him the knowledge of the law that would link them.[2]

It is evident, then, that certain qualities of an *intellectual order*, a greater or less degree of culture, a greater or less memory, may also have an influence upon

---

[1] F. Galton, *op. cit., Inquiries into Human Faculty and its Development*, pp. 88, 109-110.
[2] Maudsley, *op. cit., The Physiol. of Mind*, p. 534; H. Piéron, *op. cit., L'évolution de la mémoire*, p. 289; Dr Toulouse, *op cit., Henri Poincaré*, pp. 77-78, 101-103, 168-169; H. von Helmholtz, *op. cit., Vorträge u. Reden*, Vol. I, pp. 6-7.

LOGICAL TYPES OF MIND 281

the synthetic or analytic nature of the thinker, by helping and strengthening one or the other of these dispositions; but the preponderant influence, in the determination of this synthetic or analytic nature, nevertheless always belongs to the qualities of an *affective order*, previously discussed, namely, an intense monoaffectivism in synthetics and a calm polyaffectivism in analytics.

VI. *Visuals and Auditives*

As much may be said of the two other kinds of intellectual qualities, called the visual and the auditive qualities. They do not determine the synthetic or analytic nature of the individual, but only secondary characteristics of the mind.

"A genuine example of the auditory type", writes Meumann, "helps himself, in the evocation of his visual impressions, through the names of the things and the consciousness of having seen them in the past, even if now he does not suceeed in presenting them to his imagination ".[1]

Even for the auditives, then, we cannot say that their reasoning or thought is merely verbal ; for them also what J. S. Mill says of thought in general holds : "We think to a considerable extent by means of names ; but what we think of are the things called by those names ; and there cannot be a greater error than to imagine that thought can be carried on with nothing in our mind but names, or that we can make names think for us ".[2]

A certain independence from words, even among auditives, in the production of thought is shown by the fact that auditives also frequently "choose" their expressions. This indicates, as Bastian rightly remarks, a quite distinct process, by which the thoughts, which are already formed independently of words, call up, little by little, the respective verbal symbols.[3]

The fact, then, is simply that auditives, having a good memory for sounds, resort, in order to link together the experiments mentally performed, of which, for them also, all reasoning consists, to the aid of verbal expressions and associations which are the "transla-

---

[1] E. Meumann, *op. cit., Intell. u. Wille*, pp. 130-131.
[2] J. S. Mill, *op. cit., Logic*, Vol. I, p. 196.
[3] C. Bastian, *Le cerveau organe de la pensée*, Paris, 1888, Vol. II, Chapter XXIX.

282 THE PSYCHOLOGY OF REASONING

tion" of the corresponding concatenation of things. Yet, in some cases, the help rendered by the auditive memory is so important that they regard themselves as unable to think without the assistance of speech. The well-known aphorism of Max Müller: "No thought without language"—which we had occasion to discuss in one of our previous chapters — is in itself an indication of the distinctly marked auditive quality of the individual who enunciated and so valiantly defended it.

On the other hand, visuals do not need to have recourse to the corresponding verbal expressions in order to proceed to the concatenations of the experiments mentally performed which constitute their reasoning. They directly follow these concatenations with the "eyes of the mind." All good chess players, for instance, are clearly visuals, that is to say, they generally possess a remarkable faculty of following in imagination the movements of the pieces on the chess-board ; their reasoning "is concrete and practical, not put into words." In the same way, the old atomists and the modern electronists *saw* and *see* atoms and electrons, whose wanderings they follow in imagination, throughout the course of their thought : "The chemists who founded the atomic theory", declares Ribot, "undoubtedly *saw* atoms and visualized their architecture in compound bodies". Perrin is typical in this respect ; to convey an idea of the way in which the viscosity of gases may be explained, he adopts the analogy of two trains travelling in the same direction, with slightly different speeds, on two parallel and neighbouring ways : "The passengers might amuse themselves by leaping continuously from one to the other, receiving each time a slight shock. Owing to these shocks, those alighting upon the slower train would gradually increase its speed, while they would diminish that of the faster train when falling upon it. Thus the two speeds would in the end become equal." This touch is sufficient to enable us to lay a finger on the marked visual faculty of the eminent French physicist. The great chemist Liebig also was a reasoner who derived support from things, for he states himself that he possessed the marked faculty "of thinking by means of images (*in Anschauungen zu denken*), that is, of having

LOGICAL TYPES OF MIND   283

in the mind chemical operations instead of logical processes."[1]

When these reasoners who think only by means of images have to communicate their reasoning to others, they find themselves obliged to *translate* into corresponding verbal symbols, not hitherto employed, the imagined concatenations of facts, *after they have already been elaborated in the mind*. Often, indeed, owing to the difficulties which they have in expressing themselves, the translation is imperfect and inaccurate, though the inner reasoning has been irreproachable. "There are some", writes Maudsley, "who, with great intellectual power, never can attain to the ability of successfully expressing themselves". "Great thinkers especially", Müller-Freienfels also declares, "are frequently inept speakers. Their phrases are often ill-constructed and in bad taste; for them language is an obstacle rather than a help to thought." Thus, for example, Galton always thought "absolutely without the use of any mental words"; and he confesses the great difficulties which he experienced in translating into words all that he had thought with the help of images.[2]

More than that, words frequently express, in a large number of visuals, only detached fragments of the inner reasoning, which emerge like islets, so distant from one another that the auditor fails even to suspect the existence of the chain of submarine mountains joining them all. Darwin, for instance, "was essentially a man who thought concretely, and with his eye on the object". "He always reasons justly, but he leaves much to be inferred and supplied by the reader. His reasoning, in a word, is rarely quite explicit and rarely analytical. We are never allowed to see the bare bones of the argument." Similarly it is related of Robert Mayer that "when he spoke he was in the habit of expressing only very incompletely the intermediate

[1] Cf. Ballet, *Le langage intérieur*, Paris, 1888, p. 35; A. A. Cleveland, *art. cit.*, "The Psychology of Chess and of learning to play it", pp. 290-291; Ribot, *op. cit.*, *Essai sur l'imaginat. créatr.*, pp. 199-200; J. Perrin, "Peut-on peser un atome avec précision?", *La Revue du Mois*, 10 Nov. 1908, p. 519; W. Ostwald, *op. cit.*, *Gr. Männer*, p. 155.

[2] Maudsley, *op. cit.*, *The Physiology of Mind*, pp. 497-498: R. Müller-Freienfels *art. cit.*, "Beiträge zum Problem des wortlosen Denkens", p. 327; F. Galton, letter to Max Müller, in M. Müller, *Three Introductory Lectures on the Science of Thought*, Chicago, 1909, **Appendix, pp. 1-3.**

284 THE PSYCHOLOGY OF REASONING

stages of his own reasoning, so that his expressions frequently caused surprise by reason of the fragmentary manner in which his thought appeared to progress."[1]

Consequently, the visuals—although their imagination may be more vivid, their invention of new combinations and connections among things more diversified, and their reasoning, as well as all their thought, more solid—generally at the outset, in the verbal statement of their thought, succeed only in giving a very inadequate impression of the value of their intelligence; especially when they are face to face with the easy and brilliant conversation of auditives. *Vice versa*, it is precisely the great facility and rapidity, characteristic of auditives, with which they translate verbally what they think, or, even more, their capacity of thinking by means of this verbal translation itself, and so constructing formally correct verbal reasonings—that renders auditives more superficial and poorer in imagination, than the visuals. "Too great a facility of speech", writes Müller-Freienfels, "may be an obstacle to thought. When the formulation in words takes place too swiftly and easily, there may be the danger of the thoughts being expressed before even they have been fully elaborated, and of their remaining thus definitely imperfect in the domain of speech, to the detriment of their originality."[2]

But however great the differences may be which are observable between visuals and auditives, they nevertheless have not much influence upon the determination of the synthetic or analytic nature of the individual. The one or the other, in fact, may belong to either of the two fundamental types.

If the visual is analytic, he will be led to form, to use Galton's term, "specialized pictures" (the "plastic imagination" of Ribot); if he is synthetic, "generalized pictures", that is very clear and tangible schematizations of the conceptions or abstractions which he has discovered or adopted (the "rational imagination" of Ribot). In fact, it must never be forgotten that as we

---

[1] E. S. Russell, "The Evidence for Natural Selection", *Scientia*, 1909, No. IX-I, p. 69 ; W. Ostwald, *op. cit., Gr. Männer*, p. 62.

[2] R. Müller-Freienfels, *art. cit.*, "Beiträge zum Probl. d. wortlosen Denkens ", pp. 326-327.

LOGICAL TYPES OF MIND 285

rise in generalization or abstraction, we reach not to vacuity, as Ribot well says, but to the simple.[1] If the analytic is auditive, he will be meticulous in the choice of words, he will take a very great interest in the subtle shades of signification of different terms, he will raise interminable and useless questions about words, and so will run the danger of falling into the most complete aridity. Into this sort of aridity the visual analytic never falls, because his mental processes relying on things lead always to effective new results, though these may be of a particular order and not of special importance. If, finally, the reasoner is auditive and at the same time synthetic, he will employ only terms of general signification, with very vague and often obscure meanings, just because he is incapable of a very clear visual schematization of any one of his general concepts. He will thus run the risk of building up structures of an imposing external aspect, but resting upon fragile or even wholly chimerical foundations. Such a risk is never present in the reasoning of the visual synthetic, thanks to the *schematically concrete* representation which the latter succeeds in making for himself of each of his concepts, however abstract it may be.

A sub-class of visuals, called by Ribot typographic visuals, is also noticed by Galton, who in his inquiry found "many cases of persons mentally reading off scores when playing the pianoforte, or manuscripts when they are making speeches." Victor Hugo, for example, "never dictated, never made verses from memory, and only composed as he wrote ; for he thought that writing has its physiognomy and *wanted to see the words*."[2]

With the graphic symbol they acquire the same familiarity that the auditives acquire with the verbal symbol, so that, like them, they by no means always need to see, behind the symbol, the reality which it represents. To this category, *e.g.*, belong most of the analytical mathematicians who possess so great a facility in mechanical calculation. In them, "the process (of reasoning) is wholly dependent upon the use of symbols."[3]

---

[1] Cf. Fr. Galton, *op. cit., Inquiries into Hum. Faculty*, pp. 109-114 ; and Th. Ribot, *op. cit., Essai sur l'imagin. créatr.*, pp. 160-162.

[2] Ribot, *op. cit., L'évolution des idées générales*, pp. 136 et seq. ; F. Galton, *op. cit., Inquiries*, etc. p. 96 ; Ribot, *op. cit., Essai sur l'imag. créatr.*, p. 157.

[3] Hastings Berkeley, *op. cit., Mysticism in Modern Mathematics*, p. 5.

286 THE PSYCHOLOGY OF REASONING

Consequently, just like the auditives, the typographic visuals are distinguished from the visualisers *of things*, whose reasoning is grounded on really imagined tangible experiences, by greater speed, but, at the same time, by greater superficiality. It is, for example, to this category of typographic visuals that the analysts certainly belong, who, as we have seen in one of our preceding chapters on the higher forms of reasoning, were the first—in spite of the just protests of mathematicians who based their reasoning upon things, and for that very reason were less superficial — to introduce and employ the graphic symbols of the imaginary numbers, although no signification had yet been successfully attached to those symbols. To the same category, also, undoubtedly belong the mathematicians who are familiar with the calculus of quaternions and with what is called symbolic algebra in general, as well as the inventors and promoters of mathematical logic.[1]

On the other hand, the mathematical visuals *of things* do not conceal their dislike for an exaggerated symbolism and for excessively long calculations. It is well known, for instance, how vigorously and insistently Comte fought the analysts *à outrance*. Mach confesses that in his youth he always revolted against every deduction made by means of symbols, the significance of which did not appear to him entirely clear and capable of being represented in the imagination. All the work of Poinsot was likewise a reaction against the excessive use of calculation, and he sought to substitute, for the dry equations of analytical mechanics, concrete and intuitive conditions of equilibrium and movement. "It is possible by these calculations", he wrote, *e.g.*, in his *Théorie nouvelle de la rotation des corps* (1834), "to determine the place where a body will be found after a given time ; but it can by no means be seen how the body arrives there ; it is lost to sight entirely, *whereas one would wish to observe and follow it, with the eyes so to speak, during the whole course of its rotation.*"[2]

Hermite, on the other hand, a great analyst, was ill at ease in all reasoning that demanded representa-

---

[1] *Cf.*, e.g., P. Duhem, *op. cit.*, *La théorie physique*, etc. pp. 120-122.
[2] E. Mach, *op. cit.*, *Erkenntnis und Irrtum*, p. 36 ; L. Brunschvicg, *op. cit.*, *Les étapes de la philosophie mathématique*, p. 306.

LOGICAL TYPES OF MIND 287

tions of things: "I cannot tell you", he wrote, "what efforts I am obliged to make in order to understand something in the working drawings of the descriptive geometry which I detest." Analysis for him was "a science of objects which exist independently of the signification given to them, and which the mathematician ought to treat by a method exactly comparable with the observation of the naturalist."[1]

But here again, the synthetic predisposition as well as the analytic predisposition of the thinker may very well coexist with this visual-typographic faculty. Large and comprehensive views of given processes of calculation ; the discovery of new analogies between given forms of functions or, more generally, of algorithmic expressions whatsoever ; the extension to other theories of given analytical methods which are valid for a particular theory ; and so on : these are so many acts of generalization of which the typographic visual may likewise be capable, if he is synthetic. Abel and Poincaré are characteristic types of such synthetic analysts. Of the two fundamental dispositions of the human mind, however, it is probably the analytic disposition which this visual typographic faculty tends to favour.

VII. *Constructive Reasoners and Intentional Reasoners Positivists and Metaphysicians*

What has been said hitherto refers chiefly to the different psychological aptitudes with respect to *constructive* reasoning, or reasoning properly so-called. There is very little to add concerning these aptitudes in relation to the two principal forms of *intentional* reasoning, which were considered in our two last chapters. For, in the same characteristics then noticed of these two forms of intentional reasoning—the dialectical and the metaphysical—we showed how preponderant is the *rôle* played by the affective part of the individual, which dominates the intellectual part and reduces it to the state of a humble servant.

It seems also unnecessary to point out that *the affective unilaterality*, which constitutes the indispensable presupposition of all intentional reasoning, whatever it

[1] L. Brunschvicg, *op. cit.*, pp. 444-445.

288 THE PSYCHOLOGY OF REASONING

may be, possesses nothing in common with *the affective intensity and concentration,* which we previously saw to be greater in the synthetic constructive reasoner than in the analytic. Because the synthetic's intense and exclusive interest in a particular question implies—if the object he is seeking remain that of constructing a "history of things" in complete correspondence with reality, so that he may thus increase his own faculty of prevision—no affective prepossession in favour of any one manner of solving the question. Whereas it is exactly the keen desire to arrive at any cost at a certain predetermined conclusion—a conclusion which, as we have already seen, is the classification or presentation of certain phenomena in a certain way, to the exclusion of every other—that impels and moulds, so to speak, all intentional reasoning, dialectical no less than metaphysical.

It is this purpose to be attained at any cost that impels one and the same dialectic reasoner sometimes to become analytic, by noticing the smallest details of a certain object or phenomenon, in order to attempt to bring it into the desired conceptual category, and at other times, to adopt a synthetic attitude, by defining very broadly, *e.g.,* a certain legal concept, so as to render it capable of including the offence which is desired to be brought into the concept. It is likewise this singleness of aim, for which his conscience with all its strength strives, that impels one and the same metaphysician, sometimes to ascend to grand and nebulous concepts, capable of encompassing the whole of reality, and sometimes to descend to the most minute and artificial sophisms to "demonstrate" the existence of God, or the immortality of the soul.

Let it suffice to note here how favourable the *auditive* faculty is to any form of intentional reasoning, in comparison with the *visual*; though the latter is, as we have seen, of great advantage in constructive reasoning.

As for the dialectician, this auditive quality serves in debate to give him a facility and swiftness in the refutation of an adversary's arguments and sophisms by counter-arguments and counter-sophisms; a facility and speed of repartee of so much importance from the influence they exercise on the mind of the impartial listener, be he judge, juryman, or the public of a meeting.

LOGICAL TYPES OF MIND 289

To the metaphysician, it is of service in making him acquire so great a familiarity with the verbal symbol, and with the purely formal linkings involved, that he feels no need of always seeing, behind the symbols, the reality which they ought to represent; so that he finds easy the gradual and continual elimination of every intellectual content, to which he unconsciously submits the verbal conceptual symbol, as a last and desperate defence of his own metaphysical hypothesis against the incessant contradictions of reality. " Nonsense in grammatical form "—writes James, and the observation is chiefly true for auditives—"sounds half rational." " Nonsense ", Stöhr finely observes, " becomes possible only by language. Nonsense can be expressed by words, but cannot be thought." [1]

In this connection it is enough to point out how the Germans—whose musical powers testify to a predominance of the auditive type, confirmed by the absence among them of the visual æsthetic sense—have always been the most inclined of all European peoples to metaphysical speculation; and how, amongst them alone this speculation could be pushed to the high degree of nebulosity and nonsense attained, for instance, by its most typical representative, Hegel, an auditive *par excellence*. Whereas the French and the English, not very musical, or even unmusical, whose high visual qualities, on the other hand, were so vividly set in relief by Galton and by Taine, have always manifested against metaphysics the most lively and consistent reaction, which has ended in triumph.

VIII. *Conclusion*

We have now come to an end of this rapid survey of the various logical types, the general conclusion being that in the determination of the different characteristics of the logical faculty which above all one would call *intellectual, the affective nature* of the individual has yet a very great importance. In fact, to this, is chiefly due, as we saw in our chapter on metaphysical reasoning, the main division of thinkers into positivists and meta-

---

[1] W. James, *op. cit., The Principles of Psychology*, Vol. I, p. 264 ; A. Stöhr, *Leitfaden der Logik in psychologisierender Darstellung*, Wien, 1905, p. 89.

T

290 THE PSYCHOLOGY OF REASONING

physicians. The former, resigned to the ineluctable necessities of reality and yet energetic in dealing with that part of reality which may be transformed in the direction of their own aspirations; the latter, on the other hand, rebelling against the ineluctability of the real, and in this vain effort exhausting all their best energies. The first, usefully stimulated in their intellectual faculties from the affective side, which urges them to create " histories of things " corresponding to reality, and at the same time permits and even encourages in them the counter-action of the secondary controlling affectivity of a true and proper state of attention that aims at never losing contact with reality; the second, on the other hand, carried away by the violence of their more intimate feelings, which reduces their intellectual faculty to the *rôle* of a humble servant, even to the point of inhibiting all inner control which might imperil the object to be attained at any cost. And it is likewise to the affective nature, as we have shown in the present chapter, that in the same positive field, namely, in the domain of pure constructive reasoning, is due the main division of logical minds into synthetics and analytics. For the synthetic faculty depends upon the greatest affective intensity and affective singleness and concentration which ensue in relation to a certain question or to a certain order of phenomena; while the analytic faculty derives from a calmer and colder affective nature, which, just because of that calmness and coldness, admits of a greater multiplicity and variety of affective points of view, from which this question or that order of phenomena may be considered. So that on the intellectual elements properly so-called—more or less memory, more or less culture, a visual or auditory faculty, visual of things or typographically, etc. — there depends only the determination of the various sub-classes into which the two main branches of synthetics and analytics are ultimately sub-divided.

We shall see that this fundamental predominance of affective over intellectual elements subsists also in the determination of *the various pathological forms of reasoning*. And to these, now that we have reviewed the principal normal forms of reasoning, we finally proceed.

CHAPTER XIII

THE PATHOLOGY OF REASONING

Part I : The Incoherence and Illogicality of Dreams

DREAMS have always had for psychologists the fascination of a great enigma. How in dreams a sane mind can give the strangest, the most incoherent, the most illogical manifestations, to return afterwards in the waking state to the most normal functioning :—this is the great problem which has remained unsolved, we may say, until to-day.

The reason is perhaps that the phenomenon of sleep and that of the dream have not been considered sufficiently in relation to one another.

1. *The Different Theories of Sleep*

There are numerous theories as to the nature of sleep: *circulatory* (for example, through cerebral anæmia), *neurodynamic* (for example, through retraction of the ramifications of the neurones or by the inhibition of cerebral activity), *biochemical* (which we shall examine later), *biological* (the sleep instinct of Claparède), and *energetic* (on which we shall dwell particularly). But in general they are all at fault in their method ; they proceed, that is to say, to the study of sleep without sufficient consideration of one of its fundamental products, the dream—whose characteristics the nature of sleep should be used to explain.

According to theories stated in terms of energy, sleep would be due to the exhaustion of nervous energy expended during the waking state, and renewed during sleep itself. Thus, Wundt attributes it "to the exhaustion of disposable energies in the central nervous system". According to Pflüger: "The waking state is characterised by the fact that the living substance

292 THE PSYCHOLOGY OF REASONING

of the nervous cells decomposes ceaselessly. If this continues for a certain time, the quantity of substance capable of decomposing in each of the cells diminishes more and more, and decomposition itself is then produced in a more and more reduced measure. As soon as it descends below a certain level, we get sleep". Similarly Verworn: "During the waking state, the action of the external world to which the senses are submitted, continually maintains strong dissimilatory stimulations in the ganglion cells of the cerebral cortex, and, through exhaustion and fatigue, diminishes their excitability", until sleep supervenes. "By the law of the auto-regulation of material metabolism, restoration takes place automatically during sleep through the prevalence of the assimilatory processes and the elimination of the fatigue products, and so efficiently that little by little the excitability again increases. In the morning recovery is achieved, excitability has attained its physiological maximum, and the feeblest stimulation of the senses wakes us up".[1]

As a proof of this, various experiments have been cited; among others those of Legendre and Piéron (1911-1912), on dogs kept awake till the need of sleep overcame them. These dogs were killed before they actually fell asleep, and an examination of their brains revealed the complete destruction of the chromatic substance (Nissl's substance) in certain nervous cells; while those killed after a short sleep showed this substance completely or almost completely restored.[2]

To these theories are added, or for them are substituted, the biochemical and toxic theories (we pass over the others referred to above), according to which sleep would be due to a periodic asphyxiation of the brain or to a carbonic auto-narcosis, or to an intoxication of the nervous centres by the ponogenic substances (products of fatigue), which accumulate during the day and exercise a hypnotic influence on the nervous centres themselves. "But how can the hypnotic influence either of darkness and silence, or of monotonous noises",

---

[1] W. Wundt, op. cit., Grundzüge der physiologischen Psychologie, Vol. III, pp. 649, 668 ; M. Verworn, Die Mechanik des Geisteslebens, 3rd edition, Leipzig, 1914, pp. 71, 76-77.

[2] L. Luciani, I fenomeni psico-fisici della veglia e del sonno (Extract from the 4th volume of the 4th edition of the Fisiologia dell' uomo), Milan, 1913, p. 508 (English Translation, London, 1920).

INCOHERENCE OF DREAMS 293

asks Luciani, "be interpreted on the chemical theory of sleep? How explain that voluntary effort, interest connected with a certain order of ideas, can retard sleep for several hours, while on the other hand the fact of being disinterested in what surrounds us, voluntary consent,or simple suggestion, suffices to produce sleep?"[1] And how can dreams—we add—which indicate intense psychical activity, be explained either by the theories of exhaustion, by those of the hypnotic action of toxic substances, or by the others, circulatory, neurodynamic, etc., according to which this activity would be excluded?

2. *The Non-affectivity of Sleep and Dreams*

It is the starting-point that has been badly chosen ; that is to say, psychical activity has been considered as an indivisible whole that could be suspended 'en bloc' by sleep, instead of being split up into its fundamental elements for an investigation as to which of them are really suspended. Now, if we distinguish in the psychical activities two fundamental kinds, the affective (including the will, the attention, etc.), and the intellectual proper (*i.e.* the simple evocation of sensory elements, images), we see at once that it is only the first and not the second that are suspended by sleep.

In other words, the functional rest of the mind during sleep relates only to the affective life. And it is natural that this should be so. Numerous though the sensations or sensory evocations may be in the waking state, they are *diverse throughout*. None of them, save in exceptional cases, persists long enough, or is repeated with sufficient insistence, to exhaust the nervous energy of the respective nervous centres ; so that, while a certain system of neurones or nervous centres is in activity for certain sensations or sensory evocations, all the other neurones or nervous centres devoted to the activation of other sensory elements, remain completely at rest ; and have accordingly more than sufficient time to restore the specific nervous energy expended in activating earlier sensations or evocations. But with the affective activity it is different. The daily

---

[1] Luciani, *loc. cit.*, pp. 509-516 ; *cf.* also, for example, N. Vaschide, *Le Sommeil et le Rêve*, Paris, 1911, pp. 5-7.

294 THE PSYCHOLOGY OF REASONING

work of any individual is, in fact, incited and guided by a very limited number of fundamental affective tendencies, which, for this reason, are always or nearly always in action *during the whole day*. The farmer, earnestly engaged in cultivating his fields, the artisan whose capacity is taxed to the utmost by his task, the business man spurred on from morning till evening by the desire for wealth, the scientist keenly interested in the solution of a problem or the experimental verification of certain of his theories, do indeed accomplish the most diverse acts, receive the most varied impressions of the external world, and evoke the most varied succession of images in virtue of their particular experience of the past ; but always under the urge of their respective professional affectivity. Besides this, in every individual there is always active another affectivity, in some ways even more prolonged and more persistent, namely the desire not to be deceived, the fear of not working in the most efficient way, the pre-occupation with not behaving in the most proper manner : it is, in a word, the secondary affectivity of control, which holds momentarily in suspense the impulsion to action and so constitutes the state of attention by which the action is performed, and on which its efficiency more or less depends.

The restoration of substance consumed during the functional activity can, then, so far as the centres activating the purely sensory elements are concerned, keep pace with the wear and tear of the substance even during the waking state, because these centres are alternately in activity so that some rest while others function. But it cannot occur, in the waking state, in the centres activating the fundamental affectivities of the individual, *because they are continually in functional activity from morning to night ;* restoration can only take place in them during the suspension of all affective activity of the mind, a suspension which constitutes sleep.

This essential difference between the centres which activate purely sensory elements, and those activating affective tendencies has not even been suspected by the advocates of the theory of exhaustion. " During the continual action of sense stimulations ", says Verworn, " the auto-regulation of material metabolism cannot keep pace with the wear and tear of the living substance ".

INCOHERENCE OF DREAMS 295

On the contrary, this can and does take place in the centres that activate the purely sensory elements, while it cannot do so in those concerned with the affective activity of the mind.[1]

If the psychical activity is partly intellectual (sensory and mnemonico-sensory) and partly affective, and if it is the latter only which gets fatigued during the day and rests during sleep ("The mind that sleeps", writes Purkinje, "does not wish to continue the tensions of the waking state, but to relax and refresh itself"), we now begin to understand how it is that during sleep there is an intense psychical activity, constituted by dreams, and how it is that dreams differ so substantially from mental phenomena of the waking state. But first let us examine whether other aspects of sleep itself can be explained by our hypothesis, particularly the way in which it is produced.

We have just seen how Luciani draws attention on the one hand to the hypnotic influence of darkness, silence, monotonous noises, disinterestedness in what surrounds us, and on the other to the suspension or postponement of sleep by the work of the will or by some specific interest. Now it is evident that to a certain degree of exhaustion of the potential nervous energy, whose activity occasions the manifestation of affective tendencies, there should correspond a certain degree of obtuseness of the tendencies to be excited, so that the more this exhaustion and the subsequent degree of obtuseness are increased, the more stimulating ought the surrounding situation to be, from the affective point of view, in order to continue to keep awake the interest directed towards it.[2]

The fact that sleep depends, not on the absolute degree of affective exhaustion, but rather on the relation between this and the intensity of the exciting factor, that is to say, the interest that the surrounding situation has for the individual at the moment, explains the particular differences in the way sleep is produced.

[1] Verworn, *op. cit.*, p. 72.

[2] Litwer, who also notes how sleep depends on the relation between the excitable and the exciting factor, is equally unaware that the only excitable factor in play is the affective excitability. (H. Litwer, "Sur la physiologie du sommeil", *Archives Néerlandaises de physiologie de l'homme et des animaux*, Vol. I, Section 3, 20th April 1917, p. 438).

296 THE PSYCHOLOGY OF REASONING

Thus, in spite of great need for sleep, one can remain awake a whole night to help a friend who is ill, while at a certain extreme degree of exhaustion not even an environment dangerous to life can prevent sleep (Piéron's experiments on the dogs referred to above). The increasing incapacity to sustain attention, to be interested in what goes on around us, when we are " very sleepy," is characteristic. On the other hand, darkness, silence, and any other elimination of external stimuli which suppresses the occasion for arousing such and such an affective tendency not less than boredom, monotony and other environmental situations not exciting interest, can provoke sleep, even if the affective exhaustion is not pronounced or has scarcely begun. Thus certain domestic animals such as cats and dogs, which are never worried by the anxious search for food or the fear of enemies from which they must defend or save themselves, spend almost the whole day in sleep. We may also instance cretins, who sleep to excess, because they are not interested in anything that goes on around them. A tedious discourse or a dull book produces sleep, precisely because it does not succeed in keeping awake any interest whatever in the listener or reader. The rôle of " dodo, dodo ", with which the mother rocks her child to sleep, is first to concentrate his interest on the song, distracting him from his other objects of desire, such as sucking, and then, while the interest is thus monopolised, to gradually weaken and exhaust him by the monotonous repetition.

All these characteristics of the ways in which sleep is produced or suspended are evidence in favour of the theory that natural or physiological sleep is due to the suspension of every affective activity of the mind, following the gradual exhaustion of the respective potential nervous energy, on the activation of which the affective manifestations depend ; this process of exhaustion being assisted by the greater or less intensity of the affective stimulus of the environmental factor.

If sleep is thus characterised by " affective silence ", it follows that there will be a relaxation during sleep of all attentional, volitional and motor activity. " Sleep ", writes Nayrac, " is a more or less complete suspension or interruption of conscious and voluntary activity. Sleep is the antagonist of the waking state : the latter

INCOHERENCE OF DREAMS 297

is characterised by a general muscular tension, the former can only exist in virtue of a general relaxation of the muscles ".[1]

And it is in consequence of this affective, attentional, volitional rest, that sleep is really restorative: "If it were not", writes Ellis, "a period in which desire were ordinarily relaxed, sleep would cease to be a period of rest and recuperation ".[2]

From which it follows that one of the first and most fundamental characteristics of dreams is that they are *non-affective*. This is proved indirectly by the fact, already observed by several writers, that "one never dreams about what has made the most impression during the waking state " (Yves Delage). "It is quite rare ", writes De Sanctis, "for a normal individual who loses his father, mother, children, or wife that he loves, to experience the sad emotion again in dreams in the nights immediately succeeding his grief." And the preoccupations of the waking state are scarcely ever renewed in the dream. So that usually we only dream about "the most insignificant " facts (Bergson), about facts "of a secondary order and an indifferent nature", rather than about important facts which have greatly interested us during the waking state.[3]

But the non-affective state of dreams is also directly demonstrated by the absence of desire, and by the indifference with which the dreamer takes part in the events of the dream: "What is always astonishing in dreams ", Freud observes, "is finding that the images presented do not affect us as we should expect they necessarily would do in the waking state". Certain very common dreams (finding ourselves partially or totally undressed in the presence of strangers, seeing as dead intimate friends who are still in life, and other

---

[1] J. P. Nayrac, *Physiologie et psychologie de l'attention*, Paris, 1906, pp. 55, 71.

[2] H. Ellis, *The World of Dreams*, London, 1911, pp. 171, 173; see also, for example, Th. Ribot, *op. cit.*, *Psychologie de l'attention*, p. 159; H. Henning, *Der Traum ein assoziativer Kurzschluss*, Wiesbaden, 1914, p. 16.

[3] See the numerous quotations by Freud in this connection, *Die Traumdeutung*, 3rd Edit., Leipzig, 1911, pp. 4, 11, 12, 13, 28, 57; S. De Sanctis, *I Sogni*, Turin, 1899, pp. 269-273; H. Bergson, *art. cit.*, *Le rêve*, pp. 120-121; Vaschide, *op. cit.*, *Le Sommeil et le rêve*, p. 89; J. Pérès, "La logique du rêve et le rôle de l'association et de la vie affective", *Revue Philosophique*, Dec. 1913, p. 611; M. Foucault, *Le rêve*, Paris, 1906, p. 217; and many more

298 THE PSYCHOLOGY OF REASONING

analogous dreams) "frequently deal", writes Coriat, "with unpleasant or painful situations, without any unpleasant emotion in the dream itself; in fact, the dreamer may remain totally indifferent to the situation ". " Events," Ellis observes, "which in real life would overwhelm us, may, in dreams, be accepted as matters of course ". Foucault relates that his wife, when her daughter told her in a dream that she was going to bed because she felt ill, did not experience "any anxiety" and began, without more ado, to occupy herself with other quite insignificant things. " A young girl", Freud records, "sees in a dream her sister's baby lying dead in its coffin, but does not experience any grief or sadness ". And Freud himself sees one of his friends die suddenly in front of him, without feeling any impression.[1]

In dreams we commit immoral actions without remorse. This "complete absence of the moral sense" that so many writers have remarked in dreams, this absolute lack of "sittliche Gefühle", is only a consequence of the fact that all the higher affective tendencies are silent. "The higher moral faculties", writes Foucault, "are suspended during sleep; the sleeping mind no longer criticises its actions." "In dreams, we commit in imagination," writes Maury, "reprehensible acts, even crimes, of which we would never be guilty in real life". "Conscience", confirms Jessen, quoted by Freud, "seems to be silent in the dream, since we never experience pity, and can commit the gravest offences, even thefts and homicides, with complete indifference and without any remorse". A person of a very gentle disposition told Maury that he had killed several people in dreams. Havelock Ellis describes how a lady dreamed that she killed a woman and then quietly went to a lecture.[2]

In dreams we no longer experience any feeling of surprise, even at events which in the waking state would arouse it very keenly. "The mind is hardly astonished", Vaschide observes, "at the strange and

[1] J. H. Coriat, *The Meaning of Dreams*, London, 1916, p. 122; Ellis, *op. cit.*, p. 104; Foucault, *op. cit.*, p. 52; Freud, *op. cit.*, pp. 308, 310, 311.
[2] Foucault, *op. cit.*, p. 181; A. Maury, *Le sommeil et les rêves*, Paris, 1878, pp. 112-113, 115; Freud, *op. cit.*, p. 46; Ellis, *op. cit.*, p. 122.

INCOHERENCE OF DREAMS 299

bizarre content of its dreams ". Foucault also notes in the dream "the absence of surprise in circumstances in which we would ordinarily be surprised ". So too when we dream that we are flying in the air: "The experience", writes Ellis, "usually evokes no marked surprise, occurring as a familiar and accustomed pleasure ". "In a dream of my own", he adds, "I saw little creatures, a few inches high, moving about and acting on a diminutive stage. Though I regarded them as really living creatures and not marionettes, the spectacle caused me no surprise". Another time "I dreamed that I had a conversation with a cat, who spoke with fair clearness and sense, though the whole of her sentences were not intelligible. I was not surprised at this relative lack of intelligibility, but neither was I surprised at hearing her speaking at all ".[1]

In the same way, the astonishing metamorphoses in which dreams make us take part never cause us any feeling of surprise. It seemed to Patini, in a dream, that he found himself in an ancient Roman theatre : "And here comes a waiter in a tail-coat with a large tray full of glasses and ices, and the whole is transformed into a kind of café. *Not a vestige of astonishment* at the contradiction between the original situation and the subsequent change ". De Sanctis dreams of disputes in the Court of the Assizes : "While I dreamt, however, the hall of the Assizes changed into the examination hall of the University, as it was in my time. *The transformation did not surprise me, any more than it changed my state of mind, which remained indifferent*". The same indifference occurs to him in another dream when the Shah of Persia gradually changed into one of his sons.[2]

Lack of surprise, absence of all remorse or repentance for immoral actions we commit in dreams, indifference in the face of events which should afflict us deeply, the non-existence of any true and proper desire: all this strengthens the theory that the fundamental characteristic of dreams is, as we maintain, that of being *non-affective*. There is one fact, however, which at first sight would seem to contradict this theory, viz. that

[1] Vaschide, *op. cit.*, p. 161 ; Foucault, *op. cit.*, p. 300 ; Ellis, *op. cit.*, pp. 132, 271, 273.
[2] E. Patini, " La psicologia del sonno ", *La Cultura Filosofica*, Jan.-Feb. 1916, p. 23 ; S. De Sanctis, " Il sogno " *Volume giubilare in onore di G. Sergi*, Rome, 1916, p. 34.

300 THE PSYCHOLOGY OF REASONING

many dreams are strongly emotive, as every one knows. We have only to recall the commonest nightmares to realise what strong emotions certain dreams can arouse. Now this apparent contradiction disappears if we consider the nature of emotions and their possible double origin. In our waking life, according to the well-known theory of Lange and James, it is the intense and sudden activation of some affectivity that produces a somatic or visceral orgasm, which is then reflected psychically as emotion. In dreams, on the contrary, it is the somatic orgasm, that is to say, a severe physiological disturbance, which produces the emotion, entirely in consequence of certain cenæsthetic conditions, and thus produces an emotional state without previous existence and without the coming into play of any affective tendency. We know, moreover, that when we are awake also, in certain conditions, emotive states such as anxiety can exist that are *unjustified*, i.e. are due not to any affective cause, but simply to somatic causes. And such is precisely the origin of all emotions that are produced in dreams and that give rise to emotive dreams, which are also for the most part those of anxiety, terror, and the like. "When we are awake", Galasso well says, "the starting-point of every emotive state is principally a fact of a psychological order ; in sleep, on the contrary, the opposite happens, in the sense that the emotions generally owe their origin to facts of a somatic order". "We do not experience terror", Ellis writes in his turn, speaking of emotive dreams, "because we think we have committed a crime, but we think we have committed a crime because we experience terror". Thus under the burden of indigestion, a woman dreams that her husband kills a man and that he calls her to help him wrap up the corpse in paper, and carry it downstairs in order to put it in a carriage and go to hide it somewhere. All through this dream, the dreamer had been full of apprehension lest the deed should be discovered, and the last thing she remembered having dreamt before waking up terrified, was looking out of the window and seeing a large and threatening crowd which surrounded the house and shouted for the assassin.[1]

---

[1] J. Galasso, "Nuova ipotesi sul sonno fisiologico ", *Rivista di Psicologia applicata*, May-June 1911, p. 26 ; Ellis, *op. cit.*, pp. 109, 111-112.

INCOHERENCE OF DREAMS 301

"I believe", writes Kollarits, "that dreams of examinations are dreams of fear, pure and simple" (that is to say, of a purely visceral origin), "*without the least trace of desire*. The desire to succeed, which may be associated with fear, is active the whole day preceding the examination, and continues after waking. But, curiously enough, *there is no trace of this desire in the dream itself*." According to Wundt also, "the uncomfortable position of the dreamer, the oppression of respiration and other similar factors", are the exclusive cause of these painful dreams, which are so common, of having to pass an examination without being prepared.[1]

As for the fact of the mother who continues to sleep quietly through an intense noise in the street or the rumbling of thunder, though she wakes immediately at the slightest movement of her child in its cradle, this is probably due to the *reflex emotivity* that certain sensations, by daily habitude, provoke, and it is the emotion so induced by reflex means, that wakes her.

It is the usual regrettable confusion, on which we have again and again insisted, between affective tendencies and emotions, although they are of a substantially different nature, which has led some even of the most distinguished psychologists, and amongst them De Sanctis himself, to suppose that affective, even "intensely affective", dreams are frequent.[2] But in reality only emotive dreams are frequent, and they are so exclusively for somatic or visceral causes, so that a previous affective state as initiatory agent, as "starter", is in no way implied. Moreover, we should expect, in this connection, that the same degree of visceral disturbance would provoke a greater emotivity in the dream than when we are awake, precisely because the psychical repercussion does not encounter in the dream any obstacle due to preoccupations and desires, directed elsewhere, which are active during the waking state. In fact, when awake, we never find that indigestion, for example, provokes the state of terror to which it so often gives rise in dreams.

This emotivity of dreams, so easy and so exaggerated,

---

[1] J. Kollarits, "Contributions à l'étude des rêves", *Archives de Psychologie*, Aug. 1914, p. 251 ; Wundt, *op. cit.*, p. 656.
[2] De Sanctis, *art. cit.*, "Il Sogno", p. 10.

302 THE PSYCHOLOGY OF REASONING

caused by the slightest visceral disturbance, tends then, rather, to support the theory of their non-affectivity ; and this emotivity, co-existing with the absence of true and proper affective tendencies, affords at the same time the best proof that could be desired of the substantially different nature of emotive and affective phenomena.

3. *The Chief Consequences of Non-affectivity in Dreams*

The non-affectivity of dreams having thus been proved, all their characteristics are seen to be so many consequences of it.

For example, the rapid disappearance of the impressions of the dream on waking is the consequence of the feeble support, or absence of support, given to them by any affective tendency during the dream itself. "The impressions of the dream", remarks Morel, "are quickly effaced, and it is usually impossible for us to reproduce the details." Freud himself asks, like many others, why we generally forget our dreams as soon as we wake. "It has often happened", writes Foucault, "that I have been aroused during the night, or suddenly woken in the morning, my mind full of images of very clear dreams, but after a short time, often even a few minutes, nothing at all remained in my memory ; the dream was lost for ever." [1]

The continual metamorphoses to which the images of dreams are subject are also due to the fact that these images are not retained, even for an instant, on the threshold of consciousness by the persistence of some affective tendency to which they are of interest. "The most elementary fact about dream vision", writes Ellis, "is the perpetual and unceasing change which it is undergoing at every moment. . . . We are, as it were, gazing at a constantly revolving kaleidoscope in which every slightest turn produces a new pattern." Thus one dreams that one is at a theatre, at one moment as an actor, immediately afterwards as a spectator ; a castle situated by the sea becomes a castle on the bank of a narrow canal ; a fair handsome young man with a timid manner is transformed into Gambetta ; a wait-

---

[1] B. A. Morel, *Traité des maladies mentales*, Paris, 1860, p. 358 ; Freud, *op. cit.*, pp. 30-33 ; Foucault, *op. cit.*, p. 12.

INCOHERENCE OF DREAMS 303

ing-room in a station becomes a billiard-room, etc. To the same elementary sensation, Bergson observes, very different memories may correspond in the dream. "There is, for example, in the visual field (whether caused by some slight modifications which are produced in the retinal circulation, or by a certain pressure exercised by the closed eyelid on the eye-ball), a green stain with white spots. This could be a grass plot strewn with white flowers, it could be a billiard-table with billiard-balls, it could be a number of other things besides. These different memories, which can all profit by the same sensation, run after it. Sometimes they reach it one after the other, and it is thus that the lawn becomes a billiard-table, and that we take part in extraordinary transformations." But this transition from one image to another is rendered possible by the absence of all affectivity, of any desire for one object rather than for another ; if one of the images, for example that of the meadow with the white flowers, aroused in us the desire to go and run about there, it would not change into another but would remain "nailed", so to speak, in the mind all the time the respective affective tendency lasted.[1]

Hence too the great facility with which induced dreams are produced. In the waking state even the most intense external stimulations, such as those of the street or of a storm, do not succed in detaching us from the train of ideas in which we are interested ; on the other hand, the smallest stimulation is sufficient to make the dream deviate from one series of images to another and even a quite different series.[2]

But it is especially the two fundamental characteristics of dreams—those which have at all times most attracted the attention of psychologists, and have always remained a great unexplained problem—which receive the most complete explanation by our theory of non-affectivity. These are the incoherence and illogicality of the dreams themselves.

---

[1] Ellis, *op. cit.*, pp. 20, 21 ; Freud, *op. cit.*, pp. 227-228, 310 ; Y. Delage, "Le rêve et la condition psychique du rêveur", *Scientia*, April 1918, p. 267 ; Foucault, *op. cit.*, p. 242 ; Bergson, *art. cit.*, pp. 119-120.

[2] Cf., for example, Maury, *op. cit.*, pp. 154-156 ; Freud, *op. cit.*, p. 16 ; G. Stepanow, "Sogni Indotti", *Psiche*, 1915, nos. 3 and 4, e.g., pp. 5-6, 21-23, etc.

304 THE PSYCHOLOGY OF REASONING

4. *The Incoherence of Dreams*

If that which sleeps in the dream is only the affective side, then *ipso facto* there is lacking the evocative, directive, selective, inhibitory and connecting action which we have found to be exercised by the affective tendencies on the whole train of ideas of the reasoner.

There is no need to quote instances to prove this incoherence of dreams ; the "chaos of the dream", as Gruithuisen calls it, has always been its most salient phenomenon, and one noticed by all :

"There are no dreams", remarks Maury, "that do not contain some incoherence, some anachronism, some absurdity". "There are dreams", write Meunier and Masselon, "totally incoherent, where all logic is absent. Images arise, succeed one another, and are transformed, in an irregular and arbitrary manner. In dreams, the mind automatically obeys the play of the association of ideas." "Dreams", write Tanzi and Lugaro in their turn, "are a variegated tissue of images, representations, and evanescent ideas, sliding on a feeble weft, scarcely connected and often confused. Logical order is lost ; associations are dispersed along collateral and unusual ways ; the subject of the dream, even if derived from an obscure sensation of the real world, differs so excessively that it suddenly assumes an incoherent, often absurd, aspect". "According to Lemoine", says Freud, "the incoherence of images is the one essential characteristic of the dream". Dugas writes : "The dream is psychical anarchy ; it is the play of functions left to themselves and operating without control or purpose". Volkelt, also quoted by Freud, emphasises "the fragmentary nature, the dissolution and the confusion of the images, which in the waking state are kept together by the logical faculty of the ego." It is "the dissolubility, the disjointedness, the dissociation of the elements of the ego, the incapacity for cohesion that the dreaming ego presents in antithesis to the quite peculiar compactness and coherence of the waking personality" that, according to Patini, constitute the fundamental characteristic of dreams. Finally, we know how Foucault considers that the dream is made up of a great number

INCOHERENCE OF DREAMS   305

of pictures or groups of representations separate from one another and autonomous.[1]

In a dream of Charma's, for example, "*first*, he takes part in a procession in a church. *Then* he runs to the river to save a child who has fallen in from a bridge. He runs there quickly and arrives on the right bank of the Loire, at La Charité, his native town. *It is now* the sea near Ouistreham. He throws himself into the water and brings a drowned man to the shore ; but the drowned man is *now* the half-skinned carcase of an old cock." Quite disconnected also is the dream of a pupil of Foucault: "I find myself transported, I don't know how, to Besançon, near the baths of Pont-Cizeau (which are at Nevers) and I am bewildered. I see deserted gardens with billiard-tables, but I do not go in. I am in an immense corridor, the end of which I can't see. I arrive finally in a salon where a woman confronts me with sharp reproaches. I do not know exactly what she is saying to me, but I seem to understand her to ask me why I have come back to her house, when she has just shown me the right way. Then, without any transition, I am transported into a street in Besançon, etc., etc."[2]

This absence of connection, this supreme incoherence of dreams is due then to the fact that, since they lack the affective element, which in the waking-state is the chief controller and director of the intellectual material, there is no dam against the rising tide of our memories, which become active and follow each other chaotically by the merest play of the mechanical association of ideas. "It is by our actual thoughts", writes Janet, "that we resist the rising tide of our memories. Suppress this 'antagonistic reductive' and our old memories reproduce themselves, and combine in a thousand ways, easily, automatically and irresistibly. Memories, reveries, are all quite near to our consciousness ; a moment of sleep allows them to occupy the whole mind during dreams and nightmares." On which it may be observed that our actual thoughts can only function as antagonistic reducers in relation to the rising tide of our memories,

---

[1] Maury, *op. cit.*, p. 163 ; P. Meunier and R. Masselon, *Les rêves et leur interprétation*, Paris, 1910, pp. 10, 13 ; E. Tanzi and E. Lugaro, *Malattie mentali*, 2nd ed., Milano, 1914, vol. I, p. 270 ; Freud, *op. cit.*, p. 39 ; Patini, *art. cit.*, pp. 19, 25 ; Foucault, *op. cit.*, pp. 71, 132.

[2] Foucault, *op. cit.*, pp. 69-70, 117.

U

306 THE PSYCHOLOGY OF REASONING

in the degree that they are supported and held on the threshold of consciousness by the respective affectivity, by the respective interest that they arouse.[1]

"As regards the intelligence", writes Baillarger, "there are two very different states. In one, ideas are provoked and directed by the will; in the other, the influence of personal power has ceased, but the memory and imagination, freed from its dominion, continue to act, as may be observed during dreams for example." Now the absence of the will, the cessation of the influence of personal power, is nothing other than the immediate effect of the affective repose of the mind during sleep.[2]

Maury expresses himself still more explicitly: "What occurs in an intelligence that is failing, in an old man in his dotage, is almost identical with what happens to a man who is asleep: the attention is weakened, the will becomes numbed, the imagination is thus left to itself, and automatic mental activity comes more and more to replace voluntary activity. Thus it is probably by the weakening of the power of attention that the disorganisation of our mental faculties is chiefly caused." Now, the power of attention is weakened just when the primary and secondary tendencies, by whose opposition the state of attention is produced, are weakened.[3]

The dream may therefore be defined as an entrance of sensorial memories into anarchical activity ("planlos", as Wundt says), on account of the absence of any affective direction. "The dream," writes Pérès, "is a fact of inertia, *a decline of thought into the mechanical*. In the dream, we seize in its full activity the *aimless thought*. All that was held in check by the logic of thought directed towards an end, is emancipated in the dream and reverts to the first plan of consciousness. The anarchic dominion of the atomic elements of the mind replaces in dreams the dominion of the will." "Sleep", write Toulouse and Mignard, "realises an intellectual activity with *weakness of auto-conduction*, which is the dream." And Lehmann: "The irregular and often meaningless stream of images in the dream proves that *there is no longer any directive action on the part of the*

[1] P. Janet, *Névroses et idées fixes*, Paris, 1904, 2nd ed., Vol. I, p. 153.

[2] M. Baillarger, *Recherches sur les maladies mentales*, Vol. I, Paris, 1890, pp. 443-444.

[3] Maury, *op. cit.*, pp. 106-108.

INCOHERENCE OF DREAMS 307

attention." "The fact of sleeping", says Freud, "*implies the renunciation of volitional direction of the stream of images.*" And Henning: "In the dream *all determinative tendencies are lacking,* so that it becomes irrational".[1] The "loosening of mental bonds", the "series of degradations of the thinking and reasoning faculty", the "suspension of the higher intellectual faculties", that Ellis, Maury, Freud and many others have noted in the dream, are then due exclusively to this affective inactivity.[2]

This shows, moreover, that this "mental bond", this "thinking and reasoning faculty", these "higher intellectual faculties", consist simply and solely in the evocative, directive, selective, inhibitory and connective action of the affective tendencies, the one psychic activity which, in the dream, is silent and at rest.

The functioning of sensory evocation is, in fact, perfect. Different as the dream is from the real world in its totality, all its elements are nevertheless an exact repetition of those which reality offers us (Hildebrandt). The aphorism of Hervey de Saint-Denis, *nihil est in visionibus somnorum quod non prius fuerit in visu,* is equivalent to saying that the material of mnemonic reproduction is intact and that the mechanism of evocation in itself functions correctly in sleep no less than when we are awake.

In dreams, moreover, the association of ideas is notoriously much more varied and abundant than in the waking state ; just because of the absence of an affectivity which evokes only what interests it and inhibits any other image which might act as a disturbing factor. "In dreams", observes Galton, "all men commonly exhibit more vivid powers of imagination than are possessed by the greatest artists when awake."[3]

But the very fact that the mechanism of evocation pure and simple continues to function correctly, even in dreams, is what constitutes the most striking proof of

---

[1] Wundt, *op. cit.,* p. 657 ; Pérès, *art. cit.,* pp. 598, 602, 614 ; E. Toulouse et M. Mignard, " Les maladies mentales et l'autoconduction ", *Revue de Psychiatrie et de Psychologie expérimentale,* July 1911, p. 269 ; A. Lehmann, *Grundzüge der Psychophysiologie,* Leipzig, 1912, p. 512 ; Freud, *op. cit.,* p. 39 ; Henning, *op. cit.,* p. 15.

[2] Ellis, *op. cit.,* p. 66 ; Maury, *op. cit.,* p. 27 ; Freud, *op. cit.,* p. 39.

[3] Fr. Galton, *op. cit. : English men of Science, their Nature and Nurture,* p. 234 ; *cf.* also Foucault, *op. cit.,* pp. 212-213 ; Wundt, *op. cit.,* p. 656 ; Freud, *op. cit.,* p. 6.

308 THE PSYCHOLOGY OF REASONING

the erroneousness of the English associationist view, according to which the simple fact of association is sufficient to account for reasoning. Many dreams, and just some of the most incoherent, represent the typical case of a process strictly obeying the laws of the mechanical association of ideas: "There is at the basis of dreaming", writes Ellis, "a seemingly spontaneous procession of dream imagery which is always undergoing transformation into something different, yet not wholly different, from that which went before. It seems a mechanical flow of images, regulated by associations of resemblance ".[1]

There are three dreams of Maury which have become classic, where events are associated and succeed each other by the simple association of the respective names : *pélérinage, Pelletier, pelle ; jardin, Chardin, Janin ; kilomètre, kilos, Gilolo, lobélia, Lopez, loto.* It is sufficient to quote here the last of the three : "I dreamt of the word *kilomètre*, and I dreamt of it so hard that I imagined myself walking on a road where I read the milestones which mark the measured distances. Suddenly I find myself on one of the large scales which grocers use, on one of the trays of which a man was piling up *kilos*, so as to find out my weight; then, I do not quite know why, the grocer tells me that we are not in Paris, but in the island *Gilolo*, of which I confess I have hardly ever thought in my life. Then my mind turned to the other syllable of the name, I left the first and began to slide along the second : I had successively several dreams in which I saw the flower called *lobélia*, General *Lopez*, of whose deplorable end in Cuba I had read ; finally I woke up playing the game of *loto* ".[2]

There could be no better example of the inability of the law of the association of ideas to evoke of itself more than a chaotic and incoherent series of images. "The associationist psychologists", writes Toulouse and Mignard, "have shown us the mind as it would be without the forces of synthesis and direction ". Now these factors of synthesis and direction are constituted by the affective tendencies alone.[3]

---

[1] Ellis, *op. cit.*, p. 27.
[2] Maury, *op. cit.*, pp. 137-138.
[3] E. Toulouse and M. Mignard, " L'autoconduction ", *Revue de psychiatrie et de psychologie expérimentale.* Jan. 1912, p. 28.

INCOHERENCE OF DREAMS 309

We are thus able to draw the conclusion that the most incoherent dream would be exactly the one which would most approach a purely intellectual process, that is to say, with no blend of affective processes.

The assertion of Binet, then, is strange. " Reasoning ", he says, "is an organisation of images, *determined by the properties of the images alone;* it is sufficient that the images be presented for them to organise themselves, and for reasoning to result with the fatality of a reflex ". The function of the affective tendencies in rendering the series of images which form any reasoning process coherent and truly "organised ", could not be more explicitly misunderstood.[1]

In fact, the associationists failed to see what dreams confirm in the most suggestive manner, namely, that association by contiguity, resemblance, etc., can be produced and dispersed in an infinite number of directions, and that what has therefore to be explained is how, when awake, we do not get the chaotic release of images which is so typical of the dream. It is this that causes Verworn to remark : " The question arises : If associations can originate in all possible directions, how is it that a confusion of sensations and representations is not produced in the brain, and that regulated association and logical thought are possible ? " And he points out that " the processes of inhibition constitute for logical thought a condition as important as the processes of evocation "; but he does not see that in the waking state it is to the affective tendencies that the evocative function as well as the inhibitory function belong, and that it is exclusively to them that the coherence of the whole process of association is due.[2]

5. *The Illogicality of Dreams*

If the first of the two fundamental characteristics of dreams, incoherence, depends on the absence of the primary affective tendency and of its function of evoking, selecting, inhibiting and connecting images (the function which maintains *the thread* of reasoning), their second fundamental characteristic, illogicality, is derived from the absence of the secondary affective tendency, whose

---

[1] A. Binet, *La psychologie du raisonnement*, Paris, 1902, pp. 9-10.
[2] Verworn, *op. cit.*, pp. 53-54, 67.

310 THE PSYCHOLOGY OF REASONING

opposition to the primary tendency constitutes the state of attention and gives rise to the *critical sense*.

In the waking state, it is this secondary tendency of fear of deception, which, still more than the primary tendency, is continually in action ; it is the one which does not rest for an instant, from morning until night. If it were not continually awake, every one of our acts would be a "gaffe", a mistake, a blunder ; we would follow the first fortuitous idea that came into our minds without further ado, without any control. Now, this is exactly what happens in dreams, where the absolute lack of the critical sense is due essentially to the serene peacefulness of the sleeper, who is not worried by any feeling of surprise, of doubt, or of fear lest he be mistaken.

In the waking state, as Bergson well observes, contrary to what takes place in dreams, we choose among the mnemonic evocations which come before the mind, those which correspond with, and are wholly adapted to, reality. "This choice that we are always making, this continuous renewed adaptation, is the first and most essential condition of what is called common sense. But all this maintains a state of *uninterrupted tension*. We do not feel it at the time, any more than we feel the pressure of the atmosphere. But it produces fatigue in the long run. It is very tiring to have common sense".[1]

"The chief fact recognised by all", writes Delage, "is the suppression of the critical sense in the dream. What is the cause of this suppression ? If the critical sense is deficient in the dream it is because, in order to use it, we have to envisage simultaneously and compare several eventualities which are presented, consequences present and future, direct and indirect, and give to each the exact coefficient which measures its importance. In our waking life, intelligence is the more complete in proportion as the eyes of the mind can penetrate, not only further in front of them, but also in all other directions where elements of judgment may be found". "In the dreamer", he adds, "attention is deprived of the initiative, which in the waking state causes it to focus on all the points necessary in order to build up a complete judgment". On which it may be observed

[1] Bergson, *art. cit.*, p. 118.

INCOHERENCE OF DREAMS 311

that if, in the dream, the "eyes of the mind" do not penetrate in all directions, it is precisely because the secondary affective tendency of control is lacking : it is this tendency, in fact, which penetrates everywhere and turns directly on all the points necessary for the formation of a complete and exact judgment ; which, in other words, evokes, tests, retains and raises to the rank of "antagonistic reductives" all the facts of reality opposed to the erroneous ones that were the first to be fortuitously presented to the mind.[1]

"In dreams", writes Verworn, "associations of representations are produced which, if we were awake, *would be completely excluded by the control of our critical faculty*". Haffner, quoted by Freud, successfully sums up the two fundamental characteristics of the dream, the first due to the absence of the primary affectivity, the second to the absence of the secondary affectivity of control : " It is in the *lack of orientation* that the whole secret of the disorderly flight taken by our imagination in the dream resides ; and it is in the *absence of critical reflexion* that we may find the principal cause of the absurd extravagances of our judgment". This is why, rather than say with Foucault : " It is doubt that is the first manifestation of reasoning", we are inclined to reverse the terms of the aphorism, and to say that reason, *i.e.* the logical functioning of thought, is due to doubt, to the fear of deception.[2]

Very often, in fact, we frame false and absurd hypotheses even in the waking state, owing to the pure chance of the association which first presents them to our mind, but our anxiety not to be deceived and our surprise if we are led to results contrary to our ordinary experience, are quick to reject them. In the dream, on the other hand, as Wundt remarks, "*we never doubt,* whatever the contradiction between our oneiric images and the events of the waking state." " In the dream ", writes Galasso, " ideation is freed from the control of discernment and choice ".[3]

From this complete absence of doubt is derived among other things the generally erroneous interpreta-

---

[1] Delage, *art. cit.*, pp. 265, 266.
[2] Verworn, *op. cit.*, p. 79 ; Freud, *op. cit.*, p. 37 ; Foucault, *op. cit.*, p. 35.
[3] Wundt, *op. cit.*, p. 658 ; Galasso, *art. cit.*, p. 260.

312 THE PSYCHOLOGY OF REASONING

tion that we give in dreams to the elementary sensations felt while we are asleep : " Why should the mind misinterpret the nature of sense stimulations in dreams? " Freud asks. " If a dreamer's feet ", writes Ellis, " are in contact with something hot, it might seem more natural that he should think of the actual hot-water bottle ", which is the source of the stimulus, " rather than of an imaginary Etna ".[1]

The difficulty of understanding how it is that the person who dreams habitually interprets his elementary sensations in such an erroneous way, springs from the fact that we are apt to forget that all perception is essentially only *an hypothesis*. Every perception, in fact, is, as is well known, only formed to a very small extent by actual sensations, and often by only a single elementary sensation ; for the rest, it consists of images evoked to complete the elementary sensations themselves. The elementary sensation, besides being only a small part of the total perception, is at the same time common to several perceptions. When awake, we acquire the correct perception of things owing to the attention with which we observe them, that is to say, owing to doubts whether we "have seen aright", which we always experience when from a few sensations we wish to arrive by means of hypothesis at the object of which they are only a symbol. This attention results in the addition of other elementary sensations which enlarge the base on which the perceptive hypothesis is founded. In dreams, on the other hand, the first fortuitous hypothesis which comes into the mind is accepted without further examination. In the dream then, there is not, as De Sanctis maintains, a 'transformation' of certain sensations into representations of another kind, but a very simple completion of these sensations by the mnemonic elements which they evoke fortuitously and which, being due merely to chance and not selected by the critical sense, do not generally correspond to reality. " The dreamer ", says Delage, " has no other materials at his disposal than those which chance, acting through the association of ideas, brings into his consciousness ". We may then conclude that the idea of an object, evoked by an elementary sensation, is always *an hypothesis*, which, in the waking state, generally corresponds to reality

[1] Freud, *op. cit.*, p. 20 ; Ellis, *op. cit.*, p. 160.

INCOHERENCE OF DREAMS   313

because it is submitted to the critical affective control, and which, in dreams, does not usually correspond to reality because, being due to a pure chance of association, it is at the same time released from this critical affective control.[1]

But, we repeat, it is especially the extreme illogicality of dreams that may be explained by the absence in the dream of doubt, of the fear of being deceived, and of the least feeling of surprise at events openly conflicting with our experience. "The dream-world", writes Foucault, "does not conform to the world that we know according to our waking experience, it is contrary to the best established facts of experience". "What astonishing liberties", writes Hildebrandt, quoted by Freud, "the person who dreams allows himself in drawing his conclusions ! With what indifference he sees the discomfiture of the best known laws of experience ! *We are not at all surprised* if a dog recites verses to us, if a dead person walks to his grave by himself or if a piece of rock floats on water". "To dream of flying", writes Spencer, "and not to suspect any illusion, implies that thought is limited to a narrow train of simple ideas, and that there are not aroused any remembrances of those antagonistic experiences and of those general conceptions framed on them, *which are implied by scepticism and disbelief*".[2]

For example, Foucault relates that one of his pupils dreamed that he was run over by a train : " I remember very well the painful sensation caused by the wheel weighing on my chest. But it was only a weight ; my bones were not broken, and I even raised the carriage by inflating my chest." Another dream also related by Foucault, presents to the sleeper, by the introduction of the image of a sewing-establishment into that of a porcelain factory, porcelain vases and plates that could be sewn. Havelock Ellis dreams that he sees himself through his field-glass in a place different from that in which he stands, and "the dreaming consciousness accepted this situation *with perfect equanimity and solemnity*." " I dreamt once of a mill ", Mach tells us. " The water descended from the mill by a sloping canal, then it

---

[1] De Sanctis, *memoir cit.*, p. 32 ; Delage, *art. cit.*, p. 266.
[2] Foucault, *op. cit.*, p. 18 ; Freud, *op. cit.*, p. 40 ; H. Spencer, *op. cit.*, *The Principles of Psychology*, Vol. I, p. 593.

314 THE PSYCHOLOGY OF REASONING

ascended again by another of the same kind. *I was not at all surprised"*. And again : " In another dream I saw in my laboratory a glass full of water, in which a candle was quietly burning.—Where does it get the oxygen from? I asked myself.—It is absorbed from the water.—Where do the products of combustion go? —But here I see air-bubbles rising from the flame to the surface of the water, *and my mind is set at rest again."* Imagine what intense complicated affectivity of astonishment, curiosity, fear of having been mistaken and other similar feelings, facts so contradictory to ordinary experience would have aroused in Mach had he been awake ! [1]

These dreams serve remarkably well by the absurdity of their deductions, to show how illogicality consists only in the attribution, to an imagined experience or fact, of consequences or results different from those that have occurred in past experiences. If, for example, a lighted candle is put into water, it goes out ; Mach, on the contrary, imagines illogically that it continues to burn. These illogical dreams show at the same time how the absence of all feeling of surprise at such absurd results, of all fear or doubt about being mistaken, and consequently the absence of all critical sense, is exactly what allows these illogical deductions to be entertained and to remain on the threshold of consciousness, while if the secondary affectivity of control existed, efficient inhibitory agents would be opposed to each of these absurd results in the form of all those "antagonistic images " with which experience has furnished us in the past and which the secondary affectivity itself would evoke and sustain.

If then the incoherence of dreams is due to the lack of a primary affectivity following with interest the object whose vicissitudes we imagine, their illogicality depends on the absence of the secondary affectivity to control the respective results that we imagine should be the consequence of each of these vicissitudes. And the absence of the primary affectivity, the cause of incoherence, as well as the absence of the secondary affectivity, the cause of illogicality, are simply the immediate consequence of the *non-affectivity* of dreams, that is to say, of the functional rest of the affective part of the mind in

---

[1] Foucault, *op. cit.*, pp. 246, 240 ; Ellis, *op. cit.*, p. 64 ; E. Mach, *op. cit.*, *Die Analyse der Empfindungen*, p. 207.

INCOHERENCE OF DREAMS 315

the sleeper, while the purely intellectual part, whereby sensations and images are evoked, persists with the same activity as in the waking state.

We can, therefore, now reply to the questions formulated by the Academy of Moral and Political Sciences of Paris in putting up for competition in 1885 the subject of "The Theory of Sleep and Dreams": 1. "Which mental faculties continue or are suspended or considerably modified in sleep?" 2. "What is the essential difference between dreaming and thinking?"

To the first: that in sleep the pure intellective faculty of the evocation of sensory images continues to exist, while the affective faculty is suspended ; and, that consequently, dreams are the result *of an affective sleep unaccompanied by a corresponding intellective sleep ;* in other words, that they are *an anarchy of ideas due to the cessation of all affective government.* To the second: that to think or to reason is to follow with attention the history of an object imagined as submitted to a number of experiments, taking care to attribute to each the results that have already been reached by similar experiments in the past, and that would again be arrived at if the experiment were actually performed instead of being simply thought of—all of which implies a continuous action of evocation, selection, co-ordination and control on the part of the respective affective tendencies ; while to dream is to leave the mnemonic reproduction of sensory elements completely free, since every affective tendency is silent—which implies an incoherent and illogical evocation of images by the mere fortuitous play of the mechanical association of ideas.

6. *Other Theories of Dreams*

Our theory of non-affectivity as the cause of all fundamental characteristics of dreams, and especially of their incoherence and illogicality, is in agreement with several others which it collects together by a single explanation. It agrees, for example, with the theory of Foucault, quoted above, according to which the dream is only a series of separate pictures, which follow one another independently, or are even produced simultaneously and blend together ; with the theory of Toulouse and Mignard, according to whom dreams

316 THE PSYCHOLOGY OF REASONING

are due to the lack of auto-conduction; with the theory of Delage, who attributes dreams to the restriction of the mnemonic field, the person who dreams having at his disposal only the materials which are fortuitously furnished by the association of ideas; and it agrees with many other theories too, as is shown by the quotations given above with which we have been rather liberal, just because from this or that point of view they support our thesis. But all the theories of dreams that have been advanced hitherto have been *partial*, in the sense that they attribute dream characteristics to such and such a phenomenon, which in its turn requires explanation. Thus it remains for Foucault to explain why the successive or simultaneous evocation of separate pictures does not occur in the waking state also; Mignard and Toulouse should inform us why auto-conduction ceases to function during the dream; and Delage does not inquire the origin of the partial and non-systematic amnesia of the dreamer. And the same applies to many others. Now our theory completes them all, by showing how the phenomena invoked in explanation of the fundamental characteristics of dreams all depend, in their turn, on the non-affectivity of dreams themselves. This non-affectivity has, as we have seen, been emphasised by a large number of writers, but no one until now has raised it to the rank of the sole and fundamental explanation of the odd phenomena which occur in the dream state.

But on the other hand our theory is quite at variance with the psycho-analytic theory of Freud and his disciples, which would find an affective unity and a coherence and logicality in just this psychical process, the dream, which more than any other is distinguished by its non-affectivity, its incoherence, and its illogicality. This is, in our opinion, a highly paradoxical account, presenting as it does the strange phantasmagoria of dreams as the refined plan of a psychical censor who strives to hide under a symbolic veil the satisfaction that the desires of the unconscious, repressed during the waking state, would procure in the dream; and this without troubling and waking the normal mind of the sleeper, which would disapprove of such satisfaction. Great as has been the attention with which we have studied Freud's book, we have not found in it the

INCOHERENCE OF DREAMS   317

slightest proof of his assertion. The long and interminable analyses of dreams only succeed ultimately in proving that the images of the dream, even the strangest and most complex, are derived from the compositions or fusion of images or sense elements of the waking state, which we are quite disposed to admit. But not one of these analyses has offered the slightest proof that the oneiric phantasmagoria are an intentional pun, under which lurks an entirely different tale, directed to the satisfaction of some repressed instinct or desire of the unconscious. Such an " unconscious ", in the meaning that Freud gives it, and the famous "censor" begin to be myths themselves, and all the efforts of their creator cannot prove that they really exist and really act on the lines indicated by him.[1]

7. *Dreams and Madness*

Before bringing this study to a close we must say a few words about the connection, already envisaged by many writers, between dreams and madness.

As is well known, the great strangeness of dreams, especially their incoherence and illogicality, renders them comparable with some of the most notable psychical manifestations of the insane. Cabanis, Lélut, J. Moreau, Maine de Biran, Kant, Krauss, Schopenhauer, and many others have all emphasised the resemblance between dreams and madness. Maury particularly has insisted on this resemblance, comparing for example the senile dementia of a lady who imagined that she was dead and pretended to explain how, although thus defunct, she nevertheless took her chocolate every morning, with a dream of his own in which one of his colleagues dead and buried, explained to him how he was able to come back into this world ; an explanation that Maury accepts in his dream as a perfectly good one. The comparison of the two absurd explanations shows up their great similarity in a suggestive manner.[2]

" *Nihil tam praepostere* ", wrote Cicero, " *tam incondite, tam monstruose cogitari potest, quod non possimus somniare.*"

---

[1] For a critique of the psycho-analytic theories of the dream, see the author's article on " La signification des rêves," in *Scientia*, May 1918.

[2] Maury, *op. cit.*, pp. 165-166.

318 THE PSYCHOLOGY OF REASONING

Ellis emphasises that in dreams, as in insanity, " the incontinence of ideas linked together by superficial associations of resemblance or contiguity, is a linking without direction." " If we behaved when awake as we do in dreams," writes Freud, "we would appear to be mad ". Fechner had already noted that in dreams " it is as if the psychological activity were transferred from the brain of a reasonable man into that of a madman." "The ravings of madness", writes Luciani, "are like dreams in the waking state, as dreams are ravings during sleep. It is not strange then to consider the dream as *a passing madness*". And Wundt : " The incoherence of the stream of images, the errors of judgment and the mistakes that this incoherence brings with it, further increases the relationship, often observed, of dreams and insanity, which are already comparable as regards their fantastic ideas. Indeed, we can ourselves experience in dreams all the phenomena that may be observed in asylums. *This analogy between the dream and madness is without doubt due to common causes* ".[1]

But in the comparison of the dream with madness, it has not been adequately realized that in insanity there are different kinds of incoherence and illogicality and that accordingly only some kinds of madmen can be actually compared with the dreamer. And as regards these we shall find that the incoherence and illogicality are due here also *to an absence of affectivity*. We shall find too that other kinds of incoherence and illogicality are also always due to disturbances of an affective order, but of a different kind.

This will be shown in the two following chapters devoted to reasoning as it is found in the insane.

---

[1] Ellis, *op. cit.*, pp. 170-171 ; Freud, *op. cit.*, pp. 39-40 ; Luciani, *op. cit.*, pp. 519-520 ; Wundt, *op. cit.*, p. 675.

CHAPTER XIV

THE PATHOLOGY OF REASONING

Part II : Coherent but Illogical Insanity due to Mono-affectivism

THE surprise that we experience when confronted by unusual phenomena is not always in proportion to the intrinsic difficulty of their explanation. It has often happened in the history of the sciences that the curiosity aroused by a given group of phenomena owing to the apparent eccentricity of a small number, has served to emphasise how the principal difficulty did not consist so much in explaining what was strange as in accounting for what, in virtue of its being more familiar to us, we considered 'natural'. This has been the case with the various psychological phenomena that we class under the name of "mental equilibrium". At first sight it appears "natural" to us that a man should think and reason correctly, and on the other hand we are very astonished at the strangeness of madmen, of the "unbalanced". But a more mature reflection should convince us that it is much more difficult to account for mental "balance" than for its opposite.

1. *"Mental Equilibrium" is only Affective Equilibrium*

It is sufficient for this purpose to reflect on the number, the delicacy and the complications of the functioning and of the reciprocal influences of the factors in play from which the normal behaviour of the individual, his appropriate conduct, is derived.

First of all, there must be a great affective equilibrium which allows us to be interested in the different phenomena of the external world in proportion to the importance that they actually have for us. This is the chief service rendered by the brain to the organism, and

320 THE PSYCHOLOGY OF REASONING

represents the condition *sine qua non* for the adaptation of the organism to its environment; it should therefore be considered as the phylogenetic result of the moulding action of the external world. As long as the brain remains dependent on the whole organism, the affective tendencies maintain their equilibrium, that is to say, they remain adequate to the external world and proportionate to the real physiological needs of the organism. If on the other hand, the partial autonomy of the brain becomes complete independence, then some affective tendencies are enabled to assume abnormal intensity, excessive or deficient, and thus give rise to an affective unbalance in which the affective activity is no longer in relation either to the economy of the organism or to the environment.

In the second place, a mind is the more balanced the better it observes, interprets, judges and reasons, that is to say the more it maintains a close correspondence between our mental representations and the external world, present and past. For this purpose great affective equilibrium is equally necessary.

To observe well means to have perceptions which correspond to reality; but as we have already seen in the preceding chapter on dreams, all perception is only an hypothesis, which is generally founded on a very limited number of elementary sensations, completed by a large quantity of sensory evocations. Thus every over-intense affective state not only evokes exclusively those of the mnemonic sensory elements which agree with it, but further prevents the birth of the antagonistic affective state of doubt or fear of having been mistaken, which gives rise to the state of attention. It prevents, in this manner, firstly, the enlargement of the sensory basis of perception through which enter into play the "antagonistic reductives" of the sensory evocations which do not correspond to reality; and, in the second place, the equipment of this enlarged sensory base with other evocations actually corresponding with reality. Everyone knows, for example, that persons dominated by passion are subject to illusions even of a purely perceptual order.

The same equilibrium, between the two antagonistic affective tendencies which constitute the state of attention, is necessary for the correct interpretation of the acts or words of our fellow-creatures. If the traveller sitting

COHERENT INSANITY 321

before us in the carriage suddenly puts his hand into his pocket, we interpret the action by the supposition that he is going to pull out his handkerchief or cigarette-case or some other inoffensive object of the same kind, for experience teaches us that such is commonly the consequence of the act we happen to observe. But anyone overcome by an exaggerated feeling of fear at finding himself alone in the compartment with a stranger, will only evoke memories of railway assaults which the papers have detailed for him in the past, and will accordingly suspect that his travelling companion is going to draw his revolver.

In order to form a balanced and accurate opinion as to the probability of a certain event taking place, it is necessary to "evaluate" or "weigh" all the factors which contribute to produce it, and, at the same time, all the other factors, which would tend to prevent it. That is to say, it is necessary to evoke both kinds and keep them as much as possible before the mind, in order to give to those which are actually in the majority the possibility of functioning as antagonistic reducers in relation to the others. And if some are supported for example by the desire that the event may take place, it is necessary that the others should be supported by the no less intense affectivity of fear that the event may not occur, an affectivity which will evoke and support just those facts that the primary affectivity would not only not have evoked, but would have inhibited. The conflict between extreme optimists and pessimists as to the imminent or remote consequences of the same social events which are unfolded before their eyes, is due to their respective excessive affectivities, each taking into consideration only a part of the relevant factors.

Finally, in order to reason well it is necessary to follow with interest the vicissitudes of the object on which we imagine ourselves performing certain experiments or effecting certain modifications or acting in such and such a way. This interest should not be diverted, during the whole period of reasoning, by any external event or any other thought. It should, then, be a *sufficiently* intense interest, but *not too* intense. In fact, interest in the object whose history we follow with the mind's eye, usually implies also the desire that the series of imagined experiments should lead to one

X

322 THE PSYCHOLOGY OF REASONING

result rather than to another. And if this desire is too strong, then logical accuracy *ipso facto* incurs grave peril ; for the secondary affectivity of control, that is to say, of the fear of being mistaken, which holds the primary affectivity in suspense and constitutes the state of attention, will have difficulty in maintaining itself in face of this over-intense desire. It will also have difficulty in evoking the antagonistic reducers, which should be drawn by it from past experience and which would inhibit and expel the erroneous conclusions, evoked prematurely by excess of eagerness to arrive at the desired result.

From all this it can be seen that what is called "mental equilibrium", depends only on *affective equilibrium*, i.e. on an equilibrium between the primary affectivity tending to see, to interpret, to judge, to reason in a certain way, and the secondary affectivity, the fear of being deceived, the fear that the contrary of what is desired should happen, which balances the primary affectivity. This equilibrium constitutes the state of attention, and is the product, and, so to speak, the echo of continual disappointments experienced in the past through the too sudden acceptance of conclusions desired by the primary affectivity ; so that it also may be regarded as the result of the continual adaptation of the species and the individual to their environment.

It is well known that even normal people are frequently liable to errors in observation, or interpretation, or reasoning, due to the predominance at a certain moment of a somewhat lively affectivity not sufficiently counterbalanced by any antagonistic one. But such people are mostly capable of retrieving their mistake, especially if they are recalled to reality by others. On the other hand, more intense affective states render the persuasive work of the critical faculty more and more difficult, until the passionate condition is reached in which it is completely nullified. Thus the scientist who holds too strongly to his theories not only does not notice the facts which contradict them but is incapable of giving due weight to the objections of his opponents. Certain interminable disputes, especially in philosophy, never lead to any result, just because of the passionate enthusiasm of those who take part in them. And in

COHERENT INSANITY 323

our chapter on metaphysical reasoning, we saw how the intense passion of the believer for his supreme values, such as the existence of God, or the immortality of the soul, prevent him absolutely from seeing the illogicalities, the absurdities and the nonsense of the structures which he elaborates and in which he reposes peacefully, happy in continuing to believe in what he has so much at heart. "Happiness", writes William James, "has blindness and insensibility to opposing facts given it as its instinctive weapon for self protection against disturbance".[1]

Starting from the facts of affective disequilibrium in its first stage and applying to psychology the "principle of continuity", so fruitful in mechanics (Mach), the normal person can imagine as more and more intense, or more and more persistent, or more and more exclusively predominating, certain states of mind of an affective order, which do not happen to be for the moment in perfect equilibrium in himself; and if he then proceeds to verify the illogicality and the errors which, in him too, are immediately derived from it, he can succeed in understanding the similar psychical phenomena of madmen and thus convince himself that the illogicality and strangeness of thought of the latter are also only the consequences of their affective disequilibrium.

2. *The Mono-affectivism of Monomaniacs*

"Mental disequilibrium", then, always resolves itself into an affective disequilibrium. Accordingly, it is now widely recognised by psychiatrists that the insanity of monomaniacs in particular is due also to affective disturbances, which "group themselves round the fundamental instincts and passions of human nature".[2]

"The idea that the appearance of delirium in paranoia is due to a primary disorder of the intelligence", write Sérieux and Capgras, "is constantly losing ground; to-day we tend to consider affective disturbances as primitive."[3]

[1] W. James, *op. cit.*, *The Varieties of Religious Experience*, p. 88 ; *cf.* Ribot, *op. cit.*, *La logique des sentiments*, passim.
[2] E. Tanzi and E. Lugaro, *op. cit.*, *Malattie mentali*, Vol. I, p. 321.
[3] P. Sérieux and J. Capgras, *Les folies raisonnantes*, Paris, 1909, pp. 216-217, 220.

324 THE PSYCHOLOGY OF REASONING

Yet it is necessary to emphasise more than is usually done the character of *mono-affectivism* peculiar to the systematic insanity of the paranoiac. For this purpose it is enough to recall how often the passionate or jealous man, for example, develops into the chronic madman proper, in order to convince us of their substantial identity. Such a one, for example, returns to live with his wife, who had been obliged to leave him on account of his jealous persecution. " But his jealousy takes the form of insanity. At night, he does not sleep ; strange noises at the windows are for him a sign that certain persons are coming for his wife. He barricades the door of his house, he looks into all hiding-places and corners, he hermetically seals all openings, he feigns sleep in order to take the unfaithful one by surprise : *it is in vain ; she has a ' magic handkerchief', which allows her to go out without being seen.*"[1]

Morel has also noted in the systematic insanity of the monomaniac, "the passionate element that dominates his feelings " ; and he shows with what energy the single controlling affectivity tends to inhibit every fact that would be contrary to what it desires : " In megalomania, the incessant need to occupy the attention of the public with their personality is so violent that these madmen end by identifying themselves with the rôles that they adopt, and come to regard the most extravagant ideas as true and real. One of these patients worked himself up into a *strange fury*, when it was proved to him mathematically that the acts of which he assumed himself to be the agent or the hero preceded the time of his birth by more than a hundred and fifty years ".[2]

The state of continual remorse and terror of the melancholic, the continual acts of propitiation, humiliation, confession and self-accusation, and the continual anxiety, denote precisely the existence, the intensity and the persistence of one and the same affective state. In the persecuted, it is the egocentric state of offended pride, of "autophilia " (Ball), that forms the fundamental and exclusive basis : " Many observers," writes Séglas, "have already noticed the close relation between the insanity of the persecuted and their previous character.

[1] Renda, *Le passioni*, Turin, 1906, p. 73.
[2] B. A. Morel, *op. cit.*, *Traité des maladies mentales*, pp. 484, 548.

COHERENT INSANITY 325

Jealousy, overbearing egoism, vanity, etc., are the principal traits of this character that can be summed up in two words : arrogance and mistrust." [1]

"The affective state, internal in origin, of the chronic monomaniac", observes Godfernaux, "which would only be temporary in a sane subject, may here last for a period of several years. In such a case there is a re-organisation of the whole conscious mental content." And Sérieux and Capgras also draw attention to the egocentric-affective character of the interpretative paranoiac, such as is met with in passionate states. [2]

In all these cases the affective singleness is due to the violence of the fundamental affectivity, which is persistent and aggressive, and victoriously resists all antagonistic affective tendencies on their appearance, and inhibits them at birth. In other cases, however, often developed from those we have been considering, the affective unity of the monomaniac is produced not so much by the violence of the fundamental affectivity, rendering any opposed affectivity impossible, but because no attempt, however feeble, is made by any antagonistic tendency whatever to arouse itself. Provided there is no opposition the effect is the same, that is to say, there is equally a state of absolute mono-affectivism, although calm and peaceful. In these cases, systematic delirium would appear as "a direction of the mind, a habit which ends by exercising itself without any intense emotional state". [3]

If now, without dwelling further on the mono-affectivism of monomaniacs or paranoiacs, we pass on to the examination of its consequences in the intellectual domain, we should expect *a priori*, after all we have said about the nature of reasoning, to find in them *great coherence* united with *great illogicality*. And this is exactly what we have to establish *a posteriori*.

3. *The Coherence of Monomaniacs*

If the affectivity which is continually in play in the monomaniac is one and always the same, the direction

---

[1] J. Séglas, *Leçons cliniques sur les maladies mentales et nerveuses*, Paris, 1895, pp. 305, 307, 514-515, 519.
[2] A. Godfernaux, *Le sentiment et la pensée*, 2nd edit. Paris, 1906, pp. 65-66 ; Sérieux and Capgras, *op. cit.*, p. 4.
[3] Sérieux and Capgras, *op. cit.*, p. 220.

326 THE PSYCHOLOGY OF REASONING

of his thought or his phantasy will be in the closest connection with this affectivity only; which will function like a chromatic lens, causing everything in the external world to appear of the same uniform colour. "The ideas of jealous maniacs", write Sérieux and Capgras, "are all alike: they turn principally on the slightest gestures of the suspected partner. Has she a tired look? —it is a proof of adultery; a gay manner?—she comes from a rendezvous. A look, a movement of the eyebrows, lips or fingers are so many tell-tale signs; the same with smiles or tears. Should she utter the name of the supposed lover the sound of her voice leaves no doubt; should she repeat it often, it is "to accustom herself to hear it in public without blushing"; if she ceases to mention him, the motive can be guessed. In the street, the jealous man thinks that the passers-by are laughing at him; ceaseless allusions are made to his misfortune; he is taken for a complaisant husband. His wife's foot-steps on the parquet floor are so many signals to her lovers and compose a telegraphic alphabet that he can successfully interpret."[1]

"Just as I was getting into the carriage", wrote a person afflicted by persecution mania to Morel, "all the places were filled up; *then it came into my mind that this was a bad joke that they wanted to play on me.* Obliged to stay at Verdun, *I imagine* that everyone I meet is trying to annoy me, that they invent every means whereby to worry and persecute me. *I have so imprinted on my soul the idea that I am persecuted,* that my mind is incapable of asserting itself and driving these absurdities away".— "Another patient, hearing the sound of some workmen's hammers, interprets them as the riveting of the boards of the coffin that is to enclose her. Another sees a cart full of furniture stop in front of her house and flees, in the belief that it contains the guillotine which is to execute her".[2]

Such interpretations, all in unison with the single dominating affective tendency, show how the evocative process which gives rise to thought is completely dependent on this affectivity. But the great influence that the single affective tendency always in a state of tension exercises on the direction of the process of

---

[1] Sérieux and Capgras, *op. cit.,* p. 111.
[2] Morel, *op. cit.,* pp. 345-346, 352.

COHERENT INSANITY 327

association is particularly clear from the entirely strange interpretative associations to which nearly all monomaniacs are subject, and which denote at the same time how a keen affectivity sharpens the imagination : " Mme. X. . . . studies minutely the letters that she receives. Punctuation marks or spelling mistakes give rise to numerous interpretations. Her father writes to her: " We desire your cure." She observes that the stop is of an unusual size ; it must be read : " We desire your cure to stop " (nous ne desirons *point* ta guérison). Another woman imagines that her husband is announcing his intention of leaving her by putting two five-centimes stamps on a letter instead of a ten-centimes one. A look, a smile, a gesture, the shouts and songs of children, the coughing or spitting of a neighbour, the whispers of passers-by, pieces of paper found in the street, a door opened or closed, a mere nothing serves as a pretext. The more insignificant the fact in the eyes of the vulgar, the more penetrating appears their own perspicacity. Where others only see coincidences, they, thanks to their interpretative clairvoyance, know how to distinguish the truth and the secret relations of things." All the most insignificant and accidental objects and events assume the profound character of symbols (which, it may be mentioned in parenthesis, helps in the understanding of the psychology of the "symbolists" in literature and in art).[1]

If the whole evocative process thus falls under the full power of the single dominating affectivity, this forms in consequence a powerful thread uniting all the intellectual psychical states, *which thus become coherent with each other, even over-coherent to excess.* An excellent example of coherence is presented, for example, by the delirium of the melancholic described by Kraepelin : " A woman of fifty-six, who had nursed a son ill with typhus two years and three months previously, and had then herself got into a feverish condition, probably typhus also, some months later suddenly lost her husband. Soon, she began to get anxious and to reproach herself with not having looked after him better. Then she rapidly developed a very marked obsession of self-accusation. She thinks she has never

---

[1] Sérieux and Capgras, *op. cit.,* pp. 21, 23-24, 27, 29-30, 32-34, 91-92, etc.

328 THE PSYCHOLOGY OF REASONING

done anything good, she has let herself be led by the Evil One. Her prayers have never had any value ; only she did not know it before. Her husband has simply married the devil and therefore cannot go to heaven ; she and her children are damned, because of her former unchristian life. At the same time a great restlessness appeared, and almost complete insomnia ; the patient lamented, wept, and cried continually ; besides which, she would eat nothing, and accordingly had to be taken to a hospital. Here she manifested a number of the strangest ideas : she had been the serpent of the earthly paradise ; she had induced her husband to sin, and he moreover was called Adam ; she was damned, she and her children ; she had rendered everyone unhappy. That was why she would be burnt ; she had already been in hell, and seen there, in the abyss, her terrible sins. The firmament has fallen ; there is no more water, no money, nothing to eat ; she has destroyed everything, she is guilty of the ruin of the universe ; ' the whole world weighs on her soul.' In a written address to the tribunal, she accused herself of all these crimes and asked that she should be taken to prison ; on a note, she signed herself ' the devil ' ".[1]

We see here how closely connected and coherent is the association of ideas provoked by the evocative and selective action of the single affectivity in play. If she is a great sinner, then she is the devil ; if she is the devil, then her husband and children, according to religious teaching, are damned also, and so on. *No defective connection, no incoherence*, is ever manifested either in her ideas or her acts. On the other hand we observe the impossibility of any secondary affectivity of control being produced in the patient's mind, so that she might evoke images antagonistic to the insane ideas, beginning by the recall of all the praiseworthy actions she has performed, all the good feelings she has constantly experienced in the past, in a word, of all those images which immediately present themselves to the mind of a sane person when assailed by similar ideas and doubts.

In the same way, the other paranoiac described by

[1] E. Kraepelin, *Einführung in die psychiatrische Klinik*, Leipzig, 1901, pp. 8-9.

COHERENT INSANITY 329

Kraepelin, imagined himself persecuted by an American woman for over twenty years, and constructed a whole "Weltanschauung", fantastic but quite coherent.[1]

This remarkable and excessive coherence of monomaniacs is due then *to their morbid affective exclusiveness*, to the fact that, as Baillarger observes, they interpret *everything according to their fears and preoccupations*. As Toulouse and Mignard note, their over-powerful affectivities of egoism, vanity, and hate, hold their insane ideas *in too fixed a direction*.[2]

But this too fixed direction, due to the single dominating affectivity, does not prevent the deliria of paranoiacs from being chains of multiple and most varied ideas. We cannot therefore speak of *monoideism*, but only of *monoaffectivism*.

And it is just because they are monoaffective in the strictest sense of the word, and therefore irresistibly coherent, that melancholic, persecuted, persecuting and megalomaniac patients are all led to *systematise* their delusions. "The insane person", writes Morel, "makes every effort to associate his ideas ; he co-ordinates them, deduces some from others, and often succeeds, *after great efforts of reasoning*, in creating a delusive system in virtue of which he premeditates and acts. One insane notion is deduced from another by the same law that one reasonable idea engenders another. It is thus that the insane arrive, fatally but logically, at intellectual conceptions so contrary to general reason, and prepare to commit the most monstrous acts." "In the delirium of interpretation", write Sérieux and Capgras, "the ideas, co-ordinated into a whole whose different parts are linked together, form a group, a more or less organised system."[3]

If objections are raised to these forms of systematised delirium, reasoning, completely at the service of a single dominating affectivity, begins to function immediately in order to get rid of the contradiction : "When you succeed in proving to these unfortunates that there is no one hiding in the chimneys, or in the cellars where they hear voices, they invent all sorts of stories to

---

[1] Kraepelin, *ibid.*, pp. 150-153.
[2] Baillarger, *op. cit., Recherches sur les maladies mentales*, vol. I, pp. 257-258 ; Toulouse and Mignard, *art. cit., Les maladies mentales et l'autoconduction*, p. 272.
[3] Morel, *op. cit.*, p. 427 ; Sérieux and Capgras, *op. cit.*, p. 131.

330 THE PSYCHOLOGY OF REASONING

justify their delusion. They pretend that they are being tortured from a distance by means of electricity, speaking-trumpets, and other devices invented by the unbelievable malice of their persecutors ; they even invariably attribute to them a supernatural power ".[1]

The aggravation and complication of deliriums thus systematised arise from the fact that the sole affectivity in play, which is no longer restricted by any antagonistic tendency and never replaced by others that can for a time divert the thought elsewhere, constantly add new imaginative materials related to itself ; and these in their turn the *richer they are* and *the more in harmony* with the single motivating affective tendency of the delusion, reinforce it more and more.[2]

As their "systematisation" increases, the coherence of these delusions becomes more strict, so that they appear to have a perfect logical structure. The intellect of the individual suffering from persecution mania, writes Maudsley, "is amiss in so far as it accepts certain false premises, but, approving and accepting them, it reasons pretty logically from them." The monomaniac, observes Morel, "supports his delusive system by reasons with a very logical appearance ".[3]

Owing to this single affective tendency being always in a state of tension and always ready to evoke facts, however trifling, which are favourable to it, and to choose at the same time, as Tanzi and Lugaro say, " by passing them as it were through a sieve," from amongst arguments of every kind, just those and only those which support his delusive conviction—owing to this absolute mono-affectivism which is peculiar to him, the monomaniac is also a very clever and subtle dialectician. " In reasoning insanity ", Voivenel tells us, "the insane person can defend his convictions, sometimes even with great distinction". Thus Mlle. B. . . , "whose intelligence, memory, and logical faculties are perfectly preserved, makes correct use of all her attainments and education, and defends herself like a clever lawyer." "The patient often employs", Sérieux and Capgras observe in their turn, "the resources of a compact

---

[1] Morel, *op. cit.*, p. 364.

[2] Cf. for example, Godfernaux, *op. cit.*, pp. 65-66, 67, 69-70 ; Séglas, *op. cit.*, p. 507.

[3] Maudsley, *op. cit.*, *The Pathology of Mind*, pp. 312-316 ; Morel, *op. cit.*, p. 396.

COHERENT INSANITY 331

dialectic. He accumulates proof after proof, he always has an answer ready for every objection, he knows how to refute arguments, he puts dilemmas and seizes on the most insignificant fact in order to adapt it to his requirements ".[1]

Accordingly, the acts of the monomaniac are also perfectly coherent with his system of ideas. Take, for example, the measures of defence adopted by the persecuted. "The habitual reactions by which the maniac tries to defend himself against his enemies are changes of abode, deviations from the usual route in order to throw them off the track, the analysis of his foods and drinks, the partial refusal of certain dishes or their preparation by himself, denunciations to the authorities, and finally violent acts of every kind. We cannot here speak of an insane idea of defence, but only of *a reaction in some way logical*, resulting from ideas of persecution ".[2]

Finally, the character and the whole conduct are also perfectly coherent. " Paranoiacs ", write Tanzi and Lugaro, "are always animated by a tenacious passion which gives their character a firmness, a vigour, a quasi-heroic coherence, often unknown to normal individuals ". "Certain paranoiacs brave the greatest adversities for their insane ideal, and manifest an uncompromising coherence of character, an indomitable will and a spirit of sacrifice which should earn for them the title of heroes rather than madmen, if the ideal for which they sacrifice themselves were not repugnant to common sense ".[3]

We see then, in summing up, that the *intellectual* equipment of monomaniacs or paranoiacs is usually perfectly sane. In them, sensations, and their evocations, as Kraepelin also remarks, are kept in faithful conformity with reality. In the great majority of cases hallucinations are totally lacking. The memory is good, the imaginative faculty leaves nothing to be desired as regards richness of association and is no less at the service of the respective affectivity than in the most normal mind. Finally, *as regards coherence*, the logical

---

[1] Tanzi and Lugaro, *op. cit.*, Vol. I, p. 745 ; P. Voivenel, " Sur un cas de délire d'interprétation ", *L'Encéphale*, 10 June, 1912, pp. 539-540 ; Sérieux and Capgras, *op. cit.*, p. 49.
[2] Séglas, *op. cit.*, p. 785.
[3] Tanzi and Lugaro, *op. cit.*, Vol. I, pp. 379, 323.

332 THE PSYCHOLOGY OF REASONING

faculty is even more solid and subtle than that of the sane person. "We find in the reasoning insane", observe Sérieux and Capgras, "correct modes of expression, very accurate memories, a lively curiosity, and an uninjured intelligence, acute and penetrating". "There is neither disturbance of consciousness, nor confusion of ideas, nor any general alteration of the syllogistic faculties".[1]

The insane element in the systematic delusion of paranoiacs, does not even consist in the fundamental hypothesis that is at the root of the delusion. This, mistaken though it may be, is most often a "reasonable", *i.e.* not unlikely, hypothesis, as the normal person can also be driven to admit, provisionally, when he finds himself in a similar affective condition.[2]

The really morbid fact lies, we repeat, *in the keenness, the persistence, and the aggressiveness of a single affective tendency.* It is this which gives to all thought such great, and even an excessive, coherence ; and it is this which denies access to any of those antagonistic affective tendencies, which normally hold the primary affectivity in suspense, evoke facts contrary to the imagined hypothesis, and inhibit or "redress" it so that it may conform to reality. It follows that with *the strictest coherence,* due to the keenness, persistence, and aggression of the sole affectivity always in play, there is combined *the greatest illogicality,* as we shall see in what immediately follows.

4. *The Illogicality of Monomaniacs*

The absolute lack, the total absence of the critical sense in paranoiacs, its "decrease or perversion incapable of correcting the errors of the imagination", have been emphasised, one may say, by all writers : "In these patients", Sérieux and Capgras observe, "there is neither doubt nor control ; contradictory and antagonistic images cannot struggle against the pathological representation, and prevent it being objectified". "In paranoiacs", write Tanzi and Lugaro, "there is a constitutional lack of the critical faculty, side by side with

---

[1] Kraepelin, *op. cit.,* pp. 150-151 ; Sérieux and Capgras, *op. cit.,* pp. 5-6, 47-48.
[2] Cf. Sérieux and Capgras, *ibid.,* pp. 47-48 ; Tanzi and Lugaro, *op. cit.* Vol. I, p. 321.

COHERENT INSANITY 333

a superabundance of passionate motive power ". And this lack of the critical faculty, disposing as it does to the acceptance of every idea which is suggested or spontaneously presented to the mind as true, gives rise to a boundless credulity, leaves the intellect defenceless, and thus opens the way to the most illogical and absurd delusions.[1]

Indeed, the illogicality and absurdity simply consist in this, that we imagine, as the result of an experiment mentally performed, a fact different from what the past has taught us to expect, or we interpret a certain fact by a supposition which, according to our past experience, is impossible or highly improbable in the actual circumstances. In the normal state also, the tendency to attribute to an imagined experience a different result from the right one, or to invent erroneous hypotheses is very common. But whereas for normal people the affective tendency of control "redresses" the false deduction or interpretation, these correctives are lacking in the paranoiac just because of his complete mono-affectivism, amounting to a true *affective autocracy* with no counterbalancing factor.

Experience teaches us, for example, that a man cannot get through a key-hole, but the systematic lunatic may affirm that his persecutor entered his bedroom by this means during the night ; and he may do so in perfect good faith and with the deepest conviction, since he lacks any controlling affective tendency to invoke past experience and rectify the absurd supposition. Experience teaches us that it is impossible for a woman of a modest social condition to make use of all the men in the world in order to have her revenge on the man that she hates ; yet this is firmly believed by the paranoiac described by Kraepelin, and to whom we referred above as imagining himself persecuted by an American woman. "People afflicted by persecution mania", writes Morel, "are incapable of finding in their misguided intelligence *elements antagonistic* to their insane ideas."[2]

The mono-affectivism of paranoiacs, of systematic

[1] Sérieux and Capgras, *op. cit.*, pp. 47-48, 215, 220, 225 ; Tanzi and Lugaro, *op. cit.*, Vol. I, pp. 303, 323.
[2] Morel, *op. cit.*, p. 425.

334 THE PSYCHOLOGY OF REASONING

madmen, renders them so resolute in their convictions that objections put forward to them by others have no effect : "All the objections made to these ideas ", says Kraepelin of the paranoiac just mentioned who imagined himself persecuted by an American woman, "are received by the invalid with an air of superiority and incredulity, and rebound, so to speak, from his conviction, which remains as firm as a rock, without making any impression. It is at once manifest that he does not believe in the seriousness of our remarks, but thinks that all we say to dissuade him is contrary to what we actually believe ". "You are forced almost irresistibly to discuss the motives for their delusion with these patients ", adds Morel, "in order to convince them by reasoning ; *but they are incapable of paying attention to your words*, and respond only to their own delusion ".[1]

"The persecuted", Séglas writes, "accepts without discussion all the facts however slight that appear suspicious to him. They are acquired once and for all, *without criticism or control. He will never make the least intellectual effort, will not refer to his previous knowledge in order to control his delusion.* He has a profound faith in his convictions, a resolute belief which removes all power of control. So that we find intelligent, educated people, who will formulate, as positive proofs, the oddest and most obviously improbable ideas."[2]

"Considerations unfavourable to their actual pre-occupation ", D'Allonnes writes in his turn, "do not occur to the thought of the interpreter. The mechanism of association and judgment as regards everything that is opposed to the dominating sentiment is in abeyance. *The slightest trace of any other sentiment is swept away* ".[3]

Hence the great illogicality and absurdity which paranoiacs can attain in their reasoning. One, for example, will suppose, as we saw above, that his wife possesses a "magic handkerchief" which allows her to leave the bedroom without being seen ; or perhaps even that his wife's lover has entered by the key-hole. Another will relate how he took part in events of two or three centuries ago ; or he will accuse his imagined

---

[1] Kraepelin, *op. cit.*, pp. 150, 151 ; Morel, *op. cit.*, p. 714.
[2] Séglas, *op. cit.*, pp. 517-518, 520.
[3] R. D'Allonnes, "Les troubles de l'intelligence ", *Revue Philosophique*, Dec. 1914, pp. 470-471.

COHERENT INSANITY 335

persecutor of having the supernatural power to torment him physically, even from a distance. Yet another will be firmly convinced that a modest woman has succeeded in setting the whole human race in motion for her purposes of revenge ; etc. etc.

These illogical deductions, though always coherent with the starting-point of the delusion, may, by linking up with one another in a cumulative way, lead to such absurd conclusions, and, by repercussion, to such absolutely insane acts as the strange defences to which certain persecuted people have resource. Thus a persecuted woman described by Séglas, "had a habit of pulling off the bed-clothes every evening before retiring. Then she put a plate on the mattress and on this a candlestick and a candle with pins sticking in it, which fell into the plate as the candle burnt. This practice was designed to drive away 'evil spirits'. Another placed a book on her head and on the book a copper saucepan, in order to guard herself against the 'sharp plagues' which her enemies cast on her head. A third, whose brain, as she imagined, her enemies intended to injure, surrounded her head with an enormous coiffure, a veritable cardboard helmet which covered up her ears as well, in order to prevent 'earwigs' from entering. A fourth, in order to preserve herself from 'carrion', placed a poultice of fecal matter on her chest at night, and then completely covered herself up ".[1]

Insane as these acts certainly are, their studied meticulousness and their identical repetition every day indicate that they too are perfectly related and coherent with the fundamental hypothesis of a very determined persecution, which they are designed to frustrate.

5. Conclusion

We have thus brought to a close our brief and summary study of this particular class of the insane who are known under the name of paranoiacs or monomaniacs. It is a particularly interesting class because it allows us to distinguish and separate clearly the two fundamental characteristics of reasoning, coherence and

[1] Séglas, op. cit., p. 789.

336 THE PSYCHOLOGY OF REASONING

logicality, so habitually confused by psychologists and psychiatrists themselves.

We have found in these madmen the *greatest coherence* accompanied by *the greatest illogicality*, and this has enabled us to emphasise more than was possible in our preceding chapters on normal thought, how the concern of the primary affectivity, the one that impels to reasoning, is the maintenance of *coherence*, while it is the business of the secondary affectivity, antagonistic to it, to guarantee *logicality*. An excessive intensity and aggressiveness of the first, followed by the annihilation of the second, should therefore produce as a consequence the union of coherence with illogicality. This strangely assorted pair has, as we know, been called *rational insanity*, and if this seems to the profane like a contradiction in terms, it yet suggestively expresses this fact of coherence united with illogicality.

That the sole cause of these paranoiac delusions is the prevalence and aggression of one affective tendency, and that the whole *intellectual* mechanism remains perfectly sane, is proved by the fact that whenever this autocratic affectivity is absent thought becomes normal again ; and this is the case with many paranoiacs when they are momentarily torn away from their delusion by other occupations or preoccupations. Thus the hypochondriac professor mentioned by Séglas, before proceeding to the chair that he occupied in a university, used to perambulate the town in order to evade his imagined enemies, and would spit every few minutes so as not to absorb "the fell miasmas" that they launched against him, pronouncing cabalistic words and making strange gestures in order to baffle their plans ; but, once in the chair, he got on with his teaching in such a way that no one would have suspected him of being a man of unsound mind.[1]

A proof moreover, as to the affective nature of the antagonistic element of doubt or dread of deception, which gives rise to the critical sense and whose absence opens the way to the most foolish illogicality and absurdity, is to be found in the diametrically opposed morbid state represented by the "madness of doubt". Here the affective nature, disquieting and harassing, of the fear of deception, is well-marked, and this suspicion is

[1] Séglas, *op. cit.*, p. 789.

COHERENT INSANITY 337

opposed throughout to every affirmation or suggestion put forward by the primary affectivity, and prevents the latter from ever arriving at any conclusion.

Finally, that the exclusive cause of coherence is the existence and persistence of the primary affective tendency, to which the impulse to reasoning is due, becomes still more evident when we proceed to the examination of other very different classes of the insane in whom the maximum incoherence exists.

This is exactly what we shall do in the third and last part of the present pathological section.

CHAPTER XV

THE PATHOLOGY OF REASONING

Part III: Incoherent Insanity due to Instability, Impotence, or Absence of the Affective Tendencies

As opposed to the monomaniacs examined in the preceding chapter, where we found in activity a single affective tendency to whose exclusive predominance are due both their extreme coherence and their characteristic illogicality, we have now to consider those madmen whose principal characteristic is their incoherence. We shall confine ourselves here to a very rapid investigation of the maniacs, the confused, and the dements.

Maniacs

The incoherence in the acts and words of the maniac is classical. A patient exhibited by Kraepelin to his pupils, "rushes into the hall, in the grip of a violent excitement. She does not sit down, but walks round quickly briefly examining whatever she sees. She then mixes with the audience without restraint, as though to make friends with them. She has scarcely been persuaded to sit down when she springs up again, flings her shoes away, unties her apron and throws it away also, and begins to sing and dance. All at once she stops, claps her hands, goes to the blackboard, takes the chalk, and begins to write her name, but ends with an immense flourish that covers nearly the whole board in a moment. She then partially rubs it out with a sponge and again hastily starts writing some letters of the alphabet, but suddenly throws the chalk over the heads of the audience, seizes the chair, drags it round on the floor, then sits on it with all her weight, only to get up again at once with a bound, and to begin the

INCOHERENT INSANITY 339

same game in a different form. The whole time, the patient jabbers without ceasing, but the context of her hurried words is scarcely intelligible, and quite disconnected. When questioned insistently, she usually gives a brief and sane reply, but this is immediately followed by all sorts of disconnected phrases ".[1]

The behaviour described by Kraepelin in such a masterly way is evidence of an excessive affective excitability and instability, a chaotic chain of affectivities which burst forth and succeed each other in wild confusion, so that none succeeds even for a moment in asserting itself and gaining predominance. As Baillarger rightly remarks, the maniac closely resembles the man who is prey to a violent passion, only the passion changes every instant.[2]

From this excessive affective excitability and instability arise directly all the other distinctive features of this insanity, remarked by Kraepelin himself and other psychiatrists. These are the extraordinary " fluidity " of the different psychical processes, which are rapidly and easily activated but just as easily supplanted by others before even having had time to develop; the facility with which every fortuitous sensation draws attention to itself, though this is immediately distracted by some subsequent sensation ; the way in which the patient falls completely under the influence of even the most insignificant external events ; etc.

But, in particular, an immediate consequence of this excessive affective excitability and instability, that is to say of this tumultuous succession of momentary passionate states, is lack of connection in ideas and incoherence in words and acts. Indeed, in order that there may be a coherent series of acts or words, there must be the persistence of some predominating affective tendency to guide and co-ordinate them to its own purpose, by inhibiting and frustrating every other psychical process which might interfere with this. When this persistence and predominance of a single affective tendency are lacking and the affective activity, by the fact of its excessive excitability, falls under the power of quite fortuitous and changeable stimulations,

---

[1] E. Kraepelin, *op. cit.*, *Einführung in die psychiatrische Klinik*, pp. 62-66.

[2] M. Baillarger, *op. cit.*, *Recherches sur les maladies mentales*, p. 462.

340 THE PSYCHOLOGY OF REASONING

external as well as internal, then thought, still dominated by this tumultuous affective activity, becomes itself unstable and saltatory. In mania, observes Ribot, "les sentiments" follow each other with giddy rapidity. "In the maniac", Kraepelin too remarks, "the extravagance of thought and act is derived solely from the great facility with which the attention is distracted, from the rapid succession of new impulses which never attain complete development".[1]

In other words, the evocation of ideas remains in maniacs under the control of the affective tendencies and it is only the extreme variability and disorder of these latter which cause incoherence; so that the ideas, as Esquirol, quoted by Morel, had already observed, "are reproduced without any connection and with extreme rapidity". It is not, then, that there is an absence of "the internal agent that should bring order into the chaos", as Godfernaux writes; rather do the different internal agents, that is to say, the different affective tendencies capable of bringing order into the chaos, succeed each other so giddily themselves, that, far from completing the work of producing order, not one of them can even begin it. "An affective instability too rarely pointed out is at the root of the intellectual instability of maniacs", writes Revault d'Allonnes.[2]

Hence, as Morel remarks, the incoherence of ideas is the more extreme, the more excessive the maniacal excitement. "In mania", Esquirol has already observed, "everything appears as effort, violence, energy; all is disorder, commotion, and the lack of harmony is what is most remarkable in the insanity of maniacs". "What strikes the ordinary observer also in the maniac", Baillarger adds, "is his incoherent loquacity, his facial animation, and the excess of activity which dominates him and carries him away".[3]

That excitation of a purely affective order is the sole cause of the incoherence or lack of connection of the ideas of the maniac, is more or less clearly realised by all psychiatrists: "In a sane person", says Maudsley,

---

[1] Th. Ribot, *op. cit.*, *Psychologie de l'attention*, pp. 150-151; Kraepelin, *op. cit.*, p. 83.

[2] B. A. Morel, *op. cit.* : *Traité des maladies mentales*, p. 430; A. Godfernaux, *op. cit.*, *Le sentiment et la pensée*, pp. 18-25; R. d'Allonnes, *art. cit.*, *Les troubles de l'intelligence*, p. 475.

[3] Morel, *op. cit.*, p. 430; Baillarger, *op. cit.*, p. 71.

INCOHERENT INSANITY   341

"who is in good health, the feelings are more or less definite and constant in relation to circumstances, but in the maniac they are fragmentary, incoherent, tumultuous, and transient, the least stimulus, whether adapted or not, exciting them to the most irregular and uncertain explosions ". "The mind of maniacs ", write Tanzi and Lugaro, "is ready to interest itself in all subjects, even the most futile, with the same enthusiasm, and thought, following the vagaries of a too facile and ready attention, spends itself in a thousand directions which lead to no end. Whence spring an extreme volubility in association, an extreme accessibility to the distractions of countless external stimuli, a precipitation of judgment, an impossibility of meditation, and *an incapacity to· guide thought in a constant and reasonable direction* ".[1]

In consequence of this peculiar affective hyper-excitability, the intellectual activity of maniacs is also intense, and this affords still another proof of the fact that affective activity is the true and only excitant of intellectual activity : "Maniacs", writes Masselon, "give proof of an intense, although uncoordinated intellectual activity ; in the flux of words and images that crowd into their consciousness, they testify to a veritable cerebral erethism ; though the memories are not connected, the elements of thought are varied and numerous ; they present an exaggerated luxury of ideas and movements, a veritable intellectual and motor hyperactivity ".[2]

Moreover, the cerebral mechanism, within the limits prescribed by each momentary affective tendency, has lost nothing of its integrity, in the sense that the affective activity preserves intact its control over the intellective elements, as we mentioned above. In other words, throughout each of his very brief affective tendencies, the maniac is perfectly coherent. Thus Kraepelin, in the passage quoted above, observed that to questions put with emphasis so as to fix the maniac's attention on the questioner for a moment, a short and sane answer could usually be obtained. Masselon also notes that in maniacs "a logical relation between their

---

[1] Maudsley, *op. cit., The Pathology of Mind,* p. 245 ; E. Tanzi and E. Lugaro, *op. cit., Malattie mentali,* Vol. I, pp. 307, 537-538.

[2] R. Masselon, *La démence précoce,* Paris, 1904, p. 49.

342 THE PSYCHOLOGY OF REASONING

intellectual and emotional states" is noticeable. And Meeus, quoted by Masselon, observes that "violent though the impulses of the maniac may be, there may still be recognised in them some direction, some aim ".[1]

Very instructive in this connection is the fact that when one succeeds, by some trick, in securing the persistence of some affective tendency in a maniac, *ipso facto* his thought and behaviour become perfectly coherent. Thus, for example, when a maniac is strapped up, the prolonged detention which impedes the free exercise of his exuberant energy, causes an intense affective tendency aiming at his liberation to appear and persist ; and the persistence of this affective tendency makes him act as a perfectly normal man would act in his place ; that is to say he tries, with the greatest skill and perseverance to persuade his keepers that he has recovered his reason, so as to be untied.[2]

Maniacs, then, though at the opposite pole from monomaniacs or paranoiacs examined in our preceding chapter, also prove that coherence or incoherence of thought depend respectively on the persistence or non-persistence of the primary affective tendency which impels towards reasoning. And another characteristic feature of intelligence—coherence—is also thus revealed to us as the pure and simple effect of the way in which the affective activity displays itself.

The Confused

The existence and the persistence of certain affective tendencies, are not sufficient, however, to guarantee coherence. It is necessary further that these tendencies should preserve control and government of the intellectual elements. There is a whole group of the insane which proves to us that this subordination of the intellectual elements to the affective tendencies may be interrupted, and the latter may cease to retain their hold on the mnemonic sensorial elements. The greatest incoherence in ideas, the most absolute anarchy in evocation, may then result, notwithstanding the normal

---

[1] Masselon, *La démence précoce*, Paris, 1904, pp. 145-146.
[2] *Cf.*, for example, Morel, *op. cit.*, p. 31.

INCOHERENT INSANITY 343

functioning of the affective activities. This class consists of those that are called the mentally confused, with automatism of ideas.

The application and utilisation, for a certain end, of the sensory or pure intellectual elements, present in a potential state in the brain in the form of mnemonic accumulations, belong to the affective tendencies, which function in the evocation, selection, direction and support of the images or ideas leading to the appropriate end, as well as in the inhibition of those which are useless or detrimental to the attainment of this end, through given paths of nervous conduction, analogous to those by which one idea is evoked by another. If these paths of nervous conduction, which bind the zone of activity of the affective tendencies to the zones of activity of the sensory elements, cease to be sufficiently practicable, and if, in consequence, the relative associations are badly made, the faculty of affective control will suffer *ipso facto*, and the result will be automatism and incoherence of ideas, accompanied by a feeling of mental confusion of which the patient is strongly aware.

This feeling of confusion derives, in the first place, from the absence of affective classification, *i.e.* of the act of recognising, by affective association, the affective or utilitarian significance of objects and images, an action which constitutes what is called "mental synthesis" or "psychical assimilation" of perceptions or images. "In the mentally confused", writes Séglas, "the elementary sensations are normal, but the subject is incapable of grouping these sensations together, and assimilating them into the totality of psychical elements that constitutes personal consciousness. The confused patient is also always in doubt and uncertainty. Objects appear to him distorted, he is bewildered in the midst of an environment *which he cannot interpret and which seems to him quite strange.* A patient of this kind was as though absolutely lost in his own apartments. He asked continually to return home; he could not recover his bearings again and said to himself: ' I see the things that are in this room quite well, but I do not recognise any of them. I cannot account for them. I do not understand'". Another case, also quoted by Séglas, "has an air of looking for something, or trying to find himself again while looking everywhere about him.

344 THE PSYCHOLOGY OF REASONING

He is quite lost. When he asks for his father, and the latter speaks to him, he looks at him with surprise, and says that it is not he. He looks everywhere with a questioning air. He says that he sees things and does not recognise them; he declares that he sees and touches objects, but no longer understands them". "These facts show clearly", Séglas himself concludes, "that it is here a question of disorders depending on a lack of synthesis, that is to say, of disturbances bearing, not on the elementary sensations, but rather on the psychological assimilation of these sensations ".[1]

In the second place, the feeling of confusion springs from the futility of the efforts that the patient makes to co-ordinate and direct his ideas : "The root of mental confusion ", writes Chaslin, "is the loss of co-ordination of images ". The fact is made evident "by the efforts the patient makes to combine his ideas " (Delasiauve). Of a patient who had great difficulty in gathering together his ideas and finding words, Chaslin says : "He clearly makes *enormous efforts* to give an answer". Certain cases are *surprised* themselves at the mass of ideas that they do not succeed either in checking or guiding. "Some of the insane", Chaslin adds, "are surprised by the number of fresh delusions, forming a sort of intellectual whirlwind ; a phenomenon described by one of Kraepelin's patients as being a veritable battle of Huns in his mind ". "In the mentally confused", Toulouse and Mignard observe in turn, "what is disturbed is the possibility of co-ordinating the psychical processes in relation to an activity conscious of itself and adapted to its ends. Patients who have been cured express clearly the impression, shared also by the observer, *that they were as though trammelled in their mental effort,* that they had lost their power of controlling themselves, *that they could not, during their illness, direct their ideas* ".[2]

This powerlessness of the affective tendencies, though actually in existence, to direct ideas, may go so far as

[1] J. Séglas, *op. cit., Leçons cliniques sur les maladies mentales et nerveuses,* pp. 159-160, 421-422, 426-427, 447, 471, etc. ; cf., e.g., also Ph. Chaslin, *La confusion mentale primitive,* Paris, 1895, pp. 136-138, 149-151, etc.

[2] Chaslin, *op. cit.,* pp. 139, 147-148 ; Ed. Toulouse and M. Mignard, "Confusion mentale et démence. Les maladies mentales et l'autoconduction, La théorie confusionnelle et l'autoconduction ", *Revue de psychiatrie et psychologie experimentale,* Aug. 1908, p. 5, July 1911, p. 267, June 1914, pp. 34-35.

INCOHERENT INSANITY 345

to give rise to complete automatism of ideas and to the most disconnected verbiage, produced by pure verbal assonance.[1]

In mental confusion there is then a lack of "synthesis", of "psychical assimilation", that is to say, affective classification of ideas, the action of recognising the affective or utilitarian significance of objects or images, and also a lack of control, guidance, and co-ordination of the intellectual elements by the affective tendencies; not in consequence of the non-existence of the latter, as we found in dreams and shall find in dements, but rather because psychical association between the affective tendencies and intellectual elements no longer exists. If the affective tendencies did not exist, the patient *would experience no feeling of confusion* before the chaos of sensations and images which whirls around in his mind.

Mental confusion therefore has a special interest for us, because, considered in its purest form, we find the maximum incoherence of ideas, although the different manifestations of the intellectual part (sensations and evocations of sensations and images) as well as the affective part, are in themselves quite normal. This incoherence is shown by the confessions of the patient, as we saw above, to be due to the fact that the affective tendencies, probably owing to the impracticability of the paths of association relative to them, no longer exercise their function of checking and guiding, by which coherence is secured.

Here also, the "principle of continuity", applied to the transition of normal psychological manifestations to the abnormal, may help us to understand the state of the mentally confused and thus to confirm all the statements of the patient on the subject of the cause of his incoherence. Indeed, as soon as the evocation of ideas, on account of some unusual circumstance, becomes a little too rapid, and delay occurs in the satisfaction of our eager desire to dam up and order the tumult of evocations, we normal people also experience a feeling of bewilderment and confusion; and this we prove by introspection to be due to the fact that ideas rebel against our affective control and free themselves from it.[2]

[1] See, for example, Chaslin, *op. cit.*, pp. 92-93.
[2] *Cf.* Chaslin, *ibid.*, pp. 165 166.

346 THE PSYCHOLOGY OF REASONING

Though in certain points analogous to the confused, we shall neglect here, as having no very great interest for us, all those manifestations of incoherence of ideas due to the action of toxic or infectious agents, such as alcoholic insanity, acute insanity caused by meningitis, typhoid fever, and the like. For it is evident that in these cases it is the excitation of centres at the same time sensory and mnemonico-sensory, aroused by the stimulating agent, and consequently the entry into activity of the respective images with too great violence, which render the latter rebellious against all affective restriction and control (which gives rise, in a great many cases, to the same feeling of bewilderment or loss of direction that we have observed in the mentally confused); and this quite apart from the fact that the affective tendencies may for the same reason be themselves rendered tumultuously unstable and chaotic. We limit ourselves only to the observation that in such cases the tempestuous succession of ideas no longer follows the laws of psychical association by contiguity, resemblance, etc.; which shows that the different excitations and mnemonic activations depend only on the fortuitous ways in which the stimulating agent is diffused in the cortical zone.[1]

Dements

We shall rather dwell, as being of the greatest interest to us, on the last form of incoherence that we purpose to examine in this chapter, viz. that manifested in dements.

In such forms of insanity, non-affectivity, "apathy" and "gemütliche Stumpfheit", as Kraepelin calls it, are very familiar. In precocious dements and catatonics, for instance, the affective reactions are annihilated, as Tanzi and Lugaro remark : "Not only may the mind be free from all care, indifferent to all sinister forethought, but even the most fundamental reactions of self-preservation connected with the instincts may be lacking. Wants are not felt, painful excitations raise no protest, dangers and insults provoke no emotive

---

[1] *Cf.* e.g., Kraepelin, *op. cit.*, pp. 105-106, 108-109 ; Morel, *op. cit.*, p. 396 ; Séglas, *op. cit.*, pp. 376-377, 413-414 ; Tanzi and Lugaro, *op. cit.* vol. I, p. 239.

INCOHERENT INSANITY 347

reaction. And it is not only the reactions of defence and expressions of mimicry that are lacking; what is really absent is the emotion, both as subjective state and as objective phenomenon displayed in the internal circuits of the visceral, vascular, and somatic innervation and in the sensibility relative to it. Under a painful stimulation, in the presence of a danger, an insult or bad news whose significance is appreciated, neither the beating of the heart, nor the vasomotor innervation, nor that of the iris, are modified". "The affective vacuity of precocious dements is also shown by the loss of all affection for their family and their friends, by the complete disappearance of all ideals and aspirations. Self-love, pity, modesty, even the instinct of preservation are weakened or remain suppressed. The patients remain indifferent at the sight of the keenest sufferings; they experience no feeling of shame, no annoyance at their situation; they have no feeling of dignity, or pride. They seem insensible to all disgust, even in the sphere of taste and smell; they do not care for personal propriety and give themselves up without reserve and almost with delight to the filthiest acts, to the manipulation of their own excreta and that of others, even going as far as coprophagy ".[1]

Dumas announced one day to the dement Garin that his wife was dead: his pulse remained at 66. Another time someone came to tell him that in an hour he would be free to leave the asylum; even then, his pulse did not vary in the least degree; Garin simply replied: "Good, very good ", and immediately began to talk of something else. "He has lost ", writes Dumas, "and I think that such a loss is complete, the faculty of being moved. He no longer knows joy, sadness, misery, or anger; he is morally anæsthetised ".[2]

All psychiatrists agree in acknowledging non-affectivity as the fundamental characteristic of precocious dements and catatonics: "Precocious dements ", writes Masselon, "notice nothing, or almost nothing, spontaneously. They are interested in nothing, and are indifferent to everything that concerns them." Dementia praecox is announced or preannounced by the

[1] Tanzi and Lugaro, *op. cit.*, Vol. II, pp. 461-463.
[2] G. Dumas, "La logique d'un dément ", *Revue Philosophique*, Feb. 1908, p. 190.

348 THE PSYCHOLOGY OF REASONING

silence or the disappearance of the affective tendencies : "The affective feelings disappear very early, and the family sentiments are among the first to decrease". And it is worthy of remark that the weakening of the affective tone "precedes and dominates the weakening of the intellect".[1]

For us it is important to observe that this intellectual weakening is especially apparent in the increasing difficulty of preserving a certain coherence as much in acts as in words. Thought becomes more and more incapable of following the thread of reasoning, brief though it may be ; and this is exactly what happens in normal people also, in consequence of fatigue or exhaustion of the affective tendency which is in play. Digressions, too, succeed each other in a more and more chaotic way, by more and more abrupt leaps. "Sometimes", writes Baillarger, " we can find, up to a certain point, in the writings of incoherent dements the explanation of the incoherence itself. While the patient is beginning to express an idea that he wishes to develop, one of the words employed suggests an accessory idea which makes him abandon the first. Incoherence, then, is merely a succession of digressions which cause the first idea to be completely forgotten."[2]

Thus in consequence of the absence of all directive and connecting action on the part of the affective tendencies, there is constantly increasing psychical disintegration or anarchy, manifested either in stupid and disconnected acts, "devoid of all meaning, of all appropriateness, or even obviously contrary to all the primary interests of the patient", or in the "incohérence à froid" typical of these patients : "They delight in insipid phrases, even if devoid of all meaning, and they utter them with a smiling expression that seems to defy reason, as if they were pronouncing sentences highly subtle and à propos."[3]

Thus, a catatonic studied by Kraepelin, in whom " no determined affective disposition is observable ", who is completely obtuse affectively and shows no interest in what goes on around him, even in the visits of his

---

[1] Masselon, *op. cit.*, pp. 25, 43, 94, etc.
[2] Baillarger, *op. cit.*, pp. 626-627.
[3] Tanzi and Lugaro, *op. cit.*, Vol. II, pp. 452, 465, 445, Vol. I, pp. 309-310.

INCOHERENT INSANITY 349

nearest relations, "at whom he looks without either pleasure or displeasure and without saying a word", presents in addition to this complete affective indifference the most complete absence of connection in ideas. "He thinks that the meat he is served with is human flesh ; in the papers, everything refers to him ; there is a relation between him and the assassin of the Empress of Austria, between him and the Peace Conference ; his mother wants to murder him ; he is the worst creature in existence. He sees in the doctor the German Emperor, who has dyed his beard ; he takes another gentleman for Christ ; and all this is uttered in an indifferent tone, without the slighest trace of any emotive state whatever. Sometimes he pronounces rhyming words or phrases which have no sense : 'hem, bem, kem, dem, schem, rem'; or he repeats several times the same incomprehensible phrases : 'Einer für alle und alle für einen, und zwei für alle und drei für alle, hier und da und dort, überall und Allmacht und Allmacht,' and so on ". [1]

As can be seen, and as might be expected *a priori*, the association of ideas, freed from all affective control and left completely to itself, tends to follow more and more exclusively the fortuitous play of mechanical association, which gives rise, especially in the catatonic state of absolute affective zero, to the maximum incoherence, "which is translated into a veritable verbal salad ". [2]

We may thus arrive at the point where the sole guide in the process of associating ideas is the homophony of the respective phonetic symbols. Thus, a patient quoted by Parchappe and mentioned by Queyrat, was constantly making associations of this kind while speaking : "On dit que la vierge est folle, on parle de la *lier*, ce qui ne fait pas les affaires du département de *l'Allier*". One day when she was told to do her spinning, she replied that she did not know how to do it. "Je vous dis d'*en faire* ", the doctor insisted. "Il ne fait pas bon dans *l'enfer* ", she replied. And a patient studied by Kraepelin, a dement suffering from creeping paralysis, occupied herself when awake by repeating the whole night through, in a hollow and monotonous voice, senseless assonances such as "Grüner Raser, bunter Kater, grober

---

[1] Kraepelin, *op. cit.*, pp. 36-38.
[2] Masselon, *op. cit.*, p. 146.

350 THE PSYCHOLOGY OF REASONING

Aber, ewiger Raben, Raben haben, rother Kater, Bummelraber, gelber Kater, der Rosengraben ", and so on.[1]

It is interesting to note in parenthesis that this association of ideas by pure homophony may occur in normal minds also, in consequence of an affective exhaustion produced artificially. Experiments *ad hoc* have in fact shown, as Claparède relates, "that under the influence of exhaustion produced by a night of work and fasting, associative forms implying an intellectual relation were little by little replaced by those implying only a connection cemented by long habit or verbal similarity : it is the sound, not the sense of the word, which determines the association ".[2]

Now, in dementia praecox, and especially in catatonics, we have so to speak a chronic state of exhaustion of the affective tendencies giving rise, no longer temporarily but permanently, to the mechanical association of ideas, even by pure phonetic resemblance.

While in maniacs, then, each momentary affectivity instils into the thoughts and acts a corresponding momentary coherence, in dements and catatonics, on the contrary, there may be no limits to the psychical disintegration or anarchy in consequence of the absence of every affective tendency. And while in the former the association of ideas, remaining fully and absolutely under the control of the respective momentary affective tendencies, does not act according to the pure fortuitous play of mechanical association, but is always directed towards some end, in the latter, on the contrary, it is left completely to itself, and loses all meaning whatsoever so that it may come to act exclusively by verbal homophony. On account of this supreme incoherence and extravagance of thought and conduct, of this absence of any affective motive to guide and connect the intellectual material of sensory images, and of this limitless psychical disintegration which results from it, dementia constitutes "the truest and most complete incarnation of insanity ".[3]

Nevertheless, a fact which deserves to be mentioned is that the purely intellectual material in victims of

---

[1] Queyrat, *La logique chez l'enfant*, Paris, 1903, pp. 119-120 ; Kraepelin, *op. cit.*, pp. 45-46.
[2] Ed. Claparède, *op. cit.*, *L'association des idées*, pp. 243-244.
[3] Tanzi and Lugaro, *op. cit.*, Vol. II, p. 445.

INCOHERENT INSANITY 351

dementia praecox and catatonics remains in the majority of cases, as Kraepelin himself remarks, *almost intact.* For example, the disconnected writings of one of his patients "leave no doubt as to the affective vacuum being accompanied to a remarkable degree by mental disorder and weakness of judgment, *although the purely mnemonic possession of knowledge* (die rein gedächtnis-mässige Beherrschung der Kenntnisse) *has not suffered, or has suffered only very little*". Generally, in dementia praecox, "*the memory of knowledge previously acquired is much less disturbed than reasoning, and especially than the affective sentiments and the will,* which is so closely related to these latter ".[1]

The fact that the mnemonic intellectual material may often be said to remain intact and yet only give rise to a disconnected series of ideas, shows in the best way possible that the intellectual material constituted by images *does not organise itself into reasoning, into a coherent series of these images,* but that it needs for this purpose the evocative, guiding, selective and co-ordinating work of some affective tendency—which is exactly what is absent in the precocious dement and the catatonic. To use a bold metaphor, one may say that the mnemonic intellectual elements represent the elementary matter, the different threads that the affective tendencies then weave in order to make the most varied, richest, and firmest cloths, and which in their absence, only get piled up and wound round in disorder.

If, in consequence of their non-affectivity, coherence is absent in dementia praecox, *a fortiori* such patients lack the critical sense, so that nothing makes them recoil before the most illogical statements. Thus a general paralytic, in a state of dementia, relates that she has had four children in two years at different times, all being two years old ; and she states that "her husband has ten children, all nearly ten years old, whom she nurses ; they are very gentle, and do not hurt her breasts and everyone is happy ".[2]

Similarly, the dement Garin, quoted above, studied by Dumas, thinks that his wife has been false to him with several royal or titled lovers, and that her last-born is the daughter of Victor Hugo. But that is impossible,

---

[1] Kraepelin, *op. cit.,* pp. 22-24, 27.
[2] Séglas, *op. cit.,* pp. 278-279.

352 THE PSYCHOLOGY OF REASONING

Dumas remarks : Victor Hugo died in 1885 and your little daughter was born in 1894. He is dead as a poet, replies Garin, but after his death, *he was transformed* into a free-mason in the Lodge.[1]

That the incoherence and illogicality of dements depend actually and solely on the absence in them of any affective tendency, is proved by the attitude of the dement, which differs so markedly from that of the mentally confused. In the latter, as we have seen, the affective tendencies persist, except that in consequence of the interruption of the associative paths they can no longer exercise control over the intellectual elements. "In the incomplete and abortive answers of the confused, which reveal fragments of badly co-ordinated ideas, *may be recognised an obvious but insufficient effort* to group and translate them ". In the general paralytic in the state of dementia, on the contrary, "*there is no effort to understand and to answer*, and he gives, as though it were the most natural thing in the world, erroneous answers which become the occasion for associations of strange ideas and endless wanderings. These differences moreover appear also in the *bewildered, astonished, stupefied* look of the first, and the *inert, simple, serene* look of the second ".[2]

In the confused and in maniacs, in whom the affective tendencies still exist, there may be from time to time some gleam of intelligence ; but in dements, who are completely unaffective, this is impossible. Thus, in a case of dementia studied by Toulouse and Mignard, "her attention was not sufficient even for a moment to enable her to understand what we were saying in front of her. We saw always the same vacant, absent look, which makes living enigmas of these patients. When we uttered the grossest absurdities in front of her, she answered without feeling (apathy, indifference, are without doubt the most striking phenomena that our patient presents), by a number of incoherent remarks in the same vacant and far away voice, gazing into space : 'You are going to walk on your head '—' Yes, yes ! '—'Are you going to walk on your head?'—' Yes, he has hurt his foot.' The automatic mental activity of the patient never showed one of the gleams of intelli-

[1] Dumas, *art. cit.*, p. 179.
[2] Séglas, *op. cit.*, p. 248.

INCOHERENT INSANITY 353

gence which are so typical of the confused, and of maniacs."[1]

On account of this non-affectivity which is peculiar to them, patients suffering from dementia praecox and catatonics (senile dementia may be added, though here the intellectual material also, in consequence of mnemonic atrophy, is lacking to a far greater degree than in the others) constitute the class of the insane which approaches the nearest to the dream state of the normal man. For example, a dementia patient studied by Kraepelin, relates with the habitual expression of complete affective indifference (gemütliche Stumpfheit) "that he has seen up there a blue heart, and, behind, the flickering of the sunlight, then another blue heart, 'a heart of a pretty woman'; he has also seen flashes of lightning and a comet with a long tail; and the sunrise at the opposite point to where it usually rises": a string of disconnected images, such as may be produced in a dream.[2]

In dements, one gets exactly the same incoherence of ideas, the same overlapping of memories succeeding each other by the purely mechanical laws of resemblance or contiguity or assonance of the respective phonetic symbols, the same continual transformation of images, the same absence of all surprise in the presence of the most daring metamorphoses and the most blatant contradictions, the same total lack of any critical sense as in the dream. As Tanzi and Lugaro remark, in the most serious states of dementia praecox "paralysis of the critical faculty is complete and, as in dreams, gives free play to the most capricious fancy in every way". In the final stages these patients "abandon themselves to the strangest and most outlandish ideas with the same indifference and the same absence of any feeling of surprise which are characteristic of certain dreams". "And as in certain dreams we reconcile the most contradictory things without astonishment, and the personality of the dreamer may even be split into two, so this same phenomenon takes place in dementia praecox without arousing any surprise. The patient is a shoemaker and the King of France at the same time, the doctor is the doctor and the Grand Inquisitor".[3]

---

[1] Ed. Toulouse and M. Mignard, *art. cit.*, " L'autoconduction ", pp. 23-25.
[2] Kraepelin, *op. cit.*, p. 29.
[3] Tanzi and Lugaro, *op. cit.*, Vol. II, pp. 497, 465, 474.

z

354 THE PSYCHOLOGY OF REASONING

As we said then at the end of our chapter on dreams, the comparison between dreams and insanity in general is not at all accurate, in the sense that, as the various classes of insane are different from each other, the manner and the cause of their incoherence and illogicality are also different. But it is accurate as regards dements. Hence we can now give a more definite content to the statement of Wundt, quoted also at the end of our chapter on dreams, that "the analogy between dreams and insanity rests without doubt on common causes"; and can say that the analogy between the dream and dementia rests on one and the same cause, their *non-affectivity*.

But the affective tendencies serve not only to co-ordinate and connect ideas, but also to facilitate their evocation. The proof lies in the great contrast in this connection between the maniac and the catatonic. While the first, driven by stormy and momentary passions, presents great intellectual resources, "an extreme luxury", as Masselon observes, "of representations and associations of ideas", in the catatonic on the contrary, in the absence of all affective impulse, there is only "the expression of an enfeebled brain, poor in images and associations". Thus, a victim of dementia praecox, also described by Masselon, "is capable of applying the remaining elements of his intelligence when his attention is forced, but his brain is incapable of doing this spontaneously. It remains blank, to use the patient's own expression; ideas are no longer evoked or associated with each other, even with the slight connections which are found in the reverie."[1]

In this respect, dementia, especially in its more advanced stages, is then somewhat different from the dream, in which images, far from needing the affective stimulus in order to appear, crowd forward as soon as the inhibitive action of the affective tendencies, which were directed towards different ideas during the waking state, ceases. This is first of all due to the fact that the normal man, as contrasted with the dement, enriches himself continually during the waking-state with ever fresh intellectual elements, being endowed with a keen interest in so many things. And in the second place

[1] Masselon, *op. cit.*, pp. 144-145, 130.

INCOHERENT INSANITY 355

because the things perceived or imagined by the normal man in the waking state undergo habitual revivification by the affective tendencies interested and in consequence leave a much greater mnemonic accumulation, which the sole suppression of the inhibitive bonds suffices to put in action again, without the need of any affective spur. But in dementia praecox this revivification never takes place.

Moreover, the affective tendencies serve not only to place the mind in a condition favourable to its enrichment by ever fresh intellectual elements, *to facilitate evocation*, and then to connect ideas formed thereby, but also *to give to the ideas themselves thus evoked their respective significations*. Affective silence in its extreme degrees may thus *completely annihilate thought* and so lead to a state of "amentia" true and proper. This is of special importance to us, for it proves that when the affective activity is at zero, not only is intelligence "of no use", as Tanzi and Lugaro write, but *there is no longer any intelligence at all*.[1]

Indeed, the action "intelligere" only consists in associating a certain object or image with some affective tendency that they may be able to satisfy or oppose directly or indirectly. To "understand" is to connect, so to speak, such and such a group of sensory or mnemonic-sensory elements with the affective substratum of the individual; it is to give an affective tonality to what our sensations or respective memories project into us of the external world. If all affective activity ceases to appear, the significance of things, whatever they may be, ceases also, *and in consequence all thought whatever is extinguished*. The patient is thus reduced to a vegetative life, to a pure mechanism of reflexes, and is deprived for ever of intellectual light.

But here too, as soon as some affective tendency, illuminating the extinguished intelligence even for an instant, enters again into activity, a little reason begins to flicker also in word and in act. Thus the dement of the Asylum of St Anne, whom Godfernaux describes as singing continually in a monotonous air words devoid of all sense, on hearing the clock strike looked at it "and said in a weary tone : ' It is eleven o'clock already. Oh ! I couldn't be more hungry than I am '", after

---

[1] *Cf.* Tanzi and Lugaro, *op. cit.*, Vol. I, p. 329.

356 THE PSYCHOLOGY OF REASONING

which she took up her monotonous litany again. "The patient", remarks Godfernaux, "thus pronounced amid her wanderings a number of well associated and very significant words. It was not a mere phrase that escaped from the general disintegration, and got automatically repeated. The tone in which it was pronounced, the weary look which suddenly came over the patient's features, and her whole behaviour showed without doubt that not only had the patient co-ordinated her efforts at articulation and re-established order in the midst of the disorder of her impulses for an instant, *but also that the sentence had been understood, that it had a meaning for her when she pronounced it*". And the agent that provoked a flicker of reason in this poor mind, was therefore solely the affective tendency of hunger.[1]

Conclusion

We have thus brought to a close this rapid outline of the three classes of the incoherent insane which are the most interesting from our point of view. Our design has been to show how coherence of thought, whether manifested in words or in acts, depends on the existence, the persistence and the possibility of action of some affective tendency capable of directing and co-ordinating the evocation and succession of ideas ; capable, in other words, of utilising for its own ends the purely intellectual material of images which is at its disposal in the form of infinite mnemonic accumulations of all past experiences. Thus another of the fundamental characteristics of intelligence—coherence— is revealed as being of an exclusively affective nature.

If we have limited ourselves to passing rapidly in review the pathological forms of reasoning due solely to disturbances of an affective nature, this certainly does not imply that we think that *all* pathological manifestations of the mind must have a similar origin. Certain mental anomalies such as hallucinations and obsessions, for example—although here too there may be disorders of an affective nature also, as Janet has proved especially for the obsessions—should nevertheless be considered without any doubt as morbid manifestations of a principally intellectual nature, in that it is the sensory

---

[1] Godfernaux, *op. cit.*, pp. 21-24.

INCOHERENT INSANITY 357

or mnemonic-sensory elements themselves that no longer function normally. And we have already mentioned in passing the alcoholic and meningitic delusions, due to the stimulation of the mnemonic-sensory centres by toxic or infectious agents, and senile dementia, where there is an absence of affectivity combined with atrophy of mnemonic-intellectual material ; and so on. But it was important to us to prove, in support of our theory of the nature of reasoning, that the two fundamental characteristics of the highest and most complex psychical process, namely coherence and logicality, are actually and exclusively of affective origin. And it seems to us that our rapid incursion into the realm of dreams and insanity has proved this completely.

Our method, which consists in trying to resolve complex psychical phenomena into their elementary phenomena, has allowed us, in the pages devoted to normal reasoning, to understand the origin and nature of phenomena hitherto unanalysed or incompletely analysed, such as the affective tendencies themselves whether original or derived, the attention, the will, the capacity for abstraction and synthesis, reasoning itself in its different forms, intuitive and deductive, concrete and abstract, constructive and intentional. This method has also, we think, given appreciable results when applied to the pathological domain. For it has succeeded in throwing some light upon the nature, hitherto largely enigmatic, of the bizarre characters of dreams, the strange peculiarities of monomaniacs, and the disordered delusions of the maniac, the confused, and the dement.

Morel has already expressed the desire " *to see a good psychology serve as an introduction to the study of disorders of the reason* ". " The psychological method in psychopathology ", writes d'Allonnes in his turn, " has derived its inspiration and its bearings from normal psychology ; it treats the clinic only as a source of documents which generally are too concrete for it, but which it examines, separates, and groups at will, without embarrassing itself with methodological and epistemological classifications ; it is a psychology enriched by medical illustrations, a psycho-pathology for the use of philosophers." But the clinic cannot do without it : " Discerning observation of mental patients is impossible without psychology.

358 THE PSYCHOLOGY OF REASONING

Moreover, psychiatrists are in fact inspired by psychologists more than they inspire them. *It is time to adapt the psychological instrument more effectively to psychiatric requirements.*" And finally: " There is no doubt ", write Toulouse and Mignard, " that whenever we seek to discover the meaning of psychiatric evolution, there is a continuous effort *to investigate, beneath the morphology of mental disorders, the deep-lying mechanism of their production* ". For this purpose, " it is necessary to construct a general psychology of mental disorders, *to reduce the countless forms of clinical experience to simple, constant processes* ".[1]

This is exactly what we have tried to do in applying to the study of pathological forms of reasoning the results reached by breaking up normal reasoning itself into its elementary psychical factors ; and the new result that we have obtained has been to discover in the anomalies of the affective psyche, which may be reduced to three or four very simple types, the profound mechanism of the production of the most characteristic and important mental disorders. So that we can entertain the hope that our purely theoretical analysis relative to the nature of the highest psychical faculty, human reason, may also have contributed to throw a little more light on the mysteries of the abnormal psyche, and may thus have had appreciable results as regards practical psychiatry also.

---

[1] Morel, *op. cit.*, p. 393 ; Revault d'Allonnes, *art. cit.*, p. 490 ; Toulouse and Mignard, *art. cit.*, " Les Maladies et l'autoconduction ", pp. 273, 279.

CHAPTER XVI

CONSCIOUS AND UNCONSCIOUS REASONING

BEFORE proceeding to inquire whether unconscious reasoning really exists and how its existence is possible, and before examining whether there is not perhaps to-day a tendency to exaggerate the importance of unconscious as opposed to conscious reasoning in the normal man, it is necessary to be quite clear as to the meaning of the word 'consciousness'. We must also endeavour to ascertain the 'nature' of consciousness, *i.e.* to distinguish clearly the elementary psychical phenomena of which conscious states are composed.

I. *What is Consciousness?*

There is probably no word which has been more discussed, or whose meaning remains more obscure, than the word consciousness. Everyone would at once be quite clear whether any given psychical state or action should properly be called conscious or unconscious, yet when we go on to ask what constitutes this conscious character which is attributed to one state and denied to another very little is forthcoming in the way of a satisfactory answer. "Whoever", says Maudsley, "endeavours faithfully and firmly to obtain a definite idea of what is meant by consciousness, will find it no wise so easy a matter as the frequent use of the word might imply".[1]

Some psychologists have decided to regard the problem as insoluble. "As for defining the state of consciousness, the fact of being conscious", writes Ribot, "that were a vain and idle attempt; it is a datum of observation, an ultimate fact. Physiology shows that its production is always associated with the activity of the nervous system, in particular of the brain.

---

[1] Maudsley, *op. cit., The Physiology of Mind*, p. 45; *cf.* also, for example, Bain, *op. cit., The Emotions and the Will*, Chap. XI, " Consciousness ", pp. 539-546.

360 THE PSYCHOLOGY OF REASONING

But the converse proposition is not true; though all psychical activity always implies nerve activity, nervous activity does not always imply psychical activity. Nerve activity has far greater extension than psychical activity : hence consciousness is something super-added. In other words we must regard a state of consciousness as a complex event which pre-supposes a particular state of the nervous system ; nor is this nervous process an accessory but an integral part of the event—nay, its groundwork, its fundamental condition ; once produced the fact exists *in* itself; when consciousness is added, the event exists *for* itself; consciousness completes it and perfects it, gives it the finishing touch, but does not constitute it ".[1]

Others simply call consciousness an epiphenomenon and regard themselves as thereby free from any obligation to pursue the question further, as though they had thus completely settled it.[2]

Here, on the contrary, we propose to inquire whether by the study of certain examples of consciousness and unconsciousness, suitably selected, we can discover the fundamental characteristics which accompany the cases known as 'conscious', and which are not found in those described as 'unconscious'. This will be sufficient to make clear what constitutes the consciousness or unconsciousness of our psychical states.

It is useful to begin with an example which to many readers may not seem to fall under the cases in question, though closely related to them. I look at the portrait of a friend. I recognise that it represents him, but yet that it is not really he. The actual complex sensation, thanks to the association of resemblance, awakens at the same time the image of the real person. We have then on the one hand the co-existence, at any rate for a certain time, of actual sensations and past sensations now evoked and less intense ; on the other hand, metaphorically at any rate, the superposition or fusion, in virtue of identity, of some only of the first with some of the second. We might therefore be induced to admit that this co-existence and partial superposition or fusion

---

[1] Ribot, *Les maladies de la personnalité*, Paris, 1906, p. 6. English Translation, New York, 1887, p. 2.

[2] Cf. for example A. Binet, *La Psychologie du Raisonnement*, p. 165; G. Villa, *op. cit.*, *La psicologia contemporanea*, pp. 412-413.

UNCONSCIOUS REASONING 361

of the two complex systems of sensations pure and simple, are what makes me recognise in the portrait the friend in question, what makes me 'conscious' that it is really he who is represented in the portrait. But the question can also be asked whether, in the state of mind in which I find myself when I recognise that the object is the portrait of a friend, there do not appear as determining conditions not only elements of a purely sensory or perceptual order, but also elements of an affective or emotional order. On seeing the portrait I should, even without noticing it, have the same feelings of affection or dislike, of sympathy or antipathy etc., which would ordinarily accompany the sight of the original ; and it would be precisely these same feelings which would make me conscious that the portrait was that of the person in question. Other examples which will shortly be given force us to admit that this is what actually occurs, in other words that the superposition and fusion, partial or even complete, of pure sensations not accompanied by a superposition and fusion of elements of an affective or emotional order, is insufficient to give us the consciousness of any fact.

Still confining ourselves to contrasting two psychic states only, the one original and the other evoked, let us consider the case where the evocation of some past event is presented to our minds in complete isolation, entirely apart from other memories of preceding or subsequent facts.

"A lady, in the last stages of a chronic disease, was carried from London to a lodging in the country ; there her infant daughter was taken to visit her, and after a short interview carried back to town. The lady died a few days after, and the daughter grew up without any recollection of her mother till she was of mature age. At this time she happened to be taken into the room in which her mother died, without knowing it to have been so ; *she started* on entering it, and when a friend who was along with her asked the cause of her *agitation*, she replied, 'I have a distinct impression of having been in this room before, and that a lady who lay in that corner and seemed very ill, leaned over me, and wept.'"[1]

---

[1] J. Abercrombie, *Inquiries concerning the Intellectual Powers*, 1830, p. 117, cited by Ribot, *Les maladies de la mémoire*, Paris, 1901, pp. 143-144. (English Translation, New York, 1883, p. 42.)

362 THE PSYCHOLOGY OF REASONING

Similarly, a man of marked artistic temperament had no sooner reached the gate of a castle in Sussex than he experienced "*a very vivid impression*" of having seen it before; and recalled the scene in imagination in all its details, with a number of sight-seers. He learnt from his mother that he had in fact been taken there when about eighteen months old, and that his memory of the occasion was quite exact.[1]

Still more than in the case of the portrait doubts here arise as to whether the individual does not derive the impression of having been already personally present to the one or the other event from something more than the coincidence of the pure sensations actually given with some of the past sensations; and whether the emotions which were experienced afresh both by the lady on visiting the room and the artist on revisiting the house—emotions the same as or resembling those experienced in the past and preserved in memory—are not, rather, what really gives them the feeling of having lived through the event which now returns to their consciousness.

We have twice made allusion to the doubts raised by the suggestion that the mere coincidence of certain psychical elements actually present and certain others which are recalled is sufficient, when it is a case of pure sensations or perceptions, to evoke a past event and render it an object of consciousness. A typical case of distraction to which I am often subject would seem to prove the reasonableness of these doubts.

When I leave my study I usually put my notes in a drawer which I lock. On some occasions the act of locking the drawer appears as 'conscious'. On others, when I am still preoccupied by what a little before formed the object of my thoughts, the act seems to be an 'unconscious' one. In the second case, I have often hardly left my study when I feel uncertain whether I have turned the key or not, and as I am then unable to recall the fact, I feel it necessary to return to the room, and, since the drawer has no handle, to satisfy myself by re-opening it and closing it again. My desire to attain my end, viz. that the drawer shall be locked, a desire manifested in the attention which I

---

[1] Ribot, *loc. cit.*, p. 144 (E.T. p. 42), citing W. B. Carpenter, *Mental Physiology*, Fourth Edition, 1876, p. 431.

UNCONSCIOUS REASONING 363

devote to the successful attainment of the end, on this occasion accompanies the act itself, and when I leave my study the second time it now seems to be 'conscious'.

It may be noted that when I lock the drawer for the second time the similar previous act still appears to be 'unconscious'; yet it is certain that the same group of sensations, visual, auditory, tactile, muscular, etc., were then reproduced as must have accompanied the same act a few moments previously. Even so wide a common basis of elements of a purely sensory or perceptual order is therefore not sufficient to evoke an act which occurred so very recently and to render it conscious.

On the other hand, if the desire to attain my end accompanied the corresponding act on the second occasion, how does it happen that this act, when I once again leave my study, seems to be conscious? There is now no longer any common sensational element which can link my psychical state at the moment when I find myself outside my room to my state when I was actually locking the drawer. And yet, if I now once more ask myself whether I have locked the drawer, the act is immediately called to mind and I am completely conscious of it.

It seems then, that, it is the assemblage of affective elements, relative to the desired end, or an equivalent assemblage of emotional elements, that constitutes the portion of elements in common between an actual and a past psychical state, which is necessary and sufficient to evoke the past state and to render it conscious.

I use the words "necessary and sufficient to evoke the past state *and to render it conscious*", because there are some examples which seem to show beyond doubt that there can quite well be an evocation of some past event, though the event itself may remain quite unconscious for us.

Thus in his classic work on dreams which we have already cited on several occasions, Maury relates that he dreamt one night of a person entirely unknown to him even by sight, whose features remained very clearly before him even after he woke. Imagine then his astonishment at meeting in the street a few days afterwards the unknown of his dream in flesh and blood. After much thought, and several days after the incident, he succeeded in explaining this strange coincidence.

364 THE PSYCHOLOGY OF REASONING

The street where he had met the person in question was one which he had formerly often traversed, but, for more than a year, he had not had occasion to pass again that way until the day preceding the night of the dream. It then became necessary for him to resume his old route and he found that he frequently encountered this individual, who doubtless lived close by. Maury therefore considers it very probable that when a year previously he had often gone that way, he must then too have seen him frequently without paying any attention to him ; and the fact of having traversed the street itself on the day before the dream occurred, even if on this occasion he failed to meet him, would, by the association of ideas, have re-evoked the features of the individual in question.

When on the morning after his dream Maury awoke and continued to have the dream-image before his mind, this image then constituted a true mnemonic evocation of an event which had remained unconscious and which continued even now to remain such. The image evoked had now succeeded in attracting his attention and his interest, evoking feelings of sympathy or antipathy, of pleasure or aversion, and the like, but none of these feelings could then serve as a means of rendering 'conscious' that moment when he had seen the actual individual.

If on the other hand he had not been otherwise pre-occupied at this moment and so been prevented from experiencing for the person before him the same feelings as he now felt for the image, this common basis of affective or emotive elements, would not now have been lacking and would have been sufficient to render the event 'conscious' for him.

In summing up, therefore, what we have said so far, it seems allowable to admit that one cannot speak of the "consciousness" of a psychical state in itself, but only of the "consciousness" that a present psychical state has of a past one. This characteristic of "consciousness" *of a past psychical state,* now evoked, *in relation to another present psychical state* is met with each time there is *co-existence,* at any rate for a certain time, of the first with the second, and *superposition or fusion,* if only partial, *of the affective or emotive part of the one with that of the other.*

UNCONSCIOUS REASONING 365

The necessary, if not sufficient, condition for any psychical state then to appear to us as conscious is, therefore, that it should also contain, among its constituent parts, elements of an affective or emotive order.

We can get an idea *grosso modo* of the partial superposition or fusion of the two affective or emotive psychical states by imagining that there is at any rate a partial coincidence of the respective cerebral zones, to whose entry into activity the two affective or emotive states are due, namely that evoked and the present one.

And let us note here that the cerebral zone, to whose entry into activity the affective or emotive state now evoked is due, will be the same as that which entered into activity when the state was produced in the past.

Sometimes, especially in the phenomena of introspection, if the past psychical state, conscious in relation to a fresh state, has scarcely passed away, or lasts during the formation of the latter and thus produces the illusion that the two psychical states are contemporary and blend into one, it is more difficult to perceive that in this case also it is a matter of consciousness of one state in relation to the other ; we speak therefore, but here again inaccurately, of a psychical state " conscious in itself ".

From the conscious character of one psychical state in relation to another it is easy to pass to the conscious character of a whole series of successive acts or states, in relation to one another. Such a series occurs when, in relation to the present psychical state, a former state now evoked appears as conscious, and when to this in turn another previous or subsequent state appears as conscious, and so on.

It is sufficient to think of everything that one has done since the morning to convince oneself that, parallel with the series of our conscious acts, there always goes a series of corresponding complex affectivities, each of which, beginning to enter into activity before the cessation of the preceding act, lasts during the first phases or the entire development of the subsequent act and sometimes even during a whole series of successive acts. Thus the feeling of pleasure that I experience when nearing the end of a laborious task, because I taste in advance the approaching rest, serves to connect the actual state with that which follows in which I do actually rest. The desire not to break an appointment

366 THE PSYCHOLOGY OF REASONING

lasts during the whole series of acts that have first to be accomplished and that one hastens to perform so as not to arrive late. The complex feeling of pleasure and fear that the child experiences in enjoying the stolen sugar-plum is common to the moment when it eats it and that which follows, when it strives to conceal the traces of its petty theft: and this feeling constitutes the affective bridge that unites the two episodes thus experienced.

As a simple expedient for rendering our point more intelligible, let us represent time by the axis of the abscissæ, and let us suppose that the points and segments of the axis of the ordinates are capable of representing, by their position and size, the different portions of the total surface of the brain to whose entry into activity the different complex psychical states are due, as though the various sensory and affective-emotive centres could be arranged, without alteration of their reciprocal contiguity or proximity and of their reciprocal connections, along the axis of the ordinates. Then, as a schematic figure representing a series of original psychical states, a, b, c . . . capable of subsequently appearing as conscious in relation to one another—provided that lapse of time has not effaced the mnemonic impression they have left—we shall have a number of rectangles differing in size, form, and position, so connected that each, as regards its affective or emotive portion, is partly superposed on the affective or emotive portions of the one preceding and of the one succeeding it.

If above or below this series of rectangles, others were drawn similarly connected, but none of them having any part, affective or emotive, in common with any of the rectangles of the first series, this second series would represent a series of psychical states, x, y, z. . . , also conscious in relation to one another, but unconscious in relation to the principal series, a, b, c. . . , constituting the " conscious personality " properly so called of the individual. They would represent therefore, in relation to the individual, a short series of unconscious states, forming the beginning of a duplication of his personality. On the other hand, two series of rectangles, produced at different times even widely apart, will be able to form a single series

UNCONSCIOUS REASONING 367

when the respective psychic states are evoked simultaneously, provided that some state of the first series has some part, affective or emotive, in common with some state of the second series.

Short series of unconscious acts, forming the beginning of a double personality, are, as is well known, extremely frequent even in normal individuals.

During a holiday at Riva Valdobbia, at the foot of Monte Rosa, I used every day to take the Ca' di Janzo mule-path. The descent, especially at this time, was rather steep and rough ; sometimes one had to jump from one large stone to another, and these being rather shaky, care was required. At first, the descent diverted me by these little difficulties and succeeded always in keeping alive the interest necessary in order to surmount them. I would recognise the principal stones already encountered on other mornings and if on the preceding day one of them had been dislodged and threatened to fall, I took precautions that it should not happen again. At the end of the walk all the little incidents of the descent, all my most difficult steps and jumps, came back to mind and appeared as "conscious".

For some days, this walk secured me rest from my usual thoughts, because I was not interested in anything else. Little by little, however, the interest and preoccupation with the little difficulties to be overcome decreased to such a degree that I ended by making the descent quite mechanically, thinking of other things at the same time, as if I had walked on the main road. All my steps, even the most difficult ones taken to avoid dislodging the stones, had become so many unconscious acts. In fact, I found on my return to the hotel that not even the faintest memory of any of the roughest points of the path made me "conscious" of the descent performed.

Nevertheless, even during this unconscious descent, I certainly must have paid attention to the stones and to the way in which steps could be taken without causing their falling. Thanks to the difficulties of the path my steps could not have become purely reflex acts, especially as a good number of the stones did not always remain in the same place but were removed every day by people continually using the path. My

368 THE PSYCHOLOGY OF REASONING

steps must, therefore, have been guided by so many connected acts of reflection.

In this case, what appeared to me as conscious on the return from my walk was the series of my reflections, and what seemed unconscious, was the series of sensations and reactions provoked in me by the external world. The view is commonly held that sometimes the very opposite of this takes place, viz. that the series of external sensations provoked in us remains conscious, such as a pleasant walk in the open air; while the internal meditation continuing meanwhile, would be unconscious. We shall soon see, however, that the rôle attributed to this unconscious meditation, which is regarded by some writers as responsible for the unexpected solution of problems that we laboured in vain to solve in the conscious state, is largely exaggerated to-day; it cannot easily be allowed, because of the affective intensity that such meditation would involve.

Finally, the series of inward meditations sometimes remains unconscious as well as the sensations of the external world: "One day", Maury relates, "finding myself near M.V. . . ., who was very absent-minded and given to meditation, I noticed that he had become completely indifferent to my remarks and had ceased to reply. He seemed plunged in deep thought. His immobility was such that the thought struck me that he was going to lose consciousness. I shook him violently by the arm. 'What do you want?' he said. 'Are you ill?' I asked. 'No'. 'What is the matter then?' 'I am thinking'. 'What about?' 'My goodness, how strange; I know nothing about it any more, and yet I feel tired with thinking.'"[1]

In this case the series of sensations provoked in him by the words that Maury has continued to address to him for a certain time had remained unconscious as well as the series of his thoughts.

From these normal cases of temporary duplication of the personality which embrace all so called cases of absent-mindedness, we pass by degrees to the pathological cases of true duplication.

The well-known case related by Taine is very characteristic: "I have seen a lady, who, while talking and singing, writes, without looking at her paper, connected

[1] A. Maury, *op. cit.*, *Le sommeil et les rêves*, p. 228.

UNCONSCIOUS REASONING   369

sentences and even whole pages, without being conscious of what she is writing. In my opinion, she is perfectly honest; and she declares that at the end of the page she has no idea of what she has traced on the paper; when she reads it, she is astonished and sometimes alarmed. The writing is different from her ordinary writing. The movement of her fingers and of the pencil is stiff, and seems automatic. The writing always ends with a signature, that of someone dead, and bears the imprint of intimate thoughts, of a mental background that the author does not wish to divulge ".[1]

Quite analogous are the cases studied by Janet. For example, he suggested to an hysteric called Lucie, in a state of somnambulism, that when she wakes she would write some letter at a given signal. "Here is what she wrote, on waking", says Janet: "Madam, I cannot come on Sunday, as I intended; I beg you to excuse me. I should be delighted to go with you, but I cannot manage that day. Yours, Lucie. P.S. Please give my love to the children ". "This automatic letter is correct", continues Janet, "and implies a certain amount of thought. Lucie was talking of something quite different and answered several people while she was writing. Moreover, she understood nothing in the letter when I showed it to her, and thought that I had copied her signature ".[2]

In another experiment, Janet suggested to the same subject during hypnotic sleep that she would multiply 739 by 42 in writing. On waking, and at the given signal, "the right hand wrote the figures regularly, did the multiplication and did not stop until everything was finished. The whole time, Lucie, wide awake, was telling me what she had done that day, and did not once stop talking while her right hand made the correct calculation ".[3]

These true duplications of personality prove in the most obvious manner what we said above, namely that the psychical states, $x, y, z, \ldots$, unconscious in relation to the principal series $a, b, c \ldots$, may, on the contrary, if they satisfy the usual conditions set forth above, be

---

[1] H. Taine, *op. cit., De l'intelligence*, vol. I, pp. 16-17.
[2] P. Janet, *op. cit., l'automatisme psychologique*, pp. 263-264.
[3] Janet, *ibid.*, p. 263.

2 A

370 THE PSYCHOLOGY OF REASONING

conscious among themselves. In fact, dual personality is just constituted by a long complete series of acts, unconscious as regards one of the personalities, but forming a conscious series as regards the other.

Thus, for example, what the somnambulist does during one attack appears to him as unconscious in the waking-state, but becomes conscious again in a subsequent attack. Dr Mesnet's patient, for instance, continued to follow out plans of suicide conceived during a previous attack and completely forgotten in the lucid interval. She then recalled all the circumstances of the other attack. And Macario speaks of a young somnambulist whom a man had assaulted while she had an attack and who, once awake, had no memory, no idea of this attempt; it was only during a fresh attack that she revealed the outrage to her mother.[1]

Sometimes, one state is conscious of the other, but not vice versa. Thus the young woman with a double existence, of Dr Azam, "presented a normal state, though itself pathological, for she was hysterical, and one in which she appeared quite different in character and ideas. In the second state she remembered what she had done in the first, but on returning to this first state she completely lost the memory of what she had done during the other period ".[2]

Nothing is more suitable than these examples, which could be multiplied indefinitely, to show how each psychical state is, in itself, neither conscious nor unconscious, but becomes one or the other *only in relation to some other psychical state serving as a point of reference.* In other words, consciousness is not in itself a characteristic that can be assumed by a psychical state entirely on its own account, but it is the characteristic *of a relation* between two or more psychical states. A psychical state, even considered in isolation, can always be recognised, for example, as having one emotive character rather than another, as being imaginative rather than volitional, etc. ; on the other hand, so long as it is isolated, we can never say that it is conscious or unconscious. It is only if we relate it to another psychical state that we can say, it is conscious or unconscious, in relation to the latter. And

---

[1] A. Maury, *op. cit., Le sommeil et les rêves,* p. 234.
[2] *Ibid.*, pp. 237-238.

UNCONSCIOUS REASONING 371

if it is conscious in relation to a psychical state A, it can be unconscious in relation to another B.

Consciousness, therefore, is not an intrinsic or absolute property of psychical states, but rather a relative property external to them, and accompanying certain modalities of relation, of an affective nature, which these psychical states happen to have between them.

II. *The Exaggerated Importance Attributed to Unconscious Reasoning in Man*

Our study of the nature of consciousness has shown us the theoretical possibility, confirmed by psycho-pathological experience, of double or multiple independent series of psychical states, these latter being connected with each other in each series. We may now enquire whether such a duplication, or even a division of our psyche into more distinct personalities, mutually ignorant of one another, is actually a common phenomenon in the normal man also. This will lead us to examine the subject which chiefly interests us, namely, whether there is not a great deal of exaggeration in the importance now often attributed, in normal life also, to unconscious psychical activity in general and to unconscious reasoning in particular.

In our second chapter, we saw that the " unity of consciousness " to which the state of attention gives rise, is due to the fact that, normally, only one primary affective tendency can be aroused at once. The property of the affective tendencies of having a diffused, and indeed a largely diffused seat, makes it difficult, as we noted, for there to be two affective tendencies whose seats do not coincide to a certain extent, and difficult also, therefore—if these tendencies are not such as to hold each other reciprocally in suspense as in the state of attention, or to combine in part and blend with each other—for one not to exclude and inhibit the other. Hence, though several sensations or their images can enter into activity at the same time and coexist simultaneously in the same brain, because each has its seat localised in a given centre, or in a limited group of centres, this is not normally possible as regards the affective tendencies ; for by the fact of their diffused

372 THE PSYCHOLOGY OF REASONING

seats, they would inevitably "collide" with each other. Only when two affective tendencies differ so much from each other that they have no part of their seat in common, one demanding besides only a comparatively small expenditure of energy for its activation,—it is only in this case, we say, that in the normal man there can also be a simultaneous entry into activity of two independent affectivities, such as exists in all the so-called cases of absent-mindedness, which, as we have seen, represent duplications of personality in the making. But apart from this, in the normal man, there will only be one affective activity at once ; and accordingly, the present tendency to attribute to the unconscious life a considerable part in our normal mental activity, which would imply the existence of two distinct personalities knowing nothing of each other, is quite fantastical.

It is useless to pause over the metaphysical conception of Hartmann, who held that there is a second personality hidden beneath our ordinary consciousness, exactly comparable with the first, and exclusively endowed with all the truly creative qualities. He is even moved to exclaim : "Let us not despair at having a mind so practical and so lowly, so unpoetical and so little spiritual ; there is within the innermost sanctuary of each of us a marvellous something of which we are unconscious, which dreams and prays while we labour to earn our daily bread."[1]

But quite apart from this antiscientific conception of Hartmann and his associates, and the mystical view of Myers, the tendency to exaggerate the importance of the share that "the unconscious" is supposed to have in our psychical life is evident in the most recent studies on this same unconscious. "The question of knowing what rôle subconscious states play in normal minds," writes Dwelshauvers paraphrasing Morton Prince, "is one of the most poignant problems of psychology". According to Lipps, "the cause of numerous states of consciousness should be looked for", in the normal mind also, "in the unconscious". Jastrow affirms "the commanding influence of the subconscious in the mental life", and holds that "conscious utilization of sub-consciously elaborated data remains the normal formula

---

[1] Bernard Hart, in Münsterberg and others, *Subconscious Phenomena*, Boston and London, 1910, p. 106.

UNCONSCIOUS REASONING 373

of thought." According to Windelband, "our imaginative life shows in all its creative activity the continual co-operation of the unconscious ".[1]

These extreme champions of the unconscious gradually come to attribute to it the whole of our psychical activity. Every entrance into activity of affective tendencies, all their transformations, would be preceded, according to them, by a mysterious elaboration in the realm of the unconscious. To the work of the unconscious would be due even the mnemonic contribution which transforms each elementary sensation into a true perception. The images and ideas themselves, in the interval between one of their evocations and the next, would always continue to be in activity in the unconscious state: "The fundamental motive in making use of the hypothesis of the unconscious", writes Windelband, "is the state in which our memories may be presumed to be in the interval between their first appearance in consciousness and their reproduction, if this reproduction takes place once or several times. What becomes of our memories during the time when we are not thinking of them?"[2]

Evidently, in thus attributing to the unconscious a continuous activity, at the foundation of all conscious activity, so that the latter would never be anything more than the final result, the mature fruit of a mysterious elaboration on the part of the unconscious itself, an attempt is being made to reintroduce at the window the mystical idea of a soul which psychological science had driven out by the door. "According to these authors", writes Ribot, "subconscious activity is invested with almost supernatural power and constitutes in the individual an intermediate link between the human and the divine ".[3]

At the same time, to consider every conscious manifestation as the final result of an unconscious elaboration whose method of working admittedly escapes all our

[1] G. Dwelshauvers, *L'inconscient*, Paris, 1916, pp. 61, 112 ; J. Jastrow, *The Subconscious*, London, 1906, pp. 420, 449 ; W. Windelband, *Die Hypothese des Unbewussten*, Festrede gehalten in der Gesamtsitzung der Heidelberger Akademie der Wissenschaften am 24 April 1914, Heidelberg, 1914, p. 3.

[2] G. Dwelshauvers, *op. cit.*, *L'inconscient*, pp. 224, 176, 178 ; W. Windelband, *op. cit.*, *Die Hypothese des Unbewussten*, p. 10.

[3] Th. Ribot, in Münsterberg and others, *op. cit.*, *Subconscious Phenomena*, p. 35.

374 THE PSYCHOLOGY OF REASONING

investigations is to renounce the possibility of any explanation of psychical phenomena, to declare the impossibility of a science of psychology.

In order to avoid similar exaggerations on the subject of the part played by the unconscious or subconscious in our psychical life, exaggerations, which, we repeat, end by explaining nothing, it must not be forgotten that a sane scientific method should not have recourse to the unconscious, except where absolutely necessary. We should then ask ourselves as regards every psychical fact: Is the hypothesis of an unconscious psychical activity necessary in order to explain it, or can it be explained also without recourse to this hypothesis?

Now, it is evident that there is no need to have recourse to this hypothesis in order to explain the phenomenon of the evocation of our memories, that is to say, in order to explain how it is that a sensation, perception, image, or idea, after having been absent from our mind for a certain interval of time, can be represented to it again by means of mnemonic evocation. The simple conception of specific mnemonic accumulation, that is to say, of specific nervous energy which passes alternately from the actual to the potential state and vice versa, is sufficient to account completely for the phenomena of evocation. In the same way that no electric current exists in the interval when the accumulator remains inserted in an open circuit, so, in the interval between two successive evocations of the same image or idea, the latter does not remain " present in our mind, although latent in consciousness ", as Freud, following Windelband, maintains, but *it no longer exists at all, either as a psychical process or as a purely nervous process.*[1]

Nor is there any need to have recourse to this hypothesis of an unconscious activity in order to explain the entry into action of one or other of our affective tendencies or their transformation in consequence of their combination with others that enter into action at the same moment. In fact, these phenomena too, as we have seen in our first chapter, are only so many aspects of mnemonic evocation in general, that is to say

---

[1] *Cf.*, S. Freud, " A Note on the Unconscious in Psycho-Analysis ", *Proceedings of the Society of Psychical Research,* Part 66, vol. XXVI, p. 312.

UNCONSCIOUS REASONING 375

of the transition of certain specific nervous-energetic accumulations from the potential to the actual state. They are performed entirely openly, in full sight of consciousness, from the first moment of their reproduction, when the specific nervous energy which constitutes them enters into action.

On the other hand, have Windelband, Freud, Dwelshauvers and their associates reflected sufficiently on the enormous expenditure of nervous energy which would be produced if all the affective tendencies by which we can be moved at the opportune moment, all the sensations and perceptions already experienced, and all the images and ideas which are derived from them, continued, between two evocations, to remain simultaneously active in the mind, if only in the unconscious state?

Quite as useless is the hypothesis of some unconscious psychical activity as regards acts that have become completely automatic, that is to say, as regards those in which there is no more "selection" at all, and which consequently do not presuppose the entry into play of any affective tendency. However complicated, they are only pure reflex acts, that is to say purely nervous processes, and they therefore lack the necessary and sufficient condition for becoming true psychical acts, conscious or subconscious (that is to say conscious in relation to a secondary personality); which is, to be moved by some affective tendency.

Vice versa, in all cases of absence of mind which imply a "selection", even a succession of "selections",— such as my descent from Ca' di Janzo described above, or the experience of Mill, when, quite absorbed by the elaboration of his system of logic, he crossed Cheapside when at its busiest, and yet, absent-minded as he was, walked about without running into anyone and avoided the dangers which constantly threaten everyone on such occasions from the heavy traffic—in cases such as these it is no longer possible to consider this "absent-minded" behaviour as simply automatic. For in order to proceed to the "selection" which evidently contributes to determine this behaviour, corresponding affective tendencies must enter into play, and here then it becomes necessary to have recourse to the hypothesis of a beginning of true duplication of the personality : "The movements of the man who goes absent-mindedly along the street",

376 THE PSYCHOLOGY OF REASONING

writes Luciani, "are not at all comparable to a regular succession of simple reflex acts, because they are continually changing and modifying themselves so as not to run into obstacles, so as to avoid people and carts, and, in a word, so as to adapt, according to the circumstances, the muscular actions to the end desired. Now the pursuit of an end, the adaptation of actions to circumstances, the choice of means suitable for attaining a given end, constitute the only possible scientific criterion for distinguishing psychical manifestations from purely mechanical phenomena ".[1]

Naturally we pass by insensible degrees from purely automatic actions to absent-minded actions, so that in certain cases such as the unconscious copying without a mistake of a long piece of text, while the copyist thinks of something else, it would be difficult to say to which category they belonged. This gradual transition is due to the fact that in order to discharge actions, which are on the way to becoming automatic, a less and less intensity of the affective tendency which performed the "selection" in the past is sufficient ; so that the identical action can still be "discharged" to-day by an affective tendency of very little intensity and by to-morrow have become entirely mechanical. "At the outset", writes Jastrow, "each step of the performance is separately and distinctly the object of attention and effort ; and as practice proceeds and expertness is gained, the attention is suitably apportioned over the whole of the group of processes, the separate portions thereof becoming fused into larger units, which in turn make a constantly diminishing demand upon consciousness ".[2]

Now, it is precisely this continuous decrease of intensity of attention with which actions on the way to becoming automatic are performed, as well as the great difference between the kind of interest which impels us to the accomplishment of these actions and the kind of interest for the object pursued in thought by the absent-minded ; and also the fact that the seat of the first affectivity is very probably limited in extension in relation to that of the second affectivity turned to thinking

---

[1] L. Luciani, *op. cit., I fenomeni psico-fisici della veglia e del sonno*, p. 478.

[2] J. Jastrow, *op. cit., The Subconscious*, pp. 41-42 ; cf., also Dwelshauvers, *op. cit., L'inconscient*, p. 306.

UNCONSCIOUS REASONING 377

—it is all this that renders easy, even in normal individuals, the beginnings of that duplication of the personality represented by cases of absent-mindedness. In other words, when the affective tendency discharging an act that has been selected and become habitual has descended below a certain degree of intensity, so as to require for its entrance into activity a very small expenditure of energy in relation to that required by the principal affectivity which sustains the reflection of the absent-minded man, and when these two very different affectivities have no part of their seat in common, they will then be able to exist simultaneously and independently one of the other; and this is exactly what constitutes the splitting up of the personality into two totally distinct personalities.

Yet it is well known that in cases of intense concentration, absent-minded acts are also often suspended. Two people who are walking together stop at the liveliest moment of the discussion; at table, we may remain with fork or glass halfway to the mouth if someone is relating something very interesting. "It is when he becomes particularly absorbed", says Jastrow, "that the writer lets his pipe go out; and it is when they come to a particularly exciting part of their discourse that two companions, talking as they stroll, stop, apparently unable to talk and walk at the same time".[1]

In such cases, the energy absorbed by the stronger interest is so great that it no longer even allows of the feeble affective intensity which was sufficient to discharge the absent-minded act. *Vice versa*, as soon as the need of a new selection appears in an habitual but not entirely mechanised act, it can no longer be performed "absent-mindedly" and accordingly becomes conscious : " When speaking to a foreigner or to a person hard of hearing, we consciously attend to our enunciation; when at the table we are served with fish, we give enough attention to the machinery of mastication so as not to swallow the bones ; and when we wish to be sure to use the proper fork or spoon for the salad or sherbet, we deliberately stop and choose ".[2]

To sum up, therefore, three very different classes

---

[1] J. Jastrow, *op. cit.*, *The Subconscious*, pp. 57-58.
[2] *Ibid.*, p. 13.

378 THE PSYCHOLOGY OF REASONING

should be distinguished. The first concerns all the potential states capable of passing to the actual state, that is to say, of being transformed into psychical activities : affective tendencies, memories of sensations, images, ideas. *So long as they are in the potential state* they are neither conscious nor unconscious, *they do not exist* as psychical activities nor as purely nervous processes, any more than an electric current exists in the accumulator while the circuit remains open. The second concerns all organic activities, all reflexes, all groups of reflexes constituting in certain cases even very complicated behaviour (such as certain instincts in animals), in a word all mechanical activities which have become automatic and in which "selection" is no longer exercised, in which, that is to say, the "method of trial" is no longer manifested. All these kinds of automatic activity have no further need of any affective tendency in order to enter into action, and that is why they remain unconscious to us, without it being necessary to have recourse to any subconsciousness or co-consciousness in order to explain them ; they are simply nervous processes. Finally, the third class concerns all movements and associations of ideas where the action of a "selection" is evident, that is to say, which apparently proceed by "trials" or by "reflection" (which is only a system of mental trial) and which, consequently, can only take place under the stimulus or control of some affective tendency in the active state. It is only these which, when they are not conscious, require the hypothesis of a subconsciousness or co-consciousness, that is to say, a duplication of the personality, in its beginnings or in a more or less advanced stage ; but in normal individuals such a duplication only takes place on account of the very small intensities of the affective tendencies which discharge or control habitual acts, not yet wholly performed mechanically.

Here again we pass by insensible degrees from cases of absent-mindedness pure and simple, which occur in all normal individuals, to the much more pronounced duplication which is almost pathological. Such a case is that of the artiste mentioned by Erasmus Darwin, who, while she was rehearsing her singing lesson with much taste and delicacy under her master's eyes,

UNCONSCIOUS REASONING 379

accompanying herself at the piano, was at the same time exclusively preoccupied—as her emotional expression, and finally her tears, showed—with her canary that was dying in its cage in front of her.[1]

Finally we come to the true pathological cases so happily illustrated in Janet's work. If the extremists are wrong in wishing to see the action of the unconscious in cases where it is completely useless to have recourse to it, those who tend to consider even the most typical cases of doubling of personality as due to processes of a purely nervous nature, are equally mistaken. The behaviour of the somnambulist doubtless implies a consciousness as Janet rightly remarks; for it is evidently guided by a certain degree of "reflection" and constituted by a series of "selections". Thus the somnambulist of Charcot, "when the crisis came, thought he was a journalist and wrote a novel. He woke after having written two or three pages, which were taken away from him; in the next crisis, he recommenced his novel exactly at the point where he had left it."[2]

All the cases called "comitial ambulatory automatism" studied by Charcot also show the reality of acts certainly guided by reason, even if they remain unconscious in relation to the principal personality of the patient. In one of these epileptoid attacks, for example, the patient left "the rue Mazagran in Paris, about 7 o'clock in the evening, on Jan. 18. A week afterwards he awoke in the middle of a town, Brest, which he did not know, where he had no relations, and which he had never heard mentioned, without knowing how he had come there. When he awoke, his clothes were clean, his shoes not worn out. This proved that he had not done the journey on foot ; that consequently he must have taken a railway ticket to Brest, shown it several times during the journey, and finally given it up to the collector, on his arrival ; that he had not slept in the open air, and must have probably gone to an hotel and paid for his board and lodging. In the performance of all these complicated acts, he must have behaved, unconsciously or at least subconsciously,

[1] P. Janet, *op. cit.*, *L'automatisme psychologique*, p. 464.
[2] P. Janet, in Münsterberg and others, *op. cit.*, *Subconscious Phenomena*, pp. 64-65 ; the same, *Les névroses*, Paris, 1909, p. 28.

380 THE PSYCHOLOGY OF REASONING

like a man who was awake, with an undisturbed and healthy mind, acting with a deliberate purpose ".[1]

In all the most typical cases of double personality studied by Janet, Morton Prince, and others, where there are simultaneous manifestations of two personalities, the co-conscience which guides the acts of the secondary personality is not questionable at all. The products of so-called automatic writing should be sufficient to prove this ; for they often show true reasoning, as with the complicated arithmetical calculations that Janet succeeded in making Léonie and Lucie do, while they were talking about other things : " the automatic writing ", observes Morton Prince, " does not consist of words, phrases and paragraphs which might be mere repetitions or memories, whether physiological or psychical, of previous experiences, but consist of elaborate original compositions. Sometimes, these automatic writings exhibit mathematical reasoning, shown by the solution of arithmetical problems. Sometimes, they consist of ingeniously fabricated explanations in answer to questions ".[2]

Moreover, this state of co-consciousness in activity in the second personality during automatic writing is fully recognised by the patient if he is put into the hypnotic state representing the continuation of the second personality : " Let us take a case exhibiting automatic writing," writes Morton Prince himself, " where intelligence no. 1 remains impaired. We hypnotise such a subject : when asked what sort of intelligence it was that did the writing, he replies that he remembers perfectly the thoughts, sensations, and the feelings which made up the consciousness of which intelligence no. 1 was not aware, and that this consciousness did the writing ".[3]

What we are especially concerned to note here, is that in all cases of pronounced double personality, the two individualities have quite different and often, we might almost say, opposed affective fundamental dispositions : " The division into two or several distinct

[1] Charcot, *Leçons du Mardi à la Salpétrière* (1888-1889), Paris, 1890, pp. 303-305.
[2] P. Janet, *op. cit.*, *L'automatisme psychologique*, p. ex., pp. 262-263 ; Morton Prince, in Münsterberg and others, *op. cit.*, *Subconscious Phenomena*, p. 88.
[3] Morton Prince, *ibid.*, pp. 80, 84.

UNCONSCIOUS REASONING 381

personalities", write Tanzi and Lugaro, "is confirmed by curious divergences in the mood and character of the different personalities". "During their attack", Janet relates, "the insane at Morzine show a veritable fury against religion, insult the priests, the Holy Virgin etc., and always interlard their language with all the oaths that they know ; after the attack, they awake calm, polite, and religious".—"All hysterical delusions", Janet continues, "may be reduced to phenomena of the same kind : Rose abuses people who come near her during her delusion, while she is very polite in the waking-state ; Felida, who is sad and thinks about suicide in her first state, is gay and courageous in the second".—"All these people change in character and conduct at the same time as they change in sentiment and language". The well-known case of Miss Beauchamp is classic in this respect, for her different personalities, some of which were conscious of others, were actually so different and so inimical one to another, that their conflicts constituted a veritable "cat-and-dog life", as Jastrow says.[1]

This fundamental affective difference of the two or more personalities makes it probable that the cerebral seats of the respective affectivities have originally, even before the duplication appeared, had only a very small part in common, which will have facilitated the gradual complete separation of the seats. We can thus understand how the simultaneous entrance into activity of these affectivities, or, in any case, their complete reciprocal independence has become possible ; and this can and often does go so far that one of the personalities is completely unaware of the other, whether their entrance into activity takes place simultaneously or is produced successively.

Yet these very pronounced duplications are pathological phenomena. Normally, such cases are limited, as we have seen, to simple absent-mindedness, made possible by the great difference between the two respective affectivities and by the short duration and feeble intensity of that which impels towards and presides over the performance of the not entirely mechanised act ; while

---

[1] E. Tanzi and E. Lugaro, *op. cit.*, *Malattie mentali*, Vol. I, p. 281 ; P. Janet, *op. cit.*, *L'automatisme psychologique*, pp. 120-121, 123 ; J. Jastrow, *op. cit.*, *The Subconscious*, pp. 356, 368-369.

382 THE PSYCHOLOGY OF REASONING

in marked contrast with this accessory affectivity is the much greater persistence and stronger intensity of the affectivity which guides and controls conscious action and thought. Moreover, we have seen that as soon as the absent-minded act demands a more lively affective tendency for some special modality to be performed more carefully, it immediately becomes conscious again.

This should make it appear highly probable that everything which exacts a prolonged and intense activity of selection and reflection, everything that consists in a continuous application of the method of "trial and error," can only take place, in the normal man, in the conscious state. And as there is always the necessity in reasoning, for continuous selection and prolonged reflection, it may be regarded as highly probable that, in the normal man, it can very rarely or never take place in the unconscious state : "Reasoning", writes Ribot, "is not reducible to a mental automatism, which necessarily and directly would attain its end of itself. It proceeds by acceptance and elimination. According to the mechanism of association, the ideas of the reasoner irradiate in all directions. From this profusion of materials he must select what is adapted to his end. Now, is the selection explicable without consciousness?"[1]

On the other hand the psychological school referred to above, which tends unduly to enlarge the field of the unconscious, would wish to attribute to it, in the normal man also, even this faculty of reasoning, and would further reserve for it especially the higher forms of reasoning itself, that is to say those responsible for genial ideas : "Unconscious activity in invention", Dwelshauvers writes, "cannot be doubted. It has been formally recognised by certain scholars and artists and these not the least eminent, doubtless because the richness of their psychical life was considerable. And as consciousness never presents anything but the final result, it is necessary to admit that this immense spiritual richness is confined to the unconscious functions, whatever may be the interpretation given of them".[2]

Let us remark, to begin with, that if all inspiration were due to the unconscious, it should apply just as

---

[1] Th. Ribot, *op. cit.*, *La logique des sentiments*, p. 81.
[2] Dwelshauvers, *op. cit.*, *L'inconscient*, p. 156.

UNCONSCIOUS REASONING 383

much to each of those "happy ideas" which come daily to the mind of even the most ordinary man, there being no substantial difference between these and "genial ideas" properly so called. In other words, whoever attributes inventive inspiration to the unconscious or subconscious should also attribute to it everything that appears spontaneously to the mind : According to some authors, writes Ribot, "the dynamic subconscious is a latent state of activity, of incubation and elaboration. From this source comes inventive work, inspiration in all sorts of discoveries, improvisation and even—to a feebler degree and in a more modest form—sudden repartee and *bons mots* ; in short everything which sparkles forth from us spontaneously."[1]

Take, for example, the deciphering of a badly written word which has long resisted all our efforts to interpret it. It is evident that here it is only a matter of a choice between the scores of words evoked by association, some suggested by the meaning of the sentence or context of which the word forms a part and by its position in the sentence, the others obtained by starting from the resemblances that certain of the signs or ink-marks, which form part of the word to be deciphered, have with letters of the alphabet. As soon as the right word fortuitously presents itself by an evocative process identical with that which has evoked all the preceding interpretations that have been discarded, it is selected by the affective tendency desirous of understanding the whole meaning of the sentence. Everything, in this deciphering, is performed in daylight ; that is to say in the presence of consciousness. Where and what is the action that could be exercised by any subconsciousness ? It will be said that the deciphering of a word is not an inspiration. But we pass from the first to the second by insensible degrees. It is enough to think of the inspiration of Champollion which consisted precisely in deciphering a certain group of hieroglyphic signs signifying the name of Rameses ; which furnished him with the key to all the hieroglyphic scripts of the Egyptians.[2]

---

[1] Th. Ribot, in Münsterberg and others, *op. cit.*, *Subconscious Phenomena*, p. 33-34.

[2] A. Moret, "L'écriture hiéroglyphique en Egypte ", *Scientia*, Feb. 1919, pp. 5 ff.

384 THE PSYCHOLOGY OF REASONING

The selection of the genial idea which presents itself fortuitously takes place therefore in the conscious state. In virtue of the strong emotion caused by the happy discovery, it even leaves an indelible memory of the moment and manner of its presentation in whoever has had these inspirations. And beyond this selection among fortuitous evocations which appear in disorder, *there is nothing else* in " genial ideation ". Such intuitions or inspirations consist entirely and exclusively in the selection ; and this, we repeat, takes place in a state which is fully conscious.

" The unconscious in invention", writes Dwelshauvers, " is manifested by the fact that a combination long sought with attention and effort without being discovered, *suddenly* appears in consciousness when we are no longer thinking about it, or in the character assumed by the artist's inspiration, which seems to suggest ideas to him *that come of themselves*, without effort ".[1]

Now, if invention, if inspiration is nothing other than a fortuitous evocation of a certain idea which, at the moment of presenting itself, is "selected" from the rest by the corresponding affective tendency, it is natural that it should present itself *suddenly, as if it had come of itself, without effort—that it should seem to rise up from the depths of the unconscious*, as the physiologist Beaunis also expresses himself. All this is natural because we have here to do with an energy hitherto found, in the form of mnemonic accumulation, *in the potential state and which is transformed at this very moment into the actual.* It is just the fact that the idea presents itself *without effort* which shows that there is no preliminary participation of an unconscious activity, for this would always demand an expenditure of energy, producing exhaustion or fatigue.

In our chapter on different logical types of mind, we saw that synthetic inspiration, the discovery of hitherto unsuspected analogies or equivalences between two groups of phenomena, can also only be spontaneous and fortuitous. In fact, the attribute which makes the two groups of phenomena equivalent in relation to a certain result that interests us at the moment, must present itself accidentally to the mind, sensibly or mnemonically, at the same instant in both groups of

---

[1] Dwelshauvers, *op. cit., L'inconscient*, p. 770.

UNCONSCIOUS REASONING 385

phenomena; and the affectivity relative to the result in respect of which the two groups of phenomena are equivalent, must also be aroused at this moment. In such a case, too, there are then images or ideas which were previously in the potential state, and which, entering fortuitously into activity at this moment, give rise, here again in a fully conscious state, to an affective selection which alone constitutes the inspiration itself.

To this class of synthetic inspiration belong, as we saw in our chapter on different logical mentalities, all the inspired mathematical discoveries of Poincaré, whose masterly description of the modes of their appearance, where however the chief merit is attributed erroneously to unconscious mental elaboration, has contributed more than anyone else to habilitate the theory of the share of the unconscious in genial ideation in general.[1]

We on the contrary consider that in these inspirations of Poincaré also, everything took place openly, that is to say in full presence of consciousness, and that this character of "sudden illumination", of "brevity, suddenness, and immediate certainty", on which he lays so much emphasis, is here also due solely to the fact of a fortuitous combination of ideas, *entering into activity at this moment*. As we saw in the above-mentioned chapter, it is certainly necessary, in order to render more probable this fortuitous combination, that the mind should not be too tired, and that it should not at the moment be following with interest any other process of combination which would prevent its noticing this fortuitous union that must be caught on the wing. A restful, refreshed mind signifies, in fact, a mind rich with an accumulation of nervous energy that can facilitate the entry into activity of the countless ideas found in the potential state in the form of mnemonic accumulation; and if at the same time, on account of the long and hitherto fruitless study that it has already made of the problem, the mind is also rich with all the relevant mnemonic material on which the inspiration depends, this latter is very much facilitated. All this explains, without any recourse to the hypothesis of unconscious incubation, of some "subconscious maturing of

---

[1] H. Poincaré, *op. cit., Science et méthode*, Chap. III : " L'invention mathématique ", pp. 53, 66.

2 B

386 THE PSYCHOLOGY OF REASONING

thought", as Jastrow entitles one of his chapters, why these inspirations do not usually present themselves in the study, but in the open air, when one is enjoying a walk in the streets or in the country, and when the mind, free from every absorbing preoccupation, is given up to the "dolce pensar niente". For only this state of complete inactivity presents the conditions most favourable to this entry into activity and fortuitous combination of ideas, and to the spontaneous entrance into activity of the respective affective tendency which should catch the unexpected happy meeting on the wing, and make that instantaneous act of choice wherein, we repeat again, genial ideation entirely and exclusively consists. The fact that these ideas present themselves *without any effort*, the fact which all have noticed and which was particularly emphasised by the physiologist Beaunis, that the supposed "unconscious elaboration" is not in the least fatiguing, proves in our opinion, that this unconscious elaboration *does not take place at all*.

In conclusion : the unquestionable cases of double personality prove beyond doubt the *possibility* of an unconscious reasoning, differing in no way from conscious reasoning as regards the manner of its production. Nevertheless, the clearly pathological character presented by these cases, and, at the same time, the further fact that the duplication possible in the normal man amounts to simple cases of absent-mindedness—which if they too imply some choice, and so cannot be considered as mechanical movements, yet show that the duration, amplitude and intensity of the respective affective tendency which discharges and directs them are very feeble —these two considerations lead us to believe that it is very difficult for reasoning to enter in these cases of absent-mindedness of the normal man. It is hard, that is to say, to regard it as operative in the unconscious state while the conscious activity of the individual is occupied with other things, and this because of the considerable duration, amplitude and intensity of the subconscious affectivity that such an unconscious reasoning would presuppose. Much less is this possible for the sort of reasoning which is supposed to constitute the long and difficult elaboration leading to the inspiration.

UNCONSCIOUS REASONING 387

Contrary to the prevalent opinion of psychologists, we therefore consider that normal reasoning is produced almost exclusively in the conscious state and that, consequently, the share of the unconscious in reasoning itself and in inspiration is almost or entirely nil.

CONCLUSION

REASONING IN RELATION TO VITAL FINALISM

THE main conclusions of our work may be briefly summarised. The analysis of reasoning, the highest of our mental faculties, has led us to the view that it is constituted entirely by the reciprocal play of the two fundamental and primordial activities of our psyche, the intellectual and the affective. The first consist in simple mnemonic evocations of perceptions or images of the past ; the second appear as tendencies or aspirations of our mind towards a certain end to be attained, towards which reasoning itself is directed.

We have seen how the affective activity comes into play in reasoning, not only directly through the evocation, selection and exclusion of sense images, but also in the form of other mental faculties which are derived from it. Thus the faculty of paying attention to what we are thinking about and so of maintaining coherence of thought and exercising the power of criticism ; the faculty of imagining new combinations by means of old mnemonic elements ; the faculty of classifying and introducing a certain order into the chaotic mass of facts presented to our senses ; the faculty of creating concepts more and more general and abstract etc. ; all these faculties of attention,. coherence, criticism, imagination, classification and abstraction, which gradually raise the reasoning from its primordial intuitive forms to the highest deductions of science, are all shown by our analysis to have an affective substratum. Likewise of an affective origin is the deformation that reasoning undergoes when it passes from the constructive and creative to the intentional form, purely classificatory and usually sterile, the most typical manifestations of which are dialectic and metaphysical reasoning. We have further traced the influence of the affective tendencies in the determination of the different types of logical mentality. Lastly, we saw that even pathological

REASONING AND VITAL FINALISM 389

forms of reasoning are due to causes of a purely affective nature.

Affective activity therefore seems to impregnate every manifestation of our thought. It might even be said that, using the pure imaginative memories stored in our sensory-mnemonic accumulations as its intellectual material, it is then the sole architect which creates every edifice of reason, from the humblest construction of the lowest animal to the most elaborate triumph of the man of genius.

But this affective activity, thus seen to be the great artisan of our intelligence, the influence which spurs it on and restrains it at the same time, is itself due to the fundamental mnemonic property, is, moreover, the most direct and characteristic manifestation of this mnemonic property of living substance.

So that the mnemonic faculty, which, as we have shown elsewhere, explains the most fundamental biological phenomena—from the predetermined morphological adaptation of animal organisms and their behaviour-instinct with its unconscious foresight, to the transmissibility of acquired characters with its direct consequences in phylogenetic evolution and ontogenetic development—this mnemonic faculty is now revealed as able of itself to furnish us with all the most varied manifestations of the psyche. Just as Archimedes needed only a point of support in order to raise the earth, so this mnemonic quality is sufficient to enable the vital energy to give rise to all the most characteristic purposive manifestations of life and to create the whole thinking and reasoning mechanism of the intellect.

We have already seen that this mnemonic faculty may be defined as the capacity of reproducing, through internal causes, the specific physiological states, which primarily required for their production the action of the forces of the external world. We have also tried to give an accurate account of the mechanism involved, by admitting nervous energy at the base of every vital phenomenon and endowing it with the property of specific accumulation, that is to say, by supposing that each nervous accumulation gives as a "discharge" only the same specificity of the nervous current of "charge" by which the accumulation was stored. But even setting aside such an hypothesis, what is important

390 THE PSYCHOLOGY OF REASONING

at the moment is to observe that in order to account for the most fundamental biological and psychological manifestations of life it is sufficient to suppose that there exists in nervous energy, over and beyond the properties common to all the energies of the inorganic world, *nothing more than the mnemonic property.*

Indeed, what distinguishes vital energy from the energies of the inorganic world, is not, as many maintain, the property of adaptation to environment. This property of adaptation is common to all alike. This is proved by any physico-chemical system, which, if disturbed in its dynamic equilibrium by some new change in external conditions, regains a new dynamic equilibrium with them, that is to say, "reacts" and "adapts itself" to the changed environment. If, for example, we take with our fingers the cord of a swinging pendulum and hold it firmly at the middle, it adapts itself to the new conditions by beginning to swing faster. If the piers of a bridge happen to restrain a section of a river, the water will rise in the upper part of the river until the increase of its swiftness between the piers makes it continue its flow with the same volume as before. A ray of light is refracted as it enters a denser transparent medium. And the intensity of an electric current adapts itself to the resistance of the circuit, while the difference of potential at the poles remains constant. All these are forms of adaptation to new external circumstances on the part of the energies of the inorganic world ; which denotes that, instead of being converted into other energetic forms, these energies assume the most diverse modalities which allow them to continue, as far as possible, in their hitherto active form. What they lack then, in comparison with vital or nervous energy, is simply the mnemonic faculty, the faculty of reproducing these energetic modes of adaptation *solely through internal causes*, without it being necessary that the surrounding circumstances, which in the first instance *compelled* the form of energy in question to take these modes of adaptation, should be represented in their totality.

Now we have seen that this mnemonic property is exactly what gives to life its finalistic aspect, which consists in being moved by forces *a fronte* rather than by simple forces *a tergo*. The end towards which man gravitates with his affective tendencies, the future external

REASONING AND VITAL FINALISM 391

circumstances which the animal unconsciously prepares itself to face with the complex behaviour that instinct dictates, such and such a peculiarity of environment relatively to which the organ fashioned by the embryo in the maternal uterus will be adapted, now function as a *vis a fronte*; and they function thus because they were in the past *vis a tergo*, and because the physiological activities, then determined by them in the organism, have left of themselves a mnemonic accumulation which now constitutes in turn the true and actual *vis a tergo*, directing and moving the development, the instincts, and the conscious conduct of the living being.

And reasoning, set in motion by one or other of the primary affectivities, continually controlled by the secondary affectivity of the relative state of attention, and then borne towards the most abstract forms by the primary affectivity itself or by others derived from it, is the highest and most complex manifestation of this finalistic aspect of life.

Thence arises the tragic and eternal opposition between our inner life, wholly impregnated with finalism, and the inanimate external world in which centuries of anxious research have failed to reveal any purpose whatever. And in this opposition between the essentially finalistic microcosm and the purely mechanical macrocosm lies the ultimate foundation of the age-long struggle between science and religion, the first constrained by reason founded on facts to deny finality to the universe, the second urged irresistibly to affirm it by the imperious demands of feeling.

This opposition between reason and sentiment will never have an end, unless perhaps man resigns himself to search for the ultimate reason of his conduct, the supreme purpose of his existence, no longer in the whole universe but rather in the narrower domain of life, with which he has community of origin and nature. And if this community be profoundly understood, it will not fail to imbue him with a feeling of sympathy and solidarity towards all beings capable of enjoyment and of suffering, and in particular with a feeling of love and altruism towards his fellow-men, in whom, because they are at the summit of organic evolution, the rhythm of life beats stronger and more consciously. As a consequence, he will be impelled by a deep sense of duty

392 THE PSYCHOLOGY OF REASONING

to combat every cause of misery and to promote every occasion of joy—the one a diminution and the other an increase of vital activity ; and to encourage at the same time all forms of social progress, all manifestations of beauty, all aspirations towards the ideal, so that the development of human existence may be more and more complete, more and more serene, more and more exalted, and the torch of life may shine with a light even more pure and radiant.

INDEX

Aars, K. B. R., 43, 64
Abel, 287
Abercrombie, J., 361
Archimedes, 131, 389
Argand, R., 160
Azam, 370
Augustine, 249

Baillarger, M., 306, 329, 339-340, 348
Bain, A., 19, 20, 24, 33, 47, 234, 359
Baldwin, 27, 91
Ball, 324
Ballet, 283
Bastian, Ch., 281
Beaunis, 384, 386
Beltrami, 180, 182
Bergson, H., 40, 297, 303, 310
Berkeley, G., 111, 117, 172-173, 256
Berkeley, H., 119, 166, 181, 285
Bernard, C., 10
Bernouilli, Jac., 270-271
Bernouilli, Joh., 270-271
Berthelot, 216
Binet, A., 45, 309, 360
Bolyai, 179
Bonola, R., 179, 182
Boole, 200
Borel, E., 275
Boutroux, P., 151, 164
Bradley, 89
Brunschvigg, L., 147, 192-193, 199, 204, 286-287

Cabanis, 317
Capgras, J., 323 ff
Carlyle, 276
Carpenter, W. B., 51, 362
Castle, W. E., 8, 9
Cavalieri, 175
Cayley, A., 166, 186
Champollion, 383
Charcot, 379, 380
Charma, 305
Chasles, M., 166 ff
Chaslin, Ph., 344-345
Cicero, 317
Claparède, E., 62, 291, 350
Clavius, 157

Cleveland, A. A., 74, 152, 283
Clifford, W. K., 182, 184
Comte, A., 175, 177, 194, 269, 286
Coriat, J. H., 298
Couturat, L., 198 ff, 253

Dallinger, 8
D'Allonnes, R., 11, 22-23, 334, 340, 357-358
Dante, 214
Darwin, Ch., 269, 283
Darwin, Erasmus, 378
Darwin, F., 10
Davenport, C. B., 8, 9
Davy, 269
De Candolle, A., 272 ff
Delage, Y., 297, 303, 310 ff, 316
Delasiauve, 344
De Pesloüan, G. L., 207
De Sanctis, S., 297, 299, 301, 312-313
Descartes, 236 ff
Dugas, 304
Duhem, M., 164
Duhem, P., 151-152, 164, 266, 271, 273, 276, 286
Dumas, G., 347, 351-352
Dwelshauvers, G., 372 ff, 382, 384

Einstein, 185
Ellis, H., 297 ff, 307-308, 312 ff, 318
Enriques, F., 83, 131, 158, 179-180, 198, 202, 236, 242-243
Erdmann, K. O., 218 ff, 256-257
Esquirol, 340
Euclid, 179 ff
Exner, S., 51, 57, 60, 64

Fano, G., 179
Faraday, 129-130, 269
Fechner, 318
Féré, Ch., 43
Ferraris, G., 269
Flechsig, P., 11, 58
Foucault, M., 297 ff, 302 ff, 311, 313 ff
Freud, 297-298, 302 ff, 305, 307, 311 ff, 316 ff, 374-375

INDEX

Galasso, 300, 311
Galilee, 75, 122, 127 ff, 135, 268
Galton, F., 17, 59, 267, 280 ff, 289, 307
Gauss, 179, 271
Giard, A., 13 ff
Gigli, D., 158, 163
Goblot, E., 148, 162
Godfernaux, A., 325, 330, 340, 355-356
Gruthuisen, 304
Guastella, C., 229 ff, 241 ff
Guignebert, Ch., 235

Haffner, 311
Hart, B., 372
Hartmann, 372
Hegel, 242-243, 289
Helmholtz, 55 ff, 182 ff, 267-268, 271, 274, 280
Henning, H., 297, 307
Hering, 10
Hermite, 286
Hervey de Saint-Denis, 307
Hildebrandt, 307, 313
Houeel, J., 160
Hugo, V., 285

James, W., 22, 27-28, 49-50, 91, 137, 232, 237, 251, 289, 300, 323
Janet, P., 47, 305-306, 356, 369, 379 ff
Jastrow, J., 372-373, 376-377, 381, 386
Jennings, H. S., 2, 3, 6, 28, 31, 91, 98 ff
Jessen, 298
Jevons, S., 89, 94, 109-110, 114, 116, 125, 131, 203
Jourdain, P. E. B., 148, 150-151, 173

Kant, 317
Kepler, 136
Klein, 186, 266
Kohn, H. E., 48, 51, 53
Kollarits, J., 301
Kraepelin, E., 327 ff, 338 ff, 344 ff
Krauss, 317
Kroman, 125
Kuelpe, O., 37, 44, 50

Ladd, G. E., 62
Lamarck, 269
Lange, 22, 300
Lebon, E., 265
Lécaillon, A., 13
Legendre, 292
Lehmann, A., 16, 306-307

Leibnitz, 131, 173 ff, 203-204, 238, 240, 248, 271
Lélut, 317
Lemoine, 304
Leverrier, 270
Liebig, 269, 282
Lipps, 372
Litwer, H., 295
Lobatschewski, 179 ff
Locke, 104 ff, 111, 117, 226, 254
Lombroso, 267
Luciani, L., 292 ff, 318, 376
Lugaro, E., 304-305, 323, 330 ff, 341, 346 ff, 353, 355, 381

Macario, 370
Mach, E., 28. 74, 82, 84, 112, 116, 118, 125 ff, 131 ff, 143, 150-151, 205-206, 263, 265, 271, 286, 313-314, 323
Maillieux, J., 217-218
Maine de Biran, 317
Malebranche, 238, 248
Marconi, 270
Marx, 269
Masselon, R., 304-305, 341-342, 347, 348-349, 354
Maudsley, 23, 38, 43, 49, 81, 90, 265, 280, 283, 330, 340, 341, 359
Maury, 298, 303 ff, 317, 363-364, 368, 370
Maxwell, 269
Mayer, R., 268, 274-275, 283
Meeus, 342
Meray, Ch., 163
Mesnet, 370
Meumann, E., 23, 48-49, 90, 265, 276, 279, 281
Meunier, P., 41, 304, 305
Meyerson, E., 134
Mignard, M., 306 ff, 315-316, 329. 341, 352-353, 358
Milhaud, G., 143, 150, 152, 192-193, 238-239
Mill, J., 92-93
Mill, J. S., 87, 117, 123, 134, 136, 147, 151, 211 ff, 216-217, 226 ff, 234, 245, 274, 281, 375
Miller, 82, 90, 91, 108, 125
Mineo, C., 198
Mittermaier, C. G. A., 221, 222, 223, 226
Moebius, 34
Moreau, J., 317
Morel, B. A., 302, 324, 326, 329-330, 333, 334, 340, 342, 346, 357, 358
Moret, A., 383